BRUCE BAWER

Surrender

Bruce Bawer's book *While Europe Slept* was a finalist for the National Book Critics Circle Award. He is also the author of *A Place at the Table*, *Stealing Jesus*, and several books of literary criticism, including *Diminishing Fictions* and *The Aspect of Eternity*. He has written for *The New York Times*, *The Washington Post Book World*, *The Wall Street Journal*, *The New Republic*, *Wilson Quarterly*, *City Journal*, and many other periodicals.

www.brucebawer.com

SURRENDER

SURRENDER

Appeasing Islam, Sacrificing Freedom

BRUCE BAWER

ANCHOR BOOKS

A Division of Random House, Inc.

New York

FIRST ANCHOR BOOKS EDITION, MAY 2010

Copyright © 2009, 2010 by Bruce Bawer

All rights reserved. Published in the United States by Anchor Books, a
division of Random House, Inc., New York, and in Canada by Random
House of Canada Limited, Toronto. Originally published in hardcover in
slightly different form in the United States by Doubleday, a division of
Random House, Inc., New York, in 2009.

Anchor Books and colophon are registered trademarks of
Random House, Inc.

The Library of Congress has cataloged the Doubleday edition as follows:
Bawer, Bruce.
Surrender : appeasing Islam, sacrificing freedom / Bruce Bawer.—1st ed.
p.   cm.
Includes index.
1. Islam—Relations.   2. Islam—Public opinion.
3. Muslims—Public opinion.   4. Public opinion—Europe.   I. Title.
BP171.B35 2009
305.6'97—dc22
2008035743

Anchor ISBN: 978-0-7679-2837-3

Author photograph © T. Nilsen
Book design by Michael Collica

www.anchorbooks.com

Printed in the United States of America
10 9 8 7 6 5 4 3 2 1

For Tor André

"Those who can give up essential liberty to obtain a little temporary safety, deserve neither liberty nor safety."

> — Benjamin Franklin, notes for a proposition in the Pennsylvania Assembly, 1755

"A man who has nothing which he is willing to fight for, nothing which he cares more about than he does about his personal safety, is a miserable creature who has no chance of being free, unless made and kept so by the exertions of better men than himself."

> — John Stuart Mill, "The Contest in America," 1862

"In a democracy, no man's dignity is inviolate, and anyone's pretensions may be mocked."

> — Adam Bellow, *In Praise of Nepotism*

"America did not teach men the idea of freedom; she taught men how to practice it."

> — Nicolas Sarkozy, in a speech to the U.S. Congress, November 2007

"Congress shall make no law respecting an establishment of religion, or prohibiting the free exercise thereof; or abridging the freedom of speech, or of the press; or the right of the people peaceably to assemble, and to petition the Government for a redress of grievances."

> — First Amendment, United States Constitution

"Fight those who do not believe in Allah, nor in the latter day, nor do they prohibit what Allah and His Apostle have prohibited, nor follow the religion of truth, out of those who have been given the Book, until they pay the tax in acknowledgment of superiority and they are in a state of subjection."

> — The Koran, Sura 9.29

"We fell morally ill because we became used to saying something different from what we thought."

— Václav Havel, recalling life under Communism in his first New Year's address as president of Czechoslovakia, 1990

"Stop self-censoring."

— Ayaan Hirsi Ali to National Press Club, 2007

CONTENTS

ACKNOWLEDGMENTS

I am deeply indebted to John Talbot and Adam Bellow for their heartening commitment to this project; to Kristine Puopolo for taking it on in midstream and bringing to it such expertise and professionalism; to Stephanie Bowen and Katie Henderson for steering it expertly through production; and to Dan Feder and Amelia Zalcman for helping in a multitude of important ways.

Of the many online journalists and commentators who drew my attention to events I would otherwise never have known about, I especially wish to mention Charles Johnson, Hans Rustad, and B. Daniel Blatt. I also appreciate the support of several editors for whom I've written about topics covered herein: Paula Deitz and Ron Koury at the *Hudson Review*; Brian Anderson and Ben Plotinsky at *City Journal*; Roger L. Simon, Aaron Hanscom, and José M. Guardia at Pajamas Media; Dan Savage and Christopher Frizzelle at *The Stranger*; Marcia Drezon at *The New York Sun*; Clara Germani at *The Christian Science Monitor*; Hege Storhaug and Rita Karlsen at rights.no, the Web site of Human Rights Service; Lars Hedegaard and Helle Merete Brix at sappho.dk, the online magazine of Denmark's Free Press Society; Antonio Golmar at Libertad Digital; and Remco Meijer at *De Volkskrant*.

Thomas De Pietro has my profoundest gratitude for his extremely incisive and useful comments on an earlier draft of this book.

As before, my greatest debt is reflected in the dedication.

PART ONE

A New Brand of Jihad

I

"Send him to hell"

We in the West are living in the midst of a jihad, and most of us don't even realize it—because it's a brand of jihad that's barely a generation old.

Islam divides the world into two parts. The part governed by sharia, or Islamic law, is called the *Dar al-Islam*, or House of Submission. Everything else is the *Dar al-Harb*, or House of War. It's called the House of War because it, too, according to the Koran, is destined to be governed by sharia, and it will take war—holy war, jihad—to bring it into the House of Submission.

Jihad began with Muhammed himself. When he was born, the lands that today make up the Arab world were populated mostly by Christians and Jews; within a century after his death, those areas' inhabitants had been killed, driven away, subjugated to Islam as members of the underclass known as dhimmis, or converted to the Religion of Peace at the point of a sword. The Crusades of the twelfth and thirteenth centuries were not wars of conquest by Europeans but attempts to take back what had once been Christian territory. America's very first foreign conflict after the Revolutionary War was with the Barbary pirates, who, sponsored by the Muslim governments of North Africa—just as terrorist groups today enjoy the sponsorship of countries like Libya, Iran, and Syria—had for generations been preying on European ships and selling their crews and passengers into slavery. (Between the sixteenth and nineteenth centuries, over one million Europeans—including people like Cervantes, Saint Vincent de Paul, and French playwright Jean François Regnard—became chattel in North Africa, a minor detail that rarely makes it into Western history textbooks, perhaps because it would compel textbook writers to accord jihad a major role in their narratives of Western history.)

In 1786, John Adams and Thomas Jefferson, then the U.S. ambassadors to Britain and France respectively, met in London with the Tripolitanian envoy to Britain and asked him why his pirates were preying on American ships; he explained, as Adams and Jefferson reported afterward to the Continental Congress, that the pirates' actions were

> founded on the Laws of their Prophet, that it was written in
> their Koran, that all nations who should not have acknowledged
> their authority were sinners, that it was their right and duty
> to make war upon them wherever they could be found, and to
> make slaves of all they could take as Prisoners, and that every
> Musselman who should be slain in Battle was sure to go to
> Paradise.

In their own eyes, in short, as well as in the eyes of the Muslim governments of the day, the Barbary pirates were engaged not in criminality but in jihad (or, more specifically, *al-jihad fil-bahr,* "the holy war at sea"). For a time the young United States of America joined European governments in shelling out "tribute" to the pirates—that is, paying them off—to keep them from plundering ships and enslaving sailors. But once America had built up seagoing forces that were up to the job, it sent in the Navy and Marines to put an end to this brigandage in what became known as the First and Second Barbary Wars (1801–05, 1815)—thus the line in the Marine Corps hymn about "the shores of Tripoli." (These wars, too, fail to merit a mention in many American history textbooks.)

After their defeat in the Barbary Wars, the pirates left U.S. vessels alone. But the spirit of jihad, like a hardy virus, survived—quiescent, yet lethal—only to manifest itself, in later generations, in different forms. Today, piracy; tomorrow, terrorism.

In the late 1980s, a brand-new mutation of the virus appeared. The news came, most famously, in the form of an announcement made on Valentine's Day 1989 by the Grand Ayatollah Seyyed Ruhollah Khomeini. Khomeini, who in 1979 had succeeded the overthrown Shah Mohammed Reza Pahlavi as Iran's supreme leader (thereby earning a nod as *Time*'s Man of the Year) and promptly subjected that country to sharia, was a mufti—an Islamic scholar who is qualified under sharia law to issue a fatwa, an authoritative opinion that settles a question of faith. In this case the question was whether the British-Indian novelist Salman Rushdie should be killed for having insulted Islam in his recently published novel *The Satanic Verses*. Khomeini's answer? Iranians heard it over the radio: "I inform the proud Muslim people of the world that the author of *The Satanic Verses* book, which is against Islam, the Prophet and the Koran, and all those involved in its publication who are aware of its content are sentenced to death. I ask all the Muslims to execute them wherever they find them." Days later, Iran officially put a bounty on Rushdie's head. The author went into hiding. He has been guarded day and night by British police ever since.

Nothing quite like this, it's safe to say, had ever happened before.

Khomeini's fatwa reflected the recognition that jihad's proper targets don't just include Western vessels and buildings. They also, and more fundamentally, include Western freedoms—above all, the foundational freedom: freedom of speech. What has emerged from this recognition is a new phase of jihad whose advantages include not requiring jihadists to engage in combat to the death but only in such low-risk activities as the writing of letters of complaint to government officials, participating in "intercultural dialogue," and the occasional rally, march, riot, flag-burning, or act of embassy vandalism. Not only do the participants in this modern brand of jihad take virtually no chances (there is little likelihood of arrest and even less of conviction), but they also enjoy the assistance of non-Muslims who, when not supporting these New Age jihadists out of a misguided sense of sympathy or outright fear, are motivated by ideology—namely, the pernicious doctrine of multiculturalism, which teaches free people to belittle their own liberties while bending their knees to tyrants, and which, as we shall see, has proven to be so useful to the new brand of cultural jihadists that it might have been invented by Osama bin Laden himself.

In Khomeini's singling out of Rushdie, there was no little amount of irony. A son of Muslims, Rushdie was born in Bombay (now Mumbai) and educated at Cambridge. More to the point, though he resided in Britain and lived essentially as an Englishman, he was no knee-jerk critic of Islam or defender of the West. Far from it: at the time of Khomeini's fatwa, Rushdie's politics could be fairly described as more or less standard-issue British literary intellectual leftism. "It was ironic," the Islam expert Martin Kramer has noted, "that Rushdie, a postcolonial literary icon of impeccable left-wing credentials, should have been made by some Muslims into the very personification of orientalist hostility to Islam." Indeed, Rushdie had opposed the Shah and supported the Islamist revolution that brought Khomeini to power. Anyone familiar with his books at the time of the fatwa would have said that he harbored considerably less animosity toward Islam, radical or otherwise, than toward America and Britain, which he tended to identify not so much with freedom and human rights as with colonialism and imperialism. He was particularly hostile to Britain's then prime minister, Margaret Thatcher—upon whose government's protection, after the fatwa, his well-being entirely depended. (Rushdie's positions on Western values and Islamic revolution, to be sure, would shift somewhat as a result of his post-fatwa experiences.)

The Satanic Verses was Rushdie's fourth novel. Its title was taken from the commonly used name for certain passages that had supposedly been inserted into the Koran at an early date and later declared inauthentic and removed. Long, muddled, often surrealistic, and consistently overheated, the novel (which, like most of Rushdie's fiction, I personally find all but unreadable) was meant to be understood as a reflection on the experience of South Asian immigrants in the West. As Michiko Kakutani wrote in her *New York Times* review, it "deals only incidentally with Islam." Yet Khomeini and others managed to convince the Muslim world otherwise.

Khomeini was the most powerful person to charge Rushdie with blasphemy, but he wasn't the first. Three months before the fatwa, in October 1988, the *New York Times* ran an article about India's ban on *The Satanic Verses*, and published an open letter from Rushdie to that country's prime minister, Rajiv Gandhi, charging that the prohibition was meant to mollify "two or three Muslim politicians" who hadn't even read the book. Yet Khomeini's fatwa was the decisive act, persuading Muslims worldwide that killing Salman Rushdie would be a holy act of jihad. The Union of Islamic Students' Associations in Europe, for example, declared its solidarity with the ayatollah. Mellow-voiced pop singer Cat Stevens, who had converted to Islam and changed his name to Yusuf Islam, said that if Rushdie turned up at his door, he'd call Khomeini personally "and tell him exactly where this man is." British Muslim leader Iqbal Sacranie, who would later be awarded a knighthood, said of Rushdie: "Death, perhaps, is a bit too easy for him . . . his mind must be tormented for the rest of his life unless he asks for forgiveness to [sic] Almighty Allah." On May 27, 1989, Rushdie was burned in effigy at a gathering of at least fifteen thousand Muslims in London.

The Satanic Verses was banned in India, Bangladesh, Indonesia, Sudan, South Africa, Kenya, Thailand, Tanzania, Singapore, and even Venezuela, but not in any North American or European countries. There were those in the West, however—some of them in positions of enormous influence—who would doubtless have forbidden its sale if they had the power to do so. When asked about the fatwa, for example, former president Jimmy Carter didn't call for greater Muslim sensitivity to other people's freedom of speech but for greater Western sensitivity to Muslim feelings. Conservative British politician Norman Tebbit accused Rushdie of betraying "his upbringing, religion, adopted home and nationality." Both Tory Prime Minister Margaret Thatcher and Labor leader Neil Kinnock waited a week before finally criticizing the fatwa. The Archbishop of Canterbury, Robert Runcie, proposed that Britain's long-dormant blasphemy laws be extended to cover Islam. (As we shall see, Archbishops of Canterbury have become a lot more conciliatory since the day of Thomas Becket.)

One of America's then largest bookstore chains, B. Dalton, decided not to stock *The Satanic Verses* for security reasons. Other bookstores also declined to carry it, and still others had copies on hand but kept them out of sight. Several booksellers in both the United States and Britain were bombed, and dozens if not hundreds of others were threatened with bombing. Over the years, moreover, there were several attempts to kill Rushdie. But he survived. Others involved in his book's publication were less fortunate. In a single month, July 1991, the Italian translator of *The Satanic Verses* was attacked, beaten, and stabbed, and Hitoshi Igarashi, its Japanese translator, was murdered. Two years later, William Nygaard, Rushdie's Norwegian publisher, was shot several times outside his home in Oslo; though left for dead, he pulled through (and, bizarrely, lived to publish, in 2004, the memoirs of terrorist leader Mullah Krekar, for whom he threw a festive garden party). In 1989, twelve people died in a Bombay riot protesting Rushdie's book; in 1993, a fire set at a literary festival attended by Rushdie's Turkish translator claimed thirty-seven lives. (The translator survived.)

Rushdie tried to talk his way out of the fatwa, issuing a statement of regret in hopes that the death sentence would be withdrawn. No such luck. The ayatollah replied in highly unambiguous terms: "Even if Salman Rushdie repents and becomes the most pious man of all time, it is incumbent on every Muslim to employ everything he has got, his life and wealth, to send him to Hell."

Rushdie gave it another try in 1990, when he publicly reaffirmed his Muslim faith and called on his publishers not to issue a paperback edition of *The Satanic Verses* or to license translations of it. But it was to no avail: the fatwa remained in place. (Rushdie would later express regret for having crawled to Khomeini in this fashion.)

How did Rushdie's fellow writers respond to the fatwa? In various ways. His old Cambridge classmate Germaine Greer's reaction was to call him "a megalomaniac" and to say, rather cryptically, "I refuse to sign petitions for that book of his, which was about his own troubles." Historian Hugh Trevor-Roper, in a statement that foreshadowed the despicable reactions of many intellectuals and academics to neo-jihadist pressures and threats, said he "would not shed a tear if some British Muslims, deploring Mr. Rushdie's manners, were to waylay him in a dark street and seek to improve them." Other writers proclaimed their solidarity with Rushdie—though many stayed silent, and most of those who spoke up took a while to do so. Among those whose declarations of support for the novelist were particularly courageous—given that they lived in predominantly Muslim countries—were Nobel Prize winners Naguib Mahfouz of Egypt and Wole Soyinka of Nigeria. In New York, leading authors on both the political left and right—from Susan Sontag and E. L. Doctorow to Diana Trilling and Norman Podhoretz—came together at a public meeting to voice their solidarity with Rushdie. One of these authors was Leon Wieseltier, who, in acknowledging Rushdie's often caustic attacks on the West, noted that "in an open society, you defend even people who criticize that society." Richard Bernstein, in a *New York Times* article about the meeting, concluded that "the overwhelming consequence of the Khomeini death threat" had been "a clear solidifying of the writers' ranks, a refusal to be cowed."

Yet by whom or what were these writers refusing to be cowed? To read contemporaneous news articles and opinion pieces about the Rushdie case in the Western press is to notice that Islam itself is almost always strangely marginal. Though everybody understood, to be sure, that this brouhaha was in some fundamental sense all about religion, there seemed nonetheless to be an unspoken assumption that Khomeini's fatwa was a freakish departure from the usual order of things, even in the Muslim world. People talked about it as if it could be explained entirely by Khomeini's quirky personality and, perhaps, by the seemingly unique degree of fanaticism that was gripping Iran at that particular historical moment. That the fatwa might, alternatively, be understood as illuminating the eternal nature of Islam itself—and the attitudes toward freedom, especially freedom of speech, that are inextricable from the religion's theological essentials—was a possibility on which few prominent Western commentators chose to focus. In retrospect, indeed, it seems a bit strange: during the years preceding the fatwa, the West had been through the Israeli-Palestinian conflict, the 1972 Munich Olympics massacre, Iran's Islamic revolution of 1978–79 and hostage crisis of 1979–81, the Iran-Iraq War of 1980–88, and such atrocities as the 1985 murder of the elderly American tourist Leon Klinghoffer by Palestinian terrorists who dumped him and his wheelchair off the deck of a cruise ship, the *Achille Lauro*, into the Mediterranean. All these events had kept the Muslim world in the headlines for years—yet none of them had led Westerners, in meaningful numbers, to consider it necessary to educate themselves in any serious way about Islam. Even most of us who regarded ourselves as relatively well-informed about history and current events didn't yet grasp how profoundly different the Islamic worldview was from that of the secular West, or imagine how important it would soon be for us—for the sake of our own civilization—to understand that worldview, its religious foundations, and its long-term implications.

Certainly the U.S. media had done little or nothing to contribute to this understanding. On the contrary, when Khomeini had returned to Iran in 1979 to impose his tyranny, American journalists had treated him as a returning hero. Farshad Kholghi, a Bahai who in his childhood left Iraq with his family to escape Khomeini's oppression of non-Muslims, later recalled that the foreign reporters he watched on TV at the time had viewed the ayatollah "as a spiritual rallying point, a full-bearded Gandhi figure." When confronted with the Rushdie fatwa, then, few of us in the West were equipped with the tools that might help us to even begin to conceive of the kind of thinking that went on in millions of Muslim minds when they encountered a text like *The Satanic Verses*. Westerners accustomed to a public square awash in criticism and parody, even of religion—and accustomed, too, to the idea that such criticism and parody is entirely protected by freedom of speech, even if you or I might consider this lowbrow movie or that late-night TV skit to be in poor taste—could hardly imagine a mindset that rejected outright the legitimacy of criticism of religion and the very concept of free speech.

I must confess that I was one of those who at the time didn't quite see what the Rushdie fatwa might portend. And I had less excuse than most. Though I was a full-time literary critic who had ample opportunity to write about any book-related topic I might care to address, I didn't publish a word about the Rushdie case, and I don't remember giving a moment's consideration to doing so. All these years later, I recall feeling only that the key facts of the matter were so blindingly obvious that they hardly needed to be articulated—namely, that free speech is free speech; that to sentence somebody to death for writing anything whatsoever is sheer barbarism; that no remotely civilized person could view such an act with anything other than utter contempt; and that no writer or publisher or bookseller should ever give in to such bullying. Even to have to say these things seemed ridiculous—embarrassing, somehow. In any event, it then appeared to me, as it did to millions of others, that the whole business couldn't possibly have any long-term significance. The fatwa was a singular case, a freak incident. Certainly the future of Western civilization, this strong and remarkable edifice built upon generations of hard-won advances in the rights of man, was not a future of absurd fatwas by bloodthirsty old men! If anyone had suggested that, in coming years, Westerners would become accustomed to death threats founded upon claims that Islam's honor had been offended or its adherents' feelings hurt—and that leading Western media would let their editorial decisions be influenced by such threats or the possibility thereof—few, surely, would have believed it.

But we were mistaken. In fact the Rushdie fatwa marked the beginning of a new era of pressure and intimidation designed to bring down Western freedom of speech—and, with it, freedom generally. It was a terrible development, and the most terrible thing about it was that it was, whether by accident or design, exquisitely well-timed.

For the West had changed.

II

From Mill to Multiculturalism

People in the Western world were not always free. The right to think for oneself, to believe in anything or nothing, to publish one's thoughts, to criticize, to mock, to speak truth to power and say that the emperor has no clothes—all this developed over time and in some cases was taken away violently and then recovered through bitter, protracted struggle. The West's long, uneven progress from medieval serfdom to modern freedom involved untold sacrifice and generations of subtle alterations in people's understanding of what their place, and rights, in the world were. This is something that any minimally educated person knows, but it is also something that can be easy to lose sight of on a day-to-day basis. It is easy to fall into the habit of thinking that the way things are now is the way things always have been—or, perhaps, the way things were always meant to be. Yet it is vital for free people to remember that the freedoms to which they are accustomed are a precious heritage, a gift that most of our forebears could hardly have imagined and that some of them fought and died for. One of the things that those of us who have inherited this legacy of freedom can easily forget is that freedom is the single most vital prerequisite for a dignified human existence. This is perhaps especially true of the First Freedom—the freedom of all freedoms, the freedom from which all other freedoms flow, the freedom without which other freedoms are scarcely conceivable. I am referring to freedom of speech. Freedom of speech has rarely been anything close to a complete reality in any human society—on the contrary, throughout all but a tiny fraction of recorded human history, in most places on earth, speech has been severely restricted and violation of those restrictions has been brutally punished. Even in those times and places when genuine freedom of speech has been a reality, it has never gone entirely unchallenged.

Although we tend to generalize about "the West," moreover, one fact that is drastically underappreciated by people in the English-speaking countries is that they are in fact heirs to a considerably more liberal tradition of freedom, including freedom of speech, than are those in countries on the European continent. And among the English-speaking countries, America stands out above all the others for the degree of freedom of speech that its people enjoy, thanks to the First Amendment to the United States Constitution. That Constitution was the culmination of a series of landmark legal documents that gradually reduced royal power in England and expanded the rights of the individual. This process began, to be sure, not with rights for the whole people—most of whom, at the time, were peasants whose identities were defined by their subordination to God and the Pope, and to their respective kings and feudal lords—but with rights for nobles and church officials. For example, in the Charter of Liberties, proclaimed in 1100, King Henry I agreed to limit certain of his powers over his barons and churchmen. In 1215 King John, facing rebellion by his barons, felt compelled to sign the first version of Magna Carta ("Great Charter"), in which he acknowledged that his powers were not absolute and granted his subjects, among other things, the right not to be imprisoned without being charged ("habeas corpus"). Many basic rights that we take for granted today—including the right to a fair trial before a judge—originated in one or another of the various versions of Magna Carta that were issued over the course of the thirteenth century. Promulgated at a time when all power lay in the hands of the king, aristocracy, and church, and when there was not yet such a thing as a national legislature (Parliament was established later in the thirteenth century), Magna Carta is a crucial document in the history of the development of the English-speaking peoples' rights. At first intended to protect the rights of nobles, it was later interpreted to apply to all subjects.

Over the centuries, Magna Carta was supplemented by such documents as the 1627 Petition of Right, in which Parliament accused King Charles I of ordering arbitrary arrests, overriding property rights, and imposing martial law; the Habeas Corpus Act of 1679, which strengthened habeas corpus rights; and the 1689 English Bill of Rights, which limited the monarch's powers to tax or to judge, affirmed the people's right to bear arms and elect representatives to Parliament, and ensured those representatives' freedom of speech. To a remarkable extent, the history of British governance is (with only a couple of major setbacks) an account of a gradual increase in the rights of the individual and a gradual decline in the power of the state to punish individuals arbitrarily and unjustly—in other words, a steady climb from medieval feudalism to modern civil society. The most significant advances in individual liberty came during the Enlightenment of the eighteenth century, whose leading figures—among them Voltaire and Jean-Jacques Rousseau in France, Baruch de Spinoza in the Netherlands, and Edmund Burke and David Hume in Britain—wrote great works that helped reshape European consciousness in such a way that ordinary people gradually came to think of themselves less as powerless subjects of divinely ordained sovereigns and more as their rulers' natural equals. Mindless submission to the unquestioned tyranny of popes, prelates, monarchs, and nobles gave way to the rights of man; acceptance of traditional teachings and superstitions regarding the nature of man and his world yielded to reason, logic, and the scientific method. It was in this era of new insight into, understanding of, and respect for individual rights and the individual conscience that America's Declaration of Independence, Constitution, and Bill of Rights were created. The timing has proven to be an extraordinary blessing for later generations of Americans, as well as for the entire free world, which now is governed in accordance with ideas fermented during that period. Those ideas were further developed by others, notably John Stuart Mill, who in his 1859 book *On Liberty* asserted that "over himself, over his own body and mind, the individual is sovereign." Unless a human being has the freedom to think for himself and speak his mind, the freedom to make his own life choices and to form and enjoy his own tastes, and the freedom to associate with others, Mill asserted, he cannot be called truly free; the only legitimate justification for limiting his freedom, moreover, is to prevent him from harming others. To us, such truths are self-evident, but this is only because the ideas of people like

Mill shaped the world we live in and the way we think about it. It was Mill who introduced the notion of "the tyranny of the majority"; his emphasis throughout his writings was on the inviolable dignity, rights, and happiness of the individual.

Like the English, Americans have experienced a relatively steady growth in individual rights over the course of their history—from abolition to women's suffrage to the civil-rights developments of the 1950s and afterward. Though the First Amendment to the U.S. Constitution supposedly secured free-speech rights, certain limitations were for a long time placed on the publication of works that were deemed obscene; in the Republic's early days, President John Adams signed into law the patently unconstitutional Sedition Act, under which journalists critical of him and his administration were arrested; during the Civil War, President Lincoln suspended habeas corpus; there was also a significant blip during World War I, when the Wilson administration cracked down on critics of the war to an extent, and with a brutality, that Americans have not experienced before or since. (This is yet another part of American history that schoolbooks often drop down the memory hole, probably because it doesn't fit in with the image of Wilson as liberal hero.) But for the most part, no non-English-speaking country can boast of freedoms that have advanced so reliably over such a long period. (Since the first French Revolution in 1789, for example, France has undergone tumult after tumult—five republics, two empires, one kingdom, plus the wartime Nazi occupation and Vichy dictatorship—in which the rights of citizens have been guaranteed, rescinded, recovered, and rescinded again.) For Americans, the golden age of freedom of speech began around the middle of the last century; during this period, we have enjoyed a right to express ourselves that is, it seems safe to say, more extensive than any other people in the history of civilization has ever known. Is there a problem with having so much freedom for so long? Yes, a big one: complacency—the danger of taking it for granted as the natural order of things. As Mark Lilla noted in a widely discussed article in the *New York Times Magazine* in August 2007, our freedom is a freak exception to the history of mankind. But Lilla went on to suggest—wrongly—that this fact justifies sacrificing that freedom in order to pacify jihadists; on the contrary, this fact should only enhance our appreciation for that freedom and our readiness to defend it.

Among the restrictions placed on freedom during World War I was the Espionage Act of 1917, which made it a crime to criticize the U.S. government. Adjudicating the 1919 case of Abrams *v.* United States, the Supreme Court ruled this law constitutional by a vote of seven to two. One of the two nay votes was cast by Oliver Wendell Holmes, Jr., who wrote the following in his dissent:

> Persecution for the expression of opinions seems to me perfectly logical. If you have no doubt of your premises or your power and want a certain result with all your heart you naturally express your wishes in law and sweep away all opposition. To allow opposition by speech seems to indicate that you think the speech impotent . . . or that you do not care wholeheartedly for the result, or that you doubt either your power or your premises. But when men have realized that time has upset many fighting faiths, they may come to believe even more than they believe the very foundations of their own conduct that the ultimate good desired is better reached by free trade in ideas—that the best test of truth is the power of the thought to get itself accepted in the competition of the market, and that truth is the only ground upon which their wishes safely can be carried out. That at any rate is the theory of our Constitution. It is an experiment, as all life is an experiment. Every year if not every day we have to wager our salvation upon some prophecy based upon imperfect knowledge. While that experiment is part of our system I think that we should be eternally vigilant against attempts to check the expression of opinions that we loathe and believe to be fraught with death, unless they so imminently threaten immediate interference with the lawful and pressing purposes of the law that an immediate check is required to save the country.

With this dissent, Holmes introduced the concept of a free society as a "marketplace of ideas" and the principle that only speech that represents a "clear and present danger" to life and limb should be prohibited. It is America's dedication to the degree of openness Holmes espoused that has made it unique among the world's nations. Historically, Americans of all political stripes have tended to be intuitive supporters of free speech; this support is part and parcel of the American regard for the autonomy, rights, and conscience of the human individual. Indeed, it's hard to imagine America—with its emphasis on initiative, inventiveness, and independence of mind—without free speech.

To be sure, America has never been—and no country ever was—quite the shining "city on a hill" that Massachusetts Bay governor John Winthrop envisioned in his famous 1630 sermon. The fact that the land of the free kept millions in servitude until the mid-nineteenth century and oppressed their descendants for generations after that testifies sufficiently to the contrary. Yet what's distinctive about the story of American slavery isn't the slavery itself (which, of course, has been a fact of life throughout human history, and still exists in some Muslim countries) but the willingness of hundreds of thousands of Union soldiers to give their lives to liberate strangers from bondage. If slaveholding was a betrayal of America's founding values, the movement to free them, which culminated in the Civil War, was an expression of those values. Indeed, it was because America's founding ideals were so deeply rooted in its people's hearts and minds that Americans, over the generations, when compelled to examine lingering deficits of liberty in their society, or to defend or restore the liberty of people living far beyond their borders, ultimately responded by taking actions that served freedom's cause.

Another important factor in this equation is that America is the land of immigrants. Over the generations, it has welcomed extraordinarily large numbers of new Americans, first mostly from the British Isles, then northern Europe, then southern and Eastern Europe, then the world. This process—whereby Americans' sense of what kind of person could be one of them expanded over time, eventually including *everybody*—proved to be a boon not only for the immigrants themselves but also for America, because it steadily reinforced and deepened the shared understanding that in America, national identity had no connection with ethnicity. What bound Americans each to each was not ties of kinship but a common devotion to freedom; even as Europeans were persuaded, in one modern-day instance after another, to put their lives and fates in the hands of totalitarians with big promises—from the guillotine-masters of the French Revolution to Lenin and Hitler and Mussolini and Franco—most Americans, through most of the Republic's history, understood in their bones that no collectivist ideology, no European-born *ism* (however admired by some American intellectuals), and no bond rooted solely in ethnicity could be an improvement upon Americans' strong, simple commitment to individual liberty. This commitment served Americans well for generations. It's the main reason why a group of colonies on the margins of the known world became the strongest, richest, and freest nation ever.

Yet as America moved into the final third of the twentieth century, something dramatic—and dangerous—began to happen.

To be sure, it's true (as this gay American can attest) that American freedom has continued in recent decades to advance in many ways. Yet at the same time, a dangerous mentality has spread throughout American society—and throughout the Western world. For a long time I avoided using the term "politically correct," because it struck me as a lazy label that people on the right applied to anyone and anything on the left. But it's proven to be unavoidable. For what it designates isn't simply left-wing political views and/or the people who profess them, but a specific way of *thinking* about those views. In a book on the subject, *The Retreat of Reason*, the British writer Anthony Browne describes political correctness as having grown out of an attitude of "decency and consideration" toward society's more vulnerable members, but as having gradually become "more dogmatic and intolerant of dissent, until it became a betrayal of the very liberalism that first fueled it." To this I would add that political correctness is less about reality than it is about image—less, that is, about being genuinely decent and virtuous (which can often require one to confront received opinions and to endure vilification) than about being perceived by the "right people" as decent and virtuous. And to affirm this image, one must (1) affirm that Western capitalism is the great modern evil, (2) recognize and condemn America as capitalism's headquarters, chief symbol, and apotheosis, and (3) view the West's enemies as capitalism's virtuous victims and align oneself with them. There's a profound difference between classical liberalism—the philosophy of individual freedom, limited government, civil liberties, and free markets that grew out of the Enlightenment—and political correctness. Ever since the Enlightenment, being liberal has meant accepting the right to dissent and to hold unorthodox views; at the core of classical liberalism is the sentiment expressed in the celebrated line traditionally (if incorrectly) attributed to Voltaire: "I disagree with what you say, but I will defend to the death your right to say it." By contrast, political correctness is profoundly conformist and uncomfortable with differences of opinion.

To be politically correct is, among other things, to be a multiculturalist. Multiculturalism, a peculiarly Western set of attitudes about the non-Western world, doesn't mean viewing people with non-Western backgrounds as individuals and caring whether they live under governments that grant them the same liberties we enjoy; it means exalting non-Western groups, treating their collective values (however illiberal) as sacrosanct, and either choosing not to notice their lack of freedom or pretending that there's no such thing as freedom or, alternatively, taking the attitude that while freedom may be fine for us, because we're Westerners, a lack of freedom is just as good, if not better, for them, because, well, that's their culture and who are we to criticize it? That freedom is a precious, hard-won inheritance, and that it's the obligation of those of us who have inherited it to protect and preserve it for generations to come, is a concept alien to multicultural minds; rather, it's an article of faith for countless multiculturalists that individualism and individual rights are pernicious and dangerous, and that group identity is a benign phenomenon—that, indeed, group identity *is* identity.

The French writer Pascal Bruckner has called multiculturalism "a racism of the anti-racists" because it "accords the same treatment to all communities, but not to the people who form them, denying them the freedom to liberate themselves from their own traditions" even as it takes for granted Western individuals' right to self-determination. Knowing little about America and its history, and even less about the rest of the world and its history, American students are easily persuaded by multicultural-minded professors that their country is not a light unto the nations but a blight on the planet and that other cultures, if not downright admirable, can be excused for their failings, because those failings are, for some or reason or other, ultimately our fault. As Richard Bernstein noted way back in 1991, in his book *Dictatorship of Virtue: Multiculturalism and the Battle for America's Future*, the "once small voices of protest" who led the multicultural revolution in Sixties America and thereafter now form the core of America's cultural elite: they work as journalists, editors, and producers for media organizations; they teach at colleges and universities; they staff social organizations and cultural institutions; they're politicians and civil servants, authors and artists. And for all their power, they still act as if they are the outsiders, the voices on the barricades, fighting an oppressive establishment, when in fact, as Bernstein notes, "they, in the many domains where they are strong, have become the establishment themselves."

Real education means learning to think critically; but today much if not most education in the humanities and social sciences is conducted within a multicultural framework that forbids critical thinking about non-Western cultures. Students learn that as Westerners, they are guilt-burdened heirs of colonialism and imperialism and thus have no right to judge any aspect of another culture. They also learn that it's more important to show respect for differences between cultures than to be concerned about the living, breathing individuals who are the victims of these differences. Hence many Western adults nowadays, while reflexively dismissing even the noblest aspects of the Western liberal tradition, cannot bring themselves to condemn even such outrageous violations of fundamental human rights as female genital mutilation, forced marriage, and honor killing, or to acknowledge the nature, scale, and in some cases the very reality of the current encounter in the West between democracy and sharia. Europe has taken in, and is still taking in, huge numbers of people from some of the world's most illiberal states; but instead of being viewed as newly free individuals who need help to understand and fully avail themselves of their freedom, and, moreover, to understand that freedom does *not* mean the freedom to oppress one's own, these people have typically been seen, through multicultural eyes, as parts of a group that is essentially different and separate from the free people of Europe.

The revolution in sensibility that's been wrought by multiculturalism, especially in regard to attitudes toward the Muslim and Arab world, owes much to the late Palestinian-American professor and propagandist Edward Said, who with his immensely influential 1978 book *Orientalism*—in which he sweepingly dismissed virtually the entire corpus of Western scholarship on the Arab and Islamic world on the grounds that the scholars in question had viewed their subject through Western, and therefore racist and condescending, eyes—accomplished something extraordinary. He convinced a large proportion of the Western intelligentsia—and through them a generation of students of history and social sciences—that any opinions they might themselves form about any aspect of the Arab and Muslim world were by their very nature invalid because they were informed by centuries of Western colonialist prejudices and stereotypes. Westerners, precisely because they were Westerners, were constitutionally incapable of getting the truth about the Arab and Islamic world right; the best they could do, if they wanted to know and serve the truth, was to listen attentively to certain privileged male Arabs' and Muslims' accounts of their societies and cultures, and then (if they dared address these topics at all) slavishly echo those accounts.

No aspect of Western democracy is more anathema to the multicultural mentality than free speech. For multiculturalism encourages self-censorship and the condemnation of "insensitive" utterances—especially utterances that are perceived as potentially offensive to some protected group. And these days Muslims are the most highly protected group of all, handled with an extra-special level of sensitivity, partly because so many of their number have taken on America and Israel and capitalism with such ferocity, making jihad the ally, in effect, of multiculturalism itself. Yet such is the perversity of multiculturalism that its adherents are capable of treating even the most overtly brutal jihadists, fire-breathing imams, and tyrannical patriarchs as if they were delicate hothouse flowers, easily wounded by an unfriendly word from an obtuse and injudicious Westerner. On the contrary: as has been amply demonstrated ever since the cultural jihad began, these men are strong and purposeful. They know what they believe and stand for. And they're determined not to compromise. They aren't relativists. *They aren't multiculturalists.* They have a goal, a vision, a determination, and a sense of identity and values that Western multiculturalists cannot even imagine. And they know it. And in that knowledge lies their strength.

III

The Dialectical Scam

efore we explore the ways in which jihad has exploited political correctness and multiculturalism, let us first look at a few recent examples of how the politically correct react to the tellers of politically incorrect truths. A favorite approach is to claim that one's own free speech is endangered, or has been taken away—perhaps even as one is actively seeking to silence those truth tellers or to punish them for speaking. "I tested freedom of speech in America," thundered one 2005 contributor to Indymedia, a popular leftist Web site, "and found it defunct." In a 2007 essay, writer Stephen Lendman argued that "free expression is under attack . . . in the age of George [W.] Bush when dissent may be called a threat to national security, terrorism, or treason." (Lendman neglected to identify a single case in which mere dissent from Bush's policies had led to prosecution.) When Pam Spaulding began an August 2007 posting on the left-wing Pandagon blog with a reference to "the Bush administration assault on free speech," she didn't even attempt to demonstrate that such an assault was under way. She didn't have to: the reality of this assault had by that point become a truism on the left.

The folks at Indymedia and Pandagon were right: free speech *was* endangered. But it was they, and other members of the politically correct brigades, who were endangering it.

Take the case of Alvin Rosenfeld, an English professor at Indiana University. In December 2006, his essay "Progressive Jewish Thought and the New Anti-Semitism" was posted on the Web site of the American Jewish Committee (AJC). The essay, which argued that a rise in anti-Semitism is being abetted by some Jewish intellectuals' hyperbolic criticisms of Israel, was scrupulous and restrained. The only parts that weren't restrained were those that appeared within quotation marks. For example, several of the writers cited by Rosenfeld compared Israel to Nazi Germany or apartheid South Africa. "Just as Christianity may have died at Auschwitz, Treblinka and Sobibor," wrote Berkeley professor Daniel Boyarin, "so I fear that my Judaism may be dying at Nablus, Deheishe, Beteen (Beth-El) and El-Khalil (Hebron)." Michael Neumann of Trent University in Ontario accused Israel of conducting a "race war against the Palestinians" and trying to achieve "the extinction of a people." All this Israel-bashing was grotesquely at odds with the reality that it was Islamic governments and terrorist groups that wanted to destroy *Israel*.

The first major attention to Rosenfeld's essay came in the form of a *New York Times* article by Patricia Cohen on January 31, 2007, and you didn't even have to get past the headline—"Essay Linking Liberal Jews to Anti-Semitism Sparks a Furor"—to figure out her angle. As Rosenfeld later observed, "there really hadn't been much of a furor" before Cohen's piece appeared; nor had he referred even once in his AJC article to "liberal Jews." Despite the AJC's long record of liberalism, moreover, Cohen described it as "conservative"—a label that, in the *Times* mind-set, was obviously appropriate, given that the AJC, by publishing Rosenfeld's article, had associated itself with politically incorrect views. (After the AJC protested, the *Times* ran a correction.) Cohen's article unleashed a torrent of screeds whose running theme was that Rosenfeld had tried to silence other writers. *Tikkun* magazine's Michael Lerner told the *International Herald Tribune* that Rosenfeld had created an "atmosphere" that was "hysterical, verging on McCarthyism." The author Alan Wolfe accused Rosenfeld of employing "Stalinist tactics" to hinder the free exchange of ideas. And the *Forward* described Rosenfeld's essay as "a shocking tissue of slander" designed to "silence critics." (How, one wanted to ask, could quoting people verbatim be described as slandering or silencing them?) There were, to be sure, sensible voices. In *Jewish Week*, Gil Troy called Rosenfeld's essay "an honest analysis" and pointed out that nowhere in it had Rosenfeld advocated "hate laws, suppressing free speech, shunning, or any other intimidation"; rather, he'd done "what thinkers are supposed to do—identify, catalogue, analyze, explain, and challenge." As *Wall Street Journal* writer Bret Stephens put it succinctly: "How does joining a debate become an effort to suppress it?"

Yet the damage was done. Casual readers of the hostile commentaries on Rosenfeld would inevitably come away believing that he had tried to silence legitimate criticism of Israel. Surveying this sea of disinformation, Rosenfeld borrowed a term from British philosophy professor Bernard Harrison. Israel's self-styled "progressive" critics, Rosenfeld argued, were perpetrating a "dialectical scam." He outlined the procedure: First, find something about Israel to criticize; second, criticize it in the most hyperbolic manner, while warning that "'powerful' and 'repressive' Jewish institutions will try to 'silence' the critics by calling them anti-Semites"; third, when "more sober-minded critics" point out your hyperbole, "claim their censure perfectly illustrates the point that there really is a Jewish organizational conspiracy to silence 'criticism of Israel.'" *Voilà*—now you can bask in your identity as an "intellectual martyr." Indeed, though posturing as victims, the writers whom Rosenfeld had challenged were actually victimizers. They'd kicked the whole thing off by comparing Israel to Nazi Germany; now they were equating Rosenfeld with Joseph McCarthy and even Stalin. He'd quoted them fairly and criticized them responsibly; in reply, they sought to blacken his name. Who was trying to silence whom?

So it goes: a left-wing individual or group ("*A*") makes statements with which someone ("*B*") publicly disagrees, in response to which "*A*" complains that his, her, or their freedom of speech has been violated. At this point a sizable segment of the mainstream media leaps into the fray, vilifying "*B*" and agreeing that "*A*"'s freedom of speech is indeed under threat.

Another such episode was recounted by Gaby Wood of the *Observer* on February 11, 2007. On the previous October 4, Tony Judt of New York University (whom she described as a "distinguished British-born historian") had been at his home in New York, preparing a lecture on Israel to be given later that day at the Polish consulate, when the phone rang. The caller, a consular official, told Judt—perhaps the most high-profile of Israel's Jewish critics in the English-speaking world—that his lecture had been canceled. Why? It turned out that Abraham Foxman, director of the Anti-Defamation League, had made it known that, given Poland's checkered history vis-à-vis the Jewish people, he considered the idea of Judt spouting his views under the auspices of the government of Poland morally offensive, and he believed that many Americans would feel the same way. Consular authorities, realizing that Foxman might just have a point, called off the event.

An uproar ensued. In a letter published in *The New York Review of Books*, over a hundred "intellectuals" accused Foxman of depriving Judt of his freedom of speech. This theme was widely echoed. But it was sheer nonsense: by speaking his mind, Foxman had not undermined anyone's rights; he'd simply exercised his own. The Polish consulate, likewise, had been entirely within its own rights in canceling Judt's talk. The plain fact that was obscured in the Judt brouhaha (and that was equally obscured, some months later, in the controversy over Columbia University's speaking invitation to Mahmoud Ahmadinejad) was that having freedom of speech doesn't mean being guaranteed a platform. To her credit, Wood did quote a sarcastic comment by Christopher Hitchens about the PC lemmings who rushed to defend Judt's "freedom of speech." ("Absolutely conventional attacks on Israel and U.S. policy," Hitchens quite properly sneered, were being "presented as heroically original.") But the burden of Wood's argument was that Judt—whom, in her short article, she managed to characterize (or to quote others characterizing) as "brave," "exceptionally eloquent," "dazzling," "magnificent," and "talented"—had indeed been stripped of his rights. The result? Judt emerged with an even higher profile than before. Meanwhile countless people who'd never before heard of Abraham Foxman learned that he was out to destroy the First Amendment.

Then there was the case of bloggers Amanda Marcotte and Melissa McEwan, who, in early 2007, soon after being hired by John Edwards's presidential campaign, turned out to have written things to which a serious White House aspirant might not be thrilled to see his name linked. Marcotte, a contributor to the aforementioned Pandagon blog, would later characterize her own controversial postings as reflective of her "non-mainstream views on religious influence on politics." For example, in a reference to a contraceptive intended for use after unprotected sex, Marcotte had asked: "What if [the Virgin] Mary had taken Plan B after the Lord filled her with his hot, white, sticky Holy Spirit?" After Bill Donohue of the Catholic League got wind of this bit of whimsy, he demanded that the bloggers be fired. At first Edwards demurred; but after several days of intense media attention, Marcotte resigned. She didn't go quietly, however: in addition to playing the gender card (she wrote on her blog that Donohue "and his cavalcade of right wing shills don't respect that a mere woman like me could be hired for my skills"), she pulled the dialectical scam, maintaining that Donohue's "intent is to silence me" and thundering that he had no "right to curtail my freedom of speech." This sentiment was widely repeated; but loathsome though Donohue is, the very existence of the posting in which Marcotte complained about losing her freedom of speech made it clear that it remained fully intact.

These incidents illustrate a simple truth: free speech doesn't mean immunity from criticism. There would be no need for free speech, after all, if nobody disagreed about anything: only controversial speech needs protection. But controversial speech also invites disagreement and debate—and the plain truth is that just as you have freedom of speech, so do those who don't share your views. To many politically correct individuals, this is a well-nigh unacceptable fact. They're so accustomed to functioning within the cozy confines of PC-dominated environments that when they offer up comments on major issues, they don't really see themselves as taking part in an exchange of ideas with people whose opinions may differ sharply from their own; rather, they're preaching to the choir, expressing attitudes that, in their social and professional circles, are simply part of the established orthodoxy. In those circles, it's usually safe to assume that everybody they meet holds the same positions they do. As a rule, then, the articulation of opinions in such settings isn't a matter of proffering fresh and challenging insights, but of affirming a communal consensus, of reinforcing a sense of shared moral superiority. When the politically correct speak their minds, accordingly, they expect agreement, approval, nods of satisfaction, hearty pats on the back, words of congratulation; what they don't expect is to be contradicted. When they *are* contradicted, a kind of existential trauma may ensue; the speaker may experience the unaccustomed lack of reassuring accord as a violation, a wound to the soul, an infringement upon something deeply valued and utterly taken for granted. And the next thing you know, up go the cries of "censorship."

A major recent instance of this phenomenon is the case of the Dixie Chicks. On March 10, 2003, with the invasion of Iraq only ten days away, Natalie Maines, lead vocalist of this country-music trio from the Lone Star State, told a London audience: "Just so you know, we're on the good side with y'all. We do not want this war, this violence, and we're ashamed that the President of the United States is from Texas." The remark was widely reprinted. Many Americans were outraged; some radio stations boycotted the group's music. At first the Dixie Chicks seemed uncertain how to deal with the consequences. But soon enough the singers (or their PR people) seemed to realize that Maines's remark had set them apart in a spectacular way, turning them into international touchstones of opposition to Bush. They proceeded to exploit this role to the hilt—and at the heart of their efforts was the repeated invocation of the concept of freedom of speech. Although Bush himself had responded early on to the furor over Maines's remarks by affirming the singers' right to speak their minds, the Dixie Chicks continued to suggest darkly that their free-speech rights had been infringed—a charge that was echoed endlessly across the left-wing blogosphere.

In 2006, the girls released a documentary, *Dixie Chicks: Shut Up and Sing,* and recorded a song, "Not Ready to Make Nice," that further burnished their image as First Amendment champions. ("I'm not ready to make nice," went the lyric. "I'm not ready to back down.") Sales figures soared. In 2006, the trio's album *Taking the Long Way* debuted at number one on both the pop and country charts. At online message boards, the PC multitudes marveled at their "courage." But such praise was grotesque. Look again at Maines's original comment: "We're on the good side with y'all." Was this courage? Courage would've meant either pillorying Bush in front of his supporters or praising him to his enemies; as Maines's words make clear, she felt sure she was addressing people who shared her disdain for him. What she was doing, in fact, was exploiting an international crisis to bond with her fans and win cheap applause.

When a TV commercial for *Shut Up and Sing* was rejected by NBC because of its policy against running ads about political controversies (other networks ran it), the film's producer, Harvey Weinstein, was ready with a complaint: "It's a sad commentary about the level of fear in our society that a movie about a group of courageous entertainers who were blacklisted for exercising their right of free speech is now being blacklisted by corporate America." Of course, for Miramax mogul Weinstein to complain about "corporate America" was itself corporate marketing at its most brazenly cynical. As for free speech—well, by this point the notion that free speech was endangered for anti-Bush Americans was now worldwide gospel, as reflected in these representative postings from the left-wing Think Progress Web site, all responding to NBC's rejection of the *Shut Up and Sing* ad:

- "That this is being censored by NBC should be trumpeted far and wide, held up as clear and concise evidence that America is fast approaching a bona fide, demonstrable state of fascism . . ."
- "Our country has been lost. We now live under a dictatorship no better than China or Cuba. We're no longer allowed to 'disparage' our president. Free speech is only allowed if it supports the Bush regime."
- "Ben Franklin's warning has come to pass. We had a republic as long as we kept it. Now we have a fascist state like Nazi Germany."
- "Der Fuhrer and Dr. Goebbels have been resurrected in America."
- "Do we still live in America? . . . I want my REPUBLIC back! I want my Constitution back! I want my Bill of Rights back! I want my Freedoms back! LONG LIVE THE REPUBLIC!!!"
- "I can't believe this is America anymore—Is there anyone who can save us from a dictatorship? Can we save ourselves or is it too late?"

One wondered how many of these writers were being consciously hyperbolic and how many seriously had no concept of what a real dictatorship was like—of how it might feel to live in genuine terror of the late-night knock on the door. Rational thought, it seemed, had been supplanted by political correctness on a fanatical scale: people who lived safe, affluent lives, and who didn't have the slightest actual fear of being arrested for speaking their minds, felt compelled to insist ardently that America had become, or was fast becoming, a police state. It was almost as if they were suffering from something that could only be called totalitarianism envy. It was as if life in America was simply too undramatic for them, as if they perhaps felt guilty about *not* having their rights endangered, as if they lusted after the moral stature (or bragging rights?) that people now enjoyed who had spent years living under Nazism or Communism.

Shut Up and Sing: that was the title of the Dixie Chicks' documentary. But the whole point was that *nobody had shut them up*. On the contrary, the gist of many of their pronouncements was that other people, by exercising *their* free-speech rights, were denying the Dixie Chicks *their* free-speech rights. In short, the three women were basically telling their *critics* to shut up.

At the 2007 Grammy's bash the Dixie Chicks won five prizes, including best album, song, and record. Accepting the statuette for album of the year, Maines further cheapened the meaning of the First Amendment by saying: "I think people are using their freedom of speech with these awards. We get the message." This suggestion that Grammy voters, by awarding the girls a pop-music prize, had somehow struck a blow for constitutional liberties brought the whole farce to its natural consummation. "Freedom of speech" was now just a promotional slogan. Meanwhile the girls' critics were being compared to some of modern history's most formidable rogues. Senator Barbara Boxer (D-Ca.), for example, looked at the people boycotting Dixie Chicks albums and was reminded of "Nazi book-burners" and "communist dictators." Commenting on this absurd comparison in *Reason* magazine, Jacob Sullum wondered where people like Boxer had been when conservative talk-show hosts Michael Savage and Dr. Laura Schlessinger lost their radio programs (at least temporarily) after making anti-gay remarks. If Boxer and others were really operating out of a principled concern for the preservation of free speech, they should be concerned about *anybody* being silenced; but what plainly underlay the PC left's rhetoric about the Dixie Chicks was not a disinterested dedication to First Amendment freedoms, but a fierce intolerance of those who disagreed with them—and a self-righteous outrage at the idea that their own views should be subject to scrutiny and criticism by those on the other side of the fence.

"Who the hell are we to point fingers?"

Democracy relies on the free exchange of ideas. Yet to the politically correct community, the very concept of subjecting to open debate its rock-solid certitudes—whether about Israel, the Iraq war, or whatever—is heresy. Dare to question the articles of PC faith and you risk being accused of practicing a "new McCarthyism" that is "stifling debate," exerting a "chilling effect on free speech," and taking America down the slippery slope to fascism. Such rhetoric on the left, far from having anything to do with protecting free expression, is designed to intimidate those with politically incorrect thoughts into remaining silent, and thus eliminate from the public square any serious challenge to politically correct dogmas. This effort to limit debate, control its terms, and demonize dissenters from the PC playbook varies in extent and intensity, depending on the issue in question. But on no issue has the effort been more comprehensive, more passionate, and more effective than on the issue of Islam. When the subject is Islam, critical voices are systematically suppressed, views misrepresented, reputations smeared, and careers derailed. And participating in this ignominious campaign are many people who, when not busy trying to silence the tellers of truth about Islam, are weeping crocodile tears over the supposed silencing of the likes of the Dixie Chicks.

This attempt to enforce the politically correct line on Islam is, of course, a response to the new form of jihad whose first target was Salman Rushdie. To be sure, as I've noted, there were precious few of us who grasped at the time of the Rushdie fatwa that there was indeed a new form of jihad on the world scene. Rushdie's plight seemed unique, and the fatwa only a historical blip; and in the months and years that followed, though Rushdie remained in hiding and there were plots aplenty to take his life, neither Khomeini nor any other Muslim leaders followed up on the fatwa by targeting other writers. For a time, Muslim assaults on the West continued to take a more familiar form—namely, terrorism. Contrary to many people's perceptions, the 1990s were no serene interlude between the Cold War and 9/11, but a decade punctuated by brutal bombings—in 1993, the World Trade Center; in 1996, the Khobar Towers in Dhahran, Saudi Arabia; in 1998, the U.S. embassies in Kenya and Tanzania; in 2000, the USS *Cole*—that augured the horror to come. These incidents, however, didn't hold the attention of most Americans any longer than did any number of contemporaneous atrocities by such groups as the IRA in Britain and ETA in Spain. All these jihadist actions, moreover, were dwarfed in dramatic impact by the 1995 Oklahoma City bombing, which the defenders of Islam's good name seized upon as proof that every ethnic and religious group, after all, has its own violent extremists. It took 9/11 to open many Americans' eyes to the reality of the jihadist war on the West. Not until that day did many of us recognize that we had enemies in large numbers who hated our way of life—and whose hatred was rooted in a thirteen-hundred-year-old book. The 191 murders in Madrid on March 11, 2004, and the fifty-six murders in London on July 7, 2005, drove home the fact (for those who were interested in facts) that for the jihadists the enemy was not just America, or its current president, or this or that foreign-policy decision, but every country whose people lived in freedom rather than under the Koran.

For others, however, 9/11 had a different impact. Over the decades during which multiculturalism had transformed many Americans' way of thinking about society, individual freedom in America had endured largely through inertia. It was perhaps only a matter of time before some event occurred to demonstrate just how firmly the multicultural mentality had rooted itself in American minds and damaged the foundations of American freedom. The jihadist atrocity of 9/11 was that event. To be sure, in the immediate wake of the attacks on New York and Washington, there was a reflexive tendency throughout the Western world to sing freedom's praises. But words are cheap. And the gradual realization that 9/11 was not just a stand-alone event but an awakening to a daily process of cultural assault and erosion—not only by terrorists, but by millions of Muslims in the West for whom individual freedom is alien and anathema—was transformative. Muslim leaders in Western countries, keenly aware that they were living in a field that had already been seeded with multiculturalism, watered those seeds and caused a thousand flowers of guilt to bloom. In short order, many Westerners were persuaded that the individual freedom on which their societies were founded was itself an offense against Islam, and that the attempt to extend that freedom to Muslim immigrants—to say nothing of seeking to extend it to Muslim countries—was an act of cultural aggression motivated by neocolonialist arrogance. After all, if (as multiculturalism teaches) all cultures are equal, to offer freedom to immigrants from unfree countries—indeed, even to call freedom "freedom" and to lament its absence in most of the Muslim world—is to expose one's own cultural insularity and intolerance. In the face of such thinking, and in the face of the increasingly visible tensions between secular liberalism and the illiberalism of Muslim subcultures, many Westerners' resolve buckled. Many Americans, and even more Europeans, who were frightened by these tensions grasped on to the multicultural ideal as a means of resolving them and avoiding the challenges they presented. Instead of standing up for freedom, they embraced the obscene notion that compromising freedom was a necessary act of "respect" for people with other cultural backgrounds and values.

Some of us have balked at this compromise. For doing so, we've been called racists—as if the monstrous ideology with which we're expected to accept some *modus vivendi* were a skin color. We've been told that if we don't tolerate brutal cultural practices (simply because they *are* cultural practices) and the denial of equal rights to women and others in the name of respect for Islam, we're setting "us" against "them." On the contrary, it's the multiculturalists and their orthodox Muslim allies who are preoccupied with "us" and "them." It's they who think in terms of groups. Dismissing the individual, they see human beings first and foremost as members of an ethnic or religious collective; instead of recognizing all individuals as equal, they view all *groups* as equal. From this, it's only a short step to accepting the idea that no one has the right to question the guiding ideology of any group to which he or she doesn't belong—no matter how savage or primitive that ideology may be. Indeed, a good student of multiculturalism soon learns to feel squeamish even about using such words as "savage" or "primitive," because they're culturally subjective and imply criticism—which is, of course, *verboten*. Not only is assailing such practices as forced marriage, female genital mutilation, the subjugation of women, and the execution of apostates and rape victims and homosexuals out of bounds; even to mention them is to risk identifying oneself not as humane and civilized but as culturally insensitive and condescending. If we notice ourselves feeling uneasy about some aspect of the Islamic world, the multiculturalists instruct us to look in the mirror, as it were, and contemplate our own culture's worst aspects. Do Muslims stone adulteresses? Well, we execute murderers. Does Iran imprison, torture, and execute gays? Well, what about Guantánamo? Indeed, in recent years the politically correct response to every criticism of Islam could be summed up in those three words: "What about Guantánamo?"—the point being that until the West itself is morally without blemish, no one in the West has any right to criticize even the most heinous crimes against humanity by any non-Western individual, movement, group, or power. Even to report them is suspect—which explains why in November 2007 a *Times* of London article headlined "Gays should be hanged, says Iranian minister" drew online reader comments such as the following:

> When is the West going to learn not to meddle in other nations' affairs? It is none of our business what they do. It is their country, their culture. How do you justify our arrogance? As long as human rights violations in Germany, France, Canada (and they are absolutely stunning!) and the massive crimes committed by Israel are left unmentioned, are even tolerated and encouraged, who the hell are we to point fingers?

And:

> We may not agree with Iran's attitude and eventually it will change if the people want it to but it is none of our business . . . it took us a long time to learn so why not allow other countries to make their own decisions.

"Why beholdest thou the mote that is in thy brother's eye," Jesus asked, "but considerest not the beam that is in thine own eye?" Thanks largely to the influence of the Gospels, the capacity for self-criticism and self-correction is especially strong in Western culture and is a major reason for the West's success. (A culture must, after all, be able to examine itself critically if it wants to improve.) But the multicultural compulsion to switch off one's critical faculties when looking at foreign cultures is a grotesque perversion of this admirable Western virtue. And in the face of Islamic jihad, it is suicidal.

V

Fortuyn

The jihadist attacks on London, Madrid, and elsewhere that followed 9/11 didn't just drive home the fact that the jihadists, far from targeting only America, were at war with the entire free world. They also served as a reminder that not all of the Koran-besotted enemies of freedom lived in faraway places with strange-sounding names. On the contrary, during the years since the proclamation of the Rushdie fatwa, the population of Muslims living in the West had skyrocketed—and though many had migrated in search of individual liberty, others had come for purely economic reasons and had no fondness for secular government, sexual equality, or free speech. My own wake-up call about all this came in the year 2000, when I was living in Western Europe and discovered that most of its major cities were houses divided against themselves—the native Europeans and Muslim immigrants inhabiting not only different neighborhoods but, in most essential respects, different worlds, one of them free and the other governed more or less according to sharia law. In those cities, all you had to do to travel from a modern, post-Enlightenment democracy to a strict patriarchy out of seventh-century Arabia was to walk a few blocks. Western Europe's demography was changing dramatically, yet this transformation—and its grim implications—went almost entirely unmentioned in the American and European media.

Among the first prominent figures to sound the alarm about these implications was a Dutchman named Pim Fortuyn. A sociologist by training, Fortuyn warned that while his country generously subsidized Muslim families, schools, mosques, and community centers, it refused to challenge the brutal values that held sway in Muslim enclaves or to recognize the evidence that fundamentalist Islam, which was rapidly becoming the Netherlands' largest religion, was irreconcilable with Western democracy. In 1997 Fortuyn published the book *Against the Islamization of Our Culture;* only days before September 11, 2001, he wrote that communism's role as a threat to Western freedom "has been taken over by Islam." By this point Fortuyn had entered politics. Though his arguments hit home with many Dutchmen, most of his country's politicians and journalists, instead of heeding his message about the threat of Islam, saw *him* as a threat: they called him a fascist, painted him as a new Mussolini or Hitler, linked his name to such far-rightists as Jean-Marie Le Pen in France and Jörg Haider in Austria. And these lies were echoed around the world. Marlise Simons, profiling Fortuyn in a *New York Times* article whose headline described him as "Marching the Dutch to the Right," quoted one politician's characterization of him as a "dangerous man" and made sure to note the comparisons to Mussolini and Haider. There was no hint in Simons's piece, or in the great majority of the news reports and editorials about him, that (as I later wrote) Fortuyn, "by standing up against a fascist, female-oppressing ideology"—namely fundamentalist Islam—"was *resisting* the movement of the Netherlands to the right." After Fortuyn began campaigning for representation in the Dutch parliament, and it started to look as if he would be the next prime minister, the attacks grew even harsher. The result: on May 6, 2002, only nine days before the election, he was murdered by a left-wing extremist, Volkert van der Graaf, who later testified that he'd killed Fortuyn because his views on Muslim immigration made him a "danger." Van der Graaf's explanation of why he'd killed Fortuyn could have been lifted out of any one of a number of commentaries about Fortuyn that had appeared in the days before the murder.

Were journalists and politicians chastened by the knowledge that they'd contributed to Fortuyn's death? Hardly. The slurs continued unabated in the reports on the killing. "Dutch 'Le Pen' Assassinated," read the headline in the *Daily Mirror.*

Pim Fortuyn's life and death testified to a grim reality: speak the truth about Islam in the Western world today and you're a marked man. And those who paint the target on your back will be the cultural elite—the politicians, the professors, and above all the media. If the terrorist attacks in London and Madrid underscored the fact that jihadists were at war with the entire West, Fortuyn's murder can be recognized, in retrospect, as marking the resumption of the jihadist campaign to silence criticism of Islam that had begun with the Rushdie fatwa. Yet partly because van der Graaf was not himself a Muslim, partly because his declared motive was not widely reported, partly because Fortuyn was not only a writer (a rarely assassinated breed) but also a politician, and mainly because the media and others were at pains to depict Fortuyn not as a martyr for free speech but as a radical-right hatemonger who'd gotten what he had coming to him (though they were careful, of course, not to put it quite that way), the lesson of Fortuyn's murder was largely obscured. And that lesson was this: we weren't up against a "tiny" number of "extremists" who'd "hijacked" a "great and peaceful religion" (as many people, including President Bush, never tired of insisting) and who were committing "militant" (never "terrorist") acts motivated by legitimate economic and/or geopolitical grievances (as the PC left endlessly repeated), but we were, rather, facing a considerable percentage of the world's Muslims, many of them born and raised and resident in the West, who did indeed (as President Bush quite correctly put it) despise our freedoms, and who in trying to destroy those freedoms were (though Bush stubbornly refused to admit it) being entirely consistent with the tenets of their faith—and who had countless non-Muslim allies who, like van der Graaf, were steeped in PC and multicultural dogma and prepared, in the name of tolerance, to serve the jihadist effort to stifle Islam's critics.

Van Gogh

I t would take a second murder to begin to open many Western eyes to the fact that freedom of speech was, indeed, under attack by jihadists—and to accelerate efforts by politically correct Westerners to appease this new brand of jihad by shutting that freedom down.

That murder took place on an autumn morning on a busy Amsterdam street. On November 2, 2004, a heavyset, middle-aged man with a messy mop of blond hair was bicycling to work when he was shot by a young man sporting a beard and wearing a *jellaba*, a Muslim robe. Upon being struck by the bullet, the victim fell off his bike, whereupon his attacker leapt upon him, stabbed him several times, and pinned a note to his chest with a knife. The victim, Theo van Gogh, was one of the Netherlands' most famous citizens—a creative, restless, iconoclastic thinker who was at once a major celebrity and a genuine intellectual. In his inimitable TV appearances and newspaper columns, he was outrageous, clowning, self-deprecating, morally serious, passionate, and deliberately provocative. The more sacred an idea or a group was to the Dutch political and cultural establishment, the more irreverent van Gogh was about it. He was, in fact, the very personification of political incorrectness.

Few people outside the Netherlands had ever heard of him. Yet his assassination would have worldwide repercussions. For his murderer,

Mohammed Bouyeri, the Dutch-born son of Moroccan parents, was a radical Muslim whose motive for killing him was utterly straightforward: van Gogh had directed a film. Broadcast on Dutch television a few weeks earlier, it had featured a young Muslim woman who talked into the camera for approximately ten minutes about the treatment of her sex under Islam. On her nude body were scars, indicating that she had been whipped, as well as Koran verses written in Arabic—the point being that the Islamic holy books, which give Muslim men permission to confine, control, beat, rape, and even murder their wives, had indeed left their imprint on the bodies of countless Muslim women. In his lifetime (he was forty-seven), van Gogh had witnessed the transformation of Amsterdam from a mecca of individual liberty into something that increasingly resembled Mecca itself. At the time of his death, perhaps a quarter to a third of the city's residents were orthodox Muslims. Van Gogh was not alone in considering this something other than progress—but he was one of the few people in his country who were willing to say so in public. It was only natural that he ended up making a film like *Submission* (whose title is, of course, the English translation of "Islam").

Purportedly "moderate" Muslim leaders around the world issued pro forma condemnations of van Gogh's murder. But many, if not most, hastened to add that they could "understand" it, or words to that effect. What they emphasized in their statements was not their purported disapproval of the murder but their palpable disapproval of van Gogh and his film; to them, they made it clear, the murder was proof not that Western Muslims needed to adjust to the realities of free speech but that Westerners needed to assimilate traditional Muslim limitations on speech. For example, Ahmad Abu Laban of Denmark's Islamic Society (who would soon be leading efforts to pressure Denmark to curb free expression) charged that *Submission* had "crossed the limits of freedom of speech" and demanded "an open debate on these limits." Iqbal Sacranie of the Muslim Council of Britain (who would later be knighted by Queen Elizabeth) agreed. "Is freedom of expression without bounds?" he asked. "Muslims are not alone in saying 'No' and in calling for safeguards against vilification of dearly cherished beliefs." Even a Dutch Muslim actor named Farhane—who owed his career to van Gogh, and whom van Gogh had considered a friend—could not bring himself to condemn the murder. "I can see how one can be pushed into it," Farhane told writer Ian Buruma, calling *Submission* "an insult, the kind of insult I could never forget." Farhane was someone whom any casual observer would consider a model of successful assimilation—the kind of Muslim that Dutch politicians and journalists loved to hold up as proof that the immigrant experiment worked. Yet to read Farhane's comments about van Gogh's murder was to realize just how alien the mind-sets of even some "successfully assimilated" Western Muslims could be. (But then, many people had thought of van Gogh's murderer, too, as a poster boy for multiculturalism.)

What was most chilling, however, was that throughout the West, an extraordinary number of artists, actors, professors, politicians, journalists, and the like seemed more inclined to deplore van Gogh's alleged "insensitivity" to "Muslim feelings" (never mind that his film had been motivated by concern for Muslim women) than to deplore his murder. Newspapers like the *Guardian* in Britain and reflexively PC organizations such as Index on Censorship—whose purported reason for existence is to defend free speech—joined the imams and mullahs in expressing "understanding" for van Gogh's murderer. As Peter Whittle of the New Culture Forum has noted, "There were no significant expressions of outrage [over van Gogh's killing] from Britain's creative figures and institutions." In November 2004, after the two Dutch assassinations, it was far more obvious than it had been at the time of the Rushdie fatwa that there was a substantial number of Muslims in the West who wanted to see criticism of Islam stifled. Yet if in 1989 there had been, in Richard Bernstein's (perhaps somewhat rose-tinted) view, "a clear solidifying of the writers' ranks, a refusal to be cowed" by such people, in 2004 there appeared to be broad agreement among the cultural elites on the need to curb freedom of expression out of respect for Muslim sensitivities.

Many rank-and-file citizens, to be sure, didn't like the idea of such curbs ("Long live the Netherlands, long live free speech!" read a typical note placed amid the thousands of flowers at the scene of van Gogh's murder). Yet where were van Gogh's fellow writers, filmmakers, TV personalities, and newspaper columnists? When Bouyeri pumped that first bullet into van Gogh's body, it should have been the shot heard round the world; every believer in free speech should've rallied to the cause. But few did. Most looked the other way. They made excuses. They played deaf. And those who did speak up almost invariably found it necessary to chide van Gogh posthumously for his "vulgarity" and "insensitivity." They seemed not to grasp that if van Gogh had indeed sometimes been vulgar and outrageous, it was at least in part because he was trying to wake up a complacent, conformist society and remind its members that they had a right to say what they thought—and, yes, even be vulgar if they wished. Nor did they grasp that van Gogh's murder had been an attempt to silence not just one man but an entire society.

And it succeeded. Not entirely, but to a truly alarming extent. After van Gogh's murder, self-censorship in a range of professions intensified. In what might have been the bitterest irony, a screening of *Submission* at a festival of censored films was canceled out of fear of Muslim reprisal. "Does this mean I'm yielding to terror?" asked the film's producer, Gijs van de Westelaken. "Yes. But I'm not a politician or an antiterrorist police officer; I'm a film producer." This mentality was widespread, suggesting that in the privileged twenty-first-century West, many simply don't understand that the individual is the first line of defense against attacks on freedom of speech. Where people are scared to speak, there is no freedom of speech. And self-censorship was only part of it. Across Europe—as we shall see—efforts by legislatures, courts, and universities to suppress and punish public criticism of Islam intensified. Instead of motivating people to rally against the forces of censorship, in short, van Gogh's murder seemed only to advance the perpetrator's cause.

VII

The Cartoons

A mong those affected by the chill on free speech was a Danish author who, when he tried to find somebody to draw pictures of Muhammed for a children's biography, got turned down by one illustrator after another, because they were too scared of possible Muslim reprisal.

That author's name was Kåre Bluitgen, and one day a few months after van Gogh's murder, his predicament came to the attention of Flemming Rose, the culture editor of Denmark's largest newspaper, *Jyllands-Posten*. Rose was alarmed. Had the murder of Theo van Gogh already had such an adverse effect on free expression? Rose decided that something should be done to assert free people's right to express their opinions on any topic—including Islam. So he invited all forty-odd members of the Danish Cartoonists' Association to submit drawings of the prophet Muhammed. Twelve sent in submissions. On September 30, 2005, the newspaper ran them. Most of the pictures were pretty tame: a couple were provocative in the way editorial cartoons are supposed to be. But compared to the lusty Christian-baiting in movies like *Life of Brian* and in works by artists like Andres Serrano and Gilbert and George—whose "provocative" and "transgressive" and "irreverent" works have made them media darlings—Rose's cartoons were pretty pallid stuff. Three of them actually targeted not Muhammed or Islam but *Jyllands-Posten* and Bluitgen. (In one, a Danish schoolboy named Mohammed stands before a blackboard on which he has written: "*Jyllands-Posten*'s editors are a bunch of reactionary provocateurs.")

These days, when writers or artists bait Christians, the Christians (at the very most) wave signs, put out press releases, and—as we've seen in the case of the Catholic League's Bill Donohue—go on TV to complain. By contrast, when Danish Muslims saw the Muhammed cartoons, they went ballistic. Thousands protested in Copenhagen. Death threats rained down upon *Jyllands-Posten*'s editors and the twelve cartoonists, who were forced into hiding (including those who had chosen the "safe" targets, *Jyllands-Posten* and Bluitgen). Sheikh Mohammed Sayyed Tantawi, the Grand Mufti of Al-Alzhar University in Cairo and a purported liberal Muslim, called the cartoons "one of the most serious crimes ever committed" and urged the Danish government to close down the newspaper and imprison its editors. On October 12, ten ambassadors from Muslim countries (plus a Palestinian envoy), citing "the interest of inter-faith harmony, better integration and Denmark's overall relations with the Muslim world," demanded that Danish prime minister Anders Fogh Rasmussen "take all those responsible to task under the law of the land."

There was one particularly striking sentence in the ambassadors' letter (which later turned out to have been written at the instigation of Copenhagen imam Abu Laban): "Danish press and public representatives," they insisted, "should not be allowed to abuse Islam in the name of democracy, freedom of expression and human rights, the values that we all share." Yes, *the values that we all share*—an eyebrow-raising claim, given that the signatories included the envoys from Saudi Arabia (where it's forbidden to own a Bible), Pakistan (where criticism of Muhammed is a capital crime), and Iran (where gays and rape victims are executed). Of the ten countries represented by these men, six are rated by Freedom House as "not free," four as "partly free," and none as "free."

The ambassadors requested a meeting with Fogh Rasmussen to discuss the issue. He refused. His later explanation of this rebuff stands as a model of how a democratic leader should behave in such circumstances: "It is so self-evidently clear what principles Danish society is based upon," he said, "that there is nothing to have a meeting about." This blunt stance was encouraging, and so was that of *Jyllands-*

Posten's beleaguered editors, who issued this statement: "Our right to say, write, photograph and draw what we want to within the framework of the law exists and must endure—unconditionally!" Yet ranged against them was virtually the entire international political establishment, including top United Nations and European Union brass—several of whom invoked the possibility of taking official action against offensive speech. Just as the Dutch cultural elite had responded to van Gogh's murder by saying that he'd brought it on himself with his "vulgarity" and "insensitivity," so now *Jyllands-Posten* was blamed for getting itself in hot water by being—yes—vulgar and insensitive.

The crisis shifted into high gear when Abu Laban and some of his fellow imams took the cartoons on a publicity tour of the Muslim world. Their purpose: to stir up anti-Danish agitation and thus intimidate Danish authorities into curbing speech. Since *Jyllands-Posten*'s own cartoons were apparently deemed inadequate for this purpose, the imams added to their presentation other items that they dishonestly represented as having been published in *Jyllands-Posten*. One was a drawing of Muhammed being sexually violated by a dog; another, a photograph of a man in a pig mask, was actually an AP wire photo taken at a French hog-calling competition, and had nothing whatsoever to do with Muhammed or Islam. The imams plainly included these items in their arsenal because they believed their fellow Muslims would react even more strongly to them than to the actual *Jyllands-Posten* cartoons. The cynicism of this action speaks for itself. In any event, it worked. Anti-Danish protests erupted around the Muslim world; Danish embassies were vandalized, Danish businesses boycotted, Danish Web sites hacked, and scores of people killed—all of which, of course, merely proved the point of most of the cartoons. In late January, the al-Aqsa Martyrs' Brigades and Islamic Jihad ordered Scandinavians out of Palestinian areas. In February alone, Muslim reactions to the cartoons were responsible for the deaths of four people in Afghanistan, eight people in Pakistan, eleven people in Libya, sixteen people in Nigeria, and an Italian priest who was murdered in Turkey by a teenager shouting "Allahu akbar!" In March, fifty thousand protesters gathered in Karachi, many of them calling for death to the cartoonists. According to one count, well over a hundred people died as a result of the cartoon uproar.

Many Muslims obviously saw the cartoons as an opportunity to nudge an already passive Europe a step closer to full-fledged dhimmitude, or underclass status. But the Danes weren't having it. In a January 2006 poll, 79 percent of them said that Fogh Rasmussen owed no apologies for his uncompromising stand on free speech. Yet for millions of multiculturalist Europeans who had internalized sharia restrictions, Muslim acts of violence and murder in response to acts of expression were now an accepted part of life. In the view of such Europeans, the fault for any unpleasantness lay with those who "provoked" Muslim reprisals by failing to be submissive enough. When European Union Trade Commissioner Peter Mandelson complained that every republication of the cartoons by European newspapers was "adding fuel to the flames," he was, whether he was aware of it or not, giving voice to the already widespread tendency to think of Muslim masses on the rampage as if they were not human beings behaving aggressively but, rather, some phenomenon, like a forest fire, that could not itself be blamed for spreading out of control.

Across Europe, then, the same kind of secular leftists who all their lives had reflexively cheered artists for outraging Christians now insisted upon Muslims' sacred right not to be offended. Perhaps the most positive surprise in all of this was the courage with which many European newspaper editors defied the Islamists and reprinted the cartoons, in some cases with the express intention of demonstrating their support for free speech and solidarity with *Jyllands-Posten*, in other cases simply to show their readers what all the fuss was about. The cartoons appeared in scores of major dailies in Italy, Germany, Spain, and elsewhere. Even the left-wing French newspaper of record *Le Monde* ran a witty, elegant illustration in which the words "I must not draw Muhammed," scrawled several dozen times, as if by a child at a blackboard, added up to a portrait of Muhammed. Jacques Lefranc, editor of *France Soir*, reprinted the cartoons alongside a statement that "We will never apologize for having the freedom to print, to speak, and to believe . . . We've had enough of being instructed by these overly pious reactionaries." The next day the newspaper's French-Egyptian owner fired Lefranc and published an abject apology. Mohammed al-Asadi, editor of the *Yemen Observer* and a fierce critic of the cartoons, published a small reproduction of them so that readers might share his outrage—only to be sentenced to death himself.

Not all the major news media in Europe followed the example of *Le Monde* and *Die Welt*. No British newpaper ran the cartoons. Britain's Channel Four, Peter Whittle noted, "debated whether or not freedom of expression was threatened, concluded it was not, and then with spectacular absurdity refrained from showing the cartoons for fear of causing offense." Nor did *Jyllands-Posten* receive much support from its fellow news media in Scandinavia. American editors, too, proved cowardly. Only one major daily in the United States—the *Philadelphia Inquirer*—reprinted any of the cartoons. Seattle's alternate weekly, *The Stranger*, published the most famous of the cartoons—the one by *Jyllands-Posten* staff cartoonist Kurt Westergaard showing Muhammed with a bomb in his turban—to illustrate a piece by me about the cartoons. But while *The Stranger*'s editors had the guts to do this— as did innumerable bloggers—the mighty broadcast networks CBS, NBC, ABC, and Fox did not. Nor did the cable news channels CNN, MSNBC, and Fox News. In an editorial, the *New York Times* defended its refusal to print the cartoons as "a reasonable choice for news organizations that usually refrain from gratuitous assaults on religious symbols." (Describing this editorial as "a characteristically pompous and ponderous piece of chin-stroking sanctimony," Gerard Baker of the *Times* of London dryly recalled that the Gray Lady had in the past run pictures of "works of art such as a crucifix in a vat of urine or an icon of the Virgin Mary covered in elephant dung.") The magazine *Free Inquiry* reprinted the cartoons—but both the Borders Books and Waldenbooks chains refused to sell the issue in question. In all of Canada, only two marginal publications, the *Western Standard* and *Jewish Free Press*, reprinted them; both were reported to the Alberta Human Rights Commission.

While American journalists and politicians competed to see who could display the greatest sensitivity toward Muslim rioters' tender feelings (both Bill Clinton and George W. Bush condemned the cartoons), it was left to ordinary Americans to stand up for free speech. Bloggers got the word out about Denmark's plight and rallied support. In response to the Muslim boycott of Danish goods, journalist Christopher Hitchens, blogger Charles Johnson, and others organized a campaign to encourage people to buy products of Denmark. Hundreds of Web sites featured small Danish flags and such slogans as "Buy Danish" and "Support Denmark!" This campaign's spectacular success—Danish exports actually went *up*—is perhaps the most encouraging pro–free speech development of recent years. And it is no coincidence that it was from beginning to end a grassroots initiative. I am not aware of any major government body, university, or newspaper that endorsed it.

VIII

The Magazinet *Case*

While Flemming Rose and his colleagues were under siege in Denmark, in Norway another editor was watching developments with mounting concern. "Has it come this far here in Norway, too," Vebjørn Selbekk later recalled reflecting, "that Muslim threats of violence have to be taken into consideration when newspapers are deciding what to print and not print?" Selbekk, editor of a Christian newspaper, *Magazinet*, with a circulation of about four thousand, decided to publish a six-page feature on the cartoon crisis. Included was an interview with Finn Graff, Norway's most famous newspaper cartoonist. Graff, notorious for his hard-hitting cartoons, had in the past depicted both Menachem Begin and Ariel Sharon in Nazi uniforms. Now, however, he'd decided not to draw anything that might offend Muslims. "When the reaction can be threats of violence or of having your throat cut," he explained, "you've reached the limit. You've got to draw a line somewhere." To be sure, he claimed his decision was based "as much on respect for [Muslims'] religious belief as on real fear." (In short, he supposedly respected beliefs that he knew might drive people to kill him.) Given that Graff had spent decades wielding his pen with what some readers doubtless imagined was passionate moral indignation, it was interesting to discover that he was, morally speaking, a hollow vessel, with absolutely no sense of moral obligation to defend the rights of which he had made such abundant and profitable use. (In 2007, Graff would be awarded the Order of Saint Olav, the closest thing in Norway to a knighthood.)

But the highlight of *Magazinet*'s feature wasn't the interview with Graff. It was a reproduction of the *Jyllands-Posten* page containing the Muhammed cartoons. Selbekk knew that reprinting them might mean trouble, but he felt it was important for his readers to see them, and refused to be swayed by fear. As he later wrote, he felt "a fundamental unwillingness to accept that there should be danger involved in exercising freedom of speech in Norway." In an interview accompanying the cartoons, he decried the curbs on expression that were silently being introduced in Norway.

Selbekk wasn't the only Norwegian editor to reprint the cartoons. The country's newspaper of record, *Aftenposten*, ran them; so did the Web site of another major daily, *Dagbladet*. Several good-sized regional newspapers published them, too. But it was the tiny *Magazinet*, which most Norwegians had never even heard of, that became the target of PC wrath. An official at Norwegian Church Aid accused *Magazinet* of "deliberately wounding and provoking our Muslim brothers and sisters." The Socialist Youth organization in the county of West Agder reported *Magazinet* to the Norwegian government's official Press Complaints Commission. Many ordinary Norwegians faulted Selbekk as well. When he made his case on a prime-time discussion program, *Redaksjon EN*, the text messages from viewers included the following:

- "There's something wrong in a democracy when an editor can put the entire country in danger."
- "Printing a picture of Muhammed has nothing to do with freedom of expression."
- "If Jesus were presented as a terrorist I would be very insulted."
- "The editor must be blind if he can't see that the cartoons were offensive."
- "There must not be an IQ test for being editor of *Magazinet*."
- "The cartoons have been printed ONLY to provoke!"
- "How can a Christian newspaper . . . mock another religion?"

Selbekk's fellow panelists on *Redaksjon EN* characterized him as being on the far right, linked him to America, Israel, and George W. Bush (the closest thing in Norway to an Axis of Evil), and accused him of "malice toward Islam." *Magazinet*, a professor on the program complained, was destroying the intercultural harmony that he and others had spent the past ten or fifteen years working for; it didn't seem to occur to him that if printing a few cartoons could destroy this "harmony," it might not have been there to begin with.

Selbekk had one highly placed supporter: Per Edgar Kokkvold, general secretary of the Norwegian Press Association. "Freedom of expression," Kokkvold said, "is not something that comes in addition to the other human rights; it's a precondition for the other rights' existence." Noting that Muslim organizations, in response to the cartoons, had "talked about offering Danish journalists a sort of Koran course," Kokkvold offered a counter-suggestion: "We should perhaps urge the Islamic Council to offer its members a course in freedom of expression."

Though the *Jyllands-Posten* cartoons had appeared around the world, Muslim leaders used Selbekk's reprinting of them as an excuse to target Norway alongside Denmark. Norwegian flags were burned, Norwegian businesses boycotted. Yet while Denmark's leaders remained resolute in the face of anti-Danish attacks in the Middle East, Norwegian officials caved instantly. Prime Minister Jens Stoltenberg said flat out that Selbekk had been wrong to reprint the cartoons and implicitly threatened *Magazinet* with prosecution under the long-quiescent blasphemy law—a piece of legislation that Stoltenberg's own party had sought to annul.[1]

Stoltenberg wasn't alone. Condemnations of Selbekk ranged across Norway's mainstream political spectrum. The country's socialist parties slammed *Magazinet*; Dagfinn Høybråten, head of the Christian People's Party, gave voice to the multicultural prioritization of "respect" when he said that "Freedom of expression means the freedom to express oneself, not an exemption from using common sense. If one demands respect for one's own faith, one owes it to other people to respect theirs." (Forget the Enlightenment assertion of the inalienable right to criticize religion, which helped open the door to

---

[1] Both countries' leaders appeared to reflect the popular will: while Danes overwhelmingly supported Fogh Rasmussen's unequivocal defense of free speech, Norwegians believed, by a margin of 49.6 percent to 25.3 percent, that *Magazinet* had been wrong to reprint the cartoons.

the modern world of secular pluralistic democracy.) Throughout the cartoon crisis, the Norwegian Authors' Union and Norway's Freedom of Expression Foundation remained silent, while the head of Norwegian PEN, Kjell Olaf Jensen, called on Selbekk to apologize, telling *Aftenposten* that "*Magazinet* has the legal right to offend 1.3 billion people. But there's nothing morally respectable about their doing it. . . . If you're an idiot you're completely within your rights to exercise your freedom of speech, but that doesn't make the action more respectable." Thus did the head of an organization founded to defend writers' freedom of expression decide that it was now his job, instead, to pronounce on the respectability (or lack thereof) of imaginative works—at least when they addressed Islam.

Most Norwegian newspaper editors who addressed the *Magazinet* case were downright shameful. The editors of *Dagbladet*, for example, declared their refusal "to take part in a defense of freedom of speech that stops at the simple right to express oneself"—meaning, in other words, that freedom of speech needed to be qualified out of respect for Muslim sensitivities. An editorial in *Teknisk Ukeblad* (*Technical Weekly*) actually suggested that Norwegian companies that were experiencing "problems" in Pakistan "could demand economic redress from 'the brave' editor for economic loss as a result of the editor's willful smearing of Norway's reputation among the world's Muslims."

Selbekk's most outspoken critic, Foreign Affairs Minister Jonas Gahr Støre, insisted that freedom of expression "demands in our time and society a sensitivity to ethnic and religious values that mean a lot to people." When the *Jerusalem Post* reprinted the cartoons, Gahr Støre complained that "freedom of expression is there to be exercised with reason, and editors must take responsibility." It was appalling to see an official of a free country lecturing the media about their "responsibility," when he clearly had no understanding of where his own obligations lay. Gahr Støre even blamed Selbekk in part for the burning of Norway's embassy in Damascus. The rapidity with which he and Stoltenberg knuckled under to jihad could only have been read by Muslim radicals as a sign that Norway was indeed spineless—a country so in love with peace (or, perhaps, with its peace-loving and multicultural self-image) that it would sell out the highest democratic principles rather than endure any conflict whatsoever.

Selbekk has argued that the Norwegian government deliberately scapegoated him, and the evidence certainly seems to back him up. Both Stoltenberg and Gahr Støre said repeatedly that *Magazinet* was the only publication in Norway that had reprinted the cartoons; Gahr Støre kept repeating that they hadn't appeared in any of Norway's *"toneangivende"* (tone-giving) press, meaning the media that shape public discourse and whose leading editors and writers are friendly with government officials—the media, in short, that belong to the PC club. *Magazinet* didn't belong to the club—which appears to be why the Norwegian political establishment hung it out to dry. (Disgracefully, both *Aftenposten* and *Dagbladet*, instead of admitting that they'd reprinted the cartoons, too, joined in scapegoating *Magazinet*; indeed, when a Christian news bureau sent out a story pointing out that *Aftenposten* had reprinted the cartoons, an *Aftenposten* editor placed an angry phone call to the bureau.) Another reprehensible moment came when Gahr Støre sent a letter to Norwegian ambassadors instructing them to respond to any criticism of *Magazinet* by expressing regret for its actions and by stating that it was Norway's belief that free speech comes with limits. Selbekk quite justly characterized this as "prostration before some of the most totalitarian regimes in the Middle East." In the letter, Gahr Støre argued that the cartoons weren't "constructive for building the necessary bridge between cultures and religions." Kokkvold gave this the reply it deserved, explaining that "the cartoon has never had this function." "Constructive"? The cartoon's "nature is to tear down," he pointed out. "Respect"? The cartoon, he noted, "is disrespectful by its very nature." Rather than demand "constructive" behavior and "respect," Kokkvold insisted, "Muslim organizations in Norway must stand up and unequivocally defend every human being's right to express himself freely without being persecuted or threatened with murder and violence." Alas, Kokkvold was whistling in the dark.

For weeks, Selbekk defied death threats, abuse by Norway's political and media establishment, and demands from around the world that he apologize. Then, suddenly, he did an about-face. His own account of why he threw in the towel is exceedingly unconvincing. (He claims, absurdly, that he feared the news stories about the *Magazinet* case were turning people against Muslims and that if he didn't give in, there might be anti-Muslim violence.) In any event, on the morning of February 10, after several days of intense secret negotiation involving Stoltenberg, Gahr Støre, and Muslim leaders, Selbekk appeared at the press room of the Norwegian Ministry of Labor and Social Inclusion. There, standing alongside several cabinet ministers and no fewer than fourteen imams representing forty-six organizations (the largest assemblage of Muslim leaders in Norwegian history), Selbekk read to reporters a three-minute statement that Siv Jensen of the Progress Party would later call "a display of cowardice."

It's telling that Selbekk, in his memoir of the cartoon saga, neglects to quote so much as a single word from his statement, which was, after all, the climactic text of that saga's Norwegian subplot. The reason is obvious: the statement makes painful—and undoubtedly, for Selbekk, embarrassing—reading. Claiming that he hadn't completely understood "how wounding" the reprinting of the *Jyllands-Posten* cartoons was, a grotesquely abject Selbekk told the Muslim community: "Today I would like to apologize for that. I apologize deeply for the fact that you, as Muslims, have had your religious feelings hurt by what we have done." As if this weren't enough, Selbekk praised Norwegian Muslims for "deal[ing] with this situation in a dignified and restrained manner. For this they deserve honor and respect." Respect for what? No leading figure in Norway's Muslim community had said or done anything in support of free speech. Nor had there been any demonstrations by Muslims in Selbekk's defense. Not that anybody expected such things. No, apparently the best one could hope for was that Norway's Muslims would refrain from rioting, killing, and burning down buildings, as their coreligionists had done abroad, to protest the publication of a few cartoons. Only by these extremely low standards had they merited praise for their behavior. Nor did it matter that while Muslims in the Middle East had been burning Norwegian flags and a Norwegian embassy, Muslim leaders in Norway had effectively been acting in concert with them, doing what they could to try to bring both *Magazinet* and free speech to their knees.

Selbekk's prepared remarks on that dark morning leaned heavily on familiar multicultural formulas. He spoke, for example, of "understanding." It was clear that Selbekk had indeed come to an understanding: he understood that if he didn't relent, he risked physical harm for himself and his loved ones. He also spoke of "respect," a word that in this context must surely have been understood by the imams to refer not to a volitional esteem for a social equal but to the compulsory deference of a repentant infidel—a dhimmi. In addition, there was the usual banal rhetoric about how "immigrants enrich Norwegian society," how "Norwegian Muslims are peace-loving and good people," and how "we all must follow the path of dialogue." All this, of course, was hogwash, signaling that Selbekk would henceforth play nice. Selbekk also suggested that harassment and stigmatization of Norwegian Muslims had increased significantly because of the cartoon crisis. This, too, was sheer nonsense, but for Muslim and Norwegian leaders it was reassuringly consistent with their own line. Selbekk concluded by hoping that "some good can come out of the difficult things that have happened. Perhaps we all can learn something important. About freedom of speech. About dialogue. And about religion." Well, those who had followed the controversy attentively *had* learned something—they'd learned that thanks to the bullying adherents of a certain religion and their allies, freedom of speech had now been damaged.

After Selbekk had finished making his apology, Mohammed Hamdan, head of Norway's Islamic Council, accepted it on behalf of his fellow imams and declared the matter closed. Hamdan then guaranteed Selbekk's safety. It was a picture out of a sharia courtroom: the dhimmi prostrating himself before the Muslim leader, and the leader pardoning him—and, for good measure, placing Selbekk under his protection as if it were he, Hamdan, and not the Norwegian police, that held Norwegian citizens' security in his hands. "Selbekk has children the same age as my own," Hamdan said. "I want my children and his children to grow up together, live together in peace, and be friends." For many who heard this statement, and who were familiar with the subtext-rich rhetoric of many Islamists in the West, the implication seemed clear: had Selbekk *not* capitulated, the future peace of his children—who, as everyone knew, had been in hiding along with their father—might well have been jeopardized. It is also worth remembering that many Muslims, when speaking to nonbelievers, say that "Islam" means "peace"— so that one may read Hamdan's remark as implying that he looked forward to a Norway in which his and Selbekk's children would live together under Islam.

The press conference was profoundly disturbing. Yet the Norwegian government was delighted. Gahr Støre, who had responded to Selbekk's bravery with insults and threats, now congratulated him on his capitulation, which he characterized, in repulsively Orwellian terms, as an act of "responsibility" that displayed "integrity and courage." Norway's imams were ecstatic. One of them said that "the fact that Norwegians have apologized gives Norway . . . a higher status than before"—the implication plainly being that it was the prerogative of Muslim leaders to determine the "status" of non-Muslim countries. And *Aftenposten* cheered Selbekk's surrender, while denying that it constituted an admission that he'd had no right to publish the cartoons. This was, of course, a sad self-deception; in truth, Norway had taken a giant step toward a purely theoretical freedom of speech—a "freedom" of which fewer and fewer Norwegians, surely, after Selbekk's officially sanctioned act of national humiliation, would dare to avail themselves. On that day, as Selbekk himself later admitted, "Norway went a long way toward allowing freedom of speech to become the Islamists' hostage."

As if Norway hadn't already been disgraced enough, an official delegation led by the dean of the Oslo cathedral, Olav Dag Hauge, then traveled to Qatar to meet with Muslim leader Yusuf al-Qaradawi—a defender of suicide bombers and the author of an essay entitled "Our War with the Jews Is in the Name of Islam"—and implored him to accept Selbekk's apology. Lucky them; he did. "To meet Yusuf al-Qaradawi under the present circumstances," the Norwegian-Iraqi writer Walid al-Kubaisi quite rightly pronounced, "is tantamount to granting extreme Islamists and defenders of terror a right of joint consultation regarding how Norway should be governed." Apropos of Hauge's post-visit characterization of Qaradawi as "a warm person who said that he wanted peace," blogger Jan Arild Snoen pointed out that Qaradawi ran the committee responsible for the orthodoxy of the Web site islam online.net, on which one could read (among much else) that Western tolerance of homosexuality made humans lower than animals.

Some of those who played key roles in the deplorable events of February 10, 2006, were quick to deny afterward that what had happened had, in fact, happened. Bjarne Håkon Hanssen, Norway's Minister of Labor and Social Inclusion (under whose department's auspices the capitulation had taken place), insisted that Selbekk had not apologized for his freedom of speech. "It is unimaginable," Hanssen said with astonishing fatuity, "that this case could have any effect on the health of freedom of speech in Norway." Selbekk himself maintained at the time that he hadn't apologized for exercising his freedom of speech, but only for hurting feelings. But a freedom of speech that makes such a substantial exception for so-called hurt feelings is no freedom of speech at all. In an *Aftenposten* op-ed, Selbekk claimed that "we had a responsibility for the fact that the way we conducted ourselves could help quiet down a situation that was becoming rather dramatic." In other words, if the opponents of a speech act kick up enough of a fuss over it, it's the speaker's responsibility to make a display of contrition in hopes of restoring calm.

At least Norway had its brief moment of resistance. Not Sweden. Among the European officials who insisted firmly during the cartoon crisis that their nations enjoyed free speech—only to insist even more firmly that that right must be exercised "responsibly"—was Swedish foreign minister Laila Freivalds. Responding to the appearance of one of the Muhammed cartoons on the Web site of the far-right Sweden Democrats Party, Freivalds didn't just call for "responsibility" but actively enforced it, dispatching the Security Police to close down the party Web site and pronouncing it "frightful that a small group of Swedish extremists can expose Swedes to a clear danger"—as if it were the Sweden Democrats, and not jihadists, who were threatening violence. If Anders Fogh Rasmussen had sought to make it clear to Muslims that democratic governments have no power to silence the free expression of ideas, Freivalds appeared determined to show that in Sweden, at least, this was no longer the case.

The appalling conduct of the Norwegian and Swedish governments during the cartoon crisis only demonstrated how terrified they were of Muslims—and how unwilling they were to endure discomfort, take risks, or make sacrifices to preserve free speech. "For the first time in a long time," Kokkvold lamented, "there are strong forces that believe we should . . . grant the power to define [blasphemy] to those who feel offended by the blasphemy."

After the dust of the cartoon crisis had settled, those who had stood up for free speech did not feel that they had triumphed. "I would guess," said *Jyllands-Posten* editor-in-chief Juste ruefully, "that no one will draw the prophet Muhammed in Denmark in the next generation." His stark conclusion: "They have won." Kokkvold lamented that while freedom of expression is apparently "limitless when the utterances are aimed at the weak, at those who can't strike back," it's now "strongly limited when the utterances are directed at those who are strong and who reply to them with terror and murder." This, he observed, is a disaster, for

> Our civilization is built on two foundations. One of them
> is awareness of the individual human being's absolute value
> independent of race, religion, and social background. The other
> is the freedom to think and express one's thoughts. If freedom
> is to have any meaning at all, it must mean the freedom to
> say what others don't like to hear. . . . We can't have a halfway
> freedom of expression, a freedom of expression that doesn't
> apply to Islam.

As for Selbekk himself, who in the days after his apology had insisted defensively that free speech in Norway was still alive and well, he soon changed his tune. "What Norwegian editor in the future," he asked, "will voluntarily expose himself to a cacophony of death threats and unpleasantness of the sort we experienced? Not many." Many people agreed with Lars Bille, a political scientist at the University of Copenhagen, who in late 2007 told the Associated Press that "a lesson learned from the Muhammed crisis" was not "to provoke anyone for the sake of provocation." This was a nice way of saying that people had learned to hold their tongues. Many, indeed, had joined Bille in accepting the role of dhimmis—yet if you were to tell them that this was the case, they would doubtless deny it angrily. No, they would insist, *I'm just being practical; I'm just being prudent.* Perhaps the most pathetic aspect of dhimmitude is the fact that dhimmis keep telling themselves that they *aren't* dhimmis—that they're just being *sensible.*

The Norwegian authorities' handling of the *Magazinet* case was founded on a fundamental self-deception: the conceit that they were magnanimous people who were standing up against the powerful in defense of the weak. In fact they were cowards who were driven by a fear of the powerful to pick on the weak. Stoltenberg, Gahr Støre, and company bowed down to totalitarians—yet because the totalitarians didn't look like Hitler or Mussolini, it was easy to persuade good multiculturalists to see them as helpless victims. In a 2006 statement reacting to Selbekk's memoir of the *Magazinet* case, Gahr Støre reiterated the untruth that "no leading Norwegian media outlets" had reprinted the cartoons, denied that the Norwegian government had scapegoated *Magazinet*, and expressed the belief that he and Selbekk could "agree on the necessity of safeguarding the basic principles on which our society is built, such as freedom of expression and human rights, including the right to practice one's religion freely and the right for one's faith not to be insulted." To assert that last-named "right," of course—a "right" that is radically at odds with the spirit of the Enlightenment (even though blasphemy laws have survived in many Western countries, and from time to time even been enforced in isolated cases)—is to utterly abrogate freedom of expression.

Meanwhile, Mohammed Hamdan went from triumph to triumph. Appearing on Al-Jazeera shortly after accepting Selbekk's apology, he told millions of Muslims worldwide that Norwegians "believe in the freedom of the press more than we believe in God. Unfortunately freedom of speech is their religion." Given that Norwegian politicians had insisted repeatedly during the cartoon crisis that people like Hamdan were loyal, foursquare Norwegians, it was interesting to note Hamdan's use of the word "they" to refer to Norwegians; one might also note that if Hamdan's claim about Norwegians' reverence for free speech was true, then Hamdan had, in fact, managed quite a coup: he had gotten Norwegian authorities to betray their god and bow to his.

Months after Hamdan accepted Selbekk's apology—and far be it from me to suggest that there might be anything suspicious about this—Norwegian Minister of Culture and Church Affairs Trond Giske met with Hamdan for an hour or so and then announced that the government's annual support to Hamdan's Islamic Council was being raised from sixty thousand to half a million kroner. Norway's mainstream media treated this as routine news that did not warrant any puzzlement or speculation. Nor was that the end of it. In the summer of 2006, when Hamas envoys met with the Norwegian Parliament—which had decided to stop considering it a terrorist organization—Hamdan, whose brother Osama is a Hamas representative in Lebanon, took part in the meeting, though he maintained that his role was strictly that of a translator.

PART TWO

Censors and Self-Censors

The Ripple Effect

he van Gogh murder and Danish cartoon crisis had a massive ripple effect.

Motivated variously by fear, misguided sympathy, and multicultural ideology—or by a combination thereof—more and more individuals at every level of Western society have allowed concerns about what Muslims will think and do to influence their actions. Meanwhile the cultural jihad goes on, with different people contributing to it in different ways.

- European Muslim children, for example, torment their Jewish schoolmates—who in some places have been advised by teachers and political leaders to leave their yarmulkes and Stars of David at home in order to avoid "provoking trouble."

- Imams give interviews to journalists in which they insist that there's no compulsion in Islam, that Muslim women enjoy complete equality, and that jihad means striving to lead a virtuous life—and the journalists nod obediently as they take it all down.

- Silky-smooth Muslim academics persuade their infidel colleagues that it's only fair to make certain "adjustments" to democracy out of deference to Islamic sensibilities. And while street gangs in European cities commit rapes and gay-bashings —assaulting people who, their religion tells them, deserve these assaults because their clothing or conduct violates Koranic precepts—the ever so soft-spoken representatives of Islamic Councils and Muslim Associations subtly warn political leaders that unless they adjust this law or that policy to placate their "new countrymen," there may well (ahem) be even *more* violence in the streets.

Add to this steady drumbeat of low-level activity the occasional wave of mass violence—such as the one, for example, that erupted in September 2006 after Pope Benedict quoted a fourteenth-century comment about Islam in an academic lecture in Regensburg, Germany, and the one that followed the reprinting of the *Jyllands-Posten* cartoons by several Danish newspapers in early 2008 in reaction to the imposition of an Islamist death sentence on turban-bomb cartoonist Kurt Westergaard—and you get a formula for twenty-first-century jihad that, so far, has worked like a charm. It came as no surprise when the Dutch intelligence service reported in late 2007 that European imams, many of whom had earlier encouraged their congregants to join (or at least support) the terrorist war on the West, were now instead advising them to undermine Western freedoms in orderly ways, from within Western society. Plainly, the imams recognized that while dramatic, large-scale acts of terror by a few can have the unfortunate effect of rallying infidels en masse to defend their liberties (if only, perhaps, in the short term), the day-to-day efforts by a broad spectrum of Western Muslims to guilt-trip, grievance-monger, intimidate, bully, and exhaust infidels into compromising with—and, ultimately, surrendering to—sharia is proving highly effective.

It may be appropriate at this juncture to underscore an extremely important distinction in regard to religious moderation, and the point is this: that while there are such things as moderate and liberal Christianity, there is no such thing as a moderate or liberal Islam. Yes, there are millions of good-hearted individuals who identify themselves as Muslims and who have no enmity in their hearts for their non-Muslim neighbors and coworkers. Some of these Muslims are religiously observant, some are not; but their moderation is not an attribute of the brand of Islam to which they officially subscribe but is, rather, a measure of their own individual character. There are also a few extremely brave individual Muslims, such as the Canadian lesbian writer Irshad Manji, who are striving to establish a genuinely liberal Islam; but such an entity, alas, does not yet exist in practice, except in the hearts and minds and souls of a small number of revolutionary figures like Manji. Today, rather, Islam remains overwhelmingly a totalizing ideology—one whose edicts encompass all of life and are highly specific and severe in regard to adherents' belief and conduct.

This is not to deny that there exist many individual Muslims who deserve the label moderate or even liberal; it is only to say—again—that almost all of them are moderate or liberal not because they subscribe to a less conservative interpretation of their faith, but because they have chosen to put a certain distance between their own religious thought and practice and the strict tenets of institutional Islam. Some of them, indeed, may well be non-believers who have chosen to keep their non-belief to themselves in order to avoid risking the Koranic penalty for apostasy (namely, death).

As a rule, then, a moderate Muslim doesn't see extremist Muslims as getting their religion wrong in quite the way that, say, a liberal Episcopalian might feel that a conservative Southern Baptist has gotten Christianity wrong; such a Muslim, rather, even though he deeply abhors the actions of his violent coreligionists, may well be unable to shake off the feeling that they're more dedicated to Islam than *he* is. The result: a profound reluctance to criticize. Though the moderate Muslim is not motivated in the slightest to fly planes into buildings, he may well find it exceedingly difficult to criticize such actions, because when he contemplates them he can't entirely dismiss the thought that the perpetrators are better, truer, more devoted Muslims than he is.

I'm not saying that this is true of all moderate Muslims. But the fact remains that if there are indeed millions of moderate or even liberal Muslims out there, the great majority of them tend to keep an extraordinarily low profile with regard to their moderation or liberalism; and when push comes to shove (as it has with increasing frequency in recent years), few will speak up against Muslim extremists. They didn't mount the barricades in support of the Danish cartoonists' free speech;

they didn't rise up to condemn the murder of Theo van Gogh; and they don't march against terrorism. But as long as they're not building bombs, Western authorities are disinclined to ask more of them.

As the jihad advances, however, it seems increasingly (and distressingly) likely that, practically speaking, the silent majority of Muslims in the West are and will continue to be the passive allies of the active minority—which is to say that they may never, in significant numbers, put up any resistance as the Western world is gradually dragged into the House of Submission. Instead they will go about their lives more or less quietly, taking an apparently neutral posture—standing up neither for individual liberty nor for jihad and sharia, untroubled by the realization that, sooner or later, unless some resistance develops, the latter will eventually prevail.

This is profoundly unfortunate, because what we are talking about here are values that should be recognized not as Western or Christian or American, but as universal. We are speaking here of Enlightenment values—and, opposed to them, jihadist values. The former are worth defending; the latter are worth fighting against. Yet we live in a time when—whether under the influence of pernicious multicultural ideology, sheer fear, or a combination thereof—more and more free people who hold positions of responsibility in the West are irresponsibly trumpeting the equality of all ideas and all ways of life. Artists and writers avoid Islamic themes and settings; police officers avoid Muslim neighborhoods. And as for our elected leaders and government bureaucrats—well, their overall fecklessness was nicely illustrated in 2005, when French officials, alarmed by the sensational conclusion of a French Education Ministry report that Jewish children could "no longer be given an education anywhere" in France owing to harassment by Muslim classmates, shelved the thing. Fortunately, somebody leaked it onto the Internet—and a year later, a reporter who'd read about it in my book *While Europe Slept* even wrote it up in the *New York Times*. But that was the end of that; if the French educational establishment has done *anything* to make things better for Jewish pupils, I haven't heard about it.

And so it goes. To put it briefly and nakedly, the West is on the road to sharia.

The Media in the Driver's Seat

And who's in the driver's seat? The media.

How do the media help the jihadists? The easiest move is simply not to report on jihadist actions at all—or to report on them while concealing their jihadist nature. Riots gripped immigrant suburbs in France in the autumn of 2005, but weeks passed before most mainstream American media mentioned them—and when they finally did, they either covered up or drastically de-emphasized the rioters' Muslim identity. Few cited the cries of "Allahu akbar" that filled the French suburban streets. Like the cartoon riots, these uprisings—along with similar, even more widely neglected actions elsewhere in Europe—were in large part assertions of Muslim authority over Muslim neighborhoods, and thus jihadist in character; yet the media almost invariably spun them as outbursts of frustration over economic injustice. In 2007, an international wave of riots, flag-burnings, and assorted mayhem erupted over the knighting of Salman Rushdie, and Tim Rutten wrote in the *Los Angeles Times:* "If you're wondering why you haven't been able to follow all the columns and editorials in the American press denouncing all this homicidal nonsense, it's because there haven't been any." He called this "great silence . . . a great scandal." The headline said it all: "Where Is the West's Outcry?"

In recent years, the media have commissioned numerous polls and studies of Muslims only to spin the results absurdly—and/or drop them down the memory hole after a single news cycle. In 2006, a *Daily Telegraph* survey revealed that 40 percent of British Muslims wanted sharia law in Britain—yet British reporters continued afterward to write as if such sentiments are confined to a minuscule minority. In 2007, the *Times* of London reported that the leader of the organization that runs nearly half of Britain's mosques is a fervent advocate of jihad and that his sect's leading seminary teaches "a deep-rooted hatred of Western society"—yet such revelations make no permanent dent in the media's multicultural mind-set.

In May 2007, the Pew Research Center released the results of a major poll of American Muslims. Almost unanimously, the media spun the results as showing that American Muslims were well integrated and rejected terrorism. "Muslims Assimilated, Opposed to Extremism," the *Washington Post* rejoiced. The headline in *USA Today* read "American Muslims Reject Extremes." And the *Christian Science Monitor* trumpeted: "In Many Ways, US Muslims Are in Mainstream America." The survey, wrote the *Monitor*'s Jane Lampman in her lead, "tells a story that should be reassuring to Muslims and their fellow citizens alike." She called it "a surprisingly positive story" and referred to Muslims as holding "moderate views." Yet the actual results hardly gave reason for such rejoicing. Seven percent of Muslims aged eighteen to twenty-nine told the pollsters that they felt positively about al-Qaeda. In every age group, no more than 74 percent would say they felt negatively. Among the most widely celebrated findings was that 80 percent of young American Muslims said they opposed suicide bombing—even though the flip side, and the real story, was that a double-digit percentage *supported* it. The BBC, for its part, downplayed the terrorism angle, choosing to emphasize, in the report posted on its Web site, the claim that "Muslim Americans are largely integrated in US society and moderate in their views" and to focus on statistics suggesting that American Muslims were better off financially and more positive about their chances of prospering in America than other Americans (none of which, of course, speaks to their feelings about secular democracy or jihad).

The sharpest commentary on the ridiculously sunny spin that the mainstream media put on the Pew survey was provided by the Iowahawk blog, which ran a parody headlined "Midwest Lutherans Largely Reject Violence." "By an almost two-to-one margin," it began, "Midwest Lutherans voiced solid opposition to decapitation, suicide bombing, and chemical warfare . . . only 29% of all respondents agreed that 'bloody, random violence against infidels' was 'always' or 'frequently' justified. . . . Although a majority 87% of respondents agreed that 'The world should be brought to submission under global Lutheran conquest and eternal perfect rule,' there was a great deal of disagreement on the means to accomplish it."

A now-routine journalistic ploy is to recount acts of Muslim violence in abstract, sanitized terms while describing non-Muslim criticism of that violence in terms usually used to describe violence. For example, the *New York Times* report on a 2007 New York meeting between Iranian dictator Mahmoud Ahmadinejad and U.S. Christian leaders characterized Ahmadinejad, innocuously, as "a religious president of a religious nation" and approvingly contrasted the friendly tone of the meeting with "the verbal pummeling [Ahmadinejad] received at Columbia University on Monday [from university president Lee Bollinger]"—thus euphemizing away the physical brutality of the Iranian regime while describing Bollinger's frank acknowledgment of that brutality as if *it* were an act of physical brutality. Then there's the "backlash" ploy: since 9/11, the media have followed up each major terrorist act with reports about innocent Western Muslims who supposedly fear an "anti-Muslim backlash"—thus neatly shifting the focus away from real acts of violence by Muslims against non-Muslims toward imaginary acts of violence by non-Muslims against Muslims. (These "backlashes," of course, never materialize.)

III

The "American Imam"

hen there are the now-routine portrayals of "ordinary" Muslims and Muslim family life, the purpose of which is to persuade the public that there is no reason to fear Islam. A model of the genre was provided on March 5, 6, and 7, 2006, by *New York Times* reporter Andrea Elliott in the form of a three-part profile of an imam, Sheik Reda Shata, in Bay Ridge, Brooklyn. It was only one in a long line of *Times* articles published in the years after 9/11 that have plainly been intended to make Islam seem ordinary and familiar—indeed, downright cozy. Readers unfamiliar with the unwritten rules of the genre might have expected a responsible reporter to approach such a subject by seeking hard facts and asking tough questions. For example: Who is this imam? What does he stand for? What does he preach? What are his exact positions on, say, women's equality and gay rights? Instead, Elliott kicked off the first of her articles with several paragraphs of quasi-poetic scene-setting patently intended to win our sympathy and admiration for Reda Shata—to compel us to identify with him, a lone, brave figure in a strange land—even before we knew anything about what he preached or taught. "The imam begins his trek before dawn," Elliott wrote, "his long robe billowing like a ghost through empty streets. In this dark, quiet hour, his thoughts sometimes drift back to the Egyptian farming village where he was born." We read about "the sun ris[ing] over

Bay Ridge," about "the R train rattl[ing] beneath a littered stretch of sidewalk, where Mexican workers huddle[d] in the cold," about "gypsy cabs blar[ing] their horns." We followed Shata into "a plain brick building, nothing like the golden-domed mosque of his youth," where he prayed, "then climbed the cracked linoleum steps to his cluttered office" to find an answering machine "blink[ing] frantically" and stuffed with questions from his flock: "Is it halal, or lawful, to eat a Big Mac? Can alcohol be served . . . if it is prohibited by the Koran?" Such questions, Elliott informed us,

> are only a piece of the daily puzzle Mr. Shata must solve as the imam of the Islamic Society of Bay Ridge, a thriving New York mosque where several thousand Muslims worship.

One could not easily imagine the *Times* running a profile of James Dobson or Pat Robertson that started out in quite this way. No reporter would try to get away with it; no editor would accept it; readers would flood the *Times* with outraged e-mails asking why the liberal *Times* was apparently trying to get them to warm up to a fundamentalist. But these days, when the subject is a Muslim imam, the rules are different—and one of those rules is to go into soft focus, whenever possible, if the topic is Islamic belief and culture. Throughout her series on Shata, Elliott followed the rules brilliantly, underlining ad nauseam, for example, the point that Shata was a bridge-builder, a man with one foot in Islam and the other in Western culture. His story, as she spun it, was that of "the making of an American imam." He had learned, he said, "flexibility." Leading his congregation, wrote Elliott, "calls for improvisation" because it was a "diverse" group for whom life in America was "a daily clash between Islamic mores and material temptation." And "at the center of this clash stands the imam." In Elliott's view, the standard image of imams in America is "a simplistic caricature"; she wanted, rather, to show Shata as a nuanced, ambiguous figure, "neither a firebrand nor a ready advocate of progressive Islam . . . a work in progress, mapping his own middle ground between two different worlds . . . increasingly a blend of East and West, proudly walking to the mosque in a robe and sandals, while warding off the cold with a wool Yankees hat. . . . Mr. Shata is both foreign and familiar."

Elliott didn't disguise her admiration for what she viewed as Shata's balancing act. "The balance is delicate," she wrote regarding the challenge Shata supposedly faced when asked by an FBI agent to cooperate in its efforts to capture terrorists. Should he snitch or not? Where did his loyalty lie—with America's antiterrorism effort or with members of his congregation who might be involved in planning terrorist attacks? "It's like walking a tightrope," Shata said, and Elliott plainly sympathized with his dilemma. The unexplored internal contradiction here, of course, was that if Muslim Americans really were, as mainstream media such as the *Times* kept telling us, as overwhelmingly patriotic and opposed to terrorism as non-Muslim Americans, such issues wouldn't come up; counterterrorism investigators wouldn't come begging for imams' cooperation, and if they did, the imams wouldn't compare the encounter to tightrope walking. Not until near the end of the first of Elliott's articles did we learn that Shata, who had lived in the United States since 2002, could hardly speak a word of English and was obliged to converse with Elliott through a translator. Elliott didn't address the question of how someone in this position could be called an "American imam" or viewed as a "bridge-builder." We also learned in passing that Shata refused to shake women's hands and believed that "music should be forbidden if it 'encourages sexual desire.'" Exactly what else, one wondered, would he want to forbid? If he believed in prohibiting music, surely he believed in outlawing other things? Yet though Elliott's series ran to well over ten thousand words, she was too busy providing atmospheric and heartwarming details to supply a satisfactory answer to such questions.

Shata said that he rejected "suicide operations that target civilians"—but added that targeting Israeli soldiers was acceptable. Elliott didn't bother to mention that for many Muslims, no Israeli citizen can properly be categorized as a civilian since Israel itself, in their view, is an abomination—a country that should not exist and that was built on land stolen from Palestinians at gunpoint. (In the same way, some Muslims feel that no American or British citizen is a civilian, since their armies have invaded Afghanistan and Iraq and been stationed in the holy land of Saudi Arabia.) Tidily enough, Shata's argument for his support of suicide bombing was identical to the thesis of Elliott's series, namely that he's a man in the middle: "Some Muslims, if they hear this, would make me out to be a nonbeliever because they see that all these suicide operations are a must," he said. "And there are other

Muslims who feel that all of these operations are forbidden. My nature is always to be in the middle," he said.

Elliott also sympathetically quoted a lament by Shata that his out-cries against terrorism weren't being heard: "'I feel that I breathe underwater, or that I cry in a desert,' he said recently. 'That nobody responds.'"

And she quoted a speech given by Shata on September 11, 2005, in which he complained that a man "should not feel that he is under sur-veillance for every word he says, every move he makes and every piece of paper he signs." Exactly what was Shata saying here? That imams should, for example, be able to call for holy war without falling under suspicion? One wanted details. What, in particular, had inspired these remarks? Which statements was Shata referring to? By whom were they spoken? Elliott didn't explain. Then there were her references to Shata's alma mater, Al-Azhar University in Cairo, which she described in her first article as "a bastion of Islamic scholarship" and in her second as "a citadel of Islamic scholarship." What she omitted to mention was that Al-Azhar bans books, that it raids bookstores to confiscate works that violate Islamic teachings, that the sometime head of its fatwa commit-tee has issued a fatwa calling Jews "apes and pigs," that its president and leading cleric have supported suicide bombing, that its Grand Mufti demanded that Denmark close down *Jyllands-Posten* and imprison its editor, and that Al-Azhar's recent pronouncements on correct Islamic practice include the following directive about persons captured during acts of jihad: "When a child or woman is taken captive, they become slaves by the fact of capture, and the woman's previous marriage is im-mediately annulled."

Flemming Rose has also noted that Al-Azhar practices "institutional apartheid": Jews and Coptic Christians are prohibited from attending. According to Rose, "Al-Azhar has shown no willingness to abandon the part of the sharia providing Muslims with the obligation to in-sult non-Muslims' religious feelings, while at the same time insisting that non-Muslims offending Muslims' religious sensibilities should be punished." Why, in a ten-thousand-word profile of an imam, was there no room for a sentence or two explaining the kinds of things that are preached, taught, and practiced at the institution where he learned the religion that he is now himself preaching, teaching, and practicing?

Some of Shata's opinions, Elliott wrote, in yet another assertion of his role as a "man in the middle," "would offend conservative Muslims; other beliefs would repel American liberals." But she never provided a remotely explicit account of those opinions—obviously because if she had done so, the sympathy she was laboring so hard to generate would be quickly dissipated, and the image of Shata as a "man in the middle," and therefore a moderate, would be destroyed. Plainly, she was out to humanize Shata, not illuminate his thought. To this end, she churned out a boatload of lyrical (if not exactly content-rich) sentences that did a splendid job of distracting readers from what really mattered: "Islam came to him softly, in the rhythms of his grandmother's voice." She quoted lines that would be an embarrassment even in the most gushingly vapid fan-magazine celebrity profile: "I love to smile. I love to laugh. I used to think that religious people were isolated and I love to be among people." She devoted several hundred words to material about Shata's wife and family that had no other purpose than to warm the cockles of our hearts: "Mr. Shata discovered love 15 years ago. . . . 'She entered my heart,' said the imam." His wife felt the same way: "'I loved him from the moment I saw him.'" And Elliott served up a rhapsodic account of Shata's work as a matchmaker. "Nothing brings the imam more joy," she confided admiringly, "than guiding [single Muslims] to marriage. It is his way of fashioning a future for his faith. It is his most heartfelt effort—by turns graceful and comedic, vexing and hopeful—to make marriage work in America." Elliott filled several column inches with a passage (obviously intended to be charming and gently amusing) about Shata's misadventures with a man and woman whom he'd unsuccessfully sought to bring together in holy matrimony. What didn't Elliott tell us here about the successful matches Shata had arranged? Certainly she didn't breathe a word about the forced marriages that are a major feature of Islam; instead, we were given yet another poetic quotation from the imam: "The prophet said whoever brings a man and woman together, it is as if he has worshiped for an entire year." (Then again, the prophet also said that if wives "behave with open unseemliness," their husbands may "beat them but not with severity." But Elliott wasn't about to soil her pretty picture by quoting such texts.)

Elliott's article was a prime example of the way the mainstream media cover Islam today: emphasize personal and superficial details that are likely to generate sympathy while sidestepping or whitewash-

72

ing core beliefs, domestic arrangements, cultural practices, social rules, and long-term political goals that might actually inform, enlighten— and therefore alarm—readers. "He presides over a patriarchal world," Elliott wrote about Shata, "sometimes upholding it, and other times challenging it." The message was clear: this kind of "man in the middle" is the best we can hope for; the only prospect of lasting peace between Muslims and non-Muslims in the West rests in the hands of such men, because only they stand a chance of reconciling Islam and secular democracy. But what Elliott's series about Shata didn't say—what such reports in high-profile media like the *New York Times* almost never say—is that a "compromise" between Western democratic principles and the values represented by men like Shata would involve a whole-sale demolition of individual liberties.

Though the outrageous dishonesty of Elliott's profile of Shata didn't go entirely unnoticed, the criticism appeared almost entirely in media outlets at which *bien pensant* Americans have been taught to look down their noses. Both the *New York Post* and the *New York Sun* noted Elliott's failure to ask uncomfortable questions about such things as Shata's refusal to shake hands with women, and *Washington Times* columnist Diana West, for her part, reflected on Shata's line "Married life in Islam is an act of worship." Did Elliott, West inquired, ask Shata "to reconcile this ecstatic notion with the Islamic custom of arranged and forced marriages, the spate of spousal abuse and 'honor killings' within European Muslim communities . . . or the tradition of polygamy which exists to this day in portions of Islamic society?" Nope.

The irrelevance of such contrarian newspapers in the corridors of media power was neatly demonstrated when the Pulitzer Prize judges awarded Elliott their 2006 award for best feature writing. Their citation congratulated her for producing an "intimate, richly textured portrait of an immigrant imam striving to find his way and serve his faithful in America." When the *New York Sun* carped about the award, Gal Beckerman leaped to the *Times'*—and the Pulitzer jury's—defense in another pillar of the media establishment, the *Columbia Journalism Review*. Paraphrasing Elliott's tame non-admission admission that some of Shata's "beliefs would repel American liberals," Beckerman acknowledged that Shata "does possess religious opinions that would discomfit many Americans" and claimed that Elliott's article, "like the best of journalism . . . struggled to present a complex picture, full of ambiguity, of a man who falls into no easy categories." Beckerman contrasted Elliott in this regard with "the *New York Sun*, which often seems to prefer that its news fit into those easy categories." In fact what made the *Sun*'s article about Elliott's Pulitzer different from Elliott's articles on Shata is that the *Sun* didn't hesitate to place Shata in the category in which he quite plainly belonged. Beckerman actually spoke of "the considerable evidence that the Sheikh embraces very moderate viewpoints." Slurring one of Elliott's critics, Daniel Pipes, as "that reliable fount of right-wing spin on all things Middle Eastern," Beckerman sneered at his observation that "Just from the between-the-lines information Elliott provides in her articles, it is clear that the imam is no moderate but an Islamist"—meaning, in brief, a Muslim who rejects Western influence and equal rights for women, embraces theocracy and sharia law, and supports jihad. Though Beckerman dismissed this verdict outright, Pipes was absolutely correct: for all Elliott's masterly efforts to disguise the truth, any informed, careful reader of her profile could see that Shata was indeed an Islamist. "The *Sun*, it seems obvious, is simply threatened by the prospect of a Muslim moderate," insisted Beckerman, who preached that "good journalism should challenge readers with layered portraits." For Beckerman, apparently, it was perfectly all right to be non-"layered" about the *New York Sun* and Daniel Pipes, but imperative to be "layered" about the likes of Shata. To be sure, being "layered" in this case plainly meant, among other things, accepting an entirely new definition of the word "moderation." For to call a fanatic a fanatic, after all, simply sounds so . . . immoderate.

IV

Redefining Moderation

The *New York Times* stands at the red-hot center of America's mainstream media. In relation to the rest of the U.S. news media, it plays a singular role for which the mere word "influence" is hardly adequate, exerting an immense impact not only on which stories are covered and which aren't, but also on the prominence they're given and how they're spun. The *Times'* coverage of Islam in the years since 9/11 has played a unique role in shaping the way in which the American media approach this topic. Repeatedly, that coverage has seemed to reflect a conviction, not only on the part of the *Times* but throughout the Western media establishment, that if social harmony is to be achieved between Muslims and non-Muslims in the West, it's necessary for non-Muslims to undergo a radical shift in views and values. Because so much of Islamic belief and culture is intrinsically extreme, the very notion of what constitutes moderation must be transformed. If a Protestant cleric supported some if not all suicide bombing and banning some if not all music, the mainstream media would label him an extremist, if not an out-and-out lunatic; but if an imam supports them, the *Times* may well call him a moderate—because, you see, the extremist Muslims are those who support *all* suicide bombing and would ban *all* music. This is the new world order, and these are the criteria by which the mainstream media would have us distinguish moderate from radical Islam.

This media redefinition of the word "moderate," when it precedes the word "Islam" or "Muslim," has been a worldwide project. The March/April 2007 issue of the influential *Foreign Affairs* contained an essay by Robert S. Leiken and Steven Brooke entitled "The Moderate Muslim Brotherhood." While recognizing the Egypt-based organization as Islamist, Leiken and Brooke argued that "in the anxious and often fruitless search for Muslim moderates, policymakers should recognize that the Muslim Brotherhood presents a notable opportunity" because it seeks to conquer the West not through terrorism but "through gradual and peaceful Islamization." Leiken and Brooke admitted that "the Brotherhood does authorize jihad in countries and territories occupied by a foreign power," yet held up as a virtue (talk about grasping at straws) the fact that "the Brotherhood's failure to stress the religious dimension of war incenses the jihadists." The word "moderate" recurred throughout their piece, as if sheer repetition could make it stick; but to apply the word to Islamists was to radically redefine moderation. Interestingly, Leiken and Brooke's piece was followed very shortly, and echoed very closely, by an April 2007 *New York Times Magazine* article, "Islamic Democrats?," in which James Traub proposed that the U.S. government "engage the [Muslim Brotherhood] openly" and argued that it "could well be precisely the kind of moderate Islamic body that the administration says it seeks."

Similarly, a 2007 article about the European Fatwa Council in the Norwegian newspaper *Aftenposten* paraphrased Islam expert Kari Vogt to the effect that "there are no extremists on the council" (on which Yusuf al-Qaradawi is the leading voice) and that it represented "a moderate Islamism." Not "moderate Islam," mind you, but "moderate Islamism"! Even as they have been adjusting to the limits permitted to Islam's critics, then, the media have been busy resetting the boundaries of Islamic moderation: Muslim leaders are "moderate" if their approval of stoning adulteresses is couched in genteel and conciliatory-sounding terms; Islam's critics are immoderate—are, in fact, "Islamophobic" and "extreme" and "racist"—if they dare to point out how outrageous this is.

One of Elliott's three articles on Shata was headlined "To Lead the Faithful in a Faith under Fire." This headline accepted as a given that Islam has been unfairly criticized and scrutinized since 9/11. On the contrary, far from being "under fire," Islam has benefited from the determination of the mainstream media—with the *Times* in the lead—to create and reinforce a friendly, homey image of the religion. This image, far from being threatened by a massive onslaught of unjust attacks by non-Muslims, has in point of fact been challenged repeatedly by the violent and threatening behavior of Muslims themselves. Indeed, if one takes the expression "under fire" literally, the headline is nothing less than grotesque, given that in recent years violence by Muslims against non-Muslims has been far more widespread than violence in the other direction. In April 2007, Hugh Fitzgerald condemned the *Times*'s execrable coverage of the religion. "Does the *Times* even mention the Hadith and Sira? Have you learned a single thing about any teachings about Infidels in Islam from reading *The Times* over the past decade? Since 9/11/2001? Since last year? No, you have not." A reader comment at the *Dhimmi Watch* Web site noted that in an article about three Christians who had been murdered in Turkey by a Muslim group, *Times* reporter Sabrina Tavernise had used "the words 'Assailants,' 'five men,' 'attackers,' 'suspects,' and 'nationalist fringe,' but never MUSLIMS. . . . Apparently the *NYT* has the word 'Christian' in its vocabulary but not 'Muslim.'"

Of course, the *Times* does have the word "Muslim" in its vocabulary, but its policy is plainly to avoid associating it with unpleasant doings. In December 2006, the *Internet Haganah* Web site focused on a *Times* article about the Treasury Department's charge that the Islamic American Relief Agency (IARA) had funded terrorism. As the *Kansas City Star* noted, the *Times* article sought to make the charges look unfounded: while it emphasized the group's stated mission to perform "charitable work for orphans, disaster, famine relief and aid to refugees," it did not note, as the *Star* reporter put it, that "support for jihad is part and parcel of Islamic charity," that such support "is an obligation for those who cannot travel to and/or wage jihad themselves," and that the orphans who are the beneficiaries of such aid "are, in many cases, the children of deceased terrorists, aka shaheeds, glorious martyrs of the global jihad." In recounting the Treasury Department's charges, moreover, the *Times* article omitted a good deal of information that would have made it clear that those charges were far from arbitrary or whimsical. The *Times* article also reported that "no charges have been filed" against the IARA, "as though the absence of charges is somehow proof of innocence. . . . In point of fact the issue of the IARA has been before the Federal courts previously, and the IARA has lost. Repeatedly."

It can take no more than two or three well-chosen words for a skilled mainstream-media reporter to give an Islam-related story the desired spin. For instance, a July 2007 *Times* article about the terrorist action at the airport in Glasgow the previous month referred to the July 2005 London bombings as having brought "home to Britain fears of home-grown terrorist attacks among its disenfranchised South Asian population." With those three words—"disenfranchised South Asian"—the article's authors, Alan Cowell and Raymond Bonner, accomplished a great deal. The word "disenfranchised" implied that terrorism could perhaps be understood as the result of this supposed "disenfranchise-ment"; never mind that seven of the eight Glasgow suspects were priv-ileged, affluent physicians. Never mind, either, that to describe even ordinary, non-M.D. Muslims in Britain as "disenfranchised" is out-rageous; far from being disenfranchised in the U.K., many Muslims move there to *escape* disenfranchisement. Yes, most British Muslims live largely apart from mainstream British society, many of them col-lecting welfare instead of working—yet they live like this not because they have been forced to do so by some exclusionary government but because they *want* to. (To live off infidel society rather than contribute to it is, after all, an aspect of jihad.) To be sure, there *are* countless Mus-lims in Britain who are denied their full democratic rights; the people who are denying them these rights, however, are not government of-ficials but their own husbands, fathers, family patriarchs, and imams. And this disenfranchisement is a topic to which reporters like Cowell and Bonner generally prefer to turn a blind eye.

Then there is Cowell and Bonner's striking use of the term "South Asian"—a rhetorical choice that is standard practice at British news-papers. The idea was plainly to suggest that religion was not a factor in this story at all—that the perpetrators of terrorism might just as easily be Hindus or Zoroastrians (even though Muslim terrorists rou-tinely make it clear that their motives are indeed religious). *Times* edi-tors would doubtless have justified the use of the term "South Asian" by saying that they didn't want to stigmatize all Muslims; but what they ended up doing instead was stigmatize all South Asians (many of whom, in Britain, are not Muslims but Hindus, who are overwhelmingly law-abiding, hardworking, and prosperous, and whose coreligionists on the subcontinent have, in fact, suffered greatly at the hand of jihadists).

When the *Times'* Nicholas Kulish reported in September 2007 on the discovery of a bomb-making factory in a Copenhagen apartment, he told the story from the suspects' point of view. Kulish closed on what was plainly intended to be a poignant note: stating that the apartment door was "cracked where it was broken open by a police battering ram," he explained that its residents were "two brothers of Pakistani descent," both of whom were taken into custody, though the older one "was released after less than a day." Kulish quoted this older brother:

> "They came at 2 o'clock," he said. "They broke open the door. They broke everything. They came as animals." He added that he had not seen his brother since going to sleep the night before their arrest.... "I work all day," he said in a soft voice. "I don't know what my brother and his friends do."

Thus ended the article—not by focusing on the fact that Muslims in Denmark were plotting to blow their neighbors to smithereens, but with a bid for sympathy for this soft-voiced young man who, we were expected to believe, had no idea that people were making bombs in his home. Kulish's decision to quote the description of police as "animals" was particularly inspired; one cannot easily imagine a *Times* reporter using that word to describe, say, terrorists.

A similarly mendacious approach to Islam could be observed in an article that appeared in the *Tampa Tribune* on September 2, 2007. Entitled "A Family in Despair," it was about Youssef Megahed, one of two University of Florida students who had been nabbed with "a pipe bomb in the trunk of their Toyota Camry as they drove near a Naval weapons station." The *Tribune*'s reporter, Gretchen Parker, spun the story brilliantly, focusing on the "shock" and "despair" of the "teary" and "terrified" Youssef and the "anxiety" of his Egyptian immigrant parents; on the young convict's professed fear that his grandfather would die before he got out of prison; and on the effect the young man's predicament had had on his family. "They have a close family," wrote Parker, "and Samir [Youssef's father] says he is worried about all of them." Samir was also, as Parker was at pains to point out, concerned about the family, back in Egypt, of his son's codefendant: "How can I tell a father, 'You are not going to see your son again'?" As for Youssef's mother, she "tried to reassure [her son] by putting her hand on his back and rubbing it, but the tenor of the meeting was dismal." In short, it wasn't just the *Times* that was churning out this sort of nonsense: newspapers across America were taking the same irresponsible approach to the coverage of jihadist threats to national security.

In September 2007, the *Times*'s Neil MacFarquhar reported on the annual convention of the Islamic Society of North America (ISNA). Though the organization had recently been named as an unindicted coconspirator in the trial of the Holy Land Foundation on charges of aiding Hamas, the Department of Justice nonetheless chose to sponsor a recruitment booth at the convention. As terrorism expert Steve Emerson wrote in a blistering dissection of MacFarquhar's article,

> MacFarquhar not only gives a free pass to Islamists, but at the same time dismisses legitimate criticism of the Department of Justice's presence at the conference. . . . MacFarquhar completely ignores damning information about ISNA that came out during the trial, including such things as its foundations in the Muslim Brotherhood, and its multiple financial contributions to Hamas through its subsidiary, the North American Islamic Trust (NAIT).

But MacFarquhar didn't settle for just whitewashing the ISNA; his article was also, in Emerson's words, "a hit piece" against two of the ISNA's outspoken critics in Congress, Pete Hoekstra and Sue Myrick. MacFarquhar passed along without comment remarks by the convention's keynote speaker, Rep. Keith Ellison, about Hoekstra and Myrick, whose criticism of the Department of Justice's presence at the event Ellison had assailed as "ill-informed and typical of bigoted attacks that other minorities have suffered." As Emerson pointed out, Hoekstra and Myrick had not "criticized Islam or minorities" but had, rather, expressed concern about ISNA, a "Muslim Brotherhood front group with a long and documented history of support for terrorism." Contrast MacFarquhar's handling of this aspect of the story with his description of one of the speakers at the ISNA event, Zaid Shakir, whom he called "an African-American imam with rock star status among young

Muslims," and whom he quoted as lamenting that people on American talk radio "mak[e] stuff up about Islam." One would never have known from this description that Shakir is, in fact, a radical imam with a deplorable record of fiery anti-American and anti-infidel rhetoric.

The *Times* handled not only the ISNA but also the Council on American-Islamic Relations (CAIR) with kid gloves. On August 8, 2007, the Investigative Project on Terrorism reported that on the previous day, FBI agent Lara Burns had testified at the Holy Land Foundation (HLF) trial that CAIR "was listed as a member of the Muslim Brotherhood's Palestine Committee," that it had "received money from HLF" (which contradicted Congressional testimony given in 2003 by CAIR cofounder Nihad Awad), and that Awad and his fellow cofounder, Omar Ahmed, were "listed as individual members [of] the Brotherhood's Palestine Committee in America." This testimony shattered CAIR's long-standing effort to portray itself as mainstream and moderate; yet no mention of it appeared in the *New York Times* and other major newspapers, which routinely represented CAIR as a thoroughly respectable civil-rights organization. Indeed, the mainstream media virtually ignored the entire Holy Land Foundation trial. As blogger Charles Johnson wrote, "It's disgraceful how little coverage this hugely important trial is receiving in mainstream media." Yet the disgrace went even deeper: the very day after the story about Burns's testimony was posted on the Counterterrorism Blog, the *New York Times* ran a long article about Islamic financial institutions and terrorism—the angle being that some people involved in "Islamic finance" felt that they were being unfairly linked with terrorism. The article, written by Landon Thomas, Jr., was an incredible attempt at a total whitewash, and appeared only two days after testimony at the Holy Land Foundation trial had affirmed the financial connections between high-profile American Muslim institutions and terrorism. How many references did Thomas make to the Holy Land trial? None whatsoever.

It wasn't only the *Times* that gave the Holy Land trial short shrift. A *Newsweek* article about the trial by Gretel C. Kovach strove to leave the impression that it was a pure and simple case of Islamophobia—that malicious government bigots were punishing Muslims for giving to charity. ("Charitable giving," Kovach instructed readers, is "one of the five pillars of Islam.") "They are trying to marginalize the Muslim voice," complained a vice president of CAIR, whom Kovach described as "well-respected." (There was no mention of CAIR's inclusion in the government's list of unindicted coconspirators, or of CAIR communications director Ibrahim Hooper's 1993 admission that he would "like the government of the United States to be Islamic sometime in the future. . . . But I'm not going to do anything violent to promote that. I'm going to do it through education.") In a particularly audacious example of the use of an opening blatantly designed to win sympathy for some party or another, Kovach bracketed her article with quotations not from one of the accused funders of terrorism, or from any of the government investigators or prosecutors, or (needless to say) from any of the many victims of Hamas terrorism, but from Noor Elashi, the twenty-one-year-old daughter of one of the officers of the Holy Land Foundation. Kovach began her piece by inviting us to sympathize with this poor girl who was tormented by the accusations directed at her beloved father, and closed with a sentence from an essay written by the girl: "I know my father is innocent, and that his only crimes were helping feed Palestinian orphans and being an Arab-American." Blogger Charles Johnson, who quite correctly characterized the article as "deceptive and ridiculous," charged *Newsweek* with being "the public relations arm for radical Islam." There was certainly a great deal of evidence to support this statement; then again, *Newsweek* had plenty of top-level competition for that honor.

One exception was Rod Dreher, who in a *Dallas Morning News* column wrote that "the HLF trial is exposing for the first time how the international Muslim Brotherhood—whose Palestinian division is Hamas—operates as a self-conscious revolutionary vanguard in the United States. The court documents indicate that many leading Muslim-American organizations—including the Council on American-Islamic Relations, the Islamic Society of North America, and the Muslim American Society—are an integral part of the Brotherhood's efforts to wage jihad against America by nonviolent means." Yet the mainstream media essentially boycotted the trial—and, in reports on Islam, continued to refer to CAIR as if it were a respectable mainstream organization.

Only days after MacFarquhar's whitewash of ISNA, *USA Today* ran an article by Cathy Lynn Grossman about Ingrid Mattson, head of the ISNA. Unsurprisingly, Grossman's glowing portrait of Mattson—whom the headline described as "The face of Islam in America"—made no mention whatsoever of the Holy Land trial. Instead, Grossman depicted Mattson, a convert from Catholicism who had "found her spiritual home in Islam," as a hardworking woman with a "tiny, book-stuffed office" and "a snug black headscarf" who was extraordinarily devoted to her project of building (in her own words) "a strong religious and civic institutional life for Muslims in America." She was, Grossman wrote, "too liberal for some, too conservative for others." Like Elliott, Grossman served up the same kind of hyperbolic language about Islam that one never sees applied to any other religion in the Western media: "This is the faith she chose at age 23, drawn in, she says, by Islam's beauty, its ethos of service and its synthesis of life and faith in which every act relates to God." The only hint of criticism of Mattson and her organization that Grossman quoted came from Muslim political scientist M. A. Muqtedar Khan of the University of Delaware, who found her insufficiently extreme.

Carrying Islamists' Water

Public broadcasting has been no better. The 2007 PBS series *America at a Crossroads*, about Islam in America, was to have included a documentary by Martyn Burke entitled "Islam vs. Islamists." Burke said that his film, which focused on moderate and liberal Muslims who are opposed to Islamism, "attempts to answer the question: 'Where are the moderate Muslims?' The answer is, 'Wherever they are, they are reviled and sometimes attacked.'" PBS's problem with the film was that it dared to acknowledge that some American Muslims *aren't* moderate or liberal. For this reason, it was dropped from the Islam series (which otherwise was predictably propagandistic). Jeff Bieber, executive producer of *America at a Crossroads* for the Washington, D.C., public-television station WETA, called Burke's documentary "alarmist"— which has become the mainstream media's label of choice for any book or television program that is overly candid about the perils of Islam. While major newspapers ignored the story of the show's cancellation, Dennis Wagner reported in the *Arizona Republic* that an official at WETA wanted Burke to remove from the film the "claim that Muslim radicals are pushing to establish 'parallel societies' in America and Europe governed by Shariah law rather than sectarian courts." The series' message, as Brendan Bernhard wrote in the *New York Sun*, is that a military response to jihad "is futile," and that the only way to deal with it, other than through "police work," is "to grovel and plead in order to keep the 'peace.'"

Several months after *America at a Crossroads* came CNN's three-part, six-hour *God's Warriors*, perhaps *the* archetypal TV treatment of Islam in the post-9/11 era. In service of the thesis that Christian and Jewish extremism is as widespread and dangerous today as Muslim extremism, the producers seemed to have sought out the most radical Christians and Jews they could find, the cameraman filmed their gatherings in ways plainly designed to make them look even more radical, and Christiane Amanpour asked accusatory questions that emphasized their fanaticism. Meanwhile Amanpour apparently did her best to make jihadists sympathetic. Indeed, the very concept of jihad was absent from her picture of God's Muslim warriors, whom she depicted not as fighting to conquer the world for Allah but as reacting to West Bank settlements. "Muslims, like people everywhere, abhor terrorism," she said. "The small minority who resorts to violence is symptomatic of something many of us have failed to understand: the impact of God's Jewish warriors goes far beyond these rocky hills. The Jewish settlements have inflamed much of the Muslim world." In short, if it were not for *Jewish* warriors—that is, West Bank settlers—there would be no *Muslim* warriors.

Though *God's Warriors* was welcomed warmly by the mainstream media, some took a different view. Alex Safian of the Committee for Accuracy in Middle East Reporting in America noted that though there is "no counterpart among Jews and Christians to the violent jihadist Muslim campaigns under way across the globe," Amanpour "uttered the words 'Jewish warriors' five times more often than 'Muslim warrior.'" Safian took special note of "two apolitical segments" in *God's Muslim Warriors* featuring "appealing devout Muslim women who talked about why they wear a head covering and how Islam enriches their lives." There were no similar segments in the series about charmingly pious Jews or Christians.[2]

God's Warriors did receive stinging criticism from one prominent

---

[2]As a supplement to the series, CNN ran material on its Web site that represented Muslim Americans as regular objects of abuse by non-Muslims, depicted Islam as a refreshing spiritual alternative to Western decadence, and provided heartwarming images of everyday Muslim life. Here, too, there was no similar material about Christianity and Judaism.

member of the mainstream media. Calling the series "shameful advocacy masked as journalism," Dan Abrams of MSNBC accused Amanpour of equating "Jewish and Christian political movements, even Jewish lobbyists in Congress" with Muslim terrorists—the exception being that she strove to "understand" the latter. Abrams noted that even as Amanpour "portray[ed] Muslims as victims," she "accus[ed] evangelical Christians of playing the victim"—an upside-down picture that is, of course, standard in today's media. Appearing on Abrams's program, Steve Emerson called *God's Warriors* "the most dishonest series on television that I've seen in my 20 years of reporting or covering terrorism."

In July 2007, a new cartoon controversy erupted—this time in Sweden. Several drawings by the artist Lars Vilks, in which the prophet Muhammed was depicted as a dog, were removed from an exhibition in the town of Tällerud. The organizers admitted that their only motive was concern about Muslim violence. When one of the drawings was published in a local newspaper, Swedish Muslims and the Organization of the Islamic Conference protested, Vilks received death threats, and al-Qaeda offered $100,000 for his murder ($150,000 if the killer slit his throat). Unlike Selbekk in Norway, fortunately, he won widespread media support in his country. It was less heartening, though, to see how the Vilks story was reported in some high-profile English-language media. CNN reporter Paula Newton suggested that perhaps "Vilks should have known better" because of what had happened to the *Jyllands-Posten* cartoonists (whom she mistakenly conflated into a single cartoonist)—as if people who make art should naturally take their marching orders from people who make death threats. In the *Economist*, Fogh Rasmussen's refusal during the *Jyllands-Posten* crisis to hold a "dialogue" about free speech with the representatives of countries that deny that freedom was described as arrogant and "muddled" ("Denmark's prime minister . . . haughtily declined to meet a delegation of Muslim ambassadors") while Swedish prime minister Fredrik Reinfeldt's decision to "invite" *his* Muslim emissaries "in for a chat" about Vilks's drawings was portrayed as admirable. The *Economist* also depicted Vilks as an eccentric who should not be taken "too seriously." This respected weekly, then, encouraged readers to dismiss a brave, freedom-loving artist as a marginal oddball—and to view the henchmen of thuggish Islamic regimes as gentlemen who were deserving of respectful dialogue.

Another day, another cartoon controversy. Two months after the Vilks controversy, a couple of installments of the popular "Opus" comic strip by Berkeley Breathed featured a character in a burqa who declared that she had become a "radical Islamist." Even some Muslim leaders said that they didn't find the strip offensive. But several newspapers refused to print the strips. A real dhimmi doesn't take chances.

In 2008, ABC aired a program whose purpose was to reveal the supposedly high levels of anti-Muslim bigotry in the United States. A bakery clerk in rural Texas was shown being verbally abusive toward a veiled Muslim woman customer. But both the clerk and the customer were actors hired by ABC. The whole performance was a stunt designed to capture bystanders' reactions, and was carried out with help from CAIR. The bakery was just outside of Waco, a town identified in cultural elite minds with right-wing extremists and white supremacy; plainly, the producers had picked a spot where, they assumed, they could expect to find plenty of vicious anti-Muslim bigots. Instead, most of the bystanders caught on camera were supportive of the faux-Muslim woman. If there really were high levels of anti-Muslim verbal assaults in the United States, of course, ABC wouldn't have had to concoct a situation to film—it would have plenty of footage of *real* bias incidents. In any case, this was one more media effort to persuade the public that the problem is Islamophobia, not Islamic jihad.

Despite the unsensational results of its experiment, ABC pitched it as an exposé of high levels of anti-Muslim prejudice in America. A piece on ABC News's Web site quoted a Yale social psychologist as saying that "when we as Americans feel threatened from the outside, we're going to define ourselves in very rigid fashions." So let's get this straight: a woman is wearing a veil and it's not her, but those who are offended by this symbol of medieval submission, who are defining themselves "in very rigid fashions." And yes, by all means, let's forget *why* Americans feel threatened by Islam. The ABC News piece also cited statistics on "anti-Islamic hate crime incidents in the United States," which supposedly had "more than quadrupled from 28 incidents in 2000 to 150 incidents in 2006." Only 150 in a country of 300 million people? And how many cases have there been of gay bashing or rape, say, by Muslims? How many in Europe? (My partner alone has been assaulted by Muslims on four different occasions—twice in Amsterdam, twice in Oslo.)

ABC's Web page on the program included a list of "Common Misunderstandings About Muslims" in which each "Misunderstanding" was followed by the "Truth." It was staggeringly dishonest. For example, are Muslim women "oppressed and forced to wear hijab"? No, we were told. "Truth: Women often see [hijab] as empowering because they are not viewed as sexual objects but judged by their character." Does Islam promote "violence and terrorism"? No. "Truth: According to the Council on American-Islamic Relations, prominent Muslims, Islamic organizations, and Islamic scholars have repeatedly denounced the terrorist attacks of Sept 11 and terrorism in general." As for jihad, it means to "strive, struggle and exert effort" and this "includes struggle against evil inclinations within oneself." (Again, the source for this blatant lie was CAIR.) As Steven Emerson wrote, ABC "did its level best" in this piece "to carry water for the radical Islamist, and *jihadist*, movement in America."

The online encyclopedia Wikipedia has been braver than many major newspapers and TV networks in the face of Muslim pressure. After receiving more than 180,000 demands to eliminate pictures of Muhammed from its article on the prophet, the site owners refused: "no content or images will be removed because people find them objectionable or offensive." In February 2008, CAIR filed a complaint with the FBI about comments that readers of the Little Green Footballs Web site had posted on that site about a mosque that was under construction in St. Louis. Newspapers in St. Louis, plus the local CBS-TV affiliate, uncritically echoed CAIR's charges, casting CAIR as a respected civil-rights group and LGF as an extremist hate site.

In February 2008 the Web site of Norway's Human Rights Service was censored by its Web host. The company, Imbera, removed three items from the site because they were illustrated with Kurt Westergaard's famous *Jyllands-Posten* drawing of Muhammed with a bomb in his turban and a Muhammed drawing by Lars Vilks. University of Oslo law professor Jon Bing defended Imbera, saying that it had not only a right but a legal obligation to take this action. HRS commented that Norwegians are now living in a "threat culture. . . . The government, bishops, and others don't see that they have capitulated to this threat culture, but prefer to define it as a dialogue. But where the threats begin, the dialogue stops."

VI

The European Media

The role of Dhimmitude Central that is played in the United States by the *New York Times* is filled in Britain by the BBC. A few quick examples will illustrate its characteristic approach to Islam.

- In 2006, when psychotherapist John Casson reported that Manchester's top imam, Arshad Misbahi, had told him in an interview that he supported the death penalty for homosexuality, the BBC, in a dispatch headlined "Imam Accused of 'Gay Death' Slur," spun the controversy as an effort by Casson to discredit Islam. The BBC concluded its story with comments from an Islamic Human Rights Commission spokesman who equated Muslim attitudes toward homosexuality with those of "other orthodox religions, such as Catholicism" and complained that focusing on the issue was "part of demonizing Muslims."

- In 2007, BBC News reacted to a think tank's report about jihadist books purchased at British mosques by ignoring its contents and instead raising doubts about the authenticity of one or two of the book receipts.

- In 2007 a former governor of the BBC, Dame Pauline Neville-Jones, expressed outrage at a BBC children's news program that presented Muslim terrorism as a response—implicitly an understandable one—to actions by America. (There was, of course, no mention of jihad.) "How can we expect to win" in the struggle against terrorists, she asked, "when our national broadcaster is parroting their line to our own children?"

For years the BBC has regularly served up some of the most egregiously anti-American, anti-Israeli, and anti-capitalistic reportage in the business while promulgating apologetics for Islam. But not until somebody at the Beeb shifted around a few seconds of video to make it look as if Queen Elizabeth had walked out of a session with photographer Annie Leibovitz did the Corporation's credibility take a major hit among the British public. On the heels of this scandal, surprisingly, the BBC commissioned an internal report by Malcolm Balen to determine whether it did indeed suffer from institutional bias; unsurprisingly, Balen concluded that it did. But the BBC, when confronted with a request under Britain's Freedom of Information Act (FOIA) to release Balen's report, refused—and spent a six-figure sum on two court battles to keep it private. Conservative MP David Davies pointed out the hypocrisy: "An organisation which is funded partly to scrutinise governments and other institutions in Britain appears to be using tax-payers' money to prevent its customers from finding out how it is operating." In March 2007, Paul Revoir noted in the *Daily Mail* that "[t]he BBC's own website boasts of 69 stories that it says it has broken with the help of the Freedom of Information Act." Yet after the High Court sided with the BBC on the FOIA case, the elite British media dropped the whole episode down the memory hole. For example, a July 2007 *Guardian* story about the loss of public trust in the BBC mentioned the faking of TV competitions and the Annie Leibovitz flap, but made no reference to the Balen Report or to the issue of systemic political bias; on the contrary, the article's premise was that the BBC, despite a couple of slip-ups, had an unrivaled "reputation for accuracy."

In June 2005, a month before the terrorist attacks in London, the BBC aired a documentary called *Don't Panic, I'm Islamic*, which sought to portray concerns about Islamic radicalism as overblown. Whereas Charles Johnson described it on his blog, Little Green Footballs, as "a stunning whitewash of radical Islam" that "shows how the BBC helped keep the British public fast asleep, a few weeks before the bombs went off in London subways and buses," the BBC's own Web site called it an introduction to "Muslims who speak openly about what it means to be a British Muslim—at a time when the nation is fighting a 'war on terror.'... The programme also uncovers the implications of the prejudice they encounter." The BBC's show summary went on to lament that "[t]he comfortable middle ground is eroding as Muslims are asked to either accept the 'war on terror' and deny their heritage or become radicalised and condemned as 'terrorists.'" In other words, it's unfair to expect Muslims to oppose jihadists' efforts to subjugate the West, for jihad is part of "their heritage"—a claim that utterly contradicts, of course, the endlessly repeated argument that the overwhelming majority of Muslims oppose terror. Over two years later, it emerged that five of the show's participants, who had been served up on the show as archetypal examples of innocuous Muslims-next-door, had been charged in the July terrorist attacks—and that although BBC producers had been told by one of the show participants that he knew the identity of the perpetrators, they had chosen not to pass this information on to police.

In April 2008 the BBC censored a Christian Choice Party broadcast objecting to the construction of a huge London mosque. Noting that the mosque's owner, the Taliban-linked Tablighi Jamaat movement, "opposes inter-faith dialogue and preaches that non-Muslims are an evil and corrupting influence," London *Times* reporter Andrew Norfolk quoted a supporter of the sect as saying that it seeks to create "'such hatred for [Christians' and Jews'] ways as human beings have for urine and excreta.'" Compared with such rhetoric, the language used in the Christian Choice's broadcast seemed ridiculously tame: it described Tablighi Jamaat as "a separatist Islamic group" and praised "moderate Muslims" for opposing the mosque. But the BBC forced Christian Choice to change "separatist" to "controversial" and, according to Norfolk, "barred the use of 'moderate Muslims' because the phrase implied that Tablighi Jamaat was less than moderate." Norfolk noted that the independent network ITV also censored the broadcast and in fact went further, "demanding that the adjective 'controversial' be used merely to describe the planned mosque and not the group itself."

A single staggering example will suffice to illustrate the perfidy of which the French media are capable when it comes to the truths about Islam. On the evening of September 30, 2000, Charles Enderlin, the Jerusalem correspondent for the state-owned TV channel France 2, reported the death earlier that day of a twelve-year-old Palestinian boy who, he said, had been killed in a shootout in the Gaza Strip between Israeli soldiers and Palestinian gunmen. While viewers watched a fifty-five-second film clip in which the boy and his father crouched behind a barrel in terror, Enderlin explained that the boy, Mohammed al-Dura, had been killed by Israeli gunfire. In no time at all, the footage had been broadcast around the world, and al-Dura was on his way to becoming a symbol of Palestinian victimhood and Israeli barbarity. Talal Abu Rahmeh, the freelance cameraman who had photographed the incident, would later testify that Israel Defense Forces (IDF) soldiers had killed the boy "intentionally and in cold blood" and wounded his father. Though the IDF accepted responsibility and apologized, the officer who had been in command that day insisted on his soldiers' innocence, and further investigation supported him. In 2004, three reporters were permitted to view the full twenty-seven minutes of Talal's film and discovered that it mostly depicted Palestinians *acting*—that is, pretending to be shot and in pain. Contrary to Enderlin's claim, there were no scenes of the boy's death agony. Comparison with other film shot at the same time and place by other cameramen proved beyond a doubt that the al-Dura "murder" was in fact a hoax. But when several journalists and bloggers said so in print, France 2, Enderlin, and France 2's news director, Arlette Chabot, sued three of them for defamation. In the first of the ensuing trials, in October 2006, the French justice system, as in the notorious 1894 trial of Alfred Dreyfus, stood with the establishment: Philippe Karsenty was found guilty as charged. The message was clear: "good" (i.e., politically correct, jihad-whitewashing) lies were permitted; "bad" truths would be punished. Most French media, apparently fearing that the verdict would affirm France 2's deception, didn't report on the case while it was under way, but the verdict, which reinforced the press's desired public image, was reported in huge front-page headlines.

Karsenty appealed the verdict. This time around, the judge demanded to see France 2's raw footage. Enderlin handed over only eighteen minutes of film. When it was screened in court, the staged episodes were missing, and al-Dura, after he had supposedly died, could be seen "lifting his arm and peering through his fingers at the camera," according to JTA, an Israeli news agency. Enderlin's story, and France 2's case, were left in tatters. In a November 2007 article, journalist Richard Landes provided persuasive evidence that the falsity of the al-Dura footage was in fact an open secret among many Western journalists. Karsenty was finally cleared by an appeals court in May 2008, and reacted with strong words about France 2's deception: "Every French citizen should be complaining about this insult to our intelligence. In fact, very few complain because mass brainwashing works."

Instead of being chastened by the verdict, the French media establishment reacted with outrage. *Le Nouvel Observateur* took the lead, denouncing the "smear campaign" against Enderlin and collecting the signatures of several hundred journalists and intellectuals on a pro-Enderlin petition. Anne-Elisabeth Moutet, who described the petition in the *Weekly Standard* as a case of "the guild . . . closing ranks," spoke to several of its signatories and concluded that they "rated facts far below reputation." The failure of the world media to responsibly cover the al-Dura story (I followed it on blogs) suggested that they understood very well what was going on and preferred not to draw public attention to a brand of mendacity in which they themselves regularly indulge—though usually in less sensational ways.

If the Enderlin case didn't make the kind of headlines in France that it should have, another case did. On April Fools' Day 2008, a court in Lille granted a Muslim husband an annulment on the grounds that his wife had lied about being a virgin on their wedding night. Although a want of bridal chastity is sufficient justification to annul a marriage under Islam, the verdict represented a departure from traditional French jurisprudence. To their credit, high-profile Frenchwomen recognized the court's decision as a dangerous precedent. Fadela Amara, secretary of state for urban affairs and former head of the Muslim feminist group *Ni Putes ni Soumises*, called it "a fatwa against the emancipation of women"; Women's Rights Minister Valérie Létard was appalled to see French civil law "used to diminish the status of women." France's Muslim-born minister of justice, Rachida Dati, refused at first to condemn the ruling, but under public pressure eventually ordered an appeal.

There was less outcry, alas, when a French court found Brigitte Bardot guilty in June 2008 of inciting racial and religious hatred and fined 15,000 euros. In a letter sent to French President Nicolas Sarkozy, among others, Bardot had criticized the imposition of Muslim values in France and said that Muslims were "destroying our country by imposing their ways." The fact that the guilty verdict proved her point seemed lost on the prosecutor, who, in a reference to Bardot's several previous convictions on similar charges, said, according to the BBC, that "she was weary of charging Ms Bardot with offences relating to racial hatred and xenophobia." The Bardot verdict came only days after a court in Finland sentenced blogger Seppo Lehto—best known, perhaps, for a YouTube video in which he draws Muhammed as a pig—to two years and seven months in prison on charges of religious and ethnic hatred. Lehto was also ordered to pay a few thousand euros apiece in damages to several politicians, police officers, and prosecutors. The Finnish government wanted to take down Lehto's blog, but was unable to do so because it was hosted by Blogger, a U.S. company, and was therefore protected by the First Amendment.

On an April 2008 program on Norway's TV2 about the status of women today, Afshan Rafiq, a (female) Muslim member of the Norwegian parliament for the Conservative Party, told the interviewer that under Islam women enjoy the same rights as men. Now, any responsible journalist, of course, should know that this is an out-and-out untruth. It's not a matter of opinion but of objective fact that a woman's testimony in a sharia court is given less weight than a man's, that a Muslim woman can't marry four husbands, and so forth. So what did the interviewer do when Rafiq made this breathtakingly untrue statement? Absolutely nothing; the beaming, approving smile on her face didn't waver in the slightest.

I could cite innumerable examples of European media dhimmitude, but I will content myself with offering just one more, from Norway. For a while in the autumn of 2006, the political weekly *Morgenbladet* ran an ad for subscriptions along the top of each page of its Web site. Under a photograph of a white male cab driver ran the following text, which was to be understood as being spoken by him:

> You know, these Muslims, if you feed a person with the Koran
> a couple of years, give him food, security, and everything he
> needs, you can bet he'll get a good picture of humanity. Then
> there's just as big a chance of him becoming a terrorist as there

is of me becoming a millionaire at Bjerkebanen [a racetrack in Oslo]! But if he's oppressed and discriminated against, and then fed with a little Islam, what he reads can be abused to legitimize violence. What creates extremism is lousy conditions, right? You can't just say that the terrorists have to be stopped. We have to think through what kind of conditions create extremism. Where that's concerned, I totally support what Basim Ghozlan said to Simen Sætre in the article on Islam in *Morgenbladet*'s issue number 34/2006. Want a receipt?

Though this speech was put in the mouth of some nameless, gruff-looking cabbie, every bit of it—except for a few words at the beginning and end, plus the racetrack reference—was in fact a direct quote from Basim Ghozlan, and was drawn from the interview he gave to Sætre, a *Morgenbladet* writer, in the issue mentioned. Clearly, *Morgenbladet* found Ghozlan's explanation of the roots of Muslim terrorism sympathetic. To be sure, it was rather remarkable for *Morgenbladet* to put the words of an interview subject in somebody else's mouth as part of a subscription come-on. But there was nothing remarkable about the sentiments themselves—they were exactly the sort of multicultural nonsense the media served up regularly. "What creates extremism is lousy conditions, right?" Yes, forget that van Gogh's murderer and the 7/7 terrorists grew up in nice neighborhoods and attended college; forget that the 2007 terrorists in London and Glasgow were doctors. Give a Muslim immigrant "food, security, and everything he needs," and "he'll get a good picture of humanity"; yet Muslims in Europe have received more welfare-state benefits than any immigrant group any-where at any time, and yet when and where in human history have so many members of any immigrant group been so eager to destroy the source of this manna? The "cabbie's" diatribe was pure cultural-elite foolishness, put into the mouth of someone who looked like a straight-talking, no-nonsense ethnic Norwegian from central casting in order to sell it to the masses.

Who was Basim Ghozlan? He was the director of Norway's Islamic Federation and editor of the Web site islam.no—and an Islamist who had publicly supported Hamas suicide bombings of Jewish civilians, the execution of HIV-positive people, and an end to Norway's annual Holocaust commemorations. According to the Honest Thinking Web site, Ghozlan "embraces the dream of an Islamic state with Islamic law"; according to Hege Storhaug of Oslo's Human Rights Service, Ghozlan's high-profile wife, Muslim convert Lena Larsen, has said that her ideal is a sharia state. Ghozlan also has close ties to—and has praised the scholarship of—Yusuf al-Qaradawi, who looks forward to the Muslim conquest of Europe. Under the *Morgenbladet* logo in the ad appeared the words: "Don't Make Yourself Dumber than You Are." Yet the folks at *Morgenbladet* seemed determined to stay dumb, clinging to the politically correct delusion that jihadist terror is the West's fault and holding up for emulation a man who seeks to replace democracy with sharia.

VII

"Sowing Pain"

"Europe," wrote Dan Bilefsky and Ian Fisher in the *New York Times* on October 11, 2005, "appears to be crossing an invisible line regarding its Muslim minorities. More people in the political mainstream are arguing that Islam cannot be reconciled with European values." On October 3, the Norwegian newspaper *Dagbladet* claimed that the Norwegian debate had been changed by "neoconservatives" who were speaking up for Western liberties. And a reviewer of a book by one of those so-called "neoconservatives" wrote that "Something is obviously happening, not only in Norway but throughout Europe." Something most certainly *was* happening: finally, there was at least a semblance of real debate under way about the Islamization of the West. The Danish cartoon controversy and other developments had made it harder for public figures not to take a stand. Yet while a few people stepped forward and defended free speech, others—larger in both number and influence—only became more vociferous and sophisticated in their arguments for compromise and appeasement. Media commentators who for years had celebrated dialogue with pro-jihad Muslims now turned out to be less than enthusiastic about dialogue with critics of those pro-jihad Muslims. Such a debate, they argued, was dangerous. On October 23, 2005, for example, Reuters maintained that a new, more open discussion of integration "risks further isolating these minorities rather than integrating them." (One impairs Muslim integration, then, when one openly admits that it has been a failure.) Many defenders of European Islamists intensified their attacks on people like Ayaan Hirsi Ali—the courageous Somali-born woman who, instead of submitting to a forced marriage in Canada, had taken it on the lam to the Netherlands, where she was granted asylum, learned Dutch, attended college, worked with abused Muslim women, quit Islam, entered politics, and won election to Parliament, along the way becoming a blunt, eloquent teller of home truths about the religion of her birth. (Multiculturalism, Hirsi Ali would later explain, was "elevating cultures full of bigotry and hatred toward women to the stature of respectable alternative ways of life. I wanted Muslim women to be aware of just how bad, and unacceptable, their suffering was. I wanted to help them develop the vocabulary of resistance.") Some even talked about messengers such as Hirsi Ali as if they were themselves responsible for creating the problems they discussed. The default attitude seemed to be: if only they'd shut up, all the problems would go away.

As I've mentioned, Pope Benedict XVI gave an academic address at the University of Regensburg on September 12, 2006, in which he quoted a comment made by the Byzantine emperor Manuel II Paleologus in the year 1391: "Show me just what Muhammad brought that was new and there you will find things only evil and inhuman, such as his command to spread by the sword the faith he preached." Now, every day in the Muslim world, politicians, clerics, teachers, and others spew out the most abominable lies and calumnies about the West, America, Israel, Jews, Christians, Hindus, homosexuals, democracy, and so forth on TV news and entertainment programs, in the press, and in mosques, schools, and sundry venues. Only a tiny fraction of this ocean of slander is ever reported in even the most out-of-the way Western media. Yet when word got out about the Pope quoting a single sentence from an obscure medieval monarch in a lecture at a German university, the Muslim world erupted in fury—and editorialists around the Western world chided the pontiff for having behaved in such a foolish and insensitive manner. The *New York Times* accused Benedict of having "sow[n] pain" and "fomented discord between Christians and Muslims. . . . He needs to offer a deep and persuasive apology, demonstrating that words can also heal." Implicit in this editorial was the belief that it's unwise and immoral *not* to let yourself be silenced by the possibility of violence.

Among the few prominent defenses of the pontiff was an op-ed that appeared in *Le Figaro* on September 19. The author, a philosophy teacher named Robert Redeker, defended Enlightenment values, articulated some relevant truths about Islam (including the fact that many of its adherents "seek to compel Europe to yield to its vision of man"), and noted that Islam, like Communism,

> treats generosity, broadmindedness, tolerance, gentleness,
> freedom of women and of manners, democratic values, as marks
> of decadence. They are weaknesses that it seeks to exploit, by
> means of useful idiots, self-righteous consciences drowning
> in nice feelings, in order to impose the Koranic order on the
> Western world itself.

Redeker also wrote that while "Jesus is a master of love, Muhammed is a master of hate," all too many of whose followers today have consecrated their lives to violence. As if to prove his point, Redeker was quickly targeted for death by jihadist Web sites and forced to go into hiding with his family. The response by French authorities to these death threats demonstrated the degree to which a factitious respect for bullies had already taken priority, in the minds of many Westerners, over the freedom to speak one's mind about those bullies' religion. France's then prime minister, Dominique de Villepin, while calling the threats against Redeker "unacceptable," added that "everyone has the right to express their opinions freely—at the same time that they respect others, of course." For Western democracies, this was a new rule—that one had to respect everybody. The lesson of the Redeker affair, said Villepin, was "how vigilant we must be to ensure that people fully respect one another in our society"—not a word about ensuring free speech. French education minister Gilles de Robien declared "solidarity" with Redeker, but counseled that "a public employee must be prudent, moderate, and circumspect under all circumstances." *Le Figaro* editor-in-chief Pierre Rousselin similarly vowed "solidarity" with Redeker, only to apologize later—on Al-Jazeera—for having run the op-ed. Obviously, "solidarity" wasn't what it had once been. Nor was respect. Of course, when Villepin insisted that people "in our society" must "fully respect one another" he meant that non-Muslims must respect Muslims—neither he nor anybody else, it was clear, was seeking to clamp down on even the most vicious, ad hominem criticism of (say) the American president or the pope. In any case, such "respect" was really not respect at all, because respect is freely given and must be earned; when Villepin said respect, he meant submission. One journalist who dared speak the truth was *Corriere della Sera*'s Angelo Panebianco, who pointed out that the Pope's speech, like the Muhammed cartoons, had been "only a pretext" that was used by Islamists "to ignite the Islamic squares." Jihadists were showing off their strength, exposing the West's weakness, and "testing their ability to impose Muslim hegemony on the world."

But men like Redeker and Panebianco were voices in the wilderness. More common was the discreditable attitude expressed by Paul Vallely of the *Independent* in an October 4, 2006, essay. Noting the widespread furor over Benedict's speech, Redeker's piece, and other recent acts at which Muslims had taken offense, Vallely sneered at the springing up of "champions of freedom of expression and crusaders against religious darkness in the name of Western values." Calling them "simplistic" and "alarmists," Vallely argued that what was under way wasn't a conflict between free speech and oppressive religion: it was a clash "between religious and secular fundamentalists." If in Voltaire's time, he insisted, "religion was the dominant oppressive culture against which emerging rationalism struggled," in our own time "Islam embodies the identity of one of the most vulnerable, and alienated, minorities in Europe."

Even as he insensitively criticized the "narrow-minded," "triumphalis[t]" Pope, the "adolescent" and "gratuitously offensive" Redeker, and the "vile" Theo van Gogh, Vallely celebrated what he called a "new sensitivity" toward Islam (in other words, a new self-censorship) that was, he said, "developing in many quarters"—for example, in Berlin, where the Deutsche Oper had canceled a production of Mozart's *Idemeneo* that, it was feared, would offend Muslims. "In many places," Vallely wrote, "there is a growing realisation that freedom of expression is not absolute but needs to be governed by a sense of social responsibility. To elevate one right above all is the hallmark of the single-issue fanatic." Insisting upon what in America would be called one's First Amendment rights, then, makes one a "single-issue fanatic" (a position taken, of course, out of abject fear of *real* fanatics—that is, the kinds with guns and bombs). "Sometimes it is wise to choose not to exercise a right," suggested Vallely, glibly conflating wisdom with cowardice. Dismissing "the hyperbole about art and free speech being 'the elixirs of an enlightened society'" in favor of what he deemed "a more mature approach," Vallely called for the building of "common values—ones which recognise the inalienable right to freedom of expression but which, at the same time, demand it be exercised in a measured way." Meaning, of course, a "free speech" that isn't really free speech at all. It was interesting to note that in Vallely's opinion, it was inappropriate to air disagreeable truths about Islam, but thoroughly appropriate to use vicious language to characterize those—such as the Pope, Redeker, and van Gogh—who did venture to tell those truths. For Vallely, plainly, the bottom line was that if one is in possession of a truth that just might be considered offensive by some Muslims, the proper thing to do is to drop it down the memory hole.

On the same day that it ran Vallely's essay, the *Independent* published an editorial criticizing the Pope and Redeker for "adding fuel to the flames." We've already seen this metaphor used by Peter Mandelson, and in fact to accuse those who criticize or parody Islam, or who refuse to compromise with sharia law, of "fanning the flames of Muslim anger" has become a commonplace. On the contrary, what people like Hirsi Ali and Robert Redeker are doing is refusing to feed the fires of Muslim intimidation. For every time a dhimmi like Paul Vallely refuses to stand up to jihadists, the latter are encouraged to push for even more concessions.[3]

In what was by now a standard self-contradiction, the *Independent* editors followed the stirring assertion that "of course, the right to free speech cannot be circumscribed" with the weasely statement that "in a democracy, we also have a responsibility to be mindful of the sensitivities of those around us" (especially, it seems, those inclined to burn down embassies and assassinate filmmakers). "Where there is a substantial minority Muslim population," the editors explained, "that

---

[3]Another fan of the "flames" metaphor was Neal Ascherson, who on the Open Democracy Web site complained that "rights—like the freedom of the press—inherently offer us the right to decide when to use them. The grounds for that decision include common sense and prudence. I may have the right to throw away a cigarette near a pile of leaky petrol drums, but I will probably choose not to do so, and will be held criminally responsible for a conflagration."

means thinking carefully about how Islam is presented." Apparently we need not devote too much thought to how we represent other, less violent religious groups. The *Independent*'s editors called for self-censorship and praised those who had argued for finding a balance in Europe between "free speech" and "religious freedom"—as if the newly conceived "right" of Muslims not to be offended were a time-honored fundamental element of religious freedom. "We must always remember," wrote the *Independent*'s editors, "that the traditions of free speech and religious freedom can co-exist in today's Europe. And we must do everything possible to marginalise those—on both sides—who would have us believe otherwise." This last sentence amounted to an admission that it was indeed the policy of the *Independent* to exclude from its pages the opinions of Islam's critics.

In March 2008, *Washington Post* managing editor Philip Bennett delivered a speech at the University of California at Irvine in which he lamented that the media, including his own newspaper, had failed to give the American public a clear understanding of Islam. True enough; but his argument was that the image of Islam being presented is too negative—and that the solution is to hire more Muslim reporters and editors. It was the same old dhimmi line—that if non-Muslims have any concerns at all about Islam, it's a sign of ignorance, pure and simple. A particularly egregious example of media readiness to put Muslims to work reporting on Islam came to light in the same month, when it was reported that *DR*, the Danish national radio service, while producing a 2002 documentary on the radical Muslim group Hizb ut-Tahrir, had complied with that group's demand that only Muslims be allowed to work on the program.

VIII

Profiles in Courage

There are, to be sure, individual journalists in Europe who are wide-awake about Islam, and even some of the most dhimmified news organizations have occasionally slipped and put out surprisingly honest reports. In 2006, Norway's TV2 broadcast a remarkably frank documentary about Norwegian politicians' and media's betrayal of free speech during the Danish cartoon controversy. In 2007, *Der Spiegel* ran a highly informative, in-depth piece about the rising tendency of German courts to consult sharia law when adjudicating cases involving Muslims. And in February 2008, *Newsweek*—which, along with its sister publication the *Washington Post*, has been among the most accommodationist of publications—actually ran an article by George Weigel, "The War against Jihadism," in which the slug was: "Why can't we call the enemy by its name? We're going to have to in order to win." How bizarre to see such words in a newsmagazine that had been among the chief culprits in misleading the public about the reality of jihad! But most mainstream-media reports on stories involving Islam have continued to be tendentious, selective, and marked by extensive self-censorship. As noted, I had been reading on blogs and on the Web sites of French newspapers about the wave of violence in French suburbs for several weeks in 2006 before the mass media outside France began to run short, sanitized accounts of the violence. Disturbances have taken place elsewhere in Europe that few have heard about. In early 2006 there were several days of violent revolt in Windsor, near London; on October 20, 2005, a group of young Muslims in Amsterdam attacked a bus with chemical explosives. Street riots took place in Antwerp. And so on. But few Western media consumers ever heard about these episodes—except for the still relatively small numbers who are regular readers of news and opinion blogs.

It is for this reason that the Internet often feels like a godsend. It is chilling to think of all the developments in recent years that would never have gained international attention without it. Blogs have made possible the dissemination of news that media organizations like the *Times* have preferred not to cover. And they've provided a forum for the kind of open and honest discussion that the mainstream media have tried to prevent. Bloggers report on stories that the mass media pass over; they point out omissions and distortions in mass-media coverage; and sometimes, when enough of them write about a certain story, some mainstream media feel compelled to pay attention. The blog network is a splendid way of spreading news. If an important event has only been reported on in one obscure local newspaper, a blogger somewhere will have noticed it and written about it, and other interested bloggers will link to the story, and so forth, so that the news is passed on to readers of a number of blogs around the world. The Internet has brought the freedom of expression enshrined in the U.S. Constitution to a remarkable consummation, and has spread a uniquely American openness to other countries whose own traditions are somewhat less free. If the West is saved from jihad, it will be largely a result of the uninhibited nature of free speech on the Internet. This system, of course, has its enemies—many of them in the mainstream media, who recognize an encroachment upon their power when they see it. The standard response of many mainstream journalists to the entire phenomenon of blogging has been to dismiss its practitioners as substandard and unreliable. On the contrary, the best blogs have shown over and over again just how unreliable the mainstream media often is, and how useful an independent corrective can be.

It wasn't so very long ago that the major newspapers, newsmagazines, and network news organizations enjoyed extraordinary power in American society. They had a virtual monopoly on the reporting of news; a handful of editors in New York and Washington could decide what was news and what wasn't. In practice, indeed, the system was even narrower than that: to a remarkable extent, it was a few editors at *New York Times* headquarters on 43rd Street in New York who set the agenda for the U.S. news media. Those days are over, thanks to the Internet.

Take a 2007 article by Paul Williams about a Hancock, New York, compound that Williams described as a branch of Muslims of the Americas Inc., whose founder, a Pakistani cleric, he described as having links to the organization Jamaat ul-Fuqra. "Even though Jamaat ul-Fuqra has been involved in terror attacks and sundry criminal activities, recruited thousands of members from federal and state penal systems, and appears to be operating paramilitary facilities for militant Muslims," wrote Williams, "it remains to be placed on the official U.S. Terror Watch List. On the contrary, it continues to operate, flourish, and expand as a legitimate nonprofit, tax-deductible charity." Neighbors driving past the compound, reported Williams, had heard the sound of gunfire and small explosives. "We don't even dare to slow down when we drive by," one of them told Williams. "They own the mountain and they know it and there is nothing we can do about it but move, and we can't even do that. Who wants to buy a property near that?"

Williams's article provided highly valuable insight into the spread of Islamist paramilitary compounds in the United States—of which there are apparently several. But his story didn't appear in the *New York Times*. At this writing, the *Times* appears not to have published a single word about the compound. (When I searched the *Times* database for Hancock, New York, in early 2008, I found articles about fishing and trapping river eels, but not Muslim paramilitary compounds.) No, Williams' article appeared in a publication called the *Canada Free Press*. In the post-9/11 era, this pattern has become extremely familiar: time and again, important Islam-related developments go entirely unmentioned—or are, at best, very inadequately covered—in the major media. Instead, the definitive reporting turns up in some publication you've never heard of, or on a blog. Another example: in January 2008, a group of ninety-six people who were commemorating Britain's Holocaust Memorial Day by touring "sites of Jewish interest" in London were assaulted by a gang of Muslim youths in the East End who pelted them with stones. Britain had, in short, its own little version of the Intifada. The account I read appeared in the *East London Advertiser*. I searched the Web sites of all the major London newspapers, including the tabloids, for a report on the incident. Nothing.

Another story that was all but ignored by the mainstream media first came to light in July 2004 in the online newspaper WomensWall-Street.com. In an article entitled "Terror in the Skies, Again," Annie Jacobsen described a harrowing experience she'd undergone on June 29, 2004. Flying from Detroit to Los Angeles with her husband and small child on Northwest Airlines Flight 327, Jacobsen had observed fourteen fellow passengers, all of them young or middle-aged Middle Eastern men, behaving very suspiciously—congregating in small groups at the back of the plane, making consecutive trips to the lavatory, and, it appeared, sending one another signals. Toward the end of the flight, "seven of the men stood up—in unison—and walked to the front and back lavatories"; one of them took his camera into the toilet, another his cell phone; those waiting their turn spoke to one another in Arabic; eventually, when the last man emerged from the lavatory, he signaled to one of his companions and "mouthed the word no."

Several passengers were alarmed; at least one was crying. The captain and flight attendants were uneasy as well, and one of the latter told Jacobsen's husband that air marshals on board shared their concern. After the plane landed, police officers ran to the gate and detained the fourteen men, who identified themselves as members of a Syrian band and the band's Lebanese promoter. Jacobsen and her husband were interviewed by the FBI, which supposedly found their testimony very interesting but which didn't open an investigation until after Jacobsen had recounted her experience on MSNBC. Representatives of the Transportation Security Administration, a division of the Department of Homeland Security, didn't even bother reporting the case to the DHS Operations Center, which first found out about it from an article in the *Washington Times* on July 26—a month after the incident. TSA officials said that passengers from Flight 327 who had talked to the media about their experiences had overreacted and that Jacobsen was an unstable woman whose account should not be taken seriously. Indeed, both the FBI and the Federal Air Marshal Service spread disinformation to the media, suggesting that Jacobsen had overreacted and created a disruption. One reporter said that according to an unidentified source, "the air marshals on the flight were partially concerned Jacobsen's actions could have been an effort by terrorists or attackers to create a disturbance on the plane to force the agents to identify themselves."

This explanation could not have been more twisted. Yet the media readily echoed the officials' calumnies. Jacobsen saw herself labeled panicky, prejudiced, a fool. One blogger called her article "a far-fetched piece of bigoted garbage." Patrick Smith described it in *Salon* as "a story about nothing, puffed and aggrandized to appear important . . . six pages of the worst grade-school prose, spring-loaded with mindless hysterics and bigoted provocation." (On the contrary, Jacobsen's piece was well written and as straightforwardly factual as one might have wanted Elliott's ridiculously flowery and factually slippery profile of Reda Shata to be.) A commenter at Robert Spencer's "Jihad Watch" Web site wrote: "But nothing happened. *Absolutely nothing happened!* Is not the racism and Islamophobia of the Americans on the plane obvious? How do you think the innocent men felt?" As for the *New York Times*, its initial coverage of the episode came in the form of a dismissive business-travel column by Joe Sharkey. In August, Sharkey followed up with an article maintaining that Jacobsen's most important claim—that several of the men had stood up simultaneously and taken up positions by the toilets and exit doors—was untrue. Even though Sharkey acknowledged that "flight crews are being routinely warned . . . that terrorists are 'testing the system' . . . to see how crews behave," he seemed determined to leave the impression that Jacobsen's story was groundless. It was as if the mere fact that the Syrians were a musical group made all suspicions ridiculous.

Or *were* they a musical group? Authorities as well as media, eager to dispel concerns about terrorism, grasped on to the claim that this was indeed a legitimate band on a real tour. Jacobsen was told that the story had checked out. But when she looked into it herself, she discovered that nobody, either in the government or the mainstream media, had actually done the legwork required to ensure that it checked out. She did learn, however, that producers at ABC had tried to book the band on *Good Morning America*, plainly eager to prove that the challenge America faces is not jihad but anti-Muslim bigotry. But the band— very suspiciously—hadn't been interested in this extraordinary opportunity for national exposure. Why?

Jacobsen worked hard to track down the musical group. After some effort she obtained a photograph of the band. Only two of those in the picture had been on Flight 327. She sent it to fellow passengers. They agreed: with the same two exceptions, the men they had seen on the plane that day were different from those in the photograph. Indeed, the more Jacobsen looked into the supposed facts about the band, the more the story broke down and more suspicious the whole business looked. Eventually it emerged that, contrary to what she had been told and what had been reported, none of the "band" members had been detained after the flight or seriously questioned at all; in fact, agents from Immigration and Customs Enforcement (ICE), whose job it would have been to carry out such questioning, had not even shown up. "The Federal Agents who were there, the FAMS [Federal Air Marshal Service] and the FBI, neglected to interview the men separately and at length," wrote Jacobsen. "And then, with the whole world listening, they lied about it." It is an indictment of America's mainstream media that in a country crawling with journalists who should have been urgently interested in the question of how federal immigration and counterterrorist agencies are handling national security, it took one woman, Annie Jacobsen of WomensWallStreet.com, to uncover the truth.

The mentality was bizarre. Less than three years had passed since 9/11. Everyone knew how the planes had been hijacked that day. Everyone knew—or should have known—that jihadists were still at it: the bombings in Madrid had taken place only two months earlier. The *Washington Times* noted, moreover, that although the fourteen men were traveling together, they "pretended not to notice each other" and "got seats that literally put them all over the plane." There was, then, legitimate reason for suspicion. But many Americans, especially in the media, had been brainwashed by multiculturalism into feeling that it was wrong even to let oneself think such thoughts. (As a character on *Seinfeld* would put it, "I don't think we're supposed to be talking about this.") Though Jacobsen's conduct was a model of civic responsibility, one commentator after another acted as if she'd been wrong to be suspicious—or (at least) wrong not to keep her suspicions to herself. It was as if terrorism didn't exist—or as if it were not terrorism itself, but concern about terrorism, that was the real problem in the post-9/11 world.

"Terror in the Skies, Again?" appeared in July 2004. But not until May 2007, in response to a year-old Freedom of Information Act request by the *Washington Times*, was a redacted version of an inspector general's report on the Flight 327 incident finally released. The report, the result of a two-year investigation, fully supported the testimony of Jacobsen and other eyewitnesses to the effect that the fourteen men had behaved suspiciously. They had, it turned out, been traveling on expired visas. Eight of them either had criminal records or had, on previous occasions, been considered to have behaved suspiciously; the man identified as the band's promoter had been involved in a similar episode on a Frontier Airlines flight a few months before the Flight 327 incident, and in September 2006 had been detained after arriving in the United States from Istanbul. Key information was apparently omitted from the version of the report that was released to the media; evidently the government knew more about the case than it was willing to share with the public. The *Washington Times*, which had reported shortly after the incident that passengers and air marshals felt it "resembled a dry run for a terrorist attack," now wrote that air marshals who had seen the report described it as confirming those suspicions. Indeed, despite the dismissal of Jacobsen's concerns by Homeland Security, it turned out that air marshals had had an eye on the Syrians prior to boarding. One former air marshal said the report showed that Homeland Security executives had sought "to downplay and cover up an unmistakable dry run that forced flight attendants to reveal the [identity of the] air marshals and compel the pilots to open the flight deck door." Gary Boettcher, president of the Coalition of Allied Pilots Associations, had already declared his belief that Jacobsen had witnessed a dry run. "He has had many of these experiences, and so have many of his fellow captains," reported Jacobsen in her 2005 book *Terror in the Skies*. "They have been trying to speak out about this, but so far their words have been falling on deaf ears." On April 18, 2007, Jacobsen wrote in WomensWallStreet.com that the report had not been released in full "because its contents embarrass the Transportation Security Administration (TSA)." The report, Jacobsen surmised, tied "at least two of the Syrians from the dry run on Flight 327 to an earlier dry run on a different airline—Frontier Airlines Flight 577. That the TSA missed connecting these dots and instead allowed the Syrians to go free without answering some serious questions reveals a great flaw in the aviation security net."

Did the report's partial release result in a chorus of apologies to

Jacobsen by the journalists who had savaged her? On the contrary, most mainstream media outlets either ignored the report or brazenly misrepresented its findings. It was widely claimed, in fact, that the report showed Jacobsen *had* overreacted, that the musicians had been conclusively cleared of terrorist charges, and that TSA officials had behaved correctly in dismissing Jacobsen's concerns. (The TSA, too, continued to insist that it had done nothing wrong.) And how did America's newspaper of record handle the story? On May 30, 2007, the *Times* ran a brief item that took an inexplicably jaunty tone toward the incident. Under the headline "It's Not Paranoia If They're Really Out to Get You," Tobin Harshaw wrote that conservatives had responded to Jacobsen's charges by accusing the government of "falling down on the job of protecting air travelers," while liberals had told her "to take a 'chill pill.'" Almost in passing, the article acknowledged that the Syrians had indeed been carrying out "a dry run for a terror attack." Aside from treating this deeply disturbing story as if it were an amusing piece of human-interest filler, Harshaw neglected to mention that the incident had only come to light thanks to WomensWallStreet.com, which few readers were likely to have heard of, and the *Washington Times*, to which readers of the *New York Times* are encouraged to condescend.

Then there was the "flying imams" story. On November 20, 2006, in Minneapolis, six imams boarded US Airways Flight 300 to Phoenix. After a takeoff delay of several hours, all six were removed from the plane because of behavior that was considered suspicious by passengers as well as crew members. The men had not all taken their assigned seats, but had instead fanned out in much the way the Syrians had done on Northwest Flight 327, as if to cover the exits. Two sat in first class, claiming they had been upgraded, although this later turned out to be untrue. Three of the men requested seat-belt extensions, which are meant for use by overweight passengers, but which also can be used as weapons; yet none (or perhaps only one) of the men was large enough to require an extension, and in any event, instead of using them, they placed them under their seats.

After the incident, the group quickly designated a spokesman, who told the media that they'd been expelled from the plane for praying. "To practice your faith and pray is a crime in America?" he asked rhetorically. It was, of course, the perfect accusation to level if you were trawling for media support. The Muslim American Society Freedom

Foundation got involved, as did CAIR. Both organizations pushed the line that the men had been guilty of only one offense: "flying while Muslim." The ploy worked. Media reports implied that this was an open-and-shut case of Islamophobia. Non-Muslim religious leaders helped push this line. A week after the incident, Jewish, Christian, and Muslim clerics conducted a joint "pray-in" at the airport in Washington; a few days later, another ecumenical protest took place outside US Airways headquarters. Both drew considerable media attention. *Newsweek*'s account of the episode, written by Jessica Bennett and Matthew Philips, began by focusing sympathetically on one of the flying imams, Omar Shahin, president of the North American Imams Federation, who, they wrote, was "no stranger to the heightened security of a post-9/11 world"; prior to the US Airways incident, he'd already had the experience of being "picked out of a crowd by the color of his skin—interrogated, fingerprinted, or detained."

Had *Newsweek*'s reporters attempted to discover whether Shahin's claim was true? If so, when, where, and why had he been interrogated, fingerprinted, and detained? These questions weren't answered. Instead, the reporters simply informed readers that Shahin and his five brother imams were "so used to harassment" that they'd done "everything they could to avoid suspicion" at the Minneapolis airport: "they wore Western clothes." They "spoke only English." They sat apart from one another. They prayed quietly. Yet even this was not enough. These distinguished and holy men, all of them utterly innocent, ended up being escorted off the plane in handcuffs "after a passenger handed a note to a flight attendant expressing concern over the group's 'suspicious activity.'" According to *Newsweek*, the only "suspicious activity" was "the group's loud chants of 'Allah, Allah, Allah.'" This account was, simply put, a masterpiece of misrepresentation. *Newsweek* mentioned only one seat-belt extension and declared categorically that the passenger in question needed it because of his size. The multiple examples of suspicious activity were totally omitted from the story. The statement that the episode had begun with one passenger's note was plainly a deliberate attempt to conceal the fact that crew members and passengers alike (some of them Muslims) had also been concerned about the imams. *Newsweek* did cite the charge that the men had been traveling on one-way tickets, but said that Shahin denied this and that he claimed to have "the documentation to prove it." (The reporters didn't indicate whether they'd asked to see this documentation.) *Newsweek* neither quoted the anti-American remarks that witnesses reported the imams as having made, nor mentioned their defiance of the pilot's request to deboard for further screening, which had obliged officials to remove them forcibly.

The impression left by *Newsweek*, then, was that this was a case of pure prejudice. The article concluded with a quotation from Shahin (in which the charge shifted from religious to racial bias): "I do everything by the book and I'm still suspicious. I cannot change the color of my skin." Nowhere in *Newsweek's* report was there a hint that the imams might actually have been up to something. (Nor did *Newsweek* mention that Shahin, among other things, had denied Muslim responsibility for 9/11.) The report was, in short, a model of see-no-evil multiculturalism. And an Associated Press story took much the same line—the main difference being that it ended with a quotation from Shahin implicitly accusing passengers not of racism but of religious ignorance: "If up to now they don't know about prayers," he said, "this is a real problem." Racism or religious intolerance? To the journalists writing about this incident, apparently, either would do: the important thing was to leave readers believing that Muslims, in post-9/11 America, were being harassed by bigots. Yes, the facts strongly pointed to other conclusions; yet some of America's most respected media organs chose to serve up the imam's and CAIR's spin as the unvarnished truth. Once again, it was left to the contrarian press to set the record straight: the *Washington Times*, for example, quoted a pilot as saying that in the airline industry, behavior such as that displayed by the imams on Flight 300 was recognized as indicative of "a terrorist probe."

Just as WomensWallStreet.com took the lead in the Flight 327 investigation, so now it was left to another financial publication, *Investor's Business Daily*, to focus responsibly on the case of Flight 300. In an editorial, *IBD* praised US Airways for its handling of the matter and suggested that the imams, though widely treated as "victims," were in fact "provocateurs" who "chose to make a spectacle." It was *IBD* that reported that this wasn't the first time Shahin had been implicated in an incident involving suspicious behavior on an aircraft. In a case that was later cited in the *9/11 Commission Report* as having been regarded by the FBI as a dry run for 9/11, two members of Shahin's mosque in Tucson had attempted to open the cockpit door on an America West flight.

The two men, with Shahin serving as their lawyer, had sued America West for removing them from the plane. According to *IBD*, Hani Hanjour, the hijacker who on 9/11 had piloted American Airlines Flight 77 into the Pentagon, had regularly attended Shahin's mosque. *IBD* further reported that "bin Laden's onetime personal secretary" had also belonged to the mosque, and that "bin Laden's ex-logistics chief" had preceded Shahin as the mosque's president. *IBD* quoted an FBI agent as saying that "These people don't continue to come back to Tucson because they like the sunshine. . . . Something was established there, and it's been there for a long time." *IBD* added: "And Shahin appears to be in the middle of it." These were sensational facts—but *IBD* was virtually alone in reporting most of them.

IX

Buruma

In America today, no single event surrounding a book's publication—short of a booking on *Oprah*—is considered to be as important as a review in either the daily or Sunday *New York Times*. A positive review can send sales skyrocketing; and even if the review isn't entirely positive, the fact that the *Times Book Review* has deemed a book about current events worthy of reviewing puts that book on the map, signals its significance, compels others to take its arguments seriously.

In January 2005, a scholar named Bat Ye'or published *Eurabia*, an earthshaking exposé of European governments' efforts to strengthen ties with undemocratic Arab regimes and to facilitate Muslim immigration into Europe—efforts that, in practical terms, amounted to aiding and abetting jihad. It was a book of the first importance—yet it got no *Times* review. In October 2005 came Andrew Bostom's compendious *The Legacy of Jihad*, which put current events into a highly instructive historical context, making it clear that the jihadist imperative has always been at the root of the House of Submission's relations with the House of War. No *Times* review. In February 2006 came my own *While Europe Slept* and Claire Berlinski's *Menace in Europe*—two books by American expatriates concerned by the rise of Islam in Europe. No *Times* reviews. They were followed in March by *The Force of Reason*, a powerful jeremiad about Europe's Islamization by the legendary Oriana Fallaci. No *Times* review. (There hadn't been a *Times* review for Fallaci's bestselling response to 9/11, *The Rage and the Pride*, either.) In May 2006 came *Londonistan*, an authoritative account by Melanie Phillips of how the British government had allowed London to become Ground Zero for Islamic terrorism in the West. No *Times* review. September 2006 saw the publication of Robert Spencer's *The Truth About Muhammed* and Mark Steyn's *America Alone*, both of which would climb to the top of the *New York Times* bestseller list and stay there for weeks—yet neither book got a *Times* review.

This was not simply a matter of certain writers not getting the attention they felt they deserved. It was a matter of the *New York Times*, not only America's most influential newspaper, but also the one with the most comprehensive books coverage, excluding from that coverage an entire subgenre of serious new works. Why? The obvious answer was that the *Times* wanted readers to remain in the dark about the information contained in them. And the rest of the mainstream media followed suit. Generally speaking, these books were given short shrift in major newspapers. Most of the attention they received was from blogs and other Internet-based news sites. In some cases, this attention was so extensive as to compel at least some traditional media to reckon with the books' existence (if only by misrepresenting their contents and smearing their authors). For the most part, however, the response to these books took the form of silence. This was nothing less than a scandal. Nothing could be more vital today than that free people know as much as possible about what Islamization signifies and portends; yet the *New York Times* and other major media, when confronted with a raft of books intended to contribute to this crucial effort of education, chose to pretend they didn't exist.

Then, in September 2006, came yet another book—and the *Times* suddenly found its voice.

Written by Ian Buruma, it was entitled *Murder in Amsterdam: The Death of Theo van Gogh and the Limits of Tolerance*. Both the book itself and the story of its treatment by the media—with the *New York Times* in the lead—are worth examining in some detail, because both shed a great deal of light on the cultural elite's attitude toward freedom of speech about Islam in the post-9/11 world. The book's premise was simple: after van Gogh's murder, the Dutch-born Buruma, a star of the transatlantic academic jet set (he has taught at Oxford and is now a professor at Bard College in New York), returned to his homeland and talked to a number of people—some obscure, some famous; some Muslim, some not—about the cultural background of van Gogh's murder. *Murder in Amsterdam* consisted mostly of Buruma's accounts of these conversations, plus his posthumous comments about Fortuyn and van Gogh. Previously, Buruma had been critical of radical Islam and its European apologists. But now he had changed his tune dramatically. In *Murder in Amsterdam*, his profiles of Fortuyn, van Gogh, and other supporters of freedom were plainly calculated to undermine readers' admiration for them, while in his portraits of Dutch Muslims who supported jihad he pulled out all the stops to achieve the opposite effect. For example, Buruma characterized Fortuyn as a "potential menace" because of his "loathing of Islam"—hardly a fair description of a gay liberal's concern over a religion that considers homosexuality a capital offense. Similarly, writing about Ayaan Hirsi Ali, Buruma claimed (obscenely) to see "echoes" of her youthful "enthusiasm for the Muslim Brotherhood" in her fervent opposition to Islamic patriarchy—as if a young girl's religious brainwashing could be equated with her determination, as an educated and intelligent adult, to protect other young girls from such brainwashing. Fortuyn was, and Hirsi Ali is, a hero; but Buruma repeatedly made a point of their purported arrogance, fanaticism, and personal eccentricities. He even called them dangerous—while insisting that someone like Abdelhakim Chouaati, a history teacher who was convinced that "9/11 was a Jewish plot," wasn't dangerous at all. Buruma maintained that if only Muslims could be made to feel truly at home in the Netherlands, all would be well; never mind that Chouaati, who did feel at home there, still wanted to see it under sharia law.

Murder in Amsterdam was a masterpiece of slippery rhetoric. While posing as an objective observer who was simply out to discover the truth and to give each of his interlocutors a voice, Buruma labored on every page to obscure or skirt or muddle or drastically misrepresent the essential and unsettling facts—namely, that European liberty was under attack by jihadists; that a huge percentage of European Muslims shared the jihadists' goals; and that many aspects of Islam were, to say the least, not easily reconciled with Western freedoms. Consistently, Buruma relegated such phenomena as honor killing, female genital mutilation, and forced marriage to the far background, or pushed them entirely offstage; consistently, he avoided looking too closely at what it actually means to sympathize with jihad. Reading his interviews with jihad supporters, one could see him again and again delicately avoiding the ticklish fact that jihadists aim to conquer the world, crush individual freedom, strip women of equality, execute gays and apostates and adulterers and rape victims, and turn Christians and Jews into second-class citizens. Instead, Buruma sought to give the vague impression that jihadism is not aggressive but defensive—that it's an understandable, and perhaps even noble, response to Western oppression and prejudice by downtrodden people determined to restore Muslim dignity and self-respect. A movement, say, not unlike the struggle for black civil rights in 1960s America. Throughout the book, Buruma used his considerable skills as a writer to make the supporters of jihadist butchery look sensitive, reflective, and reasonable, and to make people like Hirsi Ali—who saw that butchery for what it was and who had no interest in trying to finesse it away—look inflexible, hard-nosed, and egoistic. He managed, in short, to make Islamism, for all its inhumanity, look human and to make secular humanism look inhuman.

Murder in Amsterdam was the perfect expression of the evolving posture of the transatlantic intelligentsia toward the question of Islam in the West. Though Buruma approvingly paraphrased Dutch author Geert Mak to the effect that the Netherlands' problem "is not Islam, or religion as such" but "just the usual tensions that occur when uprooted rural people start new lives in the metropolis," both men certainly had to be aware that rural Muslims, when they immigrate to Europe, pose specific challenges, rooted in religious ideology, that (for example) Hindus from rural India, Buddhists from rural Vietnam, and Christians from rural Africa don't. For another, both men also know very well that at the center of current tensions between Europe's Muslims and non-Muslims are not "uprooted rural people" but their grown-up, Dutch-born, city-bred sons who drive BMWs and who already think of Europe as part of the Muslim *umma*. Buruma agreed not only with Mak but also, deplorably, with Amsterdam mayor Job Cohen, who called for an "accommodation with the Muslims," including toleration "of orthodox Muslims who consciously discriminate against their women." The

Netherlands, Cohen argued, should accept "opinions and habits even if we do not share them, or even approve of them." Where would he draw the line? At forced marriage? Wife-beating? Rape? Honor killing? Cohen, said Buruma, "deserves the benefit of the doubt." What doubt? What Cohen proposed—and Buruma supported—was the flat-out denial of fundamental freedoms to women and children who were living in a supposedly democratic country but who happened to have been born Muslims.

"Attacking religion," contended Buruma, isn't the answer to Europe's problems. But to make such a statement was to fundamentally misrepresent what was really under way, and what Buruma himself was advocating—the whittling down of Western freedoms in order to please the advocates of sharia. "Perhaps Western civilization, with the Amsterdam red-light district as its fetid symbol, does have something to answer for," Buruma ominously proposed. No: what the West needed now was not this repulsive readiness to jettison liberty, but van Gogh's and Hirsi Ali's staunch refusal to sell out *anyone's* rights. Yet to read Buruma's book was to get the impression that the only real problem with the rise of Islam in the West lay precisely with people like van Gogh and Hirsi Ali—people who, apparently, owing to some deep-seated psychological disturbance or other, were unhelpfully preoccupied with freedom of speech and other individual liberties that stood in the way of finding a modus vivendi. Speaking one's mind, Buruma seemed to be saying, was all very well and good, but now that Muslims were an increasingly significant factor in the West, the rest of us were going to have to start exercising a certain tact, holding our tongues, showing respect. Was that too much to ask? Buruma didn't think so. In his view, apparently, freedom of speech was history; and the enemies of Western civilization were not the Muslims whose demands for "respect" had begun all this, but people like Hirsi Ali who refused to accept these new restrictions.

This, then, was the book upon which the *Times* now chose to shine a spotlight—and it was presented in such a way as to indicate that here, at last, was *the* book about Islam in the West that serious, liberal-minded people needed to read. In the days and weeks after its publication, its title and Buruma's name cropped up frequently in the *Times*. One would have thought that after van Gogh's murder, the powers that be at every responsible-minded newspaper would have seen clearly what was happening in the West, what was at stake, and where their own moral obligations lay. You'd think they would have picked up van Gogh's torch and thrown themselves wholeheartedly into defending free speech. But no: instead, the *Times* stood by Ian Buruma in his shabby attempt to wreck van Gogh's posthumous reputation and to sell out the cause for which he'd died.

X

"Angry White Men"

When my book—and Robert Spencer's and Mark Steyn's and Melanie Phillips's—finally were mentioned in the *New York Times*, it was under rather unusual circumstances. On January 20, 2007, *While Europe Slept* was named one of five finalists for the National Book Critics Circle Award in the category of criticism. The announcement took place at a reception in New York at which I was not present, and the member of the NBCC board who had been delegated the task of reading out the list of criticism finalists was a writer whom I'd never heard of. When he read off the title of my book, he took it upon himself to call it "racism as criticism." The head of the NBCC (another person whose name I had never come across during my quarter century as an active reader and writer of literary criticism) later pronounced himself "embarrassed" by the nomination of my book, which he labeled "Islamophobic." All this was dutifully reported in the *Times* on February 8, 2007, by Patricia Cohen, who mentioned that *While Europe Slept* was one of several recent books (and she listed some of them) "that ominously warn of a catastrophic culture clash between Europeans with traditional Western values and fundamentalist Muslims." It will be recalled that in her article on the Alvin Rosenfeld controversy, Cohen had described Rosenfeld as attacking "liberal Jews"; similarly, in her article on the NBCC flap, Cohen described me as criticizing "liberals' one-sided blindness." The reference was to a posting on my blog. What I'd actually written was that "many Western authors and intellectuals who pride themselves on being liberals have effectively aligned themselves with an outrageously illiberal movement."

To Cohen's credit, she did make it clear that I was not exactly a *Times* editor's idea of a conservative from central casting: though my "book jacket is covered with admiring blurbs from well-known conservatives," she noted, "he does not fit the typical red-state mold." Cohen also dutifully quoted board members of the National Book Critics Circle who had supported me; but in addition she interviewed a Danish imam, Fatih Alev, who complained that the debate about Islam in the West was being manipulated by educated people (such as myself, presumably) who "ought to know better." "In many senses," Cohen quoted Alev as saying, "it is a constructed idea that there is this very severe difference between Western values and Muslim values." Cohen identified Alev as "a board member of the Islamic-Christian Study Center in Copenhagen," from which the reader was clearly meant to understand that we were dealing here with a moderate, well-integrated, and highly placed Muslim who was an unimpeachable authority on these matters. In fact—and, of course, Cohen did not mention any of this—Alev is on record as supporting an Islamic state in Denmark, has argued that the subordination of the Muslim religion to the state is an act of discrimination against religion, and insists that sharia law cannot be changed in any essential way, not even if a majority of Muslims were to desire that change, because any state governed according to the revised law would not be truly Islamic. According to a 2006 article by Lars Hedegaard, Alev has "said several times that no matter how disagreeable stoning may seem, it is not within the power of man to do away with God's clear command that loose women should be buried halfway in the earth and pelted with stones until they are dead." This, then, was the man to whom the *New York Times* turned for a respectable Muslim opinion about my book (which, as Cohen herself acknowledged, Alev had not even read).

Cohen's *Times* piece was widely reprinted and cited. People who had never heard of my book first read about it in the context of my being labeled a racist. The attention was worldwide. In Norway, I opened a copy of the newsweekly *Ny Tid* to find an article about the controversy. Its author, Dag Herbjørnsrud, wrote that my book had "become a bible for the born-agains who are throwing themselves into the current wave of revival against 'the other,' with reference to Norwegian or 'Christian values.'" In fact, *While Europe Slept* was a brief for secular democracy in a time when Europe was falling increasingly under the shadow of Islamofascism; Herbjørnsrud's unsubtle attempt to link the book to reactionary religion was an utter lie, the truth turned 180 degrees around. Herbjørnsrud also characterized me as having praised the far-right Sweden Democrat party—another lie. But this kind of mendacity had become standard fare in the mainstream media on both sides of the pond.

Ny Tid wasn't through with me. The cover of its very next issue asked the question: "Are the Islam critics issuing a warning or are they crusaders?" The story inside was illustrated with a big drawing of Oriana Fallaci and other critics of Islam in crusader garb. Apparently the answer to the question on the cover was (b) crusaders. The piece was called "Angry White Men"—a title that seemed especially silly, given that it appeared directly under the picture of Fallaci, a female. Such is the mentality that reigns at PC institutions like *Ny Tid*, where all criticism of Islam is automatically associated with whiteness and maleness, with the forces of reaction and European nationalism, with conservative Christianity and the political right—never mind that perhaps the most high-profile critic of Islam at the moment was Ayaan Hirsi Ali, a black, female, liberal atheist. The cover story itself included a list of books on Islam that had appeared lately in Norway, and any reader who bothered to look at the sales figures could see that the country's two biggest-selling recent titles in this genre were by women, Hirsi Ali and Hege Storhaug.

"Angry White Men" pretended to be a serious consideration of recent books that were critical of Islam. Yet after the opening sentences, in which several titles were listed—among them Robert Spencer's *The Truth About Muhammed*, Andrew G. Bostom's *The Legacy of Jihad*, and my own *While Europe Slept*—the piece's author, Thomas Berg, wrote: "One does not need to read more than the titles to understand that this is not about bridge-building." There was, in fact, little evidence that Berg *had* read past the titles: instead of providing even a cursory account of these books' contents, he offered several hundred words of dismissive comments on them by three supposed authorities on these matters. First up was Islam expert Kari Vogt, who said that these books "have an idea about what is authentically 'Norwegian' or originally 'European.' Then they describe a sort of moral infection that accompanies the presence of those with different beliefs." Second was Lars Gule: "Many people are ignorant and scared, and so you have a market for simple interpretations and answers. Many of these books mix prejudices with conspiracy theories. We recognize the result from the classical anti-Semitic thought structure: Not only do 'the others'—whether Jewish or Muslim—belong to a foreign culture; they are also sly and calculating, and it is in their 'nature' to seek world domination." As if jihad had been invented by Spencer, Bostom, Bawer, and company!

Finally came Iffit Qureshi (who was identified as a "Scots-Pakistani-Norwegian social commentator and course leader for immigrants"): "The fear of Islam is great among many people. For this we can thank, among others, the Progress Party and Human Rights Service." Yes, the Progress Party (which supports stronger immigration controls of the sort Denmark has instituted) and Human Rights Service (which fights for the rights of Muslim women and girls)—that's who's responsible for people's concern about Islam. Forget the terror attacks on New York, Madrid, London, Bali, etc., etc.; forget the van Gogh murder, the death threats directed at Rushdie, Hirsi Ali, Redeker, and countless others; forget the cartoon riots, the Pope riots, the riots in the French suburbs and elsewhere; forget, in Oslo itself, the waves of gay-bashings and rapes by increasingly aggressive Muslim youth gangs. No, if people in Norway were concerned about Islam, it was the fault of the Progress Party and Human Rights Service. Throughout this breathtakingly mendacious tissue of calumnies, neither Berg nor Vogt nor Gule nor Qureshi provided anything remotely resembling a frank description of the contents of the books supposedly under discussion. And of course that's the only way to write a piece like this: for if you were to honestly discuss a book like, say, Bostom's *The Legacy of Jihad*, you'd be forced to acknowledge that it's a sober, factual, and extraordinarily informative account of the history of jihad—and that it sheds a disturbing and illuminating light on our present challenges. Better to dismiss it, and other important books, as shrill, bigoted, and racist than to grapple with the uncomfortable truths they explore.

"An Islamic superstar"

In January 2007, the *Times* and Buruma came together again, this time to produce an archetypal piece of post-9/11 journalism. Written by Buruma, and published in the *New York Times Magazine*, it was a highly respectful full-length profile of the smooth-talking Muslim intellectual Tariq Ramadan. It should perhaps be explained that a full-length *New York Times Magazine* profile is not just another celebrity puff piece; it's an Event. And its purpose is to certify that its subject has arrived—that he or she is someone to be taken seriously, someone whose ideas matter. The editors' decision to run a profile of Ramadan, and to ask Buruma to write it, suggested that they wanted something that would reinforce the message of *Murder in Amsterdam*, encouraging Westerners to look away from uneasy questions about their liberties and embrace a post-Enlightenment ethos that regards freedom of speech as only one of a range of valid considerations.

Who was this man on whom the *New York Times* was so eager to sell its readers? He was, first of all, the scion of Islamism's royal family. For many European Muslims, as Paul Berman explained in a definitive 2007 article about Ramadan in the *New Republic* (which was as frank as Buruma's *Times* profile was slippery), "a more glorious ancestry than Tariq Ramadan's does not exist." Ramadan's maternal grandfather, Hassan al-Banna, founded the Muslim Brotherhood, the world's largest and most important Islamist organization, and was, in Berman's words, "the original model for what has come to be known as Islamism," not to mention the man who introduced "the modern vogue for suicide terror." Ramadan's father, Said Ramadan, was al-Banna's disciple and secretary, and a key supporter and ally of Sayyid Qutb, a successor to al-Banna as leader of the Muslim Brotherhood. (It was Qutb whose account of the supposed decadence of small-town Colorado life, circa 1948, helped shape millions of Muslims' image of the West.) The elder Ramadan, noted Berman, "was the editor who got Qutb started on what became his most important work." Tariq Ramadan speaks often about his father and grandfather, invariably with admiration. He even wrote his thesis at the University of Geneva about al-Banna—only to see it rejected for being partisan rather than scholarly. (After he protested the decision, a second committee was formed, which granted him his degree.) Despite his reverence for his radical forebears, to be sure, Ramadan denies that he belongs to the Muslim Brotherhood; he calls himself a moderate Muslim. Yet to examine his career is to recognize that he's tried to have it both ways—to say things which suggest that he renounces the most radical aspects of his father's and grandfather's theology even as he celebrates their legacy and basks in their reflected glory. As Berman put it, Ramadan "condemns terrorism" while "lavish[ing] praise on the theoreticians of terrorism."

Indeed, Ramadan routinely cuts and pastes his grandfather's words in order to obscure the fact that he was an out-and-out fascist—and Buruma, in his *Times* profile, similarly cut and pasted Ramadan's own words in order, as Berman put it, to "make [Ramadan's] salafi reformism sound like an earnest and slightly dowdy do-good effort to adapt Islam to the modern liberal world." Yet Ramadan's so-called reformism, as Berman pointed out, "has nothing to do with liberal reformism in the conventional sense." Berman invited readers to consider the fact that although Buruma had remarked in an earlier publication on "the Nazi influence on Qutb's thinking," in the *Times Magazine* profile of Ramadan he made no reference to it; Buruma, Berman surmised, "must have arrived at the conclusion for some reason that in the *Times Magazine* it was good to ask the question about the relation to Sayyid Qutb, but bad to answer the question." Berman additionally observed that Buruma knows about "fascism's influence outside of Europe," but that in reporting "Ramadan's description of his grandfather," he "tactfully refrained from sharing any of this information with his readers." This is just one example of the fact that when the topic is Islam, Buruma's rhetoric is not unlike mercury on a tabletop—and it was eminently apparent that this strategic slipperiness was exactly what the *Times* wanted in a profile of Tariq Ramadan.

Ramadan's father and grandfather are not the only figures who loom large in Ramadan's life and thought. Another is Yusuf al-Qaradawi (the man to whom, it will be remembered, the Norwegian government sent a delegation to beg for forgiveness for Vebjørn Selbekk's reprinting of the Muhammed cartoons). This supporter of terrorism, suicide bombings, the right of Muslim husbands to beat their wives, and capital punishment for gays—this Islamist who has implored the UN to prohibit insults to the prophet—is the selfsame man whom, as Berman explained, Ramadan "reveres" as the ultimate "model of modern enlightened Islam." Yet for all this, Ramadan has been heavily promoted in Europe as the embodiment of Muslim moderation—the thinker whose prescriptions for compromise and appeasement represent the great hope for long-term concord between Islam and the West. From early in his career, he was given flattering attention by *Le Monde*, the French magazine *Politis*, and *Le Monde diplomatique*; he enjoyed the support of many of his fellow anti-capitalists on France's far left; and he has been heartily embraced by the European academy, having been awarded faculty positions at Oxford, Rotterdam's Erasmus University (where Pim Fortuyn once taught), and the University of Leiden, where he now holds the Sultan of Oman chair in Islamology. (As Hugh Fitzgerald has noted, the chair at Leiden was "entirely bought and paid" for by the Sultan of Oman, who insisted that it be offered to Ramadan.)

But Ramadan's exaltation by the European media and academy was only the prelude to his anointing in the *New York Times Magazine*. The profile came, moreover, at an opportune time for him. Reportedly owing to terrorist ties, he had been denied entry into the United States to teach at Notre Dame (only to be snapped up by Oxford); some Frenchmen, moreover, considered him to have been discredited by his refusal, in a televised debate with Nicolas Sarkozy in 2004, to condemn the stoning of adulteresses; Ramadan called, rather, for a "moratorium" on stoning adulteresses that would allow Muslims to debate the issue. (A blogger who goes by the name of Spengler has noted that what is implicit in Ramadan's position on stoning is that "were he to condemn violence against women outright, he would be unable to speak to [European] Muslim communities"—which, of course, tells us a great deal about the dominant values of European Muslim communities.) What's more, the writer Caroline Fourest had published a devastating book, *Frère Tariq*, in which she used Ramadan's own words to show that he was no moderate at all and that he was, in addition, a habitual practitioner of the Islamic art of *taqiyya*—which essentially means saying one thing in Arabic and another thing in English or French. Many Europeans were familiar with Fourest's accusations, and nearly everybody in France, it seemed, knew about the Sarkozy debate; but none of this had made major headlines in the United States—and Buruma, it appeared, in introducing Ramadan to *Times* readers, wasn't about to place these European controversies front and center. On the contrary, he (and the *Times*) seemed determined not only to help Ramadan overcome his recent setbacks but to help him establish in America at least the degree of fame and influence that he had enjoyed in Europe. The thrust of Buruma's article, accordingly, was that Ramadan, despite certain possibly infelicitous attributes, was indeed Westerners' best hope for a peaceful accommodation with the Muslims in their midst. The profile was entitled "Tariq Ramadan Has an Identity Issue," and its first two paragraphs—as well as much of the rest of the piece—essentially amounted to a repeated restatement of Ramadan's supposed position as a "bridge-builder" (yes, just like Andrea Elliott's Brooklyn imam). Ramadan's schtick is that he discovered as a young man that Islam is his spiritual home and Europe his cultural home; Buruma (who by the end of the second paragraph had already called him "a brilliant speaker" and "an Islamic superstar" and referred to "the eloquence of this Muslim thinker") put it this way: "Ramadan's intellectual struggle to bridge different traditions was a personal one too." Buruma quoted R. Scott Appleby, who had hired Ramadan for his position at Notre Dame: "He's doing something extraordinarily difficult if not impossible, but it needs to be done. . . . He is trying to bridge a divide and bring together people of diverse backgrounds and worldviews."

Yes—but what exactly were those "worldviews"? On exactly which terms did he want to bring people together? Buruma claimed that Ramadan's attempt to reconcile "what seems hard to reconcile is what makes him an interesting and sometimes baffling figure." Well, he certainly *was* "interesting." But what did he really stand for? Was he someone to welcome or to fear, a figure of hope or of danger? For all Ramadan's supposed enthusiasm for "reconciliation," even Buruma didn't try to get away with hiding the fact that this advocate of "Islamic socialism" had no desire to reconcile himself to capitalism: "For Ramadan, 'global capitalism' . . . is the 'abode of war' . . . for 'when faced with neoliberal economics, the message of Islam offers no way out but resistance.'" For Ramadan, then, the very economic system that defines the West, and that is inextricable from its freedoms, is something that Muslims are obliged to battle with all their might: "The murderous tyranny to be resisted, in Ramadan's book, is 'the northern model of development,' which means that 'a billion and a half human beings live in comfort because almost four billion do not have the means to survive.'" In other words, Ramadan preaches zero-sum economics: if Muslims (and others in the so-called developing world) are poor, it's because the West is rich. Now, it would seem to me that the last thing Muslims need is one more "leader" reinforcing an already extremely robust victim mentality by telling them that their relative poverty is the fault not of a lack of individual effort or ingenuity, or of various cultural deficiencies, but of abuse and exploitation by the evil capitalist West; in such ways are poor people brainwashed into thinking that capitalism, the engine of wealth, is somehow the wellspring of their poverty.

Yet what was striking here was this: Buruma managed to present Ramadan's apparent belief in the armed overthrow of democratic capitalistic states in the name of "Islamic socialism" in such a manner that it was easy to miss the fact that armed overthrow was, indeed, what Ramadan was talking about. Buruma's rhetorical strategy was brilliant: he described Ramadan's support for Muslim war against Western capitalism in careful, muted language, then craftily followed this with a sentence in which the not at all muted words "murderous" and "tyranny" were used not to characterize Islamist radicals bent on destroying capitalism, but to characterize capitalism itself. Buruma's essay was chockablock with such rhetorical sleight of hand; one could read the entire thing without noticing the numerous sly ways in which his word choices and sentence structures helped shape an overall picture of Ramadan that, while not quite a lie, might be fairly described as an expertly groomed and heavily made-up version of the truth—a version that made Ramadan out to be as genial and harmless as possible. For example, Buruma cited Ramadan's enthusiasm for "traditionalist" values, for "justice" and "ethics," and for "universal principles"— all of which sounded admirable enough, or at least innocuous, unless you knew what these words signify front an Islamic perspective. "The meaning of Islam," Buruma quoted Ramadan as saying, "is justice." Yes, *Koranic* justice—which is to say, the justice of sharia law. "The neoliberal order," Ramadan protested, "leads to injustice." This was, then, a man whose idea of justice was embodied not by Western democracy but by sharia. Did Buruma bother to spell this out? Did he invite the reader to reflect upon exactly what Ramadan's statement about "the neoliberal order" might tell us about the man's supposed moderation and modernity? In a word, no.

One topic that can't easily be avoided in any profile of Ramadan is the debate with Sarkozy in which he refused to condemn the stoning of adulteresses. Buruma mentioned this sensational moment—he could hardly have gotten away with *not* mentioning it—but in another deft rhetorical move, he drew the reader's attention not to Ramadan's refusal to condemn stoning but to Sarkozy's description, in the same debate, of "rioters in poor immigrant neighborhoods as 'scum.'" What about Ramadan's view of women, which was the real story of the Sarkozy debate? "We must have the struggle for equal rights of women," Buruma quoted Ramadan as saying. "But the body must not be forgotten. Men and women are not the same. In Islamic tradition, women are seen in terms of being mothers, wives or daughters . . . " Buruma followed this with the slippery remark that "I was not sure this answer left me much the wiser." On the contrary, Ramadan's comments about women were pretty much all you needed to hear in order to understand that he was hardly a "moderate." Buruma went on to quote Caroline Fourest on Ramadan's opposition to women swimming with men, participating in sports, and shaking men's hands. Ramadan's reply? That "these quotes were taken out of context." Buruma, instead of pursuing this line of inquiry (what "context"?), dropped the matter. Nor, by the way, did he mention Ramadan's fierce opposition to the courageous women of the Muslim feminist organization *Ni Putes Ni Soumises* (Neither Whores nor Submissives).

Had Buruma even read *Frère Tariq*? If he hadn't, it was an inexcusable abdication of responsibility; if he had, his statement that Ramadan's comments on women left him "none the wiser" can most kindly be characterized as disingenuous. For Fourest's book put entirely to rest the notion that Ramadan was anything other than an Islamist. Yet Buruma mentioned *Frère Tariq* only to label it "a sharp attack." It would have been more appropriate to call it a devastating exposé. Buruma did quote Fourest's argument that Ramadan was "more dangerous than the obvious extremists, precisely because he sounds more reasonable"—but Buruma then proceeded, once again, to let this statement just lie there. Why didn't Buruma second Fourest's conclusions about Ramadan—or explain why he didn't? Similarly, after quoting Ramadan's slippery account of his grandfather's views (including a denial that al-Banna's ideas "formed the basis of Al Qaeda"), Buruma had only the following to say: "This may or may not be an accurate representation of Hassan al-Banna, but it tells us a lot about the way Ramadan presents himself." In fact Ramadan's account of al-Banna's views was a wholesale misrepresentation; either Buruma didn't want to know what Ramadan really believes, or he did know and thought it best for *Times* readers *not* to know. Nor did Buruma mention a 2004 interview with the Italian magazine *Panorama* in which Ramadan was asked whether the murder of Israeli children was justified. Ramadan replied that such murders "are condemnable"—which might mean either that he condemned them himself, or merely that they were open to condemnation by others—but added that "they are contextually explicable, and not justifiable." Meaning what? Meaning, he told *Panorama*, that the Palestinians, thanks to the "international community," were politically oppressed, "which explains (not justifying it)," why Palestinians feel driven to do such things. This splendidly convoluted statement was reminiscent of the familiar line by Muslim leaders that while they didn't support the murder of Theo van Gogh or the vandalizing of Danish embassies, they "understood" them. After the *Panorama* interview was posted online, Ramadan claimed to have been misquoted; unfortunately for him, *Panorama* turned out to have taped his remarks. As Daniel Pipes memorably observed, the tape definitively put to rest the question of whether Ramadan was moderate or truthful: "He is neither one nor the other."

Buruma mentioned Ramadan's 2003 claim that several "French Jewish intellectuals," whom he named, were interested only in Israel and not in France—all of them men of far more catholic sympathies and liberal sensibilities than Ramadan himself (and one of whom, in fact, turned out not to be Jewish). For this unwarranted assault, Ramadan deserved to be condemned in the severest possible terms. But what did Buruma say about it? "Ramadan's attack was unfair." Period. No, it was far worse than "unfair"—it was repulsive. Yet Buruma, while soft-pedaling the attack itself, called the reaction to it "vastly overblown," adding that "unlike some Islamic activists, Ramadan has never expressed any hostility to Jews in general." Such are the low standards to which people like Ramadan are held in the Western media today: Ramadan isn't some wild-eyed, openly genocidal fanatic hawking *The Protocols of the Elders of Zion* on a street corner and calling openly for the mass extermination of the Jewish race—therefore he's a moderate. "There is no question," Buruma admitted, "that he is ferociously anti-Zionist." Of course, in intellectual and academic circles nowadays, as we've seen in the Alvin Rosenfeld case, ferocious anti-Zionism is pretty much the default position on Israel, and Buruma seemed to throw it out there as a way of telegraphing to *Times* readers that Ramadan's views on Jews and Israel don't really deviate significantly from those of respectable people whom they might meet at an Upper West Side dinner party.

"We are in favor of integration," said Ramadan in a speech quoted by Buruma, "but it is up to us to decide what that means. . . . I will abide by the laws, but only insofar as the laws don't force me to do anything against my religion." This is, of course, simply another way of saying that, as far as Ramadan is concerned, Muslim law trumps secular law, and implicit in this, furthermore, is that he looks forward to a Europe under sharia. Naturally, Buruma preferred not to spell this out, writing in the concluding words of his profile that Ramadan's politics "offer an alternative to violence, which, in the end, is reason enough to engage with him, critically, but without fear." But what kind of freedom-loving Westerner can responsibly view "engagement" with an advocate of peaceful transition to sharia law as an attractive "alternative to violence"? Besides which, how can someone whose theological lodestar is Yusuf al-Qaradawi be reasonably considered "an alternative to violence"? How, moreover, could Buruma speak with any credibility of engaging with Ramadan "critically," given his admission in the profile that the only public debate between himself and Ramadan (sponsored by the French magazine *Le Point*) had been congenial—

and given, too, his refusal to confront Ramadan's views, and the implications thereof, head-on in the profile itself? (Did Buruma really feel, by the way, that a gay person, say, had no reason to "fear" Ramadan and his movement?)

This wasn't the only place in his profile of Ramadan that Buruma mentioned fear: "some fearful people," he wrote, are now calling Europe "Eurabia." Well, if some of us are "fearful," it's because many influential persons have plainly decided that the West's future lies in gradual accommodation with sharia law. This is indeed a fearful prospect. But the fear of an Ayaan Hirsi Ali, a Bat Ye'or, an Anders Fogh Rasmussen, or a José María Aznar—to name a few individuals who refuse to accept Islamization without a struggle, who must swallow the outrage of being labeled "Islamophobes" by Islamofascists and their allies, and who endure death threats from people who swarm to stadiums to hear the golden words of al-Banna's grandson—their "fear" is of a different order than the fear of an Ian Buruma, who has chosen to aid in Tariq Ramadan's tireless effort to misrepresent himself. Hirsi Ali and Bat Ye'or may feel fear—they'd be fools if they didn't—but they act courageously. That's what distinguishes them from Buruma and his ilk, in whose Orwellian world bravery is cowardice, bullying is victimhood, and standing up for freedom in the face of religious totalitarians is a demonstration of racism.

Commenting wryly on Buruma's profile of Ramadan, the French writer Pascal Bruckner said: "Yes, you read it right: in 2007, a self-styled 'progressive' Muslim . . . pushes audaciousness to the point of admitting that he *shakes women's hands*." And David Thompson, by way of observing that Buruma wasn't alone in being besotted with Ramadan, recalled a 2004 interview in which reporter Rosemary Bechler gushed: "From the start, I felt in the presence of leadership: but of the style of an exiled prince, a king over the water, a president in exile, an errant soul. . . ." Elizabeth Bryant, profiling Ramadan for the *San Francisco Chronicle* in 2004, was similarly infatuated: "Charismatic, with a trim beard and movie-star looks, Tariq Ramadan is the idol of growing numbers of French Muslims. . . ." Bryant's profile provided yet another example of media misrepresentation of Ramadan's message: "Ramadan's teachings," she wrote, were "comparable to the black pride movement in the United States in the 1960s." The Muslim Brotherhood? "An

Islamic revival movement that criticized Western decadence." Bryant dutifully mentioned "Ramadan's critics," but dispatched their criticism quickly: "Ramadan denies having ties with any terrorists, a claim bolstered by several French experts." Well, that settles that!

On April 1, 2007, as if to affirm that Buruma's take on Ramadan did indeed represent the new *Times* orthodoxy, the *Times Book Review* ran a notice by Stéphanie Giry of Ramadan's book *In the Footsteps of the Prophet* that read like a précis of Buruma's profile: not only did Giry (an editor at *Foreign Affairs*) make the same points as Buruma; she also raised and refuted the same counterarguments Buruma had raised and refuted. If anything, she seemed even more eager than Buruma to exculpate Ramadan, though her defenses of him were remarkably feeble. Yes, she admitted, Ramadan had refused to condemn the stoning of adulterers; but his claim that "advocating a sweeping ban might have alienated hard-liners . . . was probably less sinister than it sounded." (Tell that to the next adulteress to get stoned.) Besides, Ramadan's refusal to condemn stoning "wasn't a tacit endorsement of stoning so much as an expression of his view that each society must decide for itself how to put into practice the values of Islam." (How elegantly so many so-called liberals today disguise the betrayal of fundamental human rights as an expression of multicultural respect for societies' right to self-determination!) And yes, Giry admitted, Ramadan had "chided French-Jewish intellectuals . . . for reflexively backing the war in Iraq and Israel's foreign policy." In fact he'd done something far more outrageous—he'd accused a group of liberal independent thinkers of being narrowly and mendaciously devoted to the interests of their own coreligionists—a description that fits Ramadan himself far more aptly than it does Alain Finkielkraut, Bernard-Henri Lévy, or Bernard Kouchner. Giry seemed to accept the possibility that Ramadan, in describing such a cabal, was motivated by anti-Semitism—but she then wrote, stupefyingly, that "even prejudice . . . needn't have undermined his warning about the danger of sectarian politics." In other words, Ramadan's accusation of narrow Jewish sectarianism may have been wildly unfair, even anti-Semitic, and doubtless motivated by his own narrow Islamic sectarianism, but it's valuable nonetheless because it reminds us of the importance of not being narrowly sectarian!

Giry had all the answers. The denial of a U.S. visa to Ramadan? She blamed "the paranoid legalism of the State Department." (How perverse to defend an Islamist by hurling the word "legalism"—the mot juste for Islamist theology—at the U.S. State Department, whose first reaction to the Muhammed cartoons had been to condemn them!) Ramadan's support of female submission? Giry's way of putting it was that Ramadan "encourages modesty among Muslim women." His wholesale misrepresentation of Muhammed? Giry: "Muhammed may not have been as sober and sensible as Ramadan writes, but why take issue with this portrayal if it can help reconcile Islam with Western liberalism today?" This one sentence not only summed up the message of Giry's entire review; it captured perfectly the default posture of the Western media toward the truth about Islam in the post-9/11 era: yes, by all means let's bury all the facts that some Muslims would prefer for us to bury, if it means (and hey, let's hope it does!) that they'll like us and live with us in peace. Giry even referred admiringly to what she called Ramadan's "classical libertarian" defense of "the right of Muslim girls to choose for themselves whether to cover up." On the contrary, Ramadan's position on this issue combined a cynical exploitation of the Western respect for individual freedom with an equally cynical misrepresentation of Muslim reality—for the question of covering up or not is hardly one that the overwhelming majority of Muslim girls are free to decide independently. Far from it: the covering up of Muslim girls and women is itself a living symbol of the denial to them by Muslim men of the freedom to decide *anything* for themselves.

That the *Times* should countenance such a classic Orwellian equation of oppression with liberty was repulsive—but such disgraceful rhetorical games were quickly becoming par for the course in media coverage of Islam. In the eyes of mainstream journalists, the words "moderate Muslim" now denoted someone who might not stone an adulteress to death himself, but who would defend to the death another Muslim's right to do so. Apropos of such Orwellianism, Paul Berman has observed that many in the media seem "to have accepted [Ramadan's] categories of analysis, as if in a stupor." They frame issues, in short, *on his terms*. Quoting Buruma's description of Ramadan as "promot[ing] the right of Muslim women to wear the veil at French schools," Berman pointed out that this bit of nonsense "could have been written by Ramadan himself." What, in other words, about the right of Muslim women and girls not to be forced by their husbands or fathers to walk around covered in tents? Thanks to the willingness of so many journalists to discuss Islamic issues entirely on Islamic leaders' terms, noted Berman, "the entire question of women's rights . . . has disappeared from a great many journalists' narratives of events," with the result that a position that is, in fact, anti-women's rights is routinely presented "as a matter of rights for Muslims."

XII

"A caricature of sweetness and light"

Even as the mainstream media have cooperated in the effort by certain intellectuals to exalt Tariq Ramadan, they've also abetted attempts to discredit Hirsi Ali. Here again Buruma, along with Oxford professor and Europe expert Timothy Garton Ash, has led the way. Berman has noted that while Buruma had "an occasional kind word for Hirsi Ali" in *Murder in Amsterdam*, but mostly painted her in that book as a foolish extremist in "pages written with an unmistakable flash of anger, relative to Buruma's normally phlegmatic manner," in his *Times Magazine* profile of Ramadan he was even nastier to her. Noting that in addition to his book Buruma had produced "three articles condemning Hirsi Ali in the *New York Times* alone," Berman suggested that Hirsi Ali's "moral indignation" and "visceral anger at oppression" were at odds with the "kind of high-minded cerebral journalism" with which Buruma and many other members of the professoriat are more comfortable. "It is always good to be subtle and nuanced," Berman commented, "but Hirsi Ali's writings have the effect of making a large number of nuanced subtleties look ridiculous." Indeed, Hirsi Ali doesn't play rhetorical games. She tells it like it is. Observing that the most conspicuous criticism of Hirsi Ali was emanating from the highest levels of the intellectual establishment, Berman commented that there was something new, and not particularly admirable, about "the calm discussions in *The New York Times* of why it would be wrong to condemn with any vigor the stoning of women to death. . . . Something like a campaign against Hirsi Ali could never have taken place a few years ago." Describing this, rightly, as "a reactionary turn in the intellectual world," Berman added: "There is something uncanny, almost creepy, about how often the journalism on these themes has led Ayaan Hirsi Ali's critics and Tariq Ramadan's defenders into the zones of the grand theoreticians of suicide terror."

The academic establishment's standard line on Hirsi Ali was neatly spelled out toward the end of Buruma's profile of Ramadan. "Her mission, too," Buruma wrote, "is to spread universal values"—as if Hirsi Ali's universal values (that is, individual liberty and secular government) could be compared with Ramadan's (brutal patriarchy and jihad). Yet Buruma's reason for bracketing Hirsi Ali with Ramadan on this score was not to praise her by linking her with the great man, but to criticize her by drawing a contrast. For while Hirsi Ali, he reminded us, had committed the offense of leaving Islam and calling it "backward and perverse," Ramadan "insists that a reasoned but traditionalist approach to Islam offers values that are as universal as those of the European Enlightenment." Once again, Buruma's rhetorical sleight of hand was masterly: "reasoned but traditionalist" sounds fine—so long as one doesn't delve too deeply into the "traditions" involved or acknowledge that this "reasoning" takes as its starting point a literal reading of the Koran. (For people like al-Qaradawi, for example, capital punishment for gay people is "reasoned," for it follows logically from the dictates of the Muslim holy books.) "Universal" sounds good too, but all it means in this context is that Islam considers its authority to be God-given and thus binding on everyone, everywhere. (All human beings, according to Muslim belief, are born into Islam; those who style themselves non-Muslims have simply fallen away from the faith to which the deity wishes them to return.) Calling something "as universal as . . . the European Enlightenment" is hence hardly the same as calling it as *enlightened* as the European Enlightenment—but to a casual reader it can sound as if it means the same thing. If Ramadan is a "scholar," a sophisticated internationalist who prides himself on assuming a "reasonable" posture (especially when defending the stoning of adulteresses), Hirsi Ali gets worked up. She makes scenes. She puts people on the spot. She doesn't have sufficient respect for the manners and mores of intellectual discourse. She makes everything awkward, uncomfortable, *real*. She's lived among and worked closely with Muslim women who have suffered Koran-sanctioned abuse, and for people like Buruma, for whom these issues are largely abstract and theoretical, this rootedness in harsh reality is itself doubtless a source of discomfort.

On March 4, 2007, the *Times* ran a review by Buruma of Hirsi Ali's book *Infidel*. In his Ramadan profile, Buruma had dismissed criticisms of Ramadan's anti-Semitic attack on those French intellectuals as "overblown"; now, reviewing Hirsi Ali, he called a statement by her about the importance of honor killings "a trifle overblown." This same man who had danced with Astaire-like elegance around Ramadan's vilest prejudices now nitpicked snidely at Hirsi Ali's description of her concern about honor killing as a "holy mission": "Why a 'holy' mission?" asked Buruma sarcastically. "By her own account in 'Infidel' she 'had left God behind years ago.'" This was not the only occasion on which Buruma seemed personally offended by Hirsi Ali's repudiation of Islam. While the tone of Buruma's profile of Ramadan had been awestruck—how brilliant he is! how eloquent!—his review of Hirsi Ali's book was arrogantly and atrociously patronizing. He mocked the fact that some of the "glimpses of a freer life" she was vouchsafed during her childhood were "imbibed from romantic novels by Danielle Steel and Barbara Cartland." Though he called her account of how a Somali girl had ended up a member of the Dutch parliament "entirely plausible" (thereby planting in the reader's mind the unworthy thought that she might be making some of it up), Buruma ascribed to her "descriptions of life in the West an idealized, almost comic-book quality that sounds as naïve as those romantic novels she consumed as a young girl." Is Buruma too sophisticated to understand what freedom looks like to people who have grown up without it? Instead of being charmed by Hirsi Ali's refreshingly frank account of the role that popular fiction had played in her discovery of the idea of freedom, Buruma skewered her for it. "Her images of the Netherlands," he sneered, "could have been lifted from some Dutch children's book: 'so well-kept, so well-planned, so smoothly run and attractive.'" Sorry, but those were exactly the attributes of the Netherlands to which I, too, responded when I first set foot in the country in 1997. Plainly, Buruma was doing his utmost to depict this exceedingly intelligent woman as a naïf whose picture of the West was "a caricature of sweetness and light." (As opposed to the sophisticated subtleties of that exquisitely nuanced defender of stoning, Professor Ramadan.) Buruma seemed incapable of appreciating how wondrously free, safe, and peaceful the Netherlands would have seemed to a smart, independent-minded young woman from the Muslim world circa 1992. He described Hirsi Ali as if she were a petulant girl: she "tends to fly into a rage when the inhabitants of this Garden of Eden [i.e., the West] fail sufficiently to appreciate their good fortune." Yet the problem we're up against today isn't excessive rage on the part of liberty's defenders (on the contrary, Hirsi Ali is astonishingly civil toward those, such as Buruma, who make common cause with people who wish her dead); it's the bland equanimity of appeasers like Buruma.

Not that Buruma's equanimity was much in evidence in his review of *Infidel*. Unable to control his impatience with Hirsi Ali, he sneered that in her view "Europeans who argue, for example, that Muslims might feel more at home in the West if we offered a modicum of respect for their religion, instead of insulting them at every turn, are 'stupid' or worse, for it is indeed Hirsi Ali's holy mission to 'wake these people up,' to convince us that the justification for 9/11 was 'the core of Islam,' and the 'inhuman act of those 19 hijackers' its 'logical outcome.'" A few questions: Why should anybody be expected to respect a religion that demands his or her submission, subordination, or even execution? Why should someone like Buruma, who has never worried in print about whether Christianity or Mormonism or Bahai gets enough respect, be upset about Islam not getting enough of it? The post-Enlightenment West isn't about respecting ideas or religions or ideologies—it's about debating them. What it respects is individual freedom—including the freedom to criticize any idea, or religion, as much as one bloody well pleases. As for "insulting"—well, exactly who's insulting who? It isn't as if European Christians and Jews are running around raping Muslim women, defacing Muslim cemeteries, shooting bullets into the façades of Muslim houses of worship, and tormenting Muslim children in school. The Western media are constantly lecturing readers about the need to respect Islam, but they rarely dare to suggest that more than a few Muslims are lacking in respect for basic democratic values.

In his closing shot, Buruma labeled Hirsi Ali an "absolutist," a word one had yet to see him attach to Ramadan. Buruma mocked what he saw as Hirsi Ali's black-and-white view of "a perfectly enlightened West at war with the demonic world of Islam." Correction: Hirsi Ali has never said that the West was "perfectly enlightened"; she's been much more openly critical of various aspects of Western civilization than Ramadan has ever been of far more barbaric aspects of Islam. But Hirsi Ali is also, unlike Ramadan, blindingly honest about the reality of the religion into which both of them happen to have been born. And to be an "absolutist," as Buruma put it, about things like honor killing and the stoning of adulteresses is to take the only decent moral position on them.

To be sure, many mainstream journalists have been careful not to dismiss Hirsi Ali as high-handedly as Buruma has done, and some have even written about her with sincere admiration. (As a black woman who was born Muslim, she is allowed by some segments of the media to say things for which others are condemned.) But Buruma has been far from alone in taking a poisonous line on this extraordinary woman. In *Newsweek*, for example, *Infidel* was reviewed by Lorraine Ali (no relation, presumably), who described Hirsi Ali as "one of Europe's most infamous critics of Islam," called her "harsh and uncompromising," said she was "more a hero among Islamophobes than [among] Islamic women," and accused her of reaching "an inflammatory conclusion tailor-made for her right-wing constituency." Sounding precisely the same deplorable moral-equivalency note as Buruma, Ali claimed to find it "ironic that this would-be 'infidel' often sounds as single-minded and reactionary as the zealots she's worked so hard to oppose." Similarly, on the BBC's *Hardtalk*, Hirsi Ali was described as "throwing a rhetorical hand grenade" and of "cultural Bin Ladenism"—a good example of how anti-jihadist rhetoric is described in violent terms by the same kinds of journalists who, when describing jihad itself, opt for delicate euphemisms.

I've mentioned Timothy Garton Ash, who is professor of European Studies at the University of Oxford, director of the European Studies Centre at Saint Antony's College at Oxford, and a senior fellow at Stanford University's Hoover Institution. Garton Ash, in his 2004 book *Free World*, actually claimed that the most important issue facing Europe today is the conflict between "Euro-Gaullists" who want Europe to counterbalance American power and "Euroatlanticists" who favor strong U.S. ties. For chapters at a time, *Free World* contained no mention whatsoever of Europe's Islamization. When Garton Ash did bring up Islam early on, he did so only to emphasize that Islam in Europe isn't a problem in and of itself; the only problem, he maintained, resides in the "populist, anti-immigrant parties," their low-life voters, and people like Oriana Fallaci, whose courageous book *The Rage and the Pride* Garton Ash called "garish." But then, toward the end of *Free World*, as I noted in a review of it,

> Garton Ash does a sudden about-face, admitting (on pages 196–7) that there *is* a problem with Islam in Europe, and that if it isn't addressed properly, "we face a downward spiral which will be the curse of the national politics of Europe for years ahead. . . . To halt this downward spiral is the single most urgent task of European domestic politics in the next decade. We may already be too late. . . ." This admission follows 196 pages of pretending that the "urgent tasks" of European politics lie elsewhere; and after he's made it, he drops the topic cold and returns to the more comfortable conceit that the *real* European dilemma is this business about Britain bringing the United States and Europe together.

Nowhere in *Free World* did Garton Ash provide anything remotely resembling an adequate account of the changes wrought upon Western European societies by their exploding Muslim populations. Then, however, came an October 2006 review essay in the *New York Review of Books* entitled "Islam in Europe." Though there were (as we have seen) many recent books that might have been discussed in an essay with this title, he confined himself to two: *Murder in Amsterdam* and Hirsi Ali's *The Caged Virgin*. The choice of Buruma's book was no surprise: Garton Ash plainly shared Buruma's determination to make one jihad sympathizer after another seem more sympathetic and harmless than Fortuyn, van Gogh, Hirsi Ali, & co., and to avoid or drastically understate any and all disquieting facts about Muslim subcultures in Europe while emphasizing the supposed failings of their European host societies. Unsurprisingly, Garton Ash gave Buruma a big thumbs-up. As for Hirsi Ali, he didn't dare dismiss her out of hand, but was breathtakingly condescending. "It's no disrespect to Ms. Ali," he wrote, "to suggest that if she had been short, squat, and squinting, her story and views might not be so closely attended to." One might similarly have noted that Tariq Ramadan "might not be so closely attended to" if he were not so good at playing the role of a suave, civilized, Westernized Muslim—but Garton Ash did not say any such thing. In fact, like Buruma, he treated Ramadan far more respectfully than he did Hirsi Ali, whom he called "slightly simplistic." No: there's nothing "simplistic" about Hirsi Ali's work. The difference between her and Garton Ash is that she writes with total honesty about some very stark, ugly, and challenging truths, while he proffers a selective, soft-focus, "nuanced" version of these truths.

Ramadan not only received more respect in Garton Ash's review essay than Hirsi Ali did; he also got more respect than Bat Ye'or, whose book *Eurabia* Garton Ash relegated (along with *While Europe Slept*) to a footnote in which he deplored Ye'or's influence and said that her argument "has a strong element of conspiracy theory." But if Ye'or is so influential, why dismiss her in a footnote? If her argument is wrong, why not refute it instead of trying to just sneer it away? You would never know from Garton Ash's dismissive treatment of her that Ye'or's "conspiracy theory" is, in fact, supported by mountains of documentation. Like Buruma, Garton Ash seemed to believe that expecting Muslims in Europe to accept secular democracy is offensive, unmannerly, "Islamophobic": "For secular Europeans to demand that Muslims adopt their faith—secular humanism—would be almost as intolerant as the Islamist jihadist demand that we should adopt theirs." This kind of repulsive, insidious thinking has become standard issue among credentialed "Europe experts," who refuse to face up to the plain fact that there is no possible middle ground between secular democracy and sharia. It is not unreasonable, let alone "intolerant," for a pluralist secular democracy to disallow enclaves in which patriarchs rule, women are subordinate, and errant daughters and apostates are subject to execution; on the contrary, such totalitarian enclaves represent infections that will, if unchecked, eventually destroy the entire organism. Or, to switch metaphors: a house divided against itself cannot stand.

To be sure, in his *New York Review of Books* essay, as in *Free World*, Garton Ash acknowledged the seriousness of the Islamization of Europe. In the past he had denied or radically minimized this problem, and had written contemptuously about Pim Fortuyn, whose only crime had been recognizing it. "It is five minutes to twelve," Fortuyn had said in February 2002. Now Garton Ash, who in *Free World* had accused Fortuyn of practicing "poisonous populist politics" and likened him to Le Pen and the Austrian Hitler-admirer Jörg Haider, echoed Fortuyn (though without giving him credit): "It's already five minutes to midnight—and we are drinking in the last chance saloon." Though it was welcome news that Garton Ash finally felt obliged to acknowledge Europe's crisis, it was dismaying that he continued to write about it in prose heavy with euphemism, equivocation, and faculty-lounge remoteness, and to demean those who dared to address it bluntly, urgently, ardently.

We've seen how Paul Vallely of the *Independent* has used the term "secular fundamentalists" to equate free-speech advocates with murderous jihadists. In a similar spirit, Garton Ash, in his *New York Review of Books* piece, called Hirsi Ali an "Enlightenment fundamentalist." Such language is problematic on several fronts. By calling Hirsi Ali a "fundamentalist" in such a context, Garton Ash was quite deliberately equating a brave defender of freedom with tyrannical patriarchs who believe that gays, apostates, and rape victims should be executed. Yet this juxtaposition was rhetorically useful, allowing Garton Ash to represent himself as occupying the reasonable center between unreasonable extremes—Osama over here, Hirsi Ali over there.

It is, of course, fundamentally wrong to call a supporter of free speech a fundamentalist. A fundamentalist, by definition, claims to have found the highest truth in some prepackaged, infallible system of thought that has codified all the answers to all the questions. That system can take the form of a religion, such as the Christianity of Biblical literalists, or a secular ideology, such as Marxism or Nazism. To support freedom of speech (as we've seen Oliver Wendell Holmes explain) is incompatible with such unshakable convictions: if, for those who feel they may yet have things to learn about the world, freedom of speech is a good thing because it makes possible the open exchange of ideas, insights, and opinions about a range of subjects that no one individual can fully understand (and thus bids fair to enhance everybody's comprehension), to the fundamentalist, free speech threatens the full and perfect truth of which he already considers himself to be in absolute possession. We've seen how, in Vallely's eyes, a person who places one right above all others is a "single-issue fanatic." One might expect the word "fanatic" to be reserved for those who, say, fly planes into towers, bomb embassies, or kill their daughters for holding somebody's hand; but, no, Vallely, like other members of the media elite that refuses to call terrorists terrorists, has no trouble calling the defenders of freedom "fanatics." By such logic, George Orwell was a "single-issue fanatic" when he wrote: "If liberty means anything at all it's the freedom to tell people what they don't want to hear."

Buruma's and Garton Ash's comments about Hirsi Ali drew serious criticism—not in the mainstream media but online. Most notably, a series of articles on the *Sign and Sight* Web site began in January 2007 with a cogent takedown of both men by the French philosopher Pascal Bruckner, who sardonically noted that "in the eyes of our genteel professors, Ayaan Hirsi Ali . . . has committed an unpardonable offence: she has taken democratic principles seriously." But then, "in the struggle of the weak against the strong, it is easier to attack the former. Those who resist will always be accused by the cowardly of exciting the hatred of the powerful." Responding on the *Sign and Sight* Web site, Buruma insisted that "I admire Ayaan Hirsi Ali and agree with most of what she stands for" (this from a man who, as Paul Berman noted, insisted in the *Times Magazine* that he had "agreed on most issues" with Ramadan in their *Le Point* debate). Yet Buruma, in his reply to Bruckner, also accused Hirsi Ali of generalizing "cultural traditions, tribal customs, historical antecedents, all of which are highly diverse, even inside the Muslim world . . . into a monolithic threat." This is the familiar "diverse Islam" card: criticize Islam in any way, and defenders of Islam can then smoothly point out that Islam is not culturally, historically, ideologically, or theologically monolithic, but is in fact a richly varied community of faith with more than a billion adherents, and that those who criticize it are being simplistic, if not downright vulgar and intolerant. Or, as Buruma put it: "Condemning Islam, without taking the many variations into account, is too indiscriminate."

This is a strategically useful ploy—saying that Islam is wondrously manifold, after all, is the first step toward nuancing away everything about it that's disturbing, offensive, and dangerous. Buruma maintained, for example, that "the issue of headscarves" is complex: "Some women wear them to ward off male aggression, others because their parents insist on it, and some by their own choice, as a defiant badge of identity, even rebellion." Sheer nonsense: the great majority of women who wear headscarves (or the even more conservative outfits that are seen more and more frequently in Europe) wear them because their families demand it. Being covered is a sign of their subordination. If the need to ward off male aggression is a factor, it's because many Muslim men have been taught that they have not only the right but the duty to discipline Muslim women who go uncovered. For many Muslim men, indeed, it's an article of faith that such women are disobeying Allah and thus deserve what they get—including rape. But "a defiant badge of identity, even rebellion"? Buruma makes it sound as if head coverings are marks of *individual* identity or rebellion; but the only kind of identity that they represent for most women who wear them is a *corporate* identity, a collective identity usually acceded to under pressure; and the only kind of rebellion they symbolize is an often forced rebellion against Western freedoms in the name of Islamic discipline and misogyny.

Buruma also rejected Bruckner's labeling of him as a "collaborator" or an advocate of "appeasement." Instead he identified himself as one of many "who seek an accommodation with the majority of Muslims." In other words, he wasn't appeasing, he was accommodating. Talk about a distinction without a difference! (While jihadists split skulls, Buruma and Garton Ash split hairs.) Buruma then broke into a sneer: "What, in any case, does Bruckner propose to do about millions of Muslim believers living in Europe? Tell them how to interpret their holy scriptures? Force them to follow Ayaan Hirsi Ali's example and renounce their faith?" Um, for starters, how about expect them to accept that they live in a secular liberal democracy rather than in the House of War? As for Bruckner's concern about the rise of Islamism in the West, Buruma said: "I regard this as too alarmist." How can it be that things are serious enough to require an "accommodation" with orthodox Islam—that is, a compromise between Western freedom and sharia— and yet for anyone to think that this is indeed a sign that things have gotten rather serious is to be "alarmist"?

Over a period of several weeks, *Sign and Sight* ran several more commentaries by various writers, some (including Garton Ash) supporting Buruma, others supporting Bruckner. Among the latter was the Muslim reformist Bassam Tibi, a professor of political science at Göttingen University in Germany, who wrote that "Euro-Islam"—a term that he had coined but that Ramadan had appropriated for his own purposes—"is impossible without cultural adaptation involving religious reforms. And this is not something Tariq Ramadan is pursuing. . . . Tariq Ramadan presents Orthodox Islam as Euro-Islam presumably with the intent to deceive." Tibi also accused Garton Ash of "kowtowing to Ramadan." In April, Buruma and Garton Ash, in a joint "final rejoinder," accused Bruckner of "violent hyperbole"—thereby demonstrating the truth of Bruckner's own observation that "those who revolt against barbarism are themselves accused of being barbarians." Once again, those who euphemize jihadist violence were describing anti-jihadist rhetoric as if it were itself an act of violence.

As time wore on, major media on both sides of the Atlantic continued to provide Ramadan with platforms. On June 4, 2007, he turned up in the *Guardian* with an op-ed in which he contended that British Muslims' response to the London attacks the previous July had been "exemplary" and that this proved they "were well integrated to [sic] society." If there were problems, he insisted, they were the fault of the British government—which was too fixated on the "terrorist threat" (which he perversely put in scare quotes, as if the attacks he'd just mentioned had never occurred) and "paternalistic" toward Muslims (as if any Western government's "paternalism" could hold a candle to Islamic patriarchy!). Tony Blair had called for minorities to adjust to "our essential values," but Ramadan asserted that "the vast majority of British Muslims have absolutely no problem with . . . British values"— a claim that one survey after another had proven utterly false. Ramadan furthermore blamed high Muslim unemployment and crime statistics, among other problems, on British racism (which, of course, raised the question of why British Hindus are such a terrific success story). This *Guardian* piece had at least one positive result: it made the scales fall from the eyes of one of Ramadan's leading admirers in the British media. David Goodhart, editor of *Prospect*, wrote in an open letter to Ramadan that he'd "spent quite a lot of time in the past year or two defending you"—by, for example, excusing Ramadan's position on stoning as "realpolitik"—but Ramadan's "grievance-seeking, responsibility-avoiding diatribe" in the *Guardian*, which for Goodhart boiled down to a familiar cry "that Muslim extremism in Britain is someone else's fault," was, in Goodhart's view, "nonsense." Goodhart criticized Ramadan for seeing the July 7 atrocities "not as an opportunity to take a long, hard look at the pathologies inside some sections of

British Muslim society but, rather, another opportunity to blame the government and complain about Islamophobia."

Even Buruma was shifting his tone a bit. Yet while Goodhart's open letter sounded utterly sincere, Buruma's comments (which came in a September 2007 review of Norman Podhoretz's *World War IV* in the *New York Review of Books*) felt calculated—more like a politician strategically backtracking (all the while pretending not to be doing anything of the kind) than like a serious writer sincerely recounting a shift in his thought. Responding to Berman's criticism of his coziness with Ramadan, Buruma was plainly out to distance himself from al-Banna's grandson, whom he now described as "a slippery figure whose leftist third-world liberationist views are not mine." This was far more critical than anything Buruma had previously written about Ramadan, and it suggested that he had perhaps felt some heat for the things he'd written about him. Even so, Buruma remained, to use his own word, as slippery as ever, writing that Ramadan's views "may or may not be compatible with liberal democracy" (there's that same fact-avoiding "may or may not" formula) and taking the opportunity to stick a few more pins into Hirsi Ali. After the requisite acknowledgment that she was "a courageous and remarkable woman," he went in for the kill, calling *Infidel* "skillfully ghostwritten," floating (again) the idea that her anti-Islam "zeal" was a holdover from her period of "religious orthodoxy," and slamming her "dogmatism." In a tone that suggested he had been chided by Hirsi Ali's admirers, Buruma complained that to criticize her was "not the same as placing her on the same moral or political level as the violent zealots she opposes"—even though this was precisely what he and Garton Ash had been doing when they slapped onto her such labels as "Enlightenment fundamentalist." Buruma added that "only . . . fanatics" would respond to a critic of Hirsi Ali by calling him a "foe . . . of free speech, democracy, the Enlightenment, and so forth"—thus displaying yet again his fondness for words like "fanatic" and his inability to apply them to *real* fanatics. Nor was this the last of Buruma's assaults on Hirsi Ali: in a syndicated piece in November 2007, he reached a new low, accusing her of having "lent respectability to bigotry."

Garton Ash, too, backtracked—and in a similar way. Debating Hirsi Ali in London in November 2007, he expressed his "huge admiration for Ayaan's tremendous courage and clarity," withdrew the "Enlightenment fundamentalist" charge (claiming, ludicrously, that it had "not occur[red] to me that anyone would be so idiotic as to imagine that one was construing any symmetry between Islamic fundamentalists and Enlightenment fundamentalists"), and maintained that he stood foursquare for Western liberties. Once all this had been said, however, he proceeded to serve up an only slightly modified version of his (and Buruma's) earlier arguments, insisting that Islam was more complex than Hirsi Ali's simplistic formulas suggested. In response to this accusation of simplicity, Hirsi Ali made the wonderfully effective point that "the great thing about the Enlightenment was its emphasis on simple language" and on strong, comprehensible ideas (as opposed, implicitly, to Buruma and Garton Ash's fog of academic equivocation and nuance). If, she added, her strong identification with the Enlightenment "makes me simplistic then I'm proud to be so, but I think what you probably mean is that I'm clear and unflinching in my recognition of the importance of liberty and will not be prepared to bargain with it." An audience member, replying to another comment by Garton Ash, also made a vital observation: "Timothy's main reason for saying Islam cannot be incompatible with liberal democracy is by saying if it is incompatible then we're in real trouble. Well, perhaps we are just in real trouble." One couldn't escape noticing, moreover, that Garton Ash, using the same word as Buruma, called for an "accommodation" with Muslims.

In the summer of 2007, Ramadan was fined 2500 euros for having flown into a rage and insulted two border agents at the airport in Roissy, France. One was reminded of the memorable occasion on which Edward Said was caught by a cameraman throwing a rock at Israeli soldiers: suddenly the curtain was pulled back on the supposedly calm, reasonable, eminently civilized Muslim intellectual in a suit, revealing the jihadist's otherwise well-hidden fury. But the news came and went in a single news cycle, leaving no apparent dent in Ramadan's reputation among the transatlantic cognoscenti.

XIII

Apologists Aplenty

One corner of the sprawling *Washington Post/Newsweek* Web site is called "On Faith." In the summer of 2007, the site featured a piece in which *Newsweek* managing editor Jon Meacham and veteran *Post* writer Sally Quinn explained the raison d'être of a feature on the subsite entitled "Muslims Speak Out." Meacham and Quinn employed the popular "rich diversity of Islam" ploy, arguing that "it can be difficult to paint anything as vast and varied as a global religion with a single brush" and professing a desire to chart a middle ground between violent jihadists and Islam's critics and thus be "what the Qu'ran called 'middle people.'" Leaving aside the fact that when the Koran speaks of "middle people" it's not counseling moderation or compromise but is, rather, speaking of Muslims as existing between the world of substance and of spirit, the "middle" between the Taliban and the defenders of secular democracy isn't a place we should want to be; and in any event, few of the contributors to "Muslims Speak Out"—and, for that matter, few of the Muslim contributors to "On Faith" (which seemed far more concerned with Islam than with any other faith)—could legitimately be described as inhabiting this "middle." Summing up the subsite's manifest objective, Charles Johnson wrote in 2007 that the *Post* and *Newsweek* appeared to be "pulling out all the stops in their promotion of radical Islamists as 'moderates.'"

Johnson particularly lamented the inclusion in the series of Mu-zammil Siddiqi, chairman of the Fiqh Council of North America and former president of the Islamic Society of North America (ISNA), both of which had been named as unindicted coconspirators in the Holy Land trial. Johnson quoted journalist Kenneth Timmermann's obser-vation, in a 2004 article, that Siddiqi had "praised suicide bombers," "openly threatened the United States with violence if it continued its support of Israel," and "called for a wider application of sharia law in the United States." Steven Emerson, who also deplored the *Post*'s and *Newsweek*'s "efforts to help sanitize radical Muslims and present them as mainstream voices" in the "On Faith" series, noted that the contribu-tor's note for Siddiqi described him "as involved in 'inter-faith initia-tives' . . . and as the 'Chairman of the Fiqh Council of North America, a body tasked with interpreting religious law throughout the conti-nent.'" But there was no mention, Emerson pointed out, of Siddiqi's statements in support of jihad, his denial that 9/11 was committed by Muslims, or his ties to Hamas leader Mousa Abu Marzook (who in 1997 had thanked the ISNA, then run by Siddiqi, for its support) and with Sheikh Omar Abdel-Rahman, who insisted that jihad must be violent and helped plot the 1993 World Trade Center bombing.

Among the features of "On Faith" was a blog by John Esposito, who was identified as "Founding director, Prince Alwaleed bin Talal Cen-ter for Muslim-Christian Understanding, Georgetown University." The fact that his title included the name of a Saudi prince (who had coughed up a princely sum to endow the center and pay his salary) gave a pretty good clue as to his blog's contents. That someone with in-timate financial ties to the royal family of the world's most oppressive Islamic state could be engaged by the *Washington Post* and *Newsweek* to write regularly about Islam spoke volumes about the mainstream media's problematic relation to the facts about that religion.

Esposito's book *The Islamic Threat: Myth or Reality?* was one of the first works that I turned to in 1999 in my attempt to understand Am-sterdam's parallel Muslim society, but I soon realized the book was ji-hadist propaganda disguised as objective reportage. Esposito's answer to the question raised in his book's title was unequivocal: the notion of an Islamic threat was pure myth, rooted in ignorance and prejudice. As little as I knew at the time, I recognized this as an out-and-out false-hood. Martin Kramer, one of the dwindling number of well-positioned

Middle East experts (he's at Harvard) who tell the unvarnished truth about Islam, has stated unequivocally that "Esposito, more than any other academic, contributed to American complacency prior to 9/11." Far from predicting 9/11, Esposito mocked those who fretted about the possibility of such acts; not only did he insist on Islam's innocuousness, he presented the religion as a positive boon for the West, and, as Kramer puts it, represented Islamists as involved in "movements of democratic reform." To be sure, it has long been common in Esposito's field to dismiss freedom: Kramer quotes Richard Bulliet, a former director of the Middle East Institute at Columbia University, as rejecting current definitions of democracy as part of "a world hegemonic discourse of Western cultural imperialism" and as calling for a "reshaping of the concept of democracy within world terms in which there is a dialogue of discourse and not simply a Western hegemonic discourse." Thus does pretentious, abstraction-ridden multicultural rhetoric succeed in whitewashing the execution of gays, apostates, adulterers, and rape victims, and in entirely removing from the picture of the Islamic world the victims of these abominations.

Through the 1990s, Esposito and his allies, rather than focusing on the jihadist terrorism that was then already well under way, condemned media coverage of it—tepid and decontextualized though it was—for supposedly inflaming Americans' hostility toward Muslims. In the eyes of these scholars, writes Kramer, the "media were the real fanatics. . . . If they [the scholars] mentioned bin Laden at all, it was to dismiss his influence." In a 1998 essay, Esposito played the diversity card, arguing that bin Laden was only one of many "international sources (state and nonstate, non-Muslim and Muslim) of terrorism," and that it was therefore a mistake to focus on him excessively. A responsible Middle Eastern Studies establishment might have helped prepare Americans for 9/11 and its aftermath; not only did Esposito and his ilk fail to do this, but they strenuously insisted that there was no Islamic threat and sought to discredit those who said that there was. 9/11 should have ended Esposito's career; instead, the media have turned increasingly to him and other propagandists to "explain" Islam to readers, embracing their distortions and obfuscations more ardently than ever. They haven't always been subtle about this: on July 22, 2007, for example, the *Washington Post* actually had the audacity to headline an article by Esposito "Want to Understand Islam? Start Here." Esposito dragged out all the familiar argumentative gambits, including the "rich diversity of Islam" ploy ("The treatment of women under Islam is . . . wildly diverse"), which of course can be used to dismiss any troubling aspect of anything, and the "jihad means struggle" ploy ("In the Koran . . . jihad means 'to strive or struggle' to realize God's will, to lead a virtuous life, to create a just society and to defend Islam and the Muslim community"), which utterly denies the historic centrality to Islam of holy war. Esposito also gave a thumbs-up to two outrageous hagiographies, Karen Armstrong's *Muhammed: A Prophet for Our Time* and Ramadan's *In the Footsteps of the Prophet*, both of which, he said, "provide fresh, perceptive views on [Muhammed's] modern-day relevance."

For their efforts, Esposito and company have been rewarded bountifully. In January 2006, noting Prince Alwaleed's $20 million gift to his eponymous center, Kramer called Esposito "a magnet for Arab and Muslim money" and "a bought and paid-for subsidiary" of the Saudis. (Pointing out that Esposito owned "a Bethesda, Maryland[,] condo," a "getaway on the Maryland shore and a 'dream home' on the Florida coast," Kramer dryly commented: "Advocating for foreign interests from within the academy can be a lucrative vocation.") But the grant to Esposito's center was only a small part of a very extensive, and expensive, effort to (in the words of an official Saudi government statement) "promote understanding and change America's perceptions of Islam in the most fertile place, the university campus." As Julia Duin wrote in the *Washington Times*, Saudi funding of "educational" institutions in the West "started around 1976" with the establishment (at a price of one million dollars) of the King Faisal Chair in Islamic Studies at USC. According to the Saudi weekly *Ain-al-Yaqeen*, there are now "some 210 Islamic centers wholly or partly financed by Saudi Arabia, more than 1,500 mosques and 22 colleges and almost 2,000 schools for educating Muslim children in non-Islamic countries in Europe, North and South America, Australia and Asia." Saudi money, then, has paid both for the instruction of European Muslim children in Islamic supremacism and jihadist ideology and for the inculcation in non-Muslim students of the idea that Islamic supremacism and jihadist ideology are Islamophobic lies.

In February 2008, Esposito gave a speech at Stanford University. Covering it for *FrontPage Magazine*, Cinnamon Stillwell wrote that he described terrorism as rooted in "political and economic grievance" and "'occupation' on the part of 'neo-colonial powers,'" insisted that "all religions produce violence," and defined jihad in a way that "downplayed violent jihad or holy war in favor of the 'personal struggle' interpretation." In answer to a question from the audience as to "why no other impoverished or oppressed group around the world resorts to suicide bombings, Esposito stonewalled for several minutes before giving one of the few straight answers of the night: 'I don't know.'" Two months later, Esposito published a new book, *Who Speaks for Islam?*, written with Dalia Mogahed. Just as the purpose of his pre-9/11 book *The Islamic Threat: Myth or Reality?* was to convince readers that Islam posed no threat to the West, the new book sought to use Gallup poll results to assure them that the overwhelming majority of Muslims in the West were moderate. In order to accomplish this, however, Esposito and his coauthor were obliged to define "moderate" as anyone who didn't consider 9/11 "completely justified." Muslims who considered 9/11 somewhat justified, in other words, would fall into the moderate category. So, as Martin Kramer pointed out, would millions of Muslims (the figure among British Muslims, for example, is 56 percent) who deny that Arabs committed 9/11.

XIV

"Secular fundamentalists"

Another contributor to "On Faith" was Paul ("new sensitivity") Vallely, who in a piece published in July 2007 did his best to persuade readers that the real problem was Islamophobia, not jihad. Vallely described "honor killings, cutting off thieves' hands or stoning adulterers to death" as "extreme practices" that only "red-neck cab drivers" would connect with "ordinary Muslims." (It's interesting that self-styled liberals who are desperately careful not to offend "ordinary Muslims" are so quick to use expressions like "red-neck cab drivers.") Vallely did not explain, however, why someone like Tariq Ramadan refuses to condemn the stoning of adulteresses or why, when a European Muslim commits an honor killing, it can be impossible for reporters to find an "ordinary Muslim" who will criticize him. Vallely would have readers believe that "ordinary Muslims" deplore social practices that are routine, and punishments that are the law of the land, in much of the Muslim world. But Vallely was less concerned with the vulgar Islamophobia of "cab drivers" than with the "more subtle and insidious kind of Islamophobia" that, he argued, is found "among secularists who purport only to be the defenders of the values of the Enlightenment." Vallely proceeded to make a now-familiar argument against free speech: the "largely liberal secularist establishment," he complained, "refuses to acknowledge the important distinction to be made between having a right and choosing to exercise it. . . . Of course there has to be a right to free speech. But most difficult decisions are not between right and wrong. They are between competing rights. There is a right to speak without censorship but there is also a right for people to exist in society without feeling as alienated, threatened and routinely derided as many Muslims now do."

This argument has been served up frequently in recent years, and there are several points to be made about it. First, I've been verbally abused and socially excluded for being gay more times than I care to remember, but it has never occurred to me that I had a "right" not to be. On the contrary, I recognize that as long as people stop short of explicitly threatening or inciting acts of bodily harm, they have a perfect right to say what they think. I would never want to live in a nation where it were otherwise: having to deal with the occasional insult is far less unsettling than the prospect of living under a government with the power to punish insults. Second, if Muslims in the West are "alienated" from mainstream society, it's largely their own doing. Third, there's a difference between honestly discussing the facts about Islam, or any ideological system, and hurling slurs at individuals in the street. Fourth, if one is talking about the latter, the amount of personal abuse aimed at Muslims in the West is dwarfed by the amount directed by Western Muslims at women, Jews, and gays. Fifth, as to "competing rights": the First Amendment guarantees freedom of speech, but nowhere in the U.S. Constitution are Americans guaranteed the "right . . . to exist in society without feeling . . . alienated"; to claim otherwise is to attempt to replace constitutional democracy with something else. If a cartoon of Muhammed or an op-ed about terrorism makes some Muslims feel "alienated" or "derided," that's unfortunate; but there are in fact very few people in the West who do not, from time to time, feel personally targeted by some speech act or another. Until Islam became a factor in the West, we all accepted this as part of the price of freedom. A great many Muslims refuse to accept it, and expect non-Muslims to display a deference that would amount to dhimmitude. Their determination to erode Western freedom amounts, as we have seen, to a new form of jihad. And when a major American newspaper runs articles of this sort by people like Vallely, while omitting from their pages the voices of those who expose such views for what they are, it is, consciously or not, aiding jihad.

To read Vallely—who complained that "secular fundamentalists," by insisting on free speech, were "throw[ing] gasoline onto the flames" (that metaphor again)—you would think that Muslims were uniquely sinned against; in fact many Muslims are uniquely insistent upon their right not to have their religion criticized—even as they heap calumny upon other faiths. (One reader of Vallely's article commented, "you have to work hard to pick a fight with Thai Buddhists, among the most friendly and peaceful people on earth, but somehow Muslims found a way.") At the *Independent*, as at other Western newspapers, criticism of religion has long been recognized as legitimate; the exceptional effort to erect a protective wall around Islam is the result not of a wave of hatred directed *at* Muslims but of fear inspired by a flood of violence *by* Muslims. Vallely essentially admitted as much: if we don't abandon "polarized positions" (such as refusing to compromise free speech), he wrote, there'll be "no peaceful way out." The question he delicately avoided asking was this: *Why* won't there be peace? Because people like Ayaan Hirsi Ali will start machine-gunning Muslims? No, because Muslims will commit more and more violence. Vallely's closing sentences, then, were an implicit acknowledgment that his position on these matters was an expression of sheer cowardice—a caving-in to blatant intimidation.

On July 25, 2007, I went to the *Washington Post/Newsweek* Web site to find Tariq Ramadan's face smiling out at me. The picture accompanied a Q & A with Ramadan that was part of the "On Faith" series. Asked about women's rights under Islam, he executed an elegant rhetorical maneuver: "For a fruitful discussion, it is imperative to change the terms of discourse"—and proceeded to serve up several hundred words that communicated virtually nothing. "We are in a dire need," he argued, "of a constructive critical reassessment of the Islamic discourse and understanding on women." Yet he didn't provide so much as a hint of that "reassessment." His statement that "female circumcision, domestic violence, forced marriages are not Islamic" sounded good, but a reader unfamiliar with his rhetorical methods might not realize that this was hardly tantamount to categorically rejecting, for instance, a Muslim husband's sacred right to corporally punish his wife. (Ramadan's hero Qaradawi, after all, has affirmed this right, and would of course explain that such necessary acts of discipline do not constitute "domestic violence.") Ramadan called for Muslims to move beyond "narrow literalist or cultural understanding," but left it up to the reader to guess what he meant by this. Indeed, most of what he said was either vague and windy or full of the usual waffle words; for example, he condemned suicide bombings that kill "innocent" people, but didn't define "innocent."

As if the support Ramadan had received from Buruma and Garton Ash weren't enough, in August 2007 he received yet another thumbs-up in the *New York Times Magazine*, this time from Mark Lilla of Columbia University. Lilla made it abundantly clear that he shared Buruma's and Garton Ash's enthusiasm for "accommodation" of Islam. His essay, "The Politics of God," began with the observation that throughout human history governance and religion have almost always been intimately intertwined, which makes modern secular democracy and the modern concept of religion as a private matter freak exceptions. Yet Lilla, instead of celebrating church-state separation, dismissed modern liberal Christianity as inert ("the liberal deity," he wrote, "turned out to be a stillborn God") and argued, essentially, that it's in the nature of *real* religion—that is, religion that inspires genuine ardor among its adherents (including, apparently, a passionate desire to pilot commercial aircraft into skyscrapers)—to seek to ground "the legitimate political order" in faith. Therefore, Lilla contended, it's futile for secular Western liberals to ally themselves with secular Muslim liberals such as Hirsi Ali, because the latter don't represent their religion's true believers; rather, we should take seriously someone like (who else?) Tariq Ramadan, because he represents "transformations in Muslim political theology that [may] ease coexistence." No, Lilla admits, the prospect is not pretty, but

> accommodation and mutual respect can help, as can clear
> rules governing areas of tension, like the status of women,
> parents' rights over their children, speech offensive to religious
> sensibilities, speech inciting violence, standards of dress in
> public institutions and the like. Western countries have adopted
> different strategies for coping, some forbidding religious
> symbols like the head scarf in schools, others permitting them.
> But we need to recognize that coping is the order of the day,
> not defending high principle, and that our expectations should
> remain low. So long as a sizable population believes in the truth

of a comprehensive political theology, its full reconciliation with modern liberal democracy cannot be expected.

Lilla's piece was so long and languorous, and written with such perfect academic dispassion, that it was possible to get to the end of it without ever quite realizing just what he was arguing. And what he was arguing was this: that *they're* not going to change, so we have to. He was throwing in the towel, suggesting that we compromise constitutional liberties in the hope that this sacrifice might save us from violent, full-scale confrontation; he was proposing, in the name of peaceful co-existence, that America, which has fought war after war to defend its freedoms, give them up without a fight on the grounds that Muslims' fierce adherence to their religion compels us to formulate a new modus vivendi. For, after all, their piety is of a piece with the whole of human history, while our secularism is an anomaly. Nowhere in his essay did Lilla acknowledge that by compromising with Islamic extremism the West would be initiating a pattern of demand and further compromise that would end in sharia. The *Times*, one noted, was now pushing two utterly different pictures of Islam in the West—the familiar Andrea Elliott version (Islam as cozy and safe), and the new Mark Lilla version (Islam as irreconcilable with freedom). Yet though the two versions contradicted each other, they shared one key aspect—both dismissed the notion that Westerners should resist Islamism and stand up for freedom. The *Times*, in other words, welcomed into its pages the arguments that "resistance is unnecessary" and "resistance is futile"; the argument that remained unwelcome was "resistance is obligatory to preserve freedom."

Still, just as one had the impression that Buruma and Garton Ash were under pressure to moderate their criticism of Hirsi Ali and tone down their rhapsodies for Tariq Ramadan, one also gathered that the *Times* might be feeling some heat regarding its relentless appeasement of jihadism. At best this conclusion might reasonably have been drawn by readers of the January 6, 2008, *Book Review*, which was devoted largely to Islam. To be sure, some of its contents were predictable. Tariq Ramadan, for example, contributed an outrageously long-winded and saccharine effusion, "Reading the Koran," the sole purpose of which seemed to be to give non-Muslim readers a warm and fuzzy feeling about Islam:

No need for studies and diplomas, for masters and guides. Here, as we take our first steps, God beckons us with the simplicity of his closeness. The Koran belongs to everyone, free of distinction and of hierarchy. God responds to whoever comes to his Word. It is not rare to observe women and men, poor and rich, educated and illiterate, Eastern and Western, falling silent, staring into the distance, lost in thought, stepping back, weeping. The search for meaning has encountered the sacred, God is near: "Indeed, I am close at hand. I answer the call of him who calls me when s/he calls."

Ramadan's entire piece—all 2,500 words of it—read more or less like the above. It was the literary equivalent of a team running out the clock. For Ramadan never got anywhere near talking about the actual *contents* of the Koran; his tribute to its deep humanity and sublimity never so much as hinted at the existence of such suras as the following:

Prophet, make war on the unbelievers and the hypocrites and deal rigorously with them. Hell shall be their home: an evil fate. (9:73)

Fight those who believe not in God and the Last Day and do not forbid what God and His Messenger have forbidden—such men as practice not the religion of truth, being of those who have been given the Book—until they pay the tribute out of hand and have been humbled. (9:29)

Those who have denied the Book and the message We sent through Our apostles shall realize the truth hereafter: when, with chains and shackles around their necks, they shall be dragged through scalding water and burnt in the fire of Hell. (40:70)

They that deny Our revelations We will burn in fire. No sooner will their skins be consumed than We shall give them other skins, so that they may truly taste the scourge. (64:10)

The unbelievers of the People of the Book and the idolators
shall be in the Fire of Gehenna, therein dwelling forever; those
are the worst of creatures. (98:6)

Such suras aside, what was Ramadan's ridiculous panegyric doing in
the *Book Review* in the first place? Was the *Times* now in the business
of reviewing centuries-old scriptures? Would a future *Book Review*
include a Pat Robertson sermon or a piece by Tom Cruise about the
joys of Scientology? Not that the publication of Ramadan's piece was
surprising; what was a surprise was that the same issue also included a
positive review by Hirsi Ali of *The Suicide of Reason*, in which Lee Harris argued that Islam is by its nature irreconcilable with Western liberty. It was bizarre to see this dose of reality in the *Times Book Review*.
What were the editors thinking?

Another writer who should be mentioned in this context is Karen
Armstrong. A former nun who has written books about Muhammed,
the Crusades, and the three Abrahamic faiths, Armstrong has ridden
the wave of media eagerness to prettify and placate Islam. When she
published *Muhammed: A Prophet for Our Time* in 2006, the *New York
Times* ran a glowing thousand-word review by Laurie Goodstein. Its
closing sentences convey the thrust of the review, as well as of Armstrong's book: "Armstrong argues that [Muhammed] prevailed by
compassion, wisdom and steadfast submission to God. This is the
power of his story and the reason that more parents around the world
name their children Muhammad than any other name."

Of course, Muhammed spread his religion through brutal military
conquest, but Armstrong was plainly determined to make him over
into a gentle Christlike figure; and Goodstein, just as plainly, had no
problem with this rewriting of history. Indeed, Goodstein defended
Muhammed by attacking his critics. "Muhammed," she lamented, "has
been defined by his detractors: who have called him a terrorist, a lunatic
and most colorfully—by the Rev. Jerry Vines, former president of the
Southern Baptist Convention—a 'demon-possessed pedophile.'" This
was neatly calculated: such a person hates Muhammed, he can't have
been all bad, can he? Goodstein complained that "Pope Benedict XVI,
whatever his intention, created an uproar" when he quoted that Byzantine emperor's critical remark about the founder of Islam. Her point:

everyone's piling on poor Muhammed! She neglected to acknowledge the real lesson of the pontiff's Regensburg speech: namely, that all it takes to make the Islamic world explode are a few words about Islam in the Western media—words far less incendiary than things that are said daily in the Muslim media about Jews and Christians.

"Several new biographies picture Muhammed through the lens of a suicide bomber," Goodstein wrote, mentioning such books as Robert Spencer's *The Truth About Muhammed* (which, as we have seen, the *Times* did not deign to review), "and ultimately these books reveal more about suicide bombers than Muhammed." No, she insisted, if we want "to glimpse how the vast majority of the world's Muslims understand their prophet and their faith," we need to read Armstrong. Never mind that Armstrong "declines to stand in judgment of events that have scandalized other biographers," such as Muhammed's taking his daughter-in-law as his fifth wife. As Armstrong herself put it, in a ridiculous sentence that Goodstein apparently considered a reasonable defense of this action: "Why should God not give his prophet a few privileges?" Goodstein's refusal to so much as raise an eyebrow over such outrageous apologetics made it clear just how desperate mainstream journalists are these days to find excuses (however feeble) for any wrongs associated with Islam, its prophet, and its adherents. What other warrior and conqueror in all of human history would the *Times* be so eager to exculpate? It was clearly no accident, moreover, that Goodstein, in her reference to "events that have scandalized other biographers," chose to mention Muhammed's marriage to his daughter-in-law rather than his even more appalling bedding of a nine-year-old girl named Aisha (a good illustration of how, when the facts about Islam are too unsavory to explain away, the media often simply ignore them).

In 1999, the Muslim Public Affairs Council of Los Angeles gave Armstrong an award for "fairness"; representative of that "fairness" is her denial of Muslim terrorists' motives. As David Thompson wrote in a definitive article entitled "Karen Armstrong: Islam's Hagiographer," the terrorists themselves admit that they act on "what they perceive as core Islamic teachings. . . . But Armstrong would have us ignore what terrorists repeatedly tell us about themselves and their motives." Indeed, at the heart of Armstrong's project is her obscuring of the meaning of jihad, which she defines as "a cherished spiritual value that, for most Muslims, has no connection with violence"; not until recently, she would have us believe, did any "Muslim thinker" consider violent jihad central to Islam. Countering this preposterous claim, Thompson notes that "most references to jihad found in the Qur'an and Sunnah occur in a military or paramilitary context, and aggressive conceptions of jihad are found in every major school of Islamic jurisprudence"; that a fifteenth-century historian summarized "the consensus of five centuries of prior Sunni theology" with the statement that "holy war is a religious duty"; and that Muslims, according to a Shia law manual, are obliged to engage in holy war against the infidel. Similarly, Armstrong insists that anti-Semitism is a Western disease that has been imported into jihad. This lie, which has been discredited at several hundred pages' length in Andrew Bostom's *The Legacy of Islamic Anti-Semitism*, is only one example of Armstrong's tendency, as Thompson puts it, to depict "the evil imperialist West . . . as boundlessly capable of spreading corruption wherever it goes" while portraying the Muslim world as "passive, devoid of agency and thereby virtuous by default." Armstrong describes Muhammed as a "peacemaker" who respected Jews; yet anybody who has paged through the Koran knows otherwise.

In a 2007 review of several books for the *Financial Times*, Armstrong sought to depict Muhammed and Islam as innocent victims of a Western hatred, bigotry, envy, and bellicosity that dates back to the Middle Ages. "The criminal activities of terrorists have given the old western prejudice a new lease on life," Armstrong lamented, thus neatly (à la Buruma) deflecting the reader's attention away from Muslim violence to non-Muslims' alleged bigotry, and slickly equating Westerners' thoroughly legitimate post-9/11 concerns about terrorism with medieval superstitions and prejudices—all the while neatly ignoring the fact that today it's the Muslim world that still lives in the Middle Ages. While whitewashing Muhammed entirely, Armstrong dug into Robert Spencer with her claws out: "He is a hero of the American right." "Like any book written in hatred. . . ." "He deliberately manipulates the evidence." No, in thunder: it's Armstrong who systematically deep-sixes the ugly parts of the Koran and foregrounds those scraps of it that can be yanked out of context and selectively quoted to make the intended impression. In her *Financial Times* piece, she proffered the familiar lie about how Christians and Jews were treated with respect in Muslim Spain (forget the dhimmi system, which gave Muslims the right to do virtually anything to a non-Muslim with utter impunity) and insisted that the Koran condemns "all warfare as an 'awesome evil.'" This is selective quotation on a breathtakingly dishonest scale. Describing the Koran, absurdly, as being all about "forgiveness and peaceful negotiation," she concluded that "[u]ntil we all learn to approach one another with generosity and respect, we cannot hope for peace"—a sentence that one couldn't help reading as an admission (in line with Stéphanie Giry's undisguised eagerness to endorse useful misrepresentations of Muhammed) that Armstrong had jettisoned completely any sense of obligation to actually tell the truth about Islam and its founder in order to serve the cause of "peace," while failing to make it clear to infidel readers that the "peace" she had in mind would require of them, as it did of seventh-century North African Christians and Jews, either dhimmitude or conversion. Or death.

One of my own first encounters with scholarly dhimmitude came in 2001—five days, in fact, before 9/11—when social anthropologist Unni Wikan, one of Norway's most respected authorities on Islam, told *Dagbladet* that if 65 percent of rapes in Norway were committed by "non-Western immigrants" (who at the time formed no more than 2 or 3 percent of the population), much of the blame fell on Norwegian women, whose manner of dress Muslim men found provocative. Norwegian women, she counseled, "must realize that we live in a multicultural society and adapt to it." In short: be a dhimmi. Years later, the song of Norway remained the same: in March 2007 Norwegian religious historian Hanne Nabintu Herland blamed the country's still-climbing rape statistics on feminism. "Is it strange," she asked rhetorically, "that Africans rape when they come to Norway and discover what a low value Western culture places on a woman's sexuality?" Herland approvingly quoted a Kenyan Muslim leader's comment that "[a] woman in Western society is like an animal; there is no respect for her body." Hence even rape, when viewed through the lens of dhimmitude, can become an act of respect.

On June 20, 2007, the *New York Times* and *Washington Post* showed just how far they'd traveled down the road of dhimmitude. It was on that day that both newspapers ran op-eds bearing the byline of Hamas spokesman Ahmed Yousef. Both pieces were pure propaganda, and the papers faced heavy criticism in the blogosphere for running them. *Times* "public editor" (ombudsman) Clark Hoyt defended his employers' decision, arguing that "good ideas prosper in the sunshine of healthy debate, and the bad ones wither." But Yousef wasn't offering "ideas" but lies. And these lies hardly required help from the *Times* to be heard. Hamas PR had long been widely disseminated by a compliant international media. "Op-ed pages are for debate, but if you get only one side, that's not debate," wrote Hoyt. This from the public editor of a newspaper that had done its best to pretend that a succession of important books on Islam didn't even exist—a newspaper that had excluded honest experts from its pages while repeatedly printing humbug by the likes of Ramadan, Esposito, and Armstrong. At the *Post*, meanwhile, the controversy over its Yousef op-ed—as the commentator Brian Hecht noted—centered not on the fact that the newspaper had run "propaganda from a designated foreign terrorist organization, but rather that its major competitor had published a similar op-ed from the same author that very day."

At its 2007 convention, the Society of Professional Journalists passed a set of guidelines for coverage of Arabs and Muslims. The gist of these guidelines—which essentially codified the unwritten rules already in place at most mainstream media organizations—was that Arabs and Muslims should not be portrayed, either in word or image, as monolithic or exotic, and that victims of anti-Arab or anti-Muslim "hate crimes" should be covered "as thoroughly as . . . victims of overt terrorist attacks." Reporters were enjoined to "[m]ake an extra effort to include olive-complexioned and darker men and women, Sikhs, Muslims, and devout religious people of all types in arts, business, society columns and other news and feature coverage, not just stories about the crisis." (When in modern times had mainstream American media ever been concerned with including "devout religious people" in such coverage?) Other rules:

- "When writing about terrorism, remember to include white supremacist, radical anti-abortionists and other groups with a history of such activity."
- "Do not lump [Muslim countries] together as in constructions such as 'the fury of the Muslim world.'"

- "Avoid using word combinations such as 'Islamic terrorist' or 'Muslim extremist.'..."
- "Avoid using terms such as 'jihad' unless you are certain of their precise meaning.... The basic meaning of 'jihad' is to exert oneself for the good of Islam and to better oneself."

PART THREE

A War on Many Fronts

Jihad on Campus

Nowhere in the Western world today is multiculturalism more deeply rooted, dhimmitude more prevalent, and free speech more imperiled than on university campuses.

This is not how it was supposed to be. In a free society, a university should be freer than free. It should be an oasis of openmindedness—a place where the most unpopular causes can be championed and the most unorthodox ideas debated without fear of arrest, ostracism, or other penalty.

In recent decades, however, multiculturalism has transformed many of these oases into swamps of PC intolerance. Scores, if not hundreds, of American institutions of higher education have instituted "speech codes" that spell out the limits of allowable speech, and some have introduced programs that indoctrinate new students, or re-educate wayward ones, in PC dogma. All this has put universities on the cutting edge of dhimmitude.

But before we look at some of the ways in which institutions of higher education have aided jihad and punished free speech, let's briefly examine a few cases that illuminate the mentality that renders the academy so susceptible to jihadist pressures. One such incident was the Duke lacrosse team scandal. When three white players were accused in March 2006 of raping a black stripper, Duke president

Richard Brodhead behaved as if they'd already been convicted—and ignored all evidence to the contrary. (As Abigail Thernstrom wrote in the *Wall Street Journal*, "He was clearly terrified of the racial and gender activists on his own faculty.") Then there's the sorry saga of Lawrence Summers, who while president of Harvard ventured to suggest at a January 2005 conference on diversity in science and engineering that if these fields were dominated by men, it might be partly because men were more innately gifted in or drawn to these areas. Controversy ensued. Two months later, Harvard's faculty officially declared that it had "no confidence" in his leadership; though he tried to ride out the storm, his power was so thoroughly eroded by the controversy that he ended up resigning. Nor was this the end of it: in September 2007, a speaking invitation to Summers by the University of California Board of Regents was withdrawn in response to a petition drive mounted by a female professor of evolution at UC Davis.

American institutions of higher education exalt diversity—but not ideological diversity. Many students are intensely aware of their obligations under the speech codes of the institutions they attend but ignorant of their free-speech rights under the U.S. Constitution. According to surveys commissioned by the Foundation for Individual Rights in Education in 2003, "one out of every four [American] undergraduates is unable to mention any freedoms protected by the First Amendment." Even the left-wing *Nation*, as far back as December 2001, ran an article by David Glenn acknowledging that "the last generation's wave of campus speech codes and antiharassment policies may have done more to suppress freedom than to remedy injustice in any meaningful way." In 2007, members of the American Historical Association unanimously passed a resolution condemning the Iraq war but rejected one denouncing speech codes. According to the *Inside Higher Ed* Web site, Pamela Smith of Columbia University complained "that the resolution didn't reflect the extent to which colleges need to 'balance the right of free speech' with 'responsibilities that go along' with free speech." The notion that authorities have the obligation and the power to "balance" free speech with certain "responsibilities" (usually vague or even unnamed) is all but universal in academia.

Many, probably most, university officials who censor speech would deny they're doing so. A vice provost at Penn State who objected to "pro-war" views posted on a professor's Web site insisted that "We are not censoring free speech. We are just asking our professors to convey their opinions with sensitivity." The conviction that it's only acceptable to speak your mind if you do it in approved ways is common on American campuses. The upshot of the Penn State case was that the offending professor was ordered to engage in "dialogue" with students who had been offended by his Web site. This sort of forced "dialogue" is recognized at many universities as thoroughly proper punishment for "inappropriate" speech.

In a June 2007 *New York Times* report on *Indoctrinate U*—a documentary about students and professors who have found themselves in the line of PC fire—Joseph Berger highlighted a 2005 conflict, covered in the film, over a Vassar student publication's criticism of the "ghettoizing" of gay and minority students. Berger praised the way in which the conflict was "resolved"—with a decision that expressing views was permissible but that "gratuitous racial insults" were not. "Ultimately," a student told Berger, "free speech was protected." But Berger's own account showed otherwise. Berger actually wrote that "Vassar deserves credit because, as students explained, the dispute was not focused on whether *The Imperialist* [the student publication] could argue that a center exclusively for minority students fragmented the community; it was over whether the language used to express the idea was offensive." Berger seemed blithely unaware that even to distinguish between having the right to express an idea and not having the right to express it in words of one's own choosing is to jettison the First Amendment. Greg Lukianoff, head of FIRE (Foundation for Individual Rights in Education), observed that Berger was "making one of censorship's most basic arguments"; John Stuart Mill himself, noted Lukianoff, had rejected arguments for banning "intemperate discussion . . . invective [and] sarcasm" on the grounds that such rhetoric is never banned unless it challenges prevailing opinions. "As Mill made clear nearly 150 years ago," wrote Lukianoff, "an exception to free speech that *only* bans free speech deemed 'offensive' is an exception that entirely swallows the rule."

Given such developments, it was no surprise that when American Muslims began complaining after 9/11 about "Islamophobic" speech, universities not only were prepared to take their side but already had all the necessary procedures in place to enable them to act quickly and effectively against unwelcome speech about Islam. And they came through with flying colors. On no topic, indeed, has academic conformism been more fiercely enforced in recent years than on Islam. Censorship of its critics is not only widely practiced but is held up as principled. In November 2006, for example, administrators at Pace University in New York responded to Muslim student protests by pressuring Hillel, the Jewish students' organization, to cancel a screening of the film *Obsession: Radical Islam's War against the West*. The purported reason, reported Karen W. Arenson in the *New York Times*, was concern that it might "spur hate crimes against Muslim students"—even though it seemed likely that university authorities were worried less about things being done *to* Muslims than about things being done *by* Muslims.

Or consider the view of Yehuda Sarna, a rabbi associated with New York University, who at a panel discussion about *Obsession* complained that "the question about radical Islam and how do we fight it is unproductive. . . . The question is how to break down the stereotypes facing the two religions." Meaning what? Apparently that the whole business of being under assault by jihadists makes us uneasy, so let's put our heads in the sand and pretend that the real problem is the misrepresentation of Muslims. In December 2007, when the Campus Republicans at the University of Florida sponsored a screening of *Obsession* and advertised it by putting up posters that said "Radical Islam Wants You Dead," Patricia Telles-Irvin, the university's vice president for student affairs, sent out a mass e-mail complaining that the posters "reinforced a negative stereotype . . . and contributed to a generalization that only furthers the misunderstanding of the religion of Islam." This in a country whose soldiers were at that moment confronting jihadists in both Afghanistan and Iraq.

At universities, free speech is often used as an excuse to provide jihadists and their defenders with a forum, while those who criticize Islam are denied one on the grounds that universities are supposed to be "safe zones" for all groups. In October 2006, for example, members of terrorist organizations were invited to debate terrorism at Trinity College in Dublin with Muslims who opposed terrorism. The event's organizer explained that there were "two valid sides" to the issue; yet he had not invited anyone who considered Islam itself a part of the problem. Supporting terrorism, then, was a "valid" position; criticizing Islam was not.

Then there's the *Clareification* case. In February 2007, a student magazine called *Clareification* at Clare College, Cambridge, published an issue satirizing religion. It took on a variety of faiths, but what got the nineteen-year-old editor in trouble was the material on Islam, which included one of the *Jyllands-Posten* cartoons and a spoof article entitled "Ayatollah rethinks stance on 'misunderstood' Rushdie." Nearly everybody at Cambridge, it seemed, was in a competition to see who could be the biggest dhimmi. Clare College authorities called the issue "abhorrent." The college's fellows summoned a Court of Discipline. Police interrogated the editor to determine whether he had violated Section 5 of the Public Order Act (which covers instances of "harassment, alarm or distress") and reported him to the Crown Prosecution Service. The *Cambridge News*—in a supposed news article—described the Islam-related humor as "anti-Islamic material" and labeled the *Jyllands-Posten* drawing "vile" and "racist." "The College chaplain," the *Independent* reported, "has also been involved in talks aimed at trying to ease racial tension and is known to have met members of the Islamic Society and a local Imam to discuss how best to quell fears over potential racial clashes." In other words, what do we have to do and say—and *not* do and say—to keep you from turning violent? (Note how acts of sheer dhimmi groveling are described in ways that make them seem reasonable and respectable.) "Clare is an open and inclusive college," the senior tutor at Clare College, Patricia Fara, said. "A student produced satirical publication has caused widespread distress throughout the Clare community. The college finds the publication and the views expressed abhorrent. Reflecting the gravity of the situation, the college immediately began an investigation and disciplinary procedures are in train." (Note how a description of an educational institution as "open and inclusive" is followed immediately by words demonstrating just how closed and exclusionary it is.) Other officials echoed Fara's red-alert rhetoric: Calum Davey, president of the Union of Clare Students, "expressed his 'deep regret' over the publication and offered his sincere apologies for causing offense." And "an insider at the college" told the *Cambridge News* that "the probe into the racist material had 'gone to the very top.'" This "insider" also said: "Some of the most senior staff are utterly distraught and disgusted at the thought of what has happened. It's the first time in living memory a Court of Discipline has been set up. The stuff this chap printed is very inflammatory indeed.

The college fears the material in the publication could be considered as causing racial incitement. It's causing real abhorrence among the staff."

"Abhorrence." "Inflammatory." "Gravity." "Racist." "Distraught." "Disgusted." The sheer institutional cowardice was breathtaking. If these cartoons had been about any religion other than Islam, nothing whatsoever would have happened. The *Cambridge News* actually described the official inquiry as a "race-hate probe." So it was that while British Muslim leaders who had cheered on jihad terrorists and supported the Rushdie fatwa were being treated with deference by British authorities, a teenager who—following a long and admirable tradition of robust British satire—dared to write sardonically about those terrorists and that fatwa was treated as if he himself were a terrorist. Nor is that the whole of the irony. Elsewhere in the city of Cambridge, there existed an institution called the Islamic Academy where, as the *Sunday Telegraph* reported in July 2007, the bombings that had taken place in London and Glasgow in late June of that year turned out to have been plotted; Kafeel Ahmed, the local organizer for the radical Islamic group Hizb ut-Tahrir, also worked at the "academy." Yet even as the editor of *Clareification* was being anathematized by all and sundry, Islamic Academy representatives were sharing a platform at a public event with none other than Archbishop of Canterbury Rowan Williams.

Compare the response of Cambridge officials to student humor about jihad to the response of officials at other universities to the presence in their midst of actual jihadists. Three months after the *Clareification* imbroglio, Britain's University and College Union rejected a government request that British universities step up efforts to monitor the spread of jihadist ideology on campuses. Why the turndown—even though it was well known that a number of terrorists and would-be terrorists had first been indoctrinated and/or recruited at universities in Leeds and Bradford? Because, in the view of the University and College Union, even advocates of jihad have freedom of speech. The same view prevailed at Kent State University in Ohio when, in March 2007, it was reported that Julio Pino, an associate professor of history at that institution, had been posting at a jihadist Web site. Pino, using the name Assad Pino, had also written to the student newspaper in 2006: "You [that is, the United States] are a nation that permits the production, trading and usage of drugs, gambling, the sex trade, spreads diseases that were unknown to man in the past, such as AIDS, and turns women into commodities for sale. . . . The ill done to the Muslim nations must be requited. The Muslim child does not cry alone; the Muslim woman does not cry alone, and the Muslim man is already at your gates." (When it came to poetic self-dramatization, it seemed, Pino could give Reda Shata himself a run for his money.) And in 2002, in the same newspaper, Pino had praised a suicide bomber. Yet when the news about the jihadist Web site broke, Pino's department head, John Jameson, rushed to his defense, defending his teaching skills and calling the charges exaggerated. Yes, said Jameson, Pino had provided material for the jihadist Web site, but he didn't own it. (As if that made a difference!) And when KSU English professor Lewis Fried asked university president Carol Cartwright to fire Pino, she refused on free-speech grounds. At both American and British universities, then, you may stand a better chance of having your free-speech rights protected if you're preaching jihadist murder than if you're criticizing or satirizing it.

Another illuminating case was that of Sami al-Arian, a professor at the University of South Florida who was accused of having connections to the terrorist organization Palestinian Islamic Jihad. In April 2008 the *New York Times*' Neil MacFarquhar wrote an ostensible news article about al-Arian that read as if it had been written by the man's defense lawyer; dismissing al-Arian's guilty plea on a terrorism charge, MacFarquhar plainly sought to convince readers that "Mr. Al-Arian's supporters" were right when they claimed that "he is nothing more sinister than an outspoken Palestinian activist." Yet despite his apparent ties to people who represent a clear threat to the lives of free people, and the fact that al-Arian himself has been quoted as calling for "Death to Israel," Phil Donahue, when interviewing him on TV, turned reality on its head, expressing concern for al-Arian's safety and saying, "I assume you have security." Yes, that's the big problem in the West nowadays: the violent murder of radical Muslims.

We've already seen how Pace University, under Muslim pressure, canceled a showing of a film about jihad. Pace was also the setting of another case which demonstrated just how far the dhimmification of American higher education has advanced. In July 2007, Stanislav Shmulevich, a Ukrainian immigrant who was a student at Pace, was arrested and slapped with "two charges of criminal mischief in the fourth degree as a hate crime." Why? Twice in the autumn of 2006 he'd put books in toilet bowls at the university. The books weren't Shmulevich's—he'd taken them from a "meditation room" at Pace—and the toilets weren't his, either. But the police weren't interested in the theft or in damage to the plumbing. What mattered to them was that the books were copies of the Koran. Would somebody who had put two copies of, say, *Death in Venice* in a toilet bowl have ended up facing two felony raps? Of course not. (Some observers pointed out that when Andres Serrano submerged a crucifix in urine, it hadn't been considered a hate crime but an artwork.) The Shmulevich case, then, represented a chilling precedent. For what was being punished was not the actual crimes—swiping a couple of books and committing minor vandalism—but the desecration of a religion's scriptures, which should not be a crime at all in a secular republic. (Interestingly, no reporters were able to find records of a single case anywhere in the United States in which someone had ever been prosecuted for a hate crime for doing anything whatsoever to a Bible. Until Shmulevich came along, the very concept did not exist in American jurisprudence.)

Shmulevich's "bias" was no crime: if he despised the Koran, that was his right. Yet the police and most of the media failed to recognize this. Indeed, it's unsettling how many Americans have internalized at least some sharia-based notions of what constitutes a criminal offense. Winfield Myers, director of the Middle East Forum's Campus Watch, said flatly, "This is Shariah, plain and simple." He was right. And just to make the picture of jihadist manipulation complete, it soon began to appear that the whole case had been orchestrated by CAIR. To be sure, Pace spokesman Chris Cory denied that there had been any contact between the university and CAIR; yet in the *Washington Times* Audrey Hudson quoted a CAIR press release indicating that officers of that organization had taken part in a "town meeting" at Pace to discuss the Shmulevich incident (and, of course, "to create a better understanding of Islam"). Hudson also cited a Pace press release signed by Cory himself, which confirmed that Pace officials had indeed consulted with CAIR. There was yet another discrepancy: Cory told the media that Pace had at first reported Shmulevich's crime "as an act of vandalism, then the police hate-crime unit came over and decided to pursue it as a hate crime"; but according to CNN, it was Pace officials who, under "pressure from Muslims and Muslim groups," decided to charge Shmulevich with a "felony hate crime." Leaving aside the legitimacy of hate-crime legislation itself (which, to some of us, seems to punish not only actions but opinions), the extension of the concept to cover assaults not only on human beings but also on certain books marked a unique, bizarre—and ominous—new chapter in Western jurisprudence.

If universities now punish actions for fear of Muslim reactions, they also cancel events for the same reason. In 2007, for example, the German Department at the University of Leeds planned a lecture and two days of seminars under the title "Hitler's Legacy: Islamic Anti-Semitism in the Middle East"; university officials called the whole thing off, however, after receiving angry e-mails from Muslims. The German author who was to have delivered the lecture and led the seminars, Matthias Küntzel, told the *Telegraph* that the plans had been scrapped for "security reasons"; university authorities, for their part, vigorously denied that the cancellation had anything to do with "academic freedom, freedom of speech, anti-semitism or Islamophobia," or that it was a response to "threats or protests from interest groups." Authorities did not address the plain fact that if the topic of the lecture and seminars had not been Islam-related, "security concerns" would never have arisen.

Today's standard academic line on Islam was illustrated by the high-profile University of Chicago philosophy professor Martha Nussbaum in a 2007 interview with Elisabetta Ambrosi of *ResetDOC*. Denying that women suffer an unusual degree of oppression in the Islamic world or that they tend to be forced into restrictive roles more often than in Western countries, Nussbaum insisted that "there is no such thing as 'the Islamic world' and thus no such thing as 'a way' to be a woman in it. There are many types of Muslims, and, like Christians and Jews, they find many different ways to be women within their traditions." This was, of course, one more version of the "diversity" ploy—the same kind of thinking that says, "Yes, there are violent Muslims, but of course there are nonviolent Muslims, just as there are violent and nonviolent Christians." Or: "Yes, there are Muslim women who are suppressed by patriarchal husbands and fathers, but there are also Christian women in similar predicaments."

It's a measure of the twisted mentality on U.S. campuses that while it was considered scandalous to invite Lawrence Summers to address the University of California's regents, a number of colleges (including at least two in the California state system) have played host to radical lawyer Lynne Stewart, famous for representing Omar Abdel-Rahman, mastermind of the 1993 World Trade Center bombing and of the 1997 massacre at Luxor, Egypt, among other atrocities. Stewart, who was disbarred in 2005 after being found guilty of passing messages between the jailed terrorist and his confederates, has in recent years, according to Walter Olson in *City Journal*, "become a regular on the college circuit . . . one Minnesota event under putatively educational auspices was later described as a 'rally for credit.'" Officials at Stanford actually wanted to give Stewart the title "Public Interest Mentor," but were overruled by law dean Kathleen Sullivan. Olson described an October 2007 conference at Hofstra Law School at which Stewart was scheduled to participate in the closing panel discussion with another of Abdel-Rahman's attorneys. The banquet speaker was a lawyer who had been one of Stewart's "most vocal defenders," and the keynote speaker had been Stewart's counsel at her own trial. What, one wondered, was the point of this gathering if not to celebrate the defense of terrorism?

A month before Stewart's appearance at Hofstra, an even more notorious figure was being given a grand welcome at Columbia University. In response to protests over the invitation to Mahmoud Ahmadinejad—who had denied the Holocaust, called for the destruction of Israel, and executed dissidents and homosexuals—university officials, including Columbia's president, First Amendment scholar Lee Bollinger, invoked the concept of freedom of speech (as if having free speech meant having an Ivy League auditorium put at your disposal). Columbia students echoed this ridiculous line. One undergraduate told the *New York Times* that "it would be going against a lot of ethics that we stand for not to invite someone just because we don't agree with what he says." Grad student Stina Reksten said Iran's "very dire human rights situation" shouldn't be confused with "the issue here," which "is freedom of speech." Of course, if Columbia had really wanted to strike a blow for free speech, it could have invited Iranian dissidents to speak and thereby helped students understand what it means to live without freedom; instead Columbia offered legitimacy to a tyrant. If the same kind of PC academics who drove Summers out of his job eagerly trotted out the First Amendment to defend Columbia's hosting of Ahmadinejad, it was because the Iranian's opinions, unlike Summers's remark about gender and science, came down on the correct side of the

PC line: Ahmadinejad, that is, opposed Bush, the Iraq invasion, and the "war on terror," and thus deserved First Amendment protection.

When the day of Ahmadinejad's speech arrived, Bollinger, in an apparent attempt either to redeem himself morally or pacify alumni donors (or both), spent the time he had been allotted to introduce the tyrant articulating a few home truths. Bollinger began as follows:

> It should never be thought that merely to listen to ideas we deplore in any way implies our endorsement of those ideas or the weakness of our resolve to resist those ideas or our naivete about the very real dangers inherent in such ideas. It is a critical premise of freedom of speech that we do not honor the dishonorable when we open our public forum to their voices. To hold otherwise would make vigorous debate impossible.

Absolutely true. But then Bollinger said this:

> Second, to those who believe that this event never should have happened, that it is inappropriate for the University to conduct such an event, I want to say that I understand your perspective and respect it as reasonable. The scope of free speech and academic freedom should itself always be open to further debate. As one of the more famous quotations about free speech goes, it is "an experiment, as all life is an experiment." I want to say, however, as forcefully as I can, that this is the right thing to do and, indeed, it is required by existing norms of free speech, the American university, and Columbia itself.

No, inviting a thug to speak is not required by any existing norm. Indeed, Bollinger then seemed to contradict himself on this score. First he made a vital point: that "this event has nothing whatsoever to do with any 'rights' of the speaker." Instead, what was at issue was "our rights to listen and speak. We do it for ourselves." In other words, Ahmadinejad had no constitutional right to a platform—but Columbia had the constitutional right to offer it to him. True—but saying that one has the right to do something is not the same as saying that one is obliged to do it, or that it's the right thing to do. When *Jyllands-Posten* published the Muhammed cartoons, it was a brave assertion of threatened free-speech rights in the face of jihadist intimidation; Bollinger had no such justification for giving a platform to Ahmadinejad. He suggested that the Ahmadinejad speech was "in the great tradition of openness that has defined this nation for many decades now"—but (again) was issuing a speaking invitation to a dissidence-crushing dictator, rather than to one of his dissident opponents, necessarily the best possible contribution to that tradition?

One could not argue with most of what Bollinger had to say in his next few sentences:

> We need to understand the world we live in, neither neglecting its glories nor shrinking from its threats and dangers. It is consistent with the idea that one should know thine enemies, to have the intellectual and emotional courage to confront the mind of evil and to prepare ourselves to act with the right temperament. In the moment, the arguments for free speech will never seem to match the power of the arguments against, but what we must remember is that this is precisely because free speech asks us to exercise extraordinary self-restraint against the very natural but often counter-productive impulses that lead us to retreat from engagement with ideas we dislike and fear. In this lies the genius of the American idea of free speech.

Fine words—but the point that Bollinger elided so gracefully here was that some ideas are best "engaged with" in mutually respectful discourse in places like university auditoriums, while other ideas are best "engaged with" by other means, in other arenas.

Bollinger made some forceful points. He told the audience that an Iranian urban planner with a degree from Columbia was being held under house arrest in Teheran, announced that Columbia would be offering him a visiting professorship, and called on Ahmadinejad to let the man leave Iran. He informed the audience that 210 people—including two children—had been executed in Iran so far in 2007. He noted Ahmadinejad's jailing of scholars and, stirringly, cited the life story of Václav Havel as a reminder that "there are not enough prisons to prevent an entire society that wants its freedom from achieving it." He asked Ahmadinejad: "Why have women, members of the Baha'i faith, homosexuals and so many of our academic colleagues become targets of persecution in your country?" And he cited Ahmadinejad's Holocaust denial, his determination to destroy Israel, his sponsorship of terrorism, his arming of Shiite militia who are killing American soldiers in Iraq, and his defiance of international nuclear sanctions. Yet the line that made worldwide headlines, and that became the featured sound bite on TV and radio reports, was the following: "Mr. President, you exhibit all the signs of a petty and cruel dictator."

Though this statement was applauded by some—both in the auditorium and elsewhere—it was also widely condemned, often in the harshest of terms. Indeed, after the event was over, the criticism of Bollinger proved considerably more vitriolic than that of Ahmadinejad. Ignoring the litany of unspeakable crimes by Ahmadinejad's regime that Bollinger had adduced in support of his accusation, Bollinger's opponents called him "rude," "offensive," "embarrassing," "undignified," "crass," "ungracious," "way out of line," and "undiplomatic." Readers posting at the *New York Times* Web site wrote that "Bollinger has disgraced Columbia," that he had "behaved like the quintessential 'ugly American,'" that "his remarks had elements of silliness," and that he practiced "'cowboy' aggression." A *Times* reader named David Townsend called Bollinger "a bonafide racist"; another, David A. Goldfarb, complained that Bollinger "came off as an inhospitable host and as culturally insensitive," and described Bollinger's remarks as "ad hominem"—utterly ignoring Bollinger's list of Ahmadinejad's offenses. ("Hospitality," lectured Goldfarb, "is a particularly important virtue in most Muslim cultures"—as if a word like hospitality could mean anything to a man who executes gay teenagers!) Many *Times* readers went even further. Jessica Hunt wrote, "Ahmadinejad was gracious and thanked the crowd . . . even after being attacked viciously by his host." A student named Leif called Bollinger's conduct "immature" and praised Ahmadinejad for behaving "like a statesman." Mike Conrad of Washington, D.C., compared Ahmadinejad favorably with George W. Bush, describing him as "this courageous, if sometimes misguided, leader of Iran," while Luke M. Drescher equated Bollinger's "dagger language" to Bush's "Axis of Evil" speech. (Here again was another example of that newly popular trope whereby it is not the murderous conduct of Islamists but the language of their critics that is characterized in terms usually used to describe acts of violence.) One reader, comparing Ahmadinejad's Holocaust denial to American politicians' denial "that Palestinians are being massacred every day," asked: "Would [Bollinger] have had the courage to say these things to George W. Bush, Henry Kissinger, John Negroponte (all responsible for thousands of deaths), or anyone else?" And someone identifying himself as "George K." complained that "a lot of Americans are very narrow minded and only want to hear opinions that support their view of the world. Sad!" This seemed to be the bottom line in most of the criticism of Bollinger and the thumbs-up for Ahmadinejad—that whatever the Iranian leader might or might not be guilty of, to criticize him for it was to be racist, xenophobic, Islamophobic, insular, nationalistic, and America-centric. It was, in short, to violate the very spirit of multiculturalism. Conversely, to welcome Ahmadinejad was to demonstrate one's own multicultural virtue. Indeed, the more odious Ahmadinejad's crimes against humanity, the greater the virtue of those Westerners who were willing to overlook them in the name of multicultural humility and intercultural harmony.

In circumstances such as this one, the politically correct position on freedom of speech was crystal clear: the invitation to Ahmadinejad was thoroughly justified on free-speech grounds, as was anything that Ahmadinejad might choose to say in his talk, however little connection it might have to the truth; but Bollinger's opening comments were simply unacceptable, the First Amendment notwithstanding. For many of Bollinger's critics, freedom of speech took a backseat in such matters to the respect and deference owed by Americans (as citizens of the Evil Empire) to guests from the Muslim world (who are, by definition, victims of the Empire's imperialism). Thus the prevailing left-wing view was that (a) freedom of speech required that the head of one of the world's most brutal regimes be invited to speak at a major university, and (b) multicultural sensitivity required that the university's president refrain from speaking the truth about that regime's offenses in the man's presence.

In all the criticism of Bollinger's "dictator" remark, not only was the rest of his introduction lost sight of; so was Ahmadinejad's speech. It was widely reported that the audience chortled derisively at his claim that there were no homosexuals in Iran—a statement that journalists, too, plainly found amusing. But few of these media reports noted that homosexuals in Iran are, in fact, subject to the death penalty—

a grim reality that perhaps didn't fit in neatly with the desire to treat Ahmadinejad's remark as a laugh line. In any event, aside from the hilarity over this single statement by Ahmadinejad, the audience was, in large part, disturbingly respectful of the visitor from Teheran. Watching excerpts of the speech, one had the impression that many of those in attendance either didn't comprehend that they were in the presence of a despot, or were willing to overlook his despotism because they were so pleased by his antagonism to the Bush administration. Many of these Ivy League folks, one gathered, had been so expertly schooled in the multicultural thesis that the world's problems can all be traced in some way to America and the capitalist West that in their view *anyone* opposed to that lineup of villains could only be, at least in some sense and to some degree, an ally.[4]

By any objective definition, Bollinger's introductory remarks should have been considered a fine example of "speaking truth to power"—a cherished concept on the American left. Yet some of the very people who had eagerly defended Ahmadinejad's "free speech" rights now venomously condemned Bollinger for exercising his. For in the PC universe, no Muslim—not Saddam in his time or Khomeini in his, not the imams who rule European Muslim neighborhoods with an iron hand or the family patriarchs who order hit jobs on their granddaughters for reasons of "honor"—is considered to have power. Only the West has power; and even the most formidable tyrant in the Muslim world is viewed, through multicultural eyes, as a sympathetic victim who is unjustly subordinated to that power.

On November 12, 2007, Columbia University's Faculty Action Committee issued a "Statement of Concern" signed by some seventy faculty members. It read, in part, as follows:

> The president's address on the occasion of President Ahmadinejad's visit has sullied the reputation of the University with its strident tone, and has abetted a climate in which incendiary speech prevails over open debate. The president's introductory remarks were not only uncivil and bad pedagogy,

---

[4]It should be noted that a few days after Ahmadinejad was greeted respectfully at Columbia, the anti-Islamist writer David Horowitz was hounded off a stage at Emory University.

they allied the University with the Bush administration's war in Iraq, a position anathema to many in the University community.

In fact, Bollinger's remarks had not done anything of the kind. Bollinger had not mentioned Iraq; he had enumerated the facts about Ahmadinejad's regime in Iran, with a focus on the abuse of human rights and individual liberties. No one with a concern for freedom and human dignity could have found Bollinger's comments about Ahmadinejad's regime inappropriate. The committee further complained: "In the name of the University, the president has publicly taken partisan political positions concerning the politics of the Middle East in particular, without apparent expertise in this area or consultation with faculty who teach and undertake research in this area."

In other words, if Columbia University were to adopt an official position on the human rights of people living under Islamic dictatorship, that position should be formulated by the university's professors of Middle Eastern studies—who could be relied on, of course, *never* to condemn any tyranny in the name of Islam. "We believe the time has come for the faculty to reassert its commitment to academic freedom and University autonomy," wrote the Committee—even as the statement itself was a clear effort to intimidate Bollinger, and anyone who shared his concern over Iran, into either shutting up or falling into lockstep with those who saw Bush, not Ahmadinejad, as the real enemy.

In 2007 Columbia University established a new Israel Studies Department whose transparent purpose, as David Bernstein wrote, was "to deflect criticism of its extremely anti-Israel Middle East Studies Department." Yet even this venture was swathed in political correctness: the search committee for the department head included prominent anti-Israelis, and their choice turned out to be Yinon Cohen, an outspoken opponent of the Israeli Defense Forces and critic of Israel's "oppression" of Palestinians. As for Harvard—which had shed Lawrence Summers to preserve its purity—in March 2008 it played host to Khaled Abou el Fadl, a UCLA law professor who, speaking at Harvard's Divinity School, rejected the question of whether sharia was compatible with human rights, pronouncing that sharia is sharia, now and eternal, and that attempts to reconcile it with lesser, man-made value systems are irrelevant. The reaction to this statement by the mostly Muslim audience of faculty and students, wrote Hillel Stavis, "was more disturbing than the actual presentation": pretty much everybody, according to Stavis, seemed to consider it perfectly reasonable. As Andrew Bostom observed, el Fadl wanted "nothing less than for our liberal democracy to willfully impose upon itself the Ur-Fascistic totalitarianism of Sharia"; and yet el Fadl was widely considered a reformist Muslim.[5]

In the post-9/11 era, it's vital that people in the West understand Islam—and especially jihad. But these days, when courses in Islam, Arab culture, and Middle Eastern history are increasingly being funded by Muslim governments and taught by Muslims or dhimmis for whom truth takes a backseat to propaganda, the fact is that for all but a dwindling handful of maverick professors in the field, Edward Said is god, and every professor his prophet. Since 1970, the percentage of Muslim members of the Middle East Studies Association (MESA) has risen from about three to about seventy. If, for these scholars, religious identity didn't affect the objectivity and veracity of their scholarship, this fact would make no difference; alas, it has proven revolutionary—for, according to Hugh Fitzgerald, "MESA has over the past two decades slowly but surely been taken over by apologists for Islam." Fitzgerald tells of a Harvard student who took a course in Islam in which the final exam was graded by Muslims; when he received a poorer grade on the exam than he deserved, it emerged that he'd been penalized for using phrases like "as Muslims believe" or "Muslims believe that . . . ," thereby implying that Muslim beliefs were not matters of historical fact. James R. Russell, a professor of Armenian Studies at Harvard, has noted that at Columbia, where he once worked, objective and scholarly Middle Eastern Studies have been gradually replaced by a propaganda operation that is ideologically driven and indifferent to facts.

Muslim Student Associations (MSA's) have become a significant feature of student life on many campuses, and play a major role in enforcing dhimmitude. At the University of Wisconsin at Milwaukee (UWM), author Walid Shoebat, a Muslim apostate, was scheduled to give a talk in December 2007 entitled "Why I Left Jihad." In a mass e-mail describing Shoebat as "a well-known Hate-Mongerer," that uni-

---

[5]El Fadl's speech at Harvard, by the way, came only days after the university gym established women-only hours so that Muslim women could work out without men being present—a kind of arrangement that has been common for years at gyms and swimming pools in Europe.

versity's Muslim Student Association reported that it was "dealing with the administration to demand the event be cancelled." A letter from the presidents of the MSA and the Palestinian Student Association (PSA) to UWM's administration called Shoebat "a well known addict of hate-speech" who "incit[ed] Americans with fear of Muslims and Arabs, associating them with terrorism." (Here, once again, we see the absurd conceit that it is not terrorists but their opponents who cause Americans to associate Islam with terrorism.) "The ramifications of allowing such hate-mongers to spread hate," insisted the MSA/PSA letter, "has been clearly driven [sic] in the physical attacks on Muslims, Arabs, or anyone with Middle-Eastern appearance following the events of September 11th. The Muslims at UWM feel that their safety will be in danger if the above mentioned event takes place on the UWM campus." This assertion—that free speech by critics of Islam will result in physical attacks on Muslims—is now routine in such circumstances, even though it turns on its head the contemporary reality in the Western world that in violent encounters between Muslims and non-Muslims it is overwhelmingly the non-Muslims who are the victims, and that when there is violence attendant upon public events involving critics of Islam, the perpetrators are nearly always Muslims. "We take such an event as a direct attack on us," wrote the presidents of the two Muslim organizations in what certainly appeared to be a threat that their members might well consider it within their rights to "attack" *back* if their demands were not met.

In May 2008, Jonathan Constantine Movroydis and Reut R. Cohen reported on a public event at which a leader of the Muslim Student Union at the University of California at Irvine ranted fiercely against America and Jews and praised Hamas and Hezbollah. At the event, belligerent MSU members were physically aggressive toward their ideological opponents and assaulted a man who tried to film the proceedings. Campus police were useless, standing idly by as the intimidation went on, and university administrators were even worse, seeking not to curb MSU's aggression but to do its bidding by trying to keep the proceedings from being filmed—a clear "application of Sharia law," as Movroydis and Cohen put it, in a place "where the Bill of Rights is applicable." A few months later the same university's history department sponsored a talk by a member of the Muslim Brotherhood, presenting him as a spokesman for "a new generation" of Muslims who were "struggling for democracy." (Yes, the kind of democracy in which exactly one election is permitted—just enough to sweep Islamists into power.)

In addition to targeting universities, the cultural jihadists—aware that the best way to change a society is through its children—have gone after elementary and secondary schools. Among those who carry out this work are Muslim "consultants" in the textbook industry, who are partly responsible for the multicultural drivel that passes for objective information about Islam. One of the more widely used history textbooks in American middle schools, for example, is entitled *History Alive! The Medieval World and Beyond*, in which one can find the following definition of jihad: "The word *jihad* means 'to strive.' Jihad represents the human struggle to overcome difficulties and do things that would be pleasing to God. Muslims strive to respond positively to personal difficulties as well as worldly challenges. For instance, they might work to become better people, reform society, or correct injustice."

After three paragraphs about jihad being "the fight against evil within oneself," the book acknowledges that "sometimes . . . jihad becomes a physical struggle. . . . Early Muslims considered their efforts to protect their territory and extend their rule over other regions to be a form of jihad. However, the Qur'an forbade Muslims to force others to convert to Islam. So, non-Muslims who came under Muslim rule were allowed to practice their faiths." There is no mention of dhimmitude. The book's account of sharia law is equally dishonest: "Shari'ah, or Islamic law, helps Muslims live by the teachings of the Qur'an. It includes practices of daily life as well as the duty to respect others."

Though the book is about the medieval world, it includes much more (whitewashed) detail about Islam than about Christianity or Judaism, and recommendations issued by the publisher urge that students be taught about Muslim "belief and practices"and about Muhammed's life. Bert Bower, founder of the Teachers' Curriculum Institute, the book's publisher, described it as a response to the need for "multicultural" teaching. But in Scottsdale, Arizona, parents who became aware of the book's contents organized to keep it out of the schools; and William J. Bennetta of the Textbook League, who described the book as "relentlessly presenting Muslim religious tales and religious beliefs as matters of historical fact," argued that it amounted to nothing less than "indoctrination in Islam."

Other ways in which schools are introducing aspects of sharia to placate Muslims range from excusing girls from sports and school trips to omitting potentially "offensive" classics from literature classes to avoiding or reinterpreting certain historical events (such as the Crusades and Holocaust) that might give offense to removing pork items from cafeteria menus. (Needless to say, no schools are eliminating beef from cafeteria menus to avoid insulting Hindus.) In 2004, two Dutch schoolboys were ordered to remove Dutch flag patches from their backpacks because Moroccan students might consider them "provocative," and two Swedish schoolgirls were sent home "for wearing sweaters showing a tiny Swedish flag." More recently, a principal in Sweden ordered pupils not to pose for class photos wearing national team shirts displaying the Swedish flag, because it might be viewed as "xenophobic."[6] In 2008, just days before it was reported in the *Daily Telegraph* that polygamy was now legal in Britain (a subject to which I shall return), it was announced that the Department for Children, Schools and Families had decided to allow a separate, presumably Muslim-dominated inspectorate for religious schools in Britain; though the inspectorate's purpose was to ensure that children are being educated properly, the new arrangement seemed designed, rather, to ensure a more hands-off government attitude toward institutions that are preparing pupils not to be loyal citizens of a free country but obedient devotees of sharia. Fortunately, a complaint by the official school inspectorate, Ofsted (Office for Standards in Education), resulted in the cancellation of this plan some months later.

In April 2008, Tyler Hurd, a student at St. Cloud State University in Minnesota, had to leave a teacher-training program at a high school because of a Muslim student's threats to harm his dog. (The dog is a "service dog" who protects Hurd when he has seizures.) School authorities called the incident a "misunderstanding" and a product of "miscommunication" (on the contrary, the Muslim student appears to have communicated his sentiments quite clearly), emphasized that the threat was not made directly to Hurd (as if that mattered), and asserted

---

[6]Such dhimmification doesn't just affect schoolchildren: the soccer club Inter Milan recently agreed to remove the distinctive red cross from its team jerseys to avoid offending Muslims, and a British garbageman was ordered to stop wearing a garment featuring Saint George's cross (from the English flag) because it was considered "racist." He was black.

that "it is important to respect different cultures." Apparently no action was taken against the Muslim student.

Later the same year, the principal of Friendswood Junior High School near Houston invited two women from CAIR to subject students to an "Islamic Awareness" presentation—which, according to reports, was actually more of an indoctrination in Muslim belief—even though he had been told by his superintendent not to do so. And in a June 2008 article for the *San Francisco Chronicle*, Cinnamon Stillwell provided several examples of how "Islamists have taken . . . the 'soft jihad' into America's classrooms." Under cover of "Arabic instruction," public schools and taxpayer-funded private and charter schools were "implement[ing] a religious curriculum." One article cited by Stillwell, from the local New Hampshire press, described a May 2007 middle-school project:

> For one night, on May 9, the quaint colonial town of Amherst, New Hampshire, was transformed into a Saudi Arabian Bedouin tent community, with the help of 80 seventh-graders at the Amherst Middle School. . . . More than 250 guests arrived at the open tent and were welcomed with an Arabic greeting of "Marhaba" by students at a Saudi customs desk.
>
> During the check-in, guests selected a traditional Arabic name for their name badge and completed an actual Saudi customs form, which warned in bold letters "Death for Drug Trafficking" at the top. . . .
>
> Flowing fabrics hung from the ceiling separated the family and men-only dining sections. . . . Only the seventh-grade boys were allowed to host the food stations and the Arabic dancing, as the traditions of Saudi Arabia at this time prevent women from participating in these public roles. . . . Seventh-grade girls hosted the hijab and veil stations, where other female guests learned how to wear the required head covering and veils. . . .

This bizarre exercise might have been admirable if it had been part of an effort to illuminate for young people and their parents the extent of the limitations placed on individual freedom, especially that of women, in Saudi Arabia and elsewhere in the Islamic world. But this was, of course, not the intention; rather, as the article explained, "the 'open tent' was created to encourage participants to reach out and learn from people around the world, and to promote curiosity and cultural understanding."

There is reason to believe that for every such incident that receives more than local attention, there are many others that are never heard about beyond the small communities in which they take place.

II

Selling Out the Sodomites

omen, Christians, Jews, Hindus, atheists: all of them stand at least a chance of surviving in a Muslim polity if they submit to Muslim authority, and if they live according to the rules set down for those of their station under sharia law. But for individuals who are known to be gay, no compromise is possible.

After all, the works called the hadith (or sayings of Muhammed), whose guidance devout Muslims still consider binding, say of homosexual acts: "Kill the one that is doing it and also kill the one that it is being done to." One school of sharia law prescribes beating as punishment for a single homosexual act and death for recidivists; another school dictates one hundred lashes for a bachelor guilty of such activity and death for a married man; a third school demands the death penalty, period. Homosexuality is punishable by death in Iran, Saudi Arabia, Sudan, Yemen, and Mauritania, and by severe physical punishment in several other Muslim countries; the United Arab Emirates, which is often described as moderate or even liberal, imprison homosexuals for up to fourteen years. In 1998, the Taliban executed two young men for committing homosexual acts by dropping a wall on them; in 2001, Saudi Arabia sentenced nine men to prison terms and to over two thousand lashes apiece for the same offense. In Iran, at least several hundred, and more likely several thousand, people have been executed for homosexuality since the Ayatollah Khomeini took power in 1980; in May 2008, the president of Gambia, Yahya Jammeh, announced plans to kill every homosexual in the country.

Many homosexuals in Islamic countries—in fact, probably the great majority—are never arrested or arraigned but are instead beaten, disowned, and/or "executed" by their families while sympathetic authorities look the other way.

While there are at least some prominent Muslims in the West, furthermore, who have publicly criticized at least some of the injustices visited upon women in Islamic societies, few if any persons of influence in Western Muslim communities have spoken up for the rights of gay people. Iqbal Sacranie, the secretary-general of the Muslim Council of Britain who was knighted in 2005 because Tony Blair reportedly considered him an exemplary "moderate Muslim," told the BBC in January 2006 that homosexuality is quite simply "not acceptable"; indeed, it is difficult to find a Muslim cleric anywhere in the West who is so "moderate" that he will actually dissent from the judgment that gays deserve, at the very least, to be thrashed within an inch of their lives. On no issue, indeed, are Muslims more nearly unanimous in their negativity. "After more than twenty-five years in the immigration field," Danish cultural psychologist Kirsten Damgaard has written, "the Muslim immigrants I have personally met who find homosexuality acceptable can be counted on one hand." In 2002, a Muslim leader in Australia called for the establishment in that country of a sharia court that would empower Muslims to execute homosexuals by stoning; in the Netherlands, many gays first became aware that their tender concern for their Muslim countrymen was not reciprocated in May 2001, when a Dutch-Moroccan imam interviewed on television about Muslim gay-bashings compared homosexuality to an infectious disease. One consequence of Muslim attitudes toward homosexuality is a staggeringly high level of closetedness in Western Muslim communities. In 2006, when someone in Norway finally decided to organize a long-overdue discussion about homosexuality and Islam, not one openly gay Muslim could be found in the entire country to participate in the discussion. (Thanks to a recently released documentary by a gay ex-Muslim living in Norway, there are now several.)

All these facts about Islam and homosexuality are well established and incontrovertible. Yet liberals in the West, including most gay-rights activists, have been almost uniformly silent about them. Gay leaders who have spent their careers replying to the anti-gay rhetoric of people like Jerry Falwell, Pat Robertson, and the last couple of popes have responded with silence to prominent Muslims whose comments about homosexuality make Robertson look like a model of tolerance and charity. Reflecting on the hanging by Iran of two gay teenagers in 2005, Rob Anderson of the *New Republic* observed that "when it comes to the Muslim world, gay and lesbian leaders are evidently uncomfortable talking in moral absolutes. But if this is not absolute evil, then what is?" In a way, this silence isn't surprising. There has long been a willingness among gay activists to subordinate the rights of gay people to supposedly progressive goals, including "solidarity" with groups that, by and large, oppose gay rights. Even to mention the high levels of hostility to gay people in black neighborhoods, for example, has long been considered off-limits: the African-American community, by virtue of its status as an oppressed minority group, is to be understood as being in solidarity with the gay community—period. This is a ridiculous fiction. Yet gay activists are now skirting the even graver issue of Islamic attitudes toward gay people in precisely the same way. While every gay person in America and Europe knows about the Christian right's attitudes toward homosexuality, many are under the dangerous illusion that Muslims are gay people's friends and allies—that they have understanding and sympathy for the situation of gay people because they, too, are an "oppressed minority." Gay activists, far from attempting to correct this untruth, have been instrumental in spreading it.

Indeed, many of these activists have for years aligned themselves with the Palestinian cause. Never mind that gay Palestinians live in fear of arrest, detention without trial, torture, and execution at the hands of Palestinian police and security services; never mind the possibility of "honor killing" by vengeful family members and beatings and murder at the hands of Hamas, Fatah, and unaffiliated vigilante mobs. In Israel, gay Palestinians can find gay-rights groups that will help them and a government that will grant them asylum. As British gay activist Peter Tatchell has pointed out, the very name of a group like Queers Undermining Israeli Terrorism (QUIT)—whose members, as the writer Richard J. Rosendall has aptly observed, are "ever eager to show their solidarity with Palestinians who despise them"—is grotesque. Equally grotesque is that the International Gay and Lesbian Human Rights Commission

(IGLHRC), which is supposed to be a serious organization, responded to QUIT's anti-Israel instigations by boycotting a 2006 gay conference in Jerusalem. "Given IGLHRC's stated commitment to promoting human rights everywhere," Rosendall noted at the time, "you might suppose that they have also boycotted notoriously oppressive countries like China and Cuba. You would be wrong." Indeed, IGLHRC was represented at the 1995 women's conference in Beijing, and at a "women's solidarity meeting" in Havana in 1998. "So totalitarian capitals like Havana and Beijing are fine," Rosendall commented, "but the sole democracy in the Middle East, which happens to be the place to which gay Arabs in the region flee, is the target of a 'queer' boycott effort."

Every bit as reprehensible as the unwillingness of many gay-rights leaders and leftist allies to criticize Muslim attitudes toward homosexuality is the fact that organizations and individuals that have spoken up about this subject have, on this account, become the targets of criticism from those same quarters. In February 2006, for example, the Gay and Lesbian Humanist Association (GALHA) in Britain ran an article in its official magazine criticizing Islam for its anti-gay doctrine, which the article described as "barmy" (i.e., crazy). Every word of the article, which was written by GALHA's secretary, George Broadhead, was demonstrably true; yet gay and leftist groups piled on, calling it "racist." According to the *Guardian*, "Peter Herbert, chairman of the London-wide Race Hate Crime Forum, said he would be writing to the Crown Prosecution Service about the remarks and would 'vigorously pursue' a prosecution of the editor or writers who had made the 'racist and degrading' comments." The uproar was so intense that GALHA caved, issuing an apology and dismissing the magazine's editor and deputy editor. As one observer commented: "Muslims appear completely free to advocate the killing of homosexuals according to Sharia, but gays cannot even utter the word 'barmy' without the threat of prosecution under 'hate speech' laws."

The response to GALHA's article by author Ghassan Makarem proved a good example of the approved PC posture on such matters. Accusing GALHA of having "chosen to shift the struggle [against anti-gay oppression] into a racist argument against Islam," Makarem claimed that "repression of gays and lesbians does exist in Muslim countries, but the Islamic traditions advocated by the majority of the ruling elites are no different than those of the TV evangelist Pat Robertson or the pope."

To equate the Islamic torture and execution of gays with even the most hurtful anti-gay pronouncements by Protestant or Catholic leaders is, of course, outrageous; but such rhetoric has become a familiar weapon in the arsenal of the apologists for jihad. "It is true that many Muslims are homophobic," wrote Makarem. "So are many Catholics, Protestants, Jews, and atheists." With equal veracity, someone in the 1930s could have written: "It's true that many Germans are anti-Semitic. So are many Americans, Englishmen, Canadians, and Australians."

Another now-common tactic is the attribution of all prejudices by Muslims to Western influence. Hence Makarem maintained that "the rhetoric of family values was first introduced in the Levant and Egypt by missionaries from the United States and Europe." Are Christian missionaries also responsible for the fact that Islamic "family values" include the right of men to have up to four wives, to rape and beat them at whim, and to commit an "honor killing" if one of them makes the mistake of being raped? Makarem's argument was easily summed up: antigay sentiments, to the extent that they do exist among Muslims, are (a) no more extreme than anti-gay sentiments among other religious groups and (b) the product of Western imperialism. Both assertions were not only grotesquely false; they were a betrayal of the thousands who have been arrested, tortured, and executed in the Muslim world simply for being gay—and of the many more who have found refuge in the West, or in Israel, from the inhuman policies of their Muslim homelands.

Yet Makarem and his ilk can't admit such facts; their multicultural ideology forbids it. For them, the capitalist United States is the number-one enemy, and Israel is its number-one puppet; and since jihadist Islam is the only potent force on the international stage today that has set itself squarely against those villains, it must be viewed as an ally by all good leftists—including gay people. Never mind that Islamists, wherever they've gained power, have set about arresting, torturing, and executing gay people; never mind that Israel is the one country in the region where gay Muslims can seek refuge. All that matters is the need to resolutely oppose and ultimately bring down the United States. Thus, while gay activists and their PC allies tend to suppress or water down the truth about the abuse and execution of gays in the Muslim world, they exaggerate out of all proportion the victimization of Muslims in the West. Responding to Irshad Manji's book *The Trouble with Islam Today*, which bravely criticizes Muslim homophobia (among much else), the *Palestine Solidarity Review* thundered: "Is she blind to the fact that thousands of Muslims in the United States are being intimidated into silence by deportations, detentions, SEVIS [Student and Exchange Visitor Information System] registration, racist attacks on the street, and state repression?"

Though such rhetoric turns reality on its head, it is given credibility by groups like the Council for American Islamic Relations, which has spread wildly inflated statistics on hate crimes against Muslims in America—statistics that the credulous media have dutifully passed on to the public. Daniel Pipes and Sharon Chadha have observed that CAIR counts "any incident, no matter how trivial, subjective or unsubstantiated," as a hate crime. David Skinner noted that when a Muslim student at the University of Houston "saw flyers and posters with false and degrading statements about the Qur'an and the prophet Muhammed," that was considered a hate crime by CAIR; when a student at Roger Williams College wrote that "a true Muslim is taught to slay infidels," that, too, was a hate crime. Furthermore, as Pipes and Chadra point out, "any reluctance to accommodate Muslim women wearing a headscarf or veil was tallied as a bias incident, even in the case of genuine quandaries (such as veiled athletes or drivers applying for their licenses)." In 2007, when a copy of the Koran was left on the steps of the Islamic Center in Clarksville, Tennessee, with two strips of bacon placed between its pages, the words "Mohammed pedophile" scrawled on its cover, and an "expletive" written inside, it was investigated as a hate crime—even though nothing remotely resembling a crime (except under sharia) had taken place.

CAIR claims that the number of anti-Muslim "hate crimes" in the United States has risen dramatically since 9/11, from "42 cases in 2002, to 93 cases in 2003, to 141 in 2004"; yet even if every one of these reported incidents were actually a legitimate "hate crime," that number—for a country of 300 million people—would have to be regarded as amazingly low, and hailed as a stirring tribute to American tolerance. Certainly 141 anti-Muslim "hate crimes" is nothing compared to the staggering amount of genuinely abusive conduct—including such firmly institutionalized and Koran-sanctioned activities as wife-beating, family rape, and "honor killing"—that occurs daily within Muslim communities in the West, or the number of gay-bashings committed by young Muslim men every year in the cities of Europe.

In 2004, a gay man named Nathan C. Walker published online an article entitled "American Islam and Queer Solidarity." It provides a near-perfect example of the attitudes of gay people who have been persuaded to see their relationship with Islam exclusively through the prism of PC ideas about capitalist oppression and victim-group solidarity.

"I have faced a great deal of systemic discrimination," Walker wrote, "because of my sexuality—discrimination that I relate to the American Muslim experience." But what kind of discrimination have Muslims endured in the United States that can be compared to that experienced by gays? For a clear illustration of the difference between the treatment of gays and Muslims in the United States in the immediate aftermath of 9/11, just look at the conduct of the nation's commander in chief. One of the first things George W. Bush did after the destruction of the World Trade Center by Muslims acting in the name of their prophet was to rush to a mosque and praise Islam as a Religion of Peace. Thereafter, Bush frequently stood alongside Muslim leaders at public events and repeated this misrepresentation. When has he ever shared a stage with gay-rights leaders and praised gay Americans in equivalent terms? Never. Since 9/11, the major institutions of American society—its companies, churches, schools, and so forth—have striven to make it clear that they don't wish (as the saying goes) to "punish all Muslims for the acts of a few"; even as the PC left has proclaimed its solidarity with Muslims as a victim group, many on the Christian Right have embraced Muslims as fellow "people of faith."

Implicit in Walker's piece was the assumption that anything negative about Islam is a "myth." Addressing Muslims, he said: "I am called to educate you about the myths of homosexuality, just as you are called to educate me about the myths of Islam." The possibility that some "myths of Islam" might not actually be myths apparently didn't occur to him. "I call out to 21st century American Muslims," Walker wrote, "to be in solidarity with groups they might initially reject, such as the Queer community. . . . As marginalized groups, we must unite and center our efforts to emancipate society from its bigotry—to free the American who is a slave to ignorance." The notion that a group in which women are considered inferior and homosexuality punished by whipping or execution could emancipate Americans from bigotry is so disconnected from reality as to leave one speechless. To be sure, Walker acknowledged that Muslims hate gays; but he couldn't bring himself to attribute this hatred to Muslims themselves, or to Islam. (He seemed entirely ignorant of what the Koran and hadith say about homosexuality.) "You are not the one oppressing me," he insisted, addressing Muslims. "You are simply oppressed by ignorance." No, Mr. Walker, the ignorance is all yours. Thus do softheaded multiculturalists turn hatred into solidarity and the oppressor into the oppressed.

In May 2004, members of two British gay-rights groups, OutRage! and Queer Youth Alliance (QYA), took part in a London demonstration for Palestinian rights in which they carried signs reading "Israel: stop persecuting Palestine! Palestine: stop persecuting queers!" Even the politically correct attempt to draw a moral equivalence between Israel's treatment of Palestinians and Palestinians' treatment of gay people didn't mollify their fellow protesters: according to an OutRage! press release, members of the two gay groups found themselves "surrounded by an angry, screaming mob of Islamic fundamentalists, Anglican clergy, members of the Socialist Workers Party, the Stop the War coalition, and officials from the protest organizers, the Palestine Solidarity Campaign (PSC)," who attacked them as "'racists,' 'Zionists,' 'CIA and MI5 agents,' 'supporters of the Sharon government,' and accused the gays of 'dividing the Free Palestine movement.'" In response to this disgraceful event, a number of people on the gay left swung into action—by smearing OutRage! and QYA and claiming that Palestinian authorities were not opposed to homosexuality but were only concerned because many gay Palestinians are "collaborators" with Israel. The truth behind this charge is that gay Palestinians, by the mere act of accepting safe haven in Israel from the violent hatred of their fellow Palestinians, become "collaborators" in the eyes of other Palestinians; for gay activists to echo this accusation is to place solidarity with their ideological "comrades" above sympathy for fellow gays whom those "comrades" beat up and kill.

Such twisted solidarity was on display in June 2008 when the British gay Web site *Pink News* ran a piece by an anonymous writer who'd visited Iran and wanted to dispel the notion that it was a dangerous travel destination for gays; on the contrary, he insisted, the atmosphere was "so carefree and liberal . . . that I frequently forgot I was in Iran." Readers who, in their posted comments, took issue with this outrageous whitewashing of a regime that executes gay people were quickly put in their place by a phalanx of multiculturalists: one lectured them that the West's way is not "the only right way" and that Iran, as a sovereign nation, "has the right to conduct a trial in the way that it sees fit," and another witheringly dismissed the argument that "human rights are universal and inviolable" as a "schtick" that essentially translates into "screw the other culture." Few manifestations of modern-day dhimmi-tude are more grotesque and dispiriting than the spectacle of gays defending the execution of gays in the name of multicultural "respect."

In their eagerness to win Muslim votes, some politicians who were once supporters of gay rights have undergone a sea change. In July 2004, for example, then London mayor Ken Livingstone gave a hearty welcome to Yusuf al-Qaradawi, head of the European Council for Fatwa and Research, at a press conference. When Peter Tatchell and various journalists criticized the mayor for sharing a stage with Qaradawi, and quoted some of Qaradawi's less than enlightened views on women's rights, suicide bombing, and gay rights, Livingstone threw himself wholeheartedly into a defense of Qaradawi—and attacks on his critics. Livingstone wasn't alone: his assault on those who cared about gay rights (and human rights generally) was widely echoed. In a letter to the *Guardian*, Tatchell noted that not only the mayor but also "several leading black and Muslim organizations are willing to fete Dr. Qaradawi. Instead of attacking his views, they prefer to attack OutRage! over our defence of Jewish people, women and gay Muslims." As if all this weren't bizarre enough, gay Muslims joined in the attack on their own defenders. One participant in the discussion forum of a gay Muslim Web site referred to "the disgusting racism unleashed by Outrage's anti-Qaradawi campaign"; another wrote that "Outrage's campaign against Qaradawi is offensive. They are simply jumping on the anti-Muslim bandwagon. . . . As a gay Muslim, Outrage doesn't speak for me and a host of other people. . . . If Qaradawi comes to London again and Outrage and the other racists form a campaign against him, I will be out there standing against them and I will defend him." For at least some gay Muslims, then, the sense of solidarity with fellow Muslims who would execute them for being gay vanquished any sense of solidarity with fellow gay people who were standing up for their rights.

To emphasize the solidarity of his support for Qaradawi, Livingstone invited him back to London in October 2004 and refused to meet with what Tatchell described as "a coalition of Muslim, Jewish, Sikh, gay, student and women's groups" who opposed the Islamic scholar. Tatchell noted that "the Mayor justifies hosting Qaradawi on the grounds that he wants a dialogue with Muslims. But why is Ken having a dialogue with a reactionary Muslim leader? Why isn't he meeting liberal Muslims who believe in human rights?" In a letter to the *Guardian*, Tatchell wrote: "We fear for the future when sections of liberal and left opinion jettison human rights to side with the fundamentalist wing of Islam against its victims." Yet the future was already here. Commenting on Tatchell's letter, American expatriate Scott Burgess explained: "They're siding with the Islamofascists because the Islamofascists are *enemies of America*, and therefore *good*, no matter what their other beliefs and actions.... The willingness of these people to ally themselves with those who want homosexuals and women severely punished and subjugated is clear evidence of the depth of the anti-authoritarian (anti-US) psychosis at work."

Livingstone wasn't finished defending Qaradawi. In January 2005 he issued a remarkable twenty-four-page document entitled *Why the Mayor of London Will Maintain Dialogues with All of London's Faiths and Communities*. The title was deceptive, for the document's overriding purpose was to whitewash Qaradawi, who was described throughout with such adjectives as "courageous," "moderate," and "progressive," while his critics were unconscionably smeared. For example, the Middle East Media Research Institute (MEMRI), which has done an invaluable job of videotaping and translating incendiary programming from Arab-language media such as Al-Jazeera, was dismissed in Livingstone's document as engaged in practices "reminiscent of the various anti-Semitic conspiracy theories." (As it happens, it is MEMRI that has helped to expose the Arab media's dissemination of "anti-Semitic conspiracy theories.") The statement that Qaradawi seeks the establishment of Islamic law in Europe—a claim amply supported by his own published theological commentaries—was dismissed by Livingstone's document as a "conspiracy theory [taken] to laughable lengths." Livingstone also tarred the Gay and Lesbian Humanist Association with having "published a sympathetic obituary of the racist and anti-Muslim Dutch politician Pim Fortuyn." Thus did Livingstone make it clear which side he was on in the struggle between the Qaradawis of the world, who would destroy gays in the name of Islam, and the heirs of the gay liberal Fortuyn, who seek to preserve human rights in an increasingly Islamized West.

Livingstone's document about Qaradawi is a propaganda classic, making use of highly selective quotation, outright misrepresentation, and a deliberate obscuring of basic facts about Islamic belief to support the argument that Qaradawi is "progressive." In order to come to this conclusion, Livingstone was obliged to ignore a mountain of evidence to the contrary, much of it contained in Qaradawi's book *The Lawful and the Prohibited in Islam*, in which he spells out his opinions about homosexuality every bit as clearly as Hitler spelled out his view of Jews in *Mein Kampf*. Describing homosexuality as a "perverted act" that "is a reversal of the natural order, a corruption of man's sexuality, and a crime against the rights of females," Qaradawi writes that "the spread of this depraved practice in a society disrupts its natural life pattern and makes those who practice it slaves to their lusts, depriving them of decent taste, decent morals, and a decent manner of living." After telling the story of Lot, Qaradawi says that

> the jurists of Islam have held differing opinions concerning the punishment for this abominable practice. Should it be the same as the punishment for fornication, or should both the active and passive participants be put to death? While such punishments may seem cruel, they have been suggested to maintain the purity of the Islamic society and to keep it clean of perverted elements.

This was the man for whose sake Livingstone lied about MEMRI, smeared the name of Pim Fortuyn, and accused Peter Tatchell of being part of "a wave of Islamophobia." Unsurprisingly, most of the "respectable" British media helped Livingstone along by passing along his lies and covering up the facts about Qaradawi.[7]

---

[7]In early 2008, to its credit, the British government actually denied Qaradawi a visa to enter Britain for medical treatment. It was ironic that a man who had spent his life defending a primitive ideology that prevented the Islamic world's modernization was obliged to seek entry into Britain to receive modern medical care. Equally ironic was a *Guardian* essay by Inayat Bunglawala of the Muslim Council of Britain, who condemned the government's action as a violation of Qaradawi's freedom of speech—as if freedom of speech had anything to do with a democratic government's power to deny entry to foreign nationals who are declared enemies of its democracy. Bunglawala, who had praised Osama bin Laden, Sheikh Omar Abdel-Rahman, and the late Hamas leader Ahmed Yassin, had the audacity to write: "We should be prepared to defend what are surely some rather important principles. Especially if we believe that they are universal ones that we would like to see spread across the world." He was, of course, far from the first sharia supporter to appeal to Westerners' love of freedom as part of an effort to destroy it.

Livingstone was far from alone in attacking Tatchell. In August 2008, the British journalist Johann Hari, who is a gay socialist, condemned Bob Pitt's Web site *Islamophobia Watch* for "responding to every criticism" by Tatchell "of the Islamic fundamentalists who incite and perform the murder of gay people by calling him a bigot and even 'pro-Nazi.'" In response to a gay activist who asked if "it is Islamic for gay people to resist sharia law, a system that demands we should be lashed or stoned," a contributor to *Islamophobia Watch* replied that "it's not homosexuality as such that's an offense but the sexual act itself"— as if this mitigated the outrage, and as if this weren't just the kind of distinction that self-declared liberals and liberals like those at *Islamophobia Watch* would never accept from a conservative Christian.

One day in April 2005, Chris Crain, who was then the editor of the *Washington Blade*, one of America's leading gay newspapers, was walking hand in hand with his boyfriend in central Amsterdam when a young Moroccan man spit in his face. Crain stopped and asked him why. The man, who was with a friend, muttered: "Fucking fags." Suddenly, wrote Crain, "the two somehow turned into seven—and five of them were ganging up on me. . . . It seemed like every direction I turned, I got another punch to the face." Fortunately, when Crain's boyfriend came to his defense, the men fled. Crain's published account of the incident drew international attention. That May, Anthony Browne reported in the London *Times* that "the Amsterdam Tourist Board has issued a warning to gay visitors to be careful in the city. In the first country to legalise homosexual marriage, gays are increasingly fearful of holding hands in public. Some have been chased out of their houses and middle-class gays are moving to rural areas for safety." Browne quoted Crain as saying: "I didn't appreciate the depth of hostility between different groups there." (Note that even Crain, the victim of the attack, felt obliged to speak in politically correct terms of "hostility between different groups," as if gangs of gays in Amsterdam were running around beating up Muslims.) Browne told about Paul Buckley, a bartender who worked on the popular gay street Reguliersdwarstraat, who had been "chased down the Straat by a Moroccan youth shouting *flicker*—Dutch for 'faggot'—at him." For anyone familiar with that street, the idea of such a thing happening there is stunning—like a KKK member screaming the "N" word while chasing a black man down 125th Street in Harlem.

Even gay political groups in the Netherlands—which are every bit as politically correct as one would imagine—felt compelled to admit that Dutch gays had a Muslim problem. "In the last three or four years, we've seen an increase in gay people reporting incidents [of aggression against them] by members of minority groups," a spokesman for Amsterdam's Gay and Lesbian Switchboard told Browne. COC Nederland, the major Dutch gay rights organization, admitted that tolerance in Amsterdam was "slipping away like sand through the fingers." COC's Rene Soeren said: "The feeling of insecurity in Amsterdam is rising." He added: "This is a new phenomenon. . . . The group that causes the problem is more dominant in the center of town than twenty years ago—there is a struggle for public space. The gay middle class is leaving Amsterdam and living in smaller towns." (Note that Soeren, like Crain, chose to say "the group" instead of actually naming the group.) Like Livingstone, Soeren felt obliged to put down Fortuyn: "The things Fortuyn mentioned were all true and need to be mentioned, but he dealt with them in an offensive way." How? By saying "Muslims" instead of "the group"?

For his part, Scott Long, director of the Lesbian, Gay, Bisexual and Transgendered program at Human Rights Watch, served up a classic bit of multicultural blame-shifting, telling Browne that "[g]ays often become the victims of this [i.e., physical assaults] when immigrants retaliate for the inequalities they have to suffer." In other words, everything "they" do is understandable retaliation for what "we" have done to them. Crain, to his credit, rejected this analysis, saying that "Long's 'blame the society' political correctness is a distraction from the very real cultural clashes happening in Holland and elsewhere." But even to speak of "cultural clashes" was also a distraction, a euphemism; for what's happening in the West is not a "cultural clash" but a cultural assault. This wasn't the first time, by the way, that Scott Long had whitewashed Muslim homophobia: Makarem, in his *Socialist Review* article, mentioned the 2001 mass arrest and torture of gay men in Egypt, and quoted Long as insisting, absurdly, that "few if any provisions in Egyptian law dealing with sexual crimes are rooted in either *sharia* or custom." Though Long's job at Human Rights Watch was presumably to disseminate news of human-rights violations, he seemed to have decided that when those violations were committed by Muslims, it was his job to seek to excuse them or to shift responsibility for them.

Conditions for gay people in Amsterdam have continued to worsen. In November 2007, the Web site of *Der Spiegel* ran a story about the rising number of attacks on gays in that city; yet civic authorities continued to pretend not to understand the motivation for such attacks. *Der Spiegel* reported, for example, that Amsterdam mayor Job Cohen had just "commissioned the University of Amsterdam to conduct a study on the motives behind the hate crimes." As one commenter at the *Dhimmi Watch* Web site pointed out, "While they're at it, they might just as well commission studies to determine why Moroccans target the city's women, and why they target the city's Jews, and why they target the city's police, and why. . . ." According to *Der Spiegel*'s article, the Dutch researchers believed that the gay-bashers, many of whom were of Moroccan origin, "felt stigmatized by society and responded by attacking people they felt were lower on the social ladder"—in other words, the Scott Long argument. "Another working theory," reported *Der Spiegel*, "is that the attackers may be struggling with their own sexual identity." Not once did *Der Spiegel*'s article mention Islam.

On April 30, 2008, in an incident that appears not to have been reported in the United States until it came to the attention of blogger B. Daniel Blatt, an Amsterdam fashion show intended to promote tolerance of gay people was disrupted in an alarming way. Ten young Muslim men dragged nineteen-year-old model Mike du Pree down from the catwalk, which was set up in the middle of a busy downtown street, and beat him severely, breaking his nose. Though there was a large crowd of spectators—it was Queen's Day, always the busiest day in any Dutch city—only one person, a friend of du Pree's, came to his defense. The organizer of the event, Jennifer Delano, told me that du Pree was glad he had been attacked in such a public fashion: now, at least, he said, "someone listens to me" when he talks about anti-gay violence.

That same month, it was reported that owing to "the huge spike in gay bashing" since the year 2000, Dutch gays had been "flocking to the right-wing political parties"—the parties, that is, which are stronger on immigration, integration, and Islam. Noting that "several gay people" had been "attacked simultaneously in broad daylight in different parts of Amsterdam" on Gay Pride Day 2007, the same report concluded that "groups of young Muslim juveniles now prey on gays, no matter where or at what time."

In 2005, *TNR Online* ran a piece by Rob Anderson entitled "How

America's Gay Rights Establishment Is Failing Gay Iranians." Gay activists, noted Anderson, had failed to join the street protests in New York when Iranian president Mahmoud Ahmadinejad visited the UN in May of that year. "When it comes to the oppression of gays and lesbians in Muslim countries," Anderson lamented, "gay activism hasn't died; it never really existed." Activists' argument that "Americans are in no position to criticize Iranians on human rights," noted Anderson, suggested that "some gay and lesbians feel more allegiance to the relativism of the contemporary left than they do to the universality of their own cause." Indeed. Among them was Faisal Alam, founder of the gay Muslim organization Al-Fatiha. In response to the execution in Iran of two teenagers whose only crime was having sex together, Alam wrote that "while we condemn the executions of gay teens in Iran, we must remember that until March of this year, our own country was one of only five in the world that executed juvenile offenders." Thus did Alam turn the focus away from the state-ordered murder of young people in Iran simply for being gay to the admittedly illiberal but hardly comparable practice in some American states of sentencing underaged murderers to death. So it is that even gay Muslims, when they feel forced to make some comment on pitiless anti-gay acts by their fellow Muslims, either transfer the blame to Westerners or play moral-equivalency games, or both.

Even in Scandinavia, where I live, and which has long been in the forefront of gay-friendly legislation, gay rights are under Muslim assault. At a November 2007 debate organized by the gay student organization at the University of Oslo, the deputy chairman of Norway's Islamic Council, Asghar Ali, who at the time also held high-ranking positions in the ruling Labor Party and the immensely powerful Norwegian Confederation of Trade Unions and had formerly worked in an advisory capacity at the government's Equality and Anti-Discrimination Ombud—in short, an apparent model of successful assimilation—refused to reject the death penalty for homosexuals. In the ensuing weeks the government-funded Islamic Council came under pressure to clarify its position on this issue, and turned to the European Fatwa Council for guidance. When the head of the Islamic Council, Senaid Kobilica, was asked his views about executing gays, he would say only that "as a Muslim in Norway" he was bound "to respect Norwegian law." As Rita Karlsen of Human Rights Service observed, "there is a significant difference between dissociating oneself from the death penalty for homosexuals as a *Norwegian* Muslim and as a Muslim. By the very act of indicating that one is (only) dissociating oneself from it as a Norwegian Muslim, one is speaking a sharia language." Kobilica went on to say that before Norwegian Muslims could make a clear statement of where they came down on the question of executing homosexuals, they needed to discuss the issue among themselves and await the counsel of Islamic authorities. "While this process is under way, I ask for understanding and respect for the fact that I am unable to comment, either about my personal position or about the position of the Islamic Council of Norway," Kobilica told *Dagsavisen*. Understanding and respect, that is, for his unwillingness to say flat out that he did not believe gay people should be murdered for being gay.

Mohammad Usman Rana, who at the time was head of the Muslim Student Association at the University of Oslo, and who is now a medical student at the University of California at Irvine, said in the debate that he personally didn't support the death penalty for gays, but that he would not criticize other countries' practices. "I am neither a theologian nor an Islamic scholar," he later told the college newspaper *Universitas*. "I'm a Norwegian citizen and obey Norwegian law." Pressed for a clearer response, he complained: "There is unfortunately a tendency in Norway to degrade religious people. It is due to an extreme secularism among the Norwegian public. I fervently hope that our participation [in the debate on the death penalty for gays] helps to create a more nuanced view of Islam. The Norwegian public needs to become more liberal." Meaning, of course, more liberal toward Islam—and toward its mercilessly illiberal view of gays.

Far from alienating Norway's cultural elite with his views, Rana went on to win a 2008 *Aftenposten* competition for best op-ed by a younger writer on the topic "the new Norway." In his essay, "The Secular Extremist," he took on what he called "demands" that Muslims "tone down their religiosity in public and modernize and overlook the principles of belief." In Norway, he argued, "the ultimate objective is to grind away at Islam's profile as a complete way of life for Muslims and reduce the religion to a semi-secularized, relativistic, and cultural message." Rana bemoaned the appearance in the media of "ex-Muslims" and "moderate Muslims," the sweeping aside (as he called it) of true believers, and efforts to "'liberate,' 'modernize,' and 'secularize' Muslims." He made a special point of condemning those who criticize the critics of gay rights. He cited the case of conservative Church of Norway bishop Ole Christian Kvarme, whom he described as having been "nailed and crucified" in the media for his anti-gay position. Here was somebody who believes that gay people *literally* should be put to death, and he was using crucifixion imagery to describe, and condemn, the open exchange and vigorous criticism of ideas that is a foundational element of Western democracy.

Indeed, what Rana was taking on was the Enlightenment itself. Though he claimed to be an admirer of America, it was clear that his ultimate desideratum was not just American-style religious freedom but a hands-off attitude by the Norwegian state and media toward even the most extreme forms of religious expression. In denouncing what he called the "strong antipathy" of the Norwegian public square "toward views of life which insist that there exists a truth that determines right and wrong," he was essentially denouncing secular democracy itself and implicitly calling for a social order founded on that "truth"— on, that is, sharia. The title of his piece suggested that the drastic shift in the very meaning of words about Islam was taking place at lightning speed: even as supporters of jihad were now to be known as "moderates," what had until recently been called secular democracy was now "extreme secularism."

Replying to Rana's piece, Hege Storhaug of Human Rights Service toted up the ample evidence that Rana is, in fact, a firm supporter of sharia: under his direction, the Muslim Student Association and Pakistani Student Association had promoted presentations by and about a series of Islamists who support polygamy and the Taliban, condemn marriages between Muslim women and infidels, and—yes—urge the death penalty for gays and apostates. Storhaug cited a comment Rana had made to *Dagbladet* in 2006: "Islam is Islam; how can you be secular and Muslim?" It was obvious that Rana, like Tariq Ramadan, was practicing the Islamic art of *taqiyya*, pretending to agitate for greater secular pluralism when in fact his real goal was sharia. In any event, his ridiculous claim that views such as his own are unwelcome in the Norwegian media was, of course, given the lie by his *Aftenposten* prize— awarded to him, incidentally, by a panel chaired by the newspaper's openly gay op-ed editor, Knut Olav Amås. As Storhaug put it: "That the op-ed editor, who is openly gay, promotes a person who would kill him, makes the situation completely absurd and macabre."

In August 2008, it was reported that Kobilica was still awaiting word from the European Fatwa Council, though he assured the media that he was "100 percent certain that the fatwa council will not come out in favor of something which conflicts with European law." Meaning that while the death penalty for homosexuals is, indeed, an orthodox Islamic position, Western Muslim leaders, in accordance with the Koran—and with good strategy—prefer in such controversial cases not to challenge infidel law. (There would, after all, be time enough to execute gays in the coming decades, after Europe's Muslim population had attained critical balance.)

Most chilling about all this, however, was not Muslim leaders' comments but the Norwegian establishment's reactions. When it emerged that Asghar Ali was on the board of the the Oslo Arbeidersamfunn—the largest and most influential association within Norway's ruling Labor Party—its chairman, Anne Cathrine Berger, lamented that some people "can't see the difference between a board member's views and the organization's views." Ali remained on the board (though, when a new board election was held in February 2008, he chose not to run again). And when it turned out that Ali was also secretary—that is, second in command—of the 37,000-member Electricians' and IT Workers' Union, it issued a "clarification" by Ali saying that "as a Norwegian Muslim" he rejected the death penalty for gays. Like Kobilica's comment about European law, Ali's "clarification" simply affirmed that he accepts infidel law; it revealed nothing about his actual position on the question, or about whether he was, in fact, dedicated to the goal of ultimately changing Norwegian law to conform to sharia. Yet union boss Hans Olav Felix pronounced himself "satisfied" with Ali's "clarification," and Ali retained his union job.

As for the Norwegian government, there was no serious effort, as far as I know, to rescind from the Islamic Council its half million kroner a year in state support. And the media? After a news cycle or two had passed, the Norwegian media dropped the whole question of Muslims executing gays down the memory hole and resumed treating Islamic Council members as if they were model immigrants, lovers of Norway, and (that magic word) *moderates*. When Norwegian security services expressed concern in February 2008 about the possible role in terrorist funding of money sent abroad by Norwegian Muslims, *Dagsavisen* went straight to Asghar Ali for a quote pooh-poohing the idea. *Dagsavisen*'s article ended as follows: "Ali emphasizes that the Norwegian Muslim community has definitively rejected extremism." Ali's refusal to reject the death penalty for gays had already been deep-sixed.

In the same month, Muslims rioted in Denmark, and *Aftenbladet* ran a piece portraying Kobilica—who had called on Muslim youth in Norway to control themselves—as an embodiment of moderation and reason; as with Ali, his refusal to reject the death penalty for gays went unmentioned. This was followed, in April 2008, by an Andrea Elliott-style profile of Kobilica by *Aftenposten*'s Kristin Høiland. Headlined "Travel-Happy Imam," the piece glowed with enthusiasm for this exemplary "new Norwegian": "a young, modern imam, dressed in suit and tie, and available by cell phone and e-mail," Kobilica was "hospitable," a "bridge-builder." When he told Høiland that he wanted "to show that Islam is an inclusive religion," you might have expected her to ask about executing gays, but no: her next question was "Do you have any dream destinations?"

The summer of 2008 saw a brief mini-flurry of media attention to the treatment of gays under Islam, with a focus on Iraq. A UN report quoted on CNN's Web site noted that Islamist "militias" in that country were "reportedly threatening families of men believed to be homosexual, stating that they will begin killing family members unless the men are handed over or killed by the family." And *Newsweek* reported that the Iraqi "government, security forces, judiciary and religious establishment are complicit in terrorizing gays" and that "Iraqi officials scoffed at the subject" of abuse of gay people and scolded a reporter "for even asking about it." The reporters admitted that the UN's human-rights office "dodged the subject like a mine field," that "[v]irtually no government officials would sit for an interview" about it, and that even some of *Newsweek*'s staffers in Iraq "were wary of the story." Since 2003, according to a London-based Iraqi gay-rights group, "more than 430 gay men ha[d] been murdered in Iraq." Alas, this illuminating report appeared not in *Newsweek*'s print editions, but only on its Web site.

With few exceptions, Western governments have shown indifference to the fate of gay people in Muslim countries. Immigration authorities routinely send back gay asylum-seekers from Muslim countries on the grounds that they supposedly can escape punishment by hiding their homosexuality. In 2006, journalist Doug Ireland reported that Badr Corps death squads in Iraq were murdering gay people on an almost daily basis. A gay Iraqi exile in London, Ali Hili, provided Ireland with details:

> Ammar, a young gay man of 27, was abducted and shot in
> [the] back of the head in Baghdad by suspected Badr militias
> in January 2006. Haydar Faiek, aged 40, a transsexual Iraqi, was
> beaten and burned to death by Badr militias in the main street
> in the Al-Karada district of Baghdad in September 2005. Naffeh,
> aged 45, disappeared in August 2005. His family was informed
> that he was kidnapped by the Badr organization. His body
> was found in January 2006. He, too, had been subjected to an
> execution-style killing.

According to Ireland, U.S. officials responded to Iraqi gays' appeals for help "with indifference and derision." Rob Anderson of the *New Republic* wrote that "one gay Iraqi who is hiding five gay men in his home said that when he has approached American officials they have 'laughed' and have refused to provide support." Anderson added: "There really is only one way that the United States would reverse course: If a considerable amount of pressure were to be drummed up from within the United States. But if the reactions of U.S. gay and lesbian groups to Iran's gay executions are any indication, there isn't much reason for hope."

Meanwhile, at American universities, some gay professors are such true-blue multiculturalists that they've even echoed Islamist arguments against human-rights efforts in the Middle East. Take Joseph Massad, a Palestinian-American associate professor at Columbia University and a protégé of Edward Said. Massad is openly gay, but this didn't keep him from arguing, in a 2002 paper, that attempts to promote gay rights in the Middle East were part of a conspiracy by Western Orientalists to "produce homosexuals, as well as gays and lesbians, where they do not exist." Massad developed this ludicrous thesis into a 2007 book, *Desiring Arabs*, in which, as Brian Whitaker explained in a review, Massad described "a 'missionary' campaign orchestrated by what he calls the 'Gay International.'" Echoing the rhetoric of Edward Said, Massad accused this imaginary "Gay International" of being driven by an "orientalist impulse." "Massad does not deny that gay and lesbian Arabs exist," explained Whitaker, "but he sees them mainly as victims of western influence." It's hard, after having seen photographs of men and boys being executed in Muslim countries for homosexual acts, not to be utterly appalled by Massad (who also supports Hamas). As Whitaker observed,

> Massad appears . . . blinkered to the human cost of the prevailing attitudes towards homosexuality in Arab countries: the murders of gay men in Iraq, entrapment by the police in Egypt, the arrests of men who "behave like women" in Saudi Arabia, the beatings at the hands of families, the futile and potentially harmful psychiatric "cures," blackmail, the lack of state protection, and more. There is no real acknowledgment of a problem that Arabs should attend to.

Whitaker also quoted a disgusting footnote in Massad's book in which he attempted to sneer away the mistreatment of gays in the Palestinian territories. Note the words that Massad puts in scare quotes:

> Articles published in the U.S. press, written by Israelis or pro-Jewish activists, claimed that Palestinian "gays" are so oppressed that they could only find refuge in "democratic" Israel. Interviews with such "gay refugees" recounted horrid torture by PA [Palestinian Authority] elements. Indeed, the effort was inaugurated by US Congressman Barney Frank himself, who used the occasion to praise Israeli "democracy." . . .

Such rhetoric is morally comparable to that of a Jew mocking, dismissing, and denying the reality of Jewish suffering in the Holocaust. The amount of desperate denial of reality that Massad's political correctness requires is mind-boggling—it obliges him to deny the fact of Israeli democracy, of Palestinian non-democracy, of Muslim and Arab homophobia, and of the very existence of people with homosexual orientation in the Arab world.

Massad is no marginal eccentric: his book was published by the University of Chicago Press and carried blurbs from several renowned academics, including professors at City University of New York (CUNY) and Columbia. The recurring word in these blurbs was "racist"—which was deployed in such a way as to affirm that if, in fact, there's anything disturbing about Arab cultures' attitudes toward sexuality, it's the fault, in some way or other, of Western racism. As more than one commenter on amazon.com noted, this argument is itself outrageously racist: "This thesis claims that Arabs have never thought for themselves, that they are monoliths, and can only change at the behest of the west." But such is the nature of mainstream academic thinking in our time: at America's universities, Arabs and Muslims are viewed as exclusively reactive—as bearing, that is, no ultimate responsibility for anything they do. "Massad's intellectual project," concluded James Kirchick of *The New Republic*, "is a not-so-tacit apology for the oppression of people who identify openly as homosexual." Indeed, Kirchick noted that Massad, writing about the gay Egyptians who were arrested in a widely reported 2001 raid on a party boat on the Nile, "smear[ed] efforts to free the men." Massad's argument that Arab gays aren't really gays rests largely on the fact that they don't identify publicly as gays; and as Kirchick pointed out, Massad didn't "consider that the reason why Arab homosexuals may not 'express a need for gay politics' might be because they would be killed if they did."

In May 2008, Scott Long, who is in charge of gay rights for the international organization Human Rights Watch (HRW), distributed an HRW briefing paper that took issue with Dutch efforts to integrate immigrants and to test potential immigrants' "adaptability" to Dutch culture. Long rejected the argument that such policies protect gays from violence, implying (not for the first time) that anti-gay violence by Dutch Muslims is a result of "anti-immigrant xenophobia and Islamophobia." Gays, Long insisted, must help other groups to immigrate to the West "whether those groups like us or not." In short, multicultural ethics demand that gay people respond to Europe's Islamization by committing self-genocide. Both HRW's report and Long's endorsement of it were perfect examples of total enthrallment to multicultural ideology—and total indifference to the facts on the ground.

Listening to all the talk these days about the need to come to an "accommodation" with Muslims, a gay person can feel like a Czech in 1938—we're the first group to be sacrificed in order to "keep the peace." As in 1938, however, there's no realistic hope of peace down that road: to feed the monster is only to increase its strength. The situation is deeply demoralizing: if millions of Muslims can take to the streets in rage over the publication of a few cartoons, why can't more than a handful of gay people get worked up enough to open their mouths about the threat that those Muslims represent to gay people's own right to life, liberty, and the pursuit of happiness?

III

Docile Provocateurs

During World War II, Hollywood churned out scores of motion pictures that made a real contribution to the war effort, from *Casablanca* and *A Guy Named Joe* to *Thirty Seconds over Tokyo* and *The White Cliffs of Dover*. Winston Churchill famously said that the 1942 movie *Mrs. Miniver*, about a middle-class English family's experiences during the opening months of the war, was "more powerful to the war effort than the combined work of six military divisions." Even as Britain was struggling to hold out against the Nazis, its own film industry produced films, such as *The Way to the Stars* and Noël Coward's *In Which We Serve*, that celebrated its armed forces and reminded the British people of the values they were fighting for.

Before 9/11, Hollywood occasionally made movies that candidly depicted life in Islamist societies, such as *Not Without My Daughter* (1991), the true story of an American woman's effort to escape from her tyrannical Iranian husband and his Koran-besotted family in Teheran and return to the United States with her little girl. In that movie Sally Field, playing Betty Mahmoody, actually uses the word "primitive" more than once to describe the severe Iranian patriarchy under the Ayatollah Khomeini; the film treats this word choice sympathetically.

Today, however, it is hard to imagine a major studio giving the green light to a motion picture like *Not Without My Daughter*—at least not without ordering a major rewrite. Today, Hollywood producers would feel obliged to show the "other side" of Betty Mahmoody's story—to include (for example) golden-lit scenes of women sitting under beautiful shade trees and joyfully reading the Koran to their children. A twenty-first-century version of *Not Without My Daughter* would either omit the word "primitive" altogether or depict Betty Mahmoody's use of it as the act of an ignorant American who lacks cultural sensitivity. For the entertainment business has learned to treat Islam with "respect," with "understanding," with "nuance," and to either tiptoe around or whitewash the harsh reality of sharia law and jihad. Movies and television shows that dare to reflect (to at least some extent) the truth about the jihadist threat—such as the Fox series *24* and the two films about United Flight 93 (which crashed in Pennsylvania on 9/11)—are the exceptions that prove the rule.

The relatively few Hollywood scriptwriters who do tackle the subject of the "war on terror" almost uniformly toe the PC line, making villains out of U.S. leaders and viewing Muslims as victims. In Brian de Palma's *Redacted* (2007), American troops gang-rape an Iraqi woman. In George Clooney's *Syriana* (2005), the villains in the Middle East are CIA agents and American oil-company executives. Robert Redford's *Lions for Lambs* (2007) was an anti-war talkathon. The moral equivalence of *The Kingdom* (2007)—in which both the FBI agents and the terrorists they're investigating in Saudi Arabia prove to be equally amoral and bloodthirsty—is the best one can usually hope for from Hollywood. After the release of *A Mighty Heart* (2007), about the murder by terrorists in Iraq of *Wall Street Journal* reporter Daniel Pearl, the victim's father, Judea Pearl, wrote an article for *The New Republic* in which he paid the film some compliments but also accused it of moral equivalence, pointing to its "comparison of Danny's abduction with Guantánamo—it opens with pictures from the prison—and its comparison of Al Qaeda militants with CIA agents." He also cited director Michael Winterbottom's public comments about "extremists on both sides," which he considered inimical to the "moral clarity" his son's memory merited.

As Jonathan Foreman noted in an August 2007 article at *National Review Online*, Hollywood producers are blind to "the ordinary, quiet heroism of hundreds of thousands of U.S. troops who have served in

Iraq and Afghanistan" and are more interested in portraying soldiers as "rapists, murderers and torturers oppressing populations that were happy and prosperous under Saddam Hussein and the Taliban." As Foreman observed, "What Hollywood . . . 'knows' about the post–cold war military is based on *Platoon, Apocalypse Now*, and *Casualties of War*." Foreman noted that the story of Steven Vincent—the art critic who was motivated to become a war correspondent after watching the destruction of the World Trade Center from the roof of his East Village home and who ended up being kidnapped and murdered in Basra, Iraq, after writing about religious extremism in that city's police force—would "make a superb film."

Instead, we've been served such fare as *Rendition, In the Valley of Elah, Grace Is Gone*, and *Stop-Loss*—all of which view the U.S. government and military with jaundiced eyes. *Stop-Loss* (2008) encouraged us to sympathize with a soldier who goes AWOL. *Grace Is Gone* (2007) gave us, in the words of star John Cusack, a "somber drama about the costs and griefs of this whole fiasco." Cusack also starred in *War Inc.* (2008), aka *Brand Hauser*, which according to a plot summary at the Internet Movie Database, "is set in the future, when the desert country of Turaqistan is torn by a riot after a private corporation, owned by the former US president, has taken over the whole state. John Cusack plays the role of a hit man who . . . is hired by the corporation's head to kill the CEO of their competitors." What's wrong with these and other films is not that they're anti-war. What's wrong is that their worldview is founded on a breathtaking refusal to recognize the darker realities of Islam. The writers and directors of these films are determined to believe that radical Islam is not a problem, or at least not the *main* problem; in their view, the real problems are American capitalism, American warmongering, American Islamophobia, American cultural insularity.

Writing in *The Atlantic* in April 2008, Ross Douthat noted that the 2003 Bruce Willis picture *Tears of the Sun*, a "brief for moralistic interventionism" in which Navy SEALs take on violent Muslims in Africa, was "the sort of movie 9/11 was supposed to spawn: righteously patriotic, confident in American might, and freighted with old-fashioned archetypes." Yet the moment didn't last; today "the film industry's typical take on geopolitics traces all the world's evils to the machinations of a White Male enemy at home" in a manner reminiscent of such 1970s "fear the government" films as *The Conversation* and *Three Days of the Condor*. Today, as in the 1970s, the *real* enemy is virtually never Islam; it's the U.S. government, the CIA, corporate America; as Douthat puts it, "villains at home are more dangerous than any enemies abroad." Repeatedly, "terrorist baddies turn out to be Eurotrash arms dealers (2006's *Casino Royale*), disgruntled hackers (2007's *Live Free or Die Hard*), a sinister air marshal (2005's *Flightplan*), or the handsome white guy sitting next to you in the airport lounge (2005's *Red Eye*). Anyone and anybody, in other words, except the sort of people who actually attacked the United States on 9/11."

What's behind all this? It seems to me that the answer, in very large part, is this: a fear of facing up to the real enemy. For filmmakers who grew up on the fashionable paranoia of films like *Three Days of the Condor*, casting CIA agents as the enemy is like dining on comfort food. Facing up to the reality of the Islamist menace requires an authentic bravery that is hard to come by in Hollywood, where "courageous" is a label most often attached to movies (such as *Mississippi Burning*) that serve up the current consensus on long-settled social conflicts. When it comes to war, today's Hollywood wisdom doesn't go any deeper than the old Pogo cartoon: "We have found the enemy and he are us."

One of the few prominent figures in Hollywood to speak out honestly and critically about the lack of honest films about the war with Islamism was, oddly, Pat Sajak. The *Wheel of Fortune* host noted that

> the reluctance to speak out is based on more than sensitivity; *fear* also comes into play. How else can one explain Hollywood's reluctance to dramatize the brutality of those waging this war? Think about the movie industry's reaction to the Nazi menace during World War II, and contrast it to their silence now. It's hard to blame studio executives for not wanting to expose themselves to retribution or for recognizing the fact theaters would be reluctant to show anything that might be deemed "inflammatory," but it's equally hard to find anyone who will even acknowledge this climate of fear. Again, free speech has been abridged, but it doesn't seem to be of much concern to those most affected by it.

The only speech battles in which the entertainment world

seems willing to engage are in defense of sex, crudity and gratuitous violence. They can still look brave and bold by fighting those fights because they're nice, safe and familiar.

A flood of documentaries have portrayed Islamists sympathetically. Typical of the genre is the critically acclaimed *Aching Heart* by Oscar Hedin, whose curiosity as to why several of his childhood friends in Sweden had converted to Islam led him to spend three years examining the lives of young Muslim jihadists. Among the people whom Hedin thanks in the film's credits is Mullah Krekar, founder of the terrorist group Ansar al-Islam and now a resident of Oslo.

The inclination to whitewash Islam was on display in two situation comedies that debuted in 2007—*Little Mosque on the Prairie*, a production of the Canadian Broadcasting Corporation, and *Aliens in America*, which was shown on America's CW network. Both series were about Muslim immigrants living in the small-town heartland, and both aimed to communicate the idea that Muslim beliefs, values, and practices represent no challenge whatsoever to mainstream North American society—and that only an ignorant bigot would suggest otherwise. In short, there's no Islam problem in the West, only an *anti*-Islam problem. Though both shows were mediocre and painfully unfunny, both won praise from big-city newspapers for bravely taking on North American Islamophobia.

British television, too, has embraced dhimmitude. After the BBC spy drama series *Spooks* (known in the United States as *MI5*) was criticized by Muslim groups during its first season for showing radical Muslims in a mosque, the series' producers fell into line, obediently churning out shows which give the clear impression that the jihadist threat doesn't exist. Richard Littlejohn of the *Daily Mail*, who has called *Spooks* "a complete parcel of nonsense designed to peddle the Guardianista [i.e., politically correct] worldview," cited the following plotlines: one episode imagined "a fundamentalist Christian sect, hellbent on killing Muslims"; another concerned an airline bomb plot fomented not by jihadists but by "rogue elements in the security services and a deranged, Tory-supporting newspaper baron"; and a third was "a special two-parter . . . on the takeover of the Saudi Embassy" by people who at first seemed to be jihadists but who turned out to be members of the Israeli intelligence organization Mossad who were "trying to destabilise the Saudis and blame it all on peace-loving Muslim freedom fighters." To judge by *Spooks*, then, as Littlejohn wryly put it, "the threat to life and limb in Britain today comes from, in no particular order, the provisional wing of Fleet Street; renegade members of MI6; Mossad; and genocidal Christian evangelicals." Then there's *Casualty*, Britain's equivalent to *E.R.*, which has twice depicted terrorist acts by animal-rights activists. In one of these instances, according to Mark Edward Manning, the original script had depicted "a young Muslim blowing himself up at the bus station," but the BBC demanded a rewrite. Littlejohn called this "yet more evidence of the [BBC's] institutionalised bias, cowardice and cultural cringe. . . . The simple fact is that the BBC . . . is scared to death of upsetting Muslims."

In March 2008, the BBC ran a drama called *White Season—White Girl*, which was described as "the story of the clash of cultures" between a white family and the "Asian community in Bradford." In the film, eleven-year-old Leah "discovers that the culture she was initially intimidated by isn't so alien after all. She is soon seeking sanctuary in the rituals of Islam, away from the pain and strife at home. But this innocent fascination turns sour for Debbie [Leah's mother] when her daughter comes home wearing a hijab, and the family's violent reaction has explosive consequences for everyone." Such a drama might not be so objectionable if the BBC were producing a range of dramas set in Muslim communities—but it's not.[8]

July 2008 brought yet another new BBC drama series, *Bonekickers*. In good BBC fashion, its debut episode turned reality on its head by showing a Christian fundamentalist beheading a Muslim. Could anyone have been surprised when British Hindu and Sikh leaders complained, a couple of months later, that the BBC's "bias toward Islam at the expense of Hindus and particularly Sikhs is overwhelming and appears to be a part of BBC policy"?

In both America and Britain, Muslim groups have successfully pressured TV and film producers not to portray Islam as anything but a Religion of Peace. For example, CAIR successfully lobbied Paramount Pictures to change the bad guys in the Tom Clancy movie *The Sum of All Fears* (2002) from Islamist terrorists to neo-Nazis, prompting

---

[8]Bradford is the same city, by the way, where in April 2008 the traditional St. George's Parade, in honor of England's patron saint, was canceled for fear of offending Muslims and sparking Muslim riots.

Reihan Salam to ask in *Slate*: "Why is Hollywood shying away from al-Qaida-like villains?" In his 2008 autobiography, Iranian-Danish actor Farshad Kholghi noted that, despite the cartoon controversy's overwhelming impact on Denmark, "not a single movie has been made about the crisis, not a single play, not a single stand-up monologue." (Which, of course, is exactly what the cartoon jihadists wanted.) In the Netherlands, only the politician Geert Wilders, after the murder of Theo van Gogh, dared to make a film critical of Islam, and even before it was shown in early 2008 ex-union leader Doekle Terpstra—whom Dutch politician Lousewies van der Laan described as "one of our national icons of reasonableness"—called for large-scale rallies against it. "You would think," van der Laan said, "that all of Holland would rally to the defence of freedom of art and freedom of speech. The opposite is happening."

One might expect the producers of serious stage dramas and operas to be more willing to depict and defy jihad than the producers of commercial television and motion pictures. Nope. The Deutsche Oper's cancellation of a 2006 production of Mozart's *Idomeneo* involving a prop that was supposed to be the severed head of Muhammed was only the most widely reported of many such capitulations. In the *Berliner Zeitung*, Harald Jähner waxed sarcastic about the German theater's "state-subsidized courage":

Nowhere else on earth does so much stage blood flow as in our theaters. Liters of the stuff are poured over people's heads, actors shit, masturbate, and ejaculate naked on the stage. And when people run out of ideas for how to get a few people to leave the theater in anger, they stick a cross right next to the orgy so that at least the local bishop will be obliged by his congregation to write a letter of protest. Then the amassed intellectual forces of the Republic rally in defense of artistic freedom. . . . Now the Deutche Oper is giving an impressive demonstration of how little courage for such scandals there really is in our desensitized public sphere: none at all. Because as soon as people even start imagining an audience that could react differently, one that could really take offense at what's happening on stage, the performance is struck from the program.

Indeed, as early as November 2000, a production of *Aisha and the Women of Medina* by the Rotterdam theater group Onafhankelijk Toneel was canceled after Muslim clerics pressured the Moroccan composer and cast into bowing out. "We are enthusiastic about the opera," the singers wrote to the head of the theater group, "but fear reigns." (Aisha, it will be recalled, was Muhammed's nine-year-old wife.) In 2005, the Barbican Centre in London bowdlerized Marlowe's classic *Tamburlaine the Great* to avoid offending Muslims. After the Danish cartoon crisis, both the theater management and the actors "were jittery" about the very presence of a Muslim character in the play *Up on Roof* by Richard Bean, so Bean agreed to turn him into a Rastafarian. And in June 2007 London's Royal Court Theatre canceled a reading of an adaptation of *Lysistrata* that had a Muslim angle. "Our supposedly 'fearless, provocative and challenging' theatre has been reduced to this," lamented Peter Whittle of the New Culture Forum. Ramin Gray of the Royal Court told Whittle that a number of playwrights "feel they can't write openly about what they feel is maybe the most important topic facing our society at the moment." A writer that did dare to write such a play would face an uphill battle getting it produced: as Whittle noted, Nicholas Hytner of the National Theatre had resolved "that he would not put on a play attacking Islam unless it was by a Muslim."

Only one approach to the topic of Islam is totally safe: pure, shameless dhimmi celebration. Voilà: in a 2007 farce by Alastair Beaton, *King of Hearts*, a Prince William–like heir to the British throne falls in love with a Muslim girl and decides to convert to Islam—and the comedy in the play lies in the supposed foolishness and bigotry of those who find this prospect unsettling. Benedict Nightingale wrote in the London *Times* that the play "somewhat . . . idealise[s] Islam. Why, [Beaton] asks, do we demonise people who, unlike your average British 'Christian,' are so impressively serious about religion and life?" Reportedly, the members of the theater company, while so eager to lend their talents to this promotional effort on behalf of Islam, were anxious lest the poster for the play be considered offensive by Muslims.

Dhimmitude has conquered the stage Down Under as well: in June 2007, Kelsey Munro wrote in the *Sydney Morning Herald* about a new "dark satire" that "updates Dr. Strangelove's nuclear paranoia for the age of terrorism." Kirk Lynn, the author of the play, *Major Bang*, described the period after 9/11 in the United States as "all hush-hush" with "no satire." Of course the target of Lynn's satire wasn't Islam or sharia or jihad terrorists—it was those who are "paranoid" about terrorism. To hear Lynn tell it, this approach was brave and pathbreaking. In March 2008, Muslim leaders in Germany protested a planned staging in Potsdam of *The Satanic Verses*. Free speech "has its boundaries," insisted Muslim spokeswoman Nurhan Soykan, who argued that her coreligionists "can't be expected to put up with everything."

The small French town of Saint-Genis-Pouilly, on the Swiss border, provided one lonely profile in courage. Back in 1994, director Hervé Loichemol wanted to produce Voltaire's 1741 play *Fanaticism, or Mahomet the Prophet*, in Geneva to mark the tricentennial of the author's birth. But protests by Muslim activists—among them Tariq Ramadan—put the kibosh on that. In 2005, however, Loichemol revived the idea, arranging public readings of the play, a comic study of religious fanaticism and intolerance, in both Geneva and Saint-Genis-Pouilly. Once again there was an outcry from Muslims, who called Voltaire's comedy "an insult to the entire Muslim community." In a letter to Hubert Bertrand, the mayor of Saint-Genis-Pouilly, Muslim leaders demanded he cancel the play "to preserve peace"—an explicit threat. But Bertrand refused, calling in extra police to guard the theater on the night of the reading. The cops were necessary: as Andrew Higgins wrote in the *Wall Street Journal*, "a small riot broke out involving several dozen people and youths who set fire to a car and garbage cans"; Bertrand called the atmosphere "quasi-insurrectional." But he was not swayed: describing freedom of speech as the "foundation stone" of modern Europe, Bertrand told Higgins that "for a long time we have not confirmed our convictions, so lots of people think they can contest them." Given Voltaire's central role in the Enlightenment, all this Muslim pandemonium over his play seemed especially resonant: "Objecting to him [Voltaire] and his mocking of religion," noted Austin Cline of the Council for Secular Humanism, "is a good way to demonstrate that one's objections are, more broadly, to the Enlightenment as a whole."

On September 11, 2008, seven years to the day after 9/11, London theatergoers experienced a stunning break with West End dhimmitude. That night saw the opening, in the basement of London's Royal Court–Jerwood Theatre, of a play called *Now or Later* by a young

American named Christopher Shinn. It takes place on election night in the United States, and its main character is John, a gay college student who is the son of the man who is about to be declared the next president of the United States. As the play begins, photographs have surfaced online in which John is seen simulating sex with a friend while dressed up as the prophet Muhammed. John's father and his staffers panic—how can they prevent a scandal from destroying his presidency before it's even begun? John explains his stunt: coming on the heels of a campus conflict over Muhammed cartoons, it was part of an attempt to shock his politically correct classmates into understanding that the orthodox Muslims whose beliefs they were so keen not to offend were, in fact, outraged by—and determined to destroy—the very freedoms that they, his classmates, take utterly for granted. Urged by his father to apologize to fundamentalist Muslims and find common ground, John argues that it's impossible to find common ground with people who want to kill you for being gay.

Charles Spencer wrote in the *Telegraph*: "This is the play we have been waiting for—a gripping, daring work that examines the Western response to Islamic fundamentalism and the consequent threat to freedom of speech.... It's gripping stuff, and John's arguments about the way liberals cravenly surrender to the demands of radical Muslims pack a powerful and contentious dramatic punch." Other reviews, while equally enthusiastic, avoided Spencer's blunt characterization of the play's central conflict. Did *Now or Later* signal a new bravery on the part of playwrights, producers, and theater owners—or was it simply the lone exception that proved the rule about Broadway and West End cowardice? That remained to be seen.

Dhimmitude in the art world has been no less pervasive than in the theater. Postmodern artists who have striven throughout their careers to offend devout Christians and to *épater le bourgeoisie* now maintain piously that Islam deserves respect, while museums and galleries that have boasted frequently of their own daring have canceled exhibitions or taken down works that might upset Muslims. "The arts," Whittle has observed, "are increasingly censoring themselves when it comes to Islam." Tim Marlow of London's White Cube Gallery agrees: self-censorship by artists and museums, he said in late 2007, is now rife "but very few people have explicitly admitted" it. In a December 2007 article, *Spiked* editor Brendan O'Neill concurred: "Arts establishments are increasingly editing or withdrawing anything that might be judged irreligious or anti-Muslim." In 2006, for example, nude dolls by the surrealist artist Hans Bellmer were removed just before the opening of an exhibition at London's Whitechapel Art Gallery. The official excuse was "space constraints," but the real reason (as the curator of the show admitted) was fear that the nudity of the dolls would offend the gallery's Muslim neighbors. Similarly, in 2005, the World Culture Museum in Gothenburg, Sweden, withdrew from public view a painting, "Scène d'amour," that its artist, Louzla Darabi, described as a "response to Muslim hypocrisy about sexuality, above all women's sexuality." In the same year, the Tate Gallery changed its mind about displaying a work by John Latham entitled "God Is Great," which consists of copies of the Bible, Koran, and Talmud embedded in a vertical sheet of thick glass, and which is in fact considered a tribute to the so-called Abrahamic religions. The gallery's director, Stephen Deuchar, explained that the action was taken "in the light of events in London in July." It was interesting to note that Deuchar couldn't even bring himself to name those "events." (He was referring, of course, to the July 7 bombings.) "It was a very difficult decision," Deuchar stated, "but we made it due to the exceptional circumstances of this summer"—another nice touch of euphemism—"and in the light of opinions that we value regarding religious sensitivities." Deuchar's convoluted syntax suggested that not only was he scared to show Latham's work—he was scared to explain his decision in clear, direct language. An incensed Latham accused the Tate of cowardice.

Two years later, the Tate Modern mounted a video exhibit about religion. It covered all the faiths one might have expected—with a single exception.

The litany of cowardice goes on. In January 2006, officials in Middelkerke, Belgium, citing concern about Muslim reactions, canceled the exhibition of "Shark," a work by Czech artist David Cerny consisting of an underwear-clad fiberglass Saddam Hussein floating in a fish tank. Also in 2006, the *Middle East Times* (though not, apparently, any major American or British newspaper) reported that "a gang of young Muslims wielding iron rods" had protested a Paris café's exhibition of fifty-odd cartoons mocking religion (not just Islam), in response to which the café owners "placed white sheets of paper inscribed with the word 'censored' over the cartoons that were targeted by the gang."

And in August of that year, a photograph of a semi-nude, mentally ill homeless woman included in an exhibit of work by photographer Syra Miah at the Birmingham Museum and Art Gallery was removed in response to a complaint by a member of the Artists Circle, a Muslim arts group. "The Birmingham Museum and Art Gallery said it had been advised that the image, shown as part of the work included in the Art and Islam exhibition, could offend Muslims," wrote Paul Sims in the *Daily Mail*. In the *Mail*'s online comments section, one reader asked: "Does the Artists Circle now hold a veto right over the work of artists from Muslim backgrounds in Birmingham?" Another reader aptly observed: "Clearly we are moving towards a Nazi-style definition of 'Degenerate Art' and these curators in Birmingham are all too happy to collaborate."

On a visit to Amsterdam in late 2007, I read a feature article in the Dutch daily *NRC Handelsblad* about a new exhibition of work by an Iranian-born artist who lives in exile in the Netherlands and uses the pseudonym Sooreh Hera. The show, which was on display at the municipal museum in The Hague, included photographs of two gay Iranian exiles wearing masks of the prophet Muhammed and his nephew Ali. Being keenly aware of the climate of censorship in the Netherlands in the post–van Gogh era, I was surprised and impressed to discover that a Dutch museum actually had the nerve to display such work. My admiration was short-lived: the next day, back home in Oslo, I received by e-mail an unsurprising but disappointing update from a friend in Amsterdam: Hera's Muhammed and Ali photographs had been withdrawn from the show because, in the words of museum director Wim van Krimpen, "certain people in our society might perceive [them] as offensive." Krimpen said that the museum did not want "to become part of a political debate." (Usually museums love being part of debates—just not when the debate involves violent Muslims.)

The newspaper *De Volkskrant*, which at previous stages in the Dutch struggle with jihadists had conducted itself admirably, perversely praised Krimpen's removal of Hera's pictures as an act of "great professionalism." Hera disagreed: telling the *Sunday Times* that Krimpen "was very afraid," and that he had caved in to Muslim threats but was "not willing to admit it," she pulled the rest of her pictures from the show and accepted an offer to exhibit them at a museum in Gouda—whose director promptly received death threats, was placed under police guard, and withdrew its invitation. A selection of Hera's work was then accepted for display as part of an art festival, Art Amsterdam—but only on the condition that the Muhammed and Ali photographs be omitted. "Freedom of expression," a frustrated Hera told Fox News, "has become an illusion in Europe." John Voll, associate director of Esposito's Prince Alwaleed bin Talal Center for Muslim-Christian Understanding at Georgetown University, offered no sympathy: "Free speech is not absolute," he lectured, explaining that Hera's works were too offensive to deserve free-speech protection.

In Dusseldorf, a sculpture by Fleur Boecklin was withdrawn from display at a 2004 carnival because it was deemed to be "a misrepresentation of Islam as an aggressive faith." In February 2008 Reuters reported that "a group of angry Muslims" had burst into Galerie Nord in Berlin, which was displaying an exhibition of twenty-one posters entitled "Zionist Occupied Government" by a Danish man and woman who called themselves Surrend, and demanded the removal of one of the posters. "Zionist Occupied Government" satirized conspiracy theories about Israel, and the poster to which the Muslims objected depicted the Kaaba, a sacred stone in Mecca's Grand Mosque, which was labeled "Stupid Stone." The Muslims "were very aggressive," said gallery official Ralf Hartmann, "and shouted at an employee that the poster should be taken down otherwise they would throw stones and use violence." Faced with these threats, the German government closed the gallery temporarily until security could be improved.

Grayson Perry, whose work has mercilessly mocked Christianity, is one of the few artists to admit that he and his colleagues have buckled under to Muslim pressure. "The reason I haven't gone all out attacking Islamism in my art," he told the *Times* of London, "is because I feel real fear that someone will slit my throat." "It has come to the point," lamented van der Laan in December 2007, "where we don't even wait for people to feel offended." But then this is the nature of dhimmitude: in Islamic societies, non-Muslim residents who don't want trouble don't wait for Muslims to tell them they've crossed the line; they're intensely aware themselves of where that line is, keep a constant eye on it, and are exceedingly careful not to go anywhere near it.

IV

Our Fearless Leaders

Perhaps the multicultural mentality of the Western political elite is most succinctly summed up by a gesture that was observed one day in 2004 in the offices of the Norwegian government. On that day, Norway's then integration minister, Erna Solberg, welcomed a Pakistani Islamist leader by placing one hand on her chest and bowing to him. This, as Hege Storhaug quite rightly observed in recounting this fatuous act, is "just the way an Islamist expects a woman to greet him." When somebody like Solberg does such a foolish thing, she obviously thinks that it will be taken as a gesture of friendship and hospitality, that it will help her gain the Islamist's respect and trust, and that, when seen on the evening news by Muslims living in her own country, it will help her to win *their* hearts and minds (and perhaps votes) as well. What such politicians don't realize is that an Islamist perceives such a gesture as a mark of submission and a sign of weakness, and that such conduct thus breeds only contempt. An infidel who approaches a Muslim in such a manner is very likely to be pegged as a coward without beliefs, convictions, or self-respect. How, after all, can one expect any foreigner or immigrant to respect one's culture if one exhibits no respect for it oneself? Furthermore, if that foreigner or immigrant is a Muslim raised on jihadist ideology, how can one expect him to interpret such a gesture as anything but a sign that the soft jihad in which he's a soldier is proving very successful indeed—that, at least in the little corner of the House of War in which this foolish infidel has authority, there are few obstacles standing in the way of ultimate victory for the forces of Allah.

Contrast Solberg's dhimmitude with Oriana Fallaci's atttitude toward the Ayatollah Khomeini when she interviewed him in 1979. She didn't bow and scrape; instead, she complained about having to wear a chador, and when Khomeini replied that she didn't have to ("Islamic dress," he said, "is for good and proper young women"), she pulled it off, calling it a "stupid, medieval rag." Khomeini fled from the room. Margaret Talbot, in a 2006 *New Yorker* profile of Fallaci, wrote that

> When Khomeini let her return, his son Ahmed gave Fallaci some advice: his father was still very angry, so she'd better not even mention the word "chador." Fallaci turned the tape recorder back on and immediately revisited the subject. "First he looked at me in astonishment," she said. "Total astonishment. Then his lips moved in a shadow of a smile. Then the shadow of a smile became a real smile. And finally it became a laugh. He laughed, yes. And, when the interview was over, Ahmed whispered to me, 'Believe me, I never saw my father laugh. I think you are the only person in this world who made him laugh.'"

Multiculturalists say that relating to Islamists is a matter of respect. It is. But it's not about phony, dhimmi respect born of fear; it's about showing authentic, courageous respect for one's own values, rights, and individual integrity.

Another classic example of dhimmi behavior by a Western leader was provided in 2002 by the then prime minister of France, Jean-Pierre Raffarin. In a 2007 lecture, Islam expert Bernard Lewis noted that Raffarin, "who I am told is a staunch Roman Catholic," had described the twelfth-century Muslim conqueror Saladin, in a speech given in the French National Assembly five years earlier, as having "defeat[ed] the Crusaders and liberate[d] Jerusalem." As Lewis noted: "When a French prime minister describes Saladin's capture of Jerusalem from the largely French Crusaders as an act of liberation, this would seem to indicate a rather extreme case of realignment of loyalties." Lewis was so stunned by this account that he checked the parliamentary record to make sure that Raffarin had really said such a thing. He had; and only one of his colleagues had reacted aloud, calling out *"Libérer?"* ("Liberate?") But Raffarin, said Lewis, "just went straight on. That was the only interruption, and as far as I was aware there was no comment afterwards."

These incidents reflect an attitude that's deplorably widespread among Western leaders. Even as they send soldiers to risk their lives fighting jihadists in South Asia, they coddle, praise, encourage, fund, and protect from criticism Muslims at home who support jihad and who look forward to the West's absorption into the House of Submission. Pascal Bruckner has charged that "the British government and its circle of Muslim 'advisers' flirts with the credo: better fundamentalism than terrorism—unable to see that the two go hand in hand." In this regard, the UK is hardly alone. After every major terrorist act, heads of government across the Western world hurry to remind the public that the overwhelming majority of Muslims in the West are law-abiding, freedom-loving patriots who despise terrorism and reject jihad—even though relatively few of those Muslims are actually willing to say such things themselves. Many of these leaders go further, characterizing terrorism as a desperate reaction to poverty or oppression or to American or Israeli foreign policy and responding to Muslim-on-infidel rape, gay-bashing, and other crimes either by minimizing them or suggesting that they, too, are understandable responses to intolerable circumstances.

It has become routine for Western governments to cover up unpleasant facts about Islam and to try to discredit and demonize those who discuss them. I've mentioned French authorities' attempt to bury a 2005 report concluding that Jewish children could no longer receive an education in France. In Norway, the official statistics bureau has vilified the tiny, valiant Human Rights Service for demonstrating that the bureau's own marriage statistics reveal persistent low levels of marriage integration by the children and grandchildren of non-Western immigrants. As we've seen, former London mayor Ken Livingstone went to outrageous lengths to sell the Islamist scholar Qaradawi as a "progressive" and to bring into disrepute those who told the truth about him; in 2005, Queen Elizabeth II knighted Iqbal Sacranie of the Muslim Council of Britain, who had called for the death of Salman Rushdie.

Across the West, government departments and agencies spend taxpayers' money to persuade them that jihadists are their friends: in 2007, the *Pittsburgh Tribune-Review* glowingly described twelve local high-school teachers' Department of Education–sponsored trip to Egypt, where a meeting with members of the Muslim Brotherhood (preposterously described as "the leading opposition group . . . to President Hosni Mubarak") taught them "a deeper respect for Muslims." In recent years the U.S. State Department has worked on exchange programs with—and thus helped legitimize—groups suspected of involvement in terrorism-related activities. In 2008, Andrew Bostom described how Sada Cumber, America's special envoy to the Organization of the Islamic Conference (OIC), had "endorsed the OIC's fulminations over the Danish cartoons" and over the film *Fitna*, but turned a blind eye to the OIC's support of "Universal Islamic Blasphemy Law," saying that the Conference's "Muslim values" were "exactly in sync with American values."[9] In some cases when the art establishment has shown itself to be insufficiently dhimmified, government has stepped in: in 2003, for instance, the borough council in Walsall, Britain, prohibited an exhibit entitled "The Witnesses of the Future: Islamic Project" consisting of photographs of famous Western buildings and monuments to which Muslim details had been digitally added. (For example, the Statue of Liberty held a copy of the Koran.) Ironically, the exhibit's point was to mock Western fears of Islamization; Walsall Council, by its actions, only proved that those fears are justified.

In response to jihadist pressures and provocations, Western legislatures are increasingly limiting people's right to criticize Islam. Typical of these efforts is the Discrimination Law passed by Norway's parliament on April 19, 2005. It forbids "harassment on the grounds of ethnicity, national origin, ancestry, skin color, language, religion, or beliefs," and, in turn, defines harassment as "actions, omissions, *or utterances* [my emphasis] that have the effect or are intended to have the effect of being insulting, intimidating, hostile, degrading, or humiliating." Defendants may be accused not only by the individuals whom they've supposedly offended but also by semiofficial organs such as the Anti-Racist Center and the Center against Ethnic Discrimination (both of which helped formulate the law, and both of which exist less to oppose real racism and discrimination than to oppose political incorrectness

---

[9]One reflection of the reigning mentality at the State Department is the fact that in 2008—in an action that not only violated the separation of church and state but also had no connection whatsoever to State's official responsibilities—it promoted on its Web site a "Mosques of America" wall calendar.

generally) or by the government's Equality and Anti-Discrimination Ombud. Violations of the law by individuals are punishable by fine; violations by individuals in concert with at least two other persons (such as a writer conspiring with an editor and publisher, perhaps?) can be punished by up to three years' imprisonment—this in a country where murderers often get off with less. Moreover, the burden of proof is on the accused: you're guilty until proven innocent. And how does one prove oneself innocent of saying something?

Are there discriminatory actions and utterances in Norway today? Yes. In many Muslim homes in Oslo, women and girls are beaten up and raped by men who believe it's their sacred right and obligation to do these things; meanwhile, in mosques, imams spread grotesque lies about Christians, Jews, Europeans, Americans, Israelis, and gays. But—in a brilliant piece of legislative legerdemain—it's precisely such actions and utterances that are exempted from prosecution under the Discrimination Law, for it

> applies to all areas of society with the exception of family
> life and personal relationships. The prohibition against
> discrimination on grounds of religion and beliefs . . . does not
> apply to actions and activities under the auspices of faith or
> belief communities and activities with a religious or belief-
> oriented purpose, if the actions or activities are important for
> the carrying out of the community's or the activity's religious or
> belief-oriented purposes.

Thus it's permitted, for example, for an imam to preach that Norwegians are pigs, but a Norwegian who answers back risks prison; in the same way, Muslim women and girls can live as prisoners in their own homes, but a Norwegian who tries to direct attention to this social problem risks being found guilty under the law. Indeed, the law actively opens up the very real possibility that people who dare to discuss honor killings in Norway may end up being punished more severely than those who commit them. It was no coincidence that in Norway, where major proposals for legislative changes are usually debated ad nauseam in the media before any action is taken, members of parliament and the reporters who cover them maintained almost total silence about the proposed Discrimination Law, and that when it was passed (with virtually no debate, and with the support of all but one of the major political parties), the major media didn't report on this, either. In the weeks after the law's passage, I mentioned it to several Norwegians whom I considered well informed; none was aware of its existence.[10]

If I focus on Norway, that's because it's where I live and where, every time I sit down to write, I'm aware that someone in one of the country's many sprawling, dhimmified bureaucracies may decide to indict me for something I've written. But Norway is far from alone in the Western world in imposing such restrictions on speech about Islam. In 2006, Belgium's government decided that certain statements about Islam on a blog were racist and ordered them removed; in the following months the blogger was repeatedly harassed by police officers seeking to interrogate him about his writings. (Meanwhile, as Elaine Sciolino and Souad Mekhennet reported in the *New York Times* on May 28, 2008, Malika El Aroud, a "female holy warrior for Al Qaeda" based in a Brussels apartment, continued to be allowed to use her Web site to urge Muslim men to be jihadists.) Also in 2006, Alejandro de Llano, a Cuban blogger living in Spain, was hauled into court on a charge of supporting Israel and criticizing Palestinians. In France, the Constitutional Council ruled in 2007 that only professional journalists could film or broadcast acts of violence. As Peter Sayer of IDG News Service noted, the date on which this ban was imposed—March 3, 2007—was infelicitous, given that it was the sixteenth anniversary of the day when Los Angeles Police Department (LAPD) officers had beaten Rodney King, an event captured on film by George Holliday. Sayer quoted Pascal Cohet, a spokesman for Obedi, a French organization concerned with civil liberties online, as saying that "if Holliday were to film a similar scene of violence in France today he could end up in prison."

Shortly after 9/11, Britain's House of Commons approved a bill that would criminalize "words or behavior" that might "stir up racial or religious hatred." An outraged Rowan Atkinson (who plays Mr. Bean on television) commented: "For telling a good and incisive religious

[10]The government wasn't through restricting Norwegians' right to speak their minds about Islam: in February 2007, it announced a proposal to block Norwegian citizens' access to a wide range of Web sites, including those that, in the government's view, included "discriminatory and hateful statements." Given many Norwegian officials' very broad definition of this term, and their cowardice in the *Magazinet* matter, this was, to say the least, disturbing news.

joke, you should be praised. For telling a bad one, you should be ridiculed and reviled. The idea that you could be prosecuted for the telling of either is quite fantastic." Yet Atkinson was nearly alone among British authors, artists, and entertainers in his vocal criticism of the bill. Fortunately, though the law was passed by the Commons, its most restrictive provisions were rejected by the House of Lords—an ironic example of a non-democratically elected body standing up for democracy by rebuking a democratically elected body. The forces of dhimmitude persevered, however, and on October 1, 2007, a somewhat watered-down ban on religious hate went into effect in Britain. But this new law wasn't good enough for dhimmis like Archbishop of Canterbury Rowan Williams, who in January 2008 recommended yet another law—one that would "keep before our eyes the general risks of debasing public controversy by thoughtless and (even if unintentionally) cruel styles of speaking and acting." It was baffling that Williams could be so enthusiastic about giving the state such sweeping (and vague) powers, and so indifferent to the effect of such powers on the individual freedom for which Britain, in its finest hour, had stood alone against just the kind of totalitarianism that Williams and his ilk were now so eager to appease.

In March 2008, British Defense Secretary Des Browne told the *Daily Telegraph* that he supported government negotiations with the Taliban and Hezbollah. His reasoning? "People who believe that the answer to their political ambitions will be achieved through violence" need to be made to "accept that their political ambitions will be delivered by politics." In short, the way to prevent hard jihad is to give in to soft jihad—or, as David Frum put it sardonically, *"You don't have to use violence to get what you want—we'll give it to you peacefully."* As Frum noted, "The idea that it might be the 'what they want' that is itself the problem—or that the host British society might have the right to refuse it—apparently is too alien to be contemplated."

In recent years it's become commonplace in democratic countries for people in high places to issue quasi-official-sounding statements condemning others for simply opening their mouths. In the Netherlands, as the blogger Pieter Dorsman has put it, "attempts to regulate and control expression, stifle debate, and cleanse history" have only intensified since van Gogh's murder—and the attitude is, alas, encouraged by those at the very top. In June 2007 it was reported that the Dutch Labor

Party was trying to silence Ehsan Jami, a young party member who was agitating on behalf of Muslim apostates. Jami, who served on the town council in Leidschendam-Voorburg, had announced in May the formation of a Committee for Ex-Muslims which sought to make it easier for Muslims to escape their religion without reprisal. A leaked internal party e-mail revealed that a concerted effort was under way to "ideologically encapsulate" Jami and persuade him "to choose his words more carefully" lest he alienate Muslim party members. *NRC Handelsblad* quoted Aleid Wolfsen, a Labor Party member of Parliament, as saying that Jami had "a very anti-Islam agenda"; and the author of the e-mail, filmmaker Eddy Terstall, told the media that Jami used words "that act like a red rag to a bull [a nice variation on "fanning the flames"] in the Muslim community, which already has little self-confidence."

In May 2007, Dutch Crown Prince Willem-Alexander, in an apparent reference to parliament member Geert Wilders, complained about the language that some politicians use when discussing the integration of immigrants: "Not for nothing do we have the saying: 'Speech is silver, silence is golden.'" (Dutchmen still recall that the first public gesture by Willem-Alexander's mother, Queen Beatrix, after the murder of Theo van Gogh was to pay a friendly visit to a Moroccan community center—a gesture of mind-boggling dhimmitude—and that she declined to attend van Gogh's funeral.)

The saga of Wilders—who sometimes seems to be the only prominent Dutchman still alive and non-exiled who dares to criticize his country's Islamization—provided a grim case study of official dhimmitude on a national scale. In November 2007, the Associated Press reported that Wilders was making a film about the Koran and that the Dutch "interior and justice ministers said they were concerned, but believed they had no authority to prevent [Wilders] from screening his film." Implicit here, of course, was that it is even reasonable in a free country to contemplate taking such an action. On November 30, Doekle Terpstra, chairman of the Netherlands Association of Universities of Applied Science and a leading member of the Dutch cultural elite, accused Wilders of "misusing his position and freedom of speech" to divide Dutch society. Calling on "reasonable people" to oppose this "dangerous" person, Terpstra proceeded to put together a coalition of politicians, business people, Christian and Muslim clergy, and other public figures to spearhead a movement to exclude Wilders's views from the public square. "Wilders is the evil," Terpstra said, "and that evil must be stopped." Yes, *Wilders* was the evil—not the young Muslim men who idolize van Gogh's murderer and seek to make their own contributions to jihad. Politicians and journalists had talked in precisely this way about Fortuyn before his murder—*he* had been the evil who must be stopped—and Fortuyn's murderer, in explaining his motives, had echoed these calumnies.

Early in January 2008, Terpstra's efforts manifested themselves in the form of a statement that appeared on the front page of the newspaper *Trouw*. Signed by a long list of celebrated Dutchmen from various walks of life, it decried "intolerance" and called for "a new balance between the values of then and those of now"—in short, accommodation. Wilders didn't mince words: he called the signatories dhimmis. January saw other developments. The Dutch Muslim Council warned the government that if Wilders's movie was shown, "the youths on the street will have the last word. We can't stop them." (The usual not-so-veiled threat, in other words.) Amsterdam police chief Bernard Welten acknowledged that his department was holding talks about Wilders's Koran film "with imams and other leaders from the Muslim community." National counterterrorism coordinator Tjibbe Joustra suggested that Wilders leave the Netherlands for a while after his film's release. (In other words, the Netherlands could not, or would not, protect a member of its own parliament—more proof that European governments have already ceded a degree of their power to the enemies within.) And Michael van der Galiën reported in *Pajamas Media* that "private companies have joined the cry to stop Wilders . . . fearing that his movie will cost them tremendously." (Dutch business interests seemed not to understand that their own posture might end up costing them far more, and in ways they apparently didn't yet understand.)

Wilders's fellow politicians were useless. (This was, after all, a country where Piet Hein Donner, during his tenure as Dutch minister of justice, had said that if voters wanted to officially introduce sharia law in the Netherlands "it would be a disgrace to say 'This is not permitted!'") In late January, it was reported that the government had "openly distanced itself" from Wilders's film and that it feared a rerun of the Danish cartoon crisis. Amsterdam mayor Job Cohen accused Wilders's Freedom Party of aggravating tensions, dehumanizing Muslims, and inciting hatred. Foreign minister Maxime Verhagen articulated a now-familiar misconception: that "freedom of expression doesn't mean the right to offend." (What does it mean, then? The right to be innocuous?) And prime minister Jan Peter Balkenende worried that Wilders's film might precipitate a national crisis by setting off "reactions that endanger public order, security and the economy." Balkenende added that while his country had "a tradition of freedom of speech," it "also has a tradition of respect, tolerance and responsibility. Unnecessarily offending certain groups does not belong here." A report by Agence France-Presse said that Balkenende "stressed that 'provocations' have no place in the Dutch tradition of tolerance." Balkenende appeared to have forgotten that the Dutch tradition of tolerance was a product of the Enlightenment, and that the Enlightenment had itself been a major provocation. Voltaire, Descartes, Spinoza had been *provocative*—they had challenged the pre-Enlightenment worldview just as Wilders was now challenging Islam's worldview. Balkenende's example showed that members of the West's cultural elite now reflexively saw the exercise of free speech as a danger—not the presence in their midst of people who were prepared to react violently, and en masse, to that exercise. In an open letter that appeared in *de Volkskrant* on January 23, 2007, Wilders pointed out that if he had planned a film about fascist aspects of the Bible, nobody would have batted an eye; yet his plans for a Koran film had sent the Dutch cabinet into a tizzy. "The serious threats to my life and the Dutch government's panicked response to my film," he pointed out, "underline the truth of what I am saying."

In April 2007, Wilders had been called in by intelligence and security officials who, he said, intimidated him by demanding he tone down his rhetoric on Islam; a year later, in February 2008, the ministers of justice and foreign affairs called him in for another "hour of intimidation," as he put it, in connection with his impending film. A report on the *Expatica* Web site quoted sources as saying that the justice minister, Ernst Hirsch Ballin, had threatened "legal consequences for Wilders if the film contain[ed] elements that he considered hate inciting or blasphemous." That same month, *Trouw* reported that leaders of the Dutch Protestant Church wanted to speak with Wilders and his party leaders about their "polarization" of Dutch society and "stigmatization of entire population groups." In early March came news that the Dutch government was looking into the legality of forbidding Wilders's film. (Christian Democrats wanted a ban; Labor didn't.)

Meanwhile, media coverage—both in the Netherlands and abroad—tended to cast Wilders as a troublemaker and hatemonger. In February, an *Observer* profile described him as engaging in "Islam-bashing" and as part of a "new breed of right-wing populists" who were "appealing to anti-Muslim prejudice." The piece dutifully included a comment by Wilders explaining that he was not anti-Muslim but rather opposed to Islamic views on, for example, women and homosexuality; but the reporter, after quoting this explanation, proceeded to ignore Wilders's point entirely and to reiterate the identification of Wilders with "the far right." The reporter mentioned that Wilders had to live "under permanent police guard," but seemed not to recognize that this very fact confirmed Wilders's assertions about the dangers of Islamization. What was striking about the *Observer* profile was not that the reporter thought Wilders was wrong; it was that the reporter was plainly baffled by Wilders's insistence on speaking his mind even if it led to "a new bloody crisis in relations between the West and the Muslim world." "He does not seem to care" about the consequences, the reporter wrote, plainly flummoxed by Wilders's posture. The *Observer* wasn't alone. Even the usually non-dhimmi *Washington Times*, in March 2008, called Wilders's as-yet-unscreened film "anti-Muslim."

Fitna was released online on March 27. It combined graphic images of the dead of 9/11 and Madrid with quotations from the Koran which illuminated the motives of the people who had committed these murders. Its essential argument was unassailable. Yet it was pilloried all over the planet. The EU condemned it. Balkenende condemned it. The Dutch government met with Muslim ambassadors to explain that Wilders did not speak for them. The American government, according to CNN, "warned the film could spark protests and riots." After Wilders appeared on Danish TV and praised Danish Prime Minister Anders Fogh Rasmussen, he, too, condemned Wilders's film and rejected the idea that they were in any way allies. UN Secretary-General Ban Ki-moon called *Fitna* "offensively anti-Islamic," condemned it "in the strongest terms," insisted that "the right of free expression is not at stake here," and called *Fitna* "hate speech." (In fact the only parts of the film that might have qualified as hate speech were the passages Wilders quoted from Muslim scripture.) Maintaining that "freedom must always be accompanied by social responsibility," Ban said that the "fault line is not between Muslim and Western societies . . . but between small minorities of extremists on different sides"—an implicit equation of Islam's critics with those who carry out jihadist terror.

Louise Arbour, UN High Commissioner for Human Rights, agreed with her boss. So did all of the UN's "Special Rapporteurs." Jorge Sampaio, the UN High Representative for the Alliance of Civilizations, called *Fitna* "an insulting film on the Holy Qur'an" that "seems to serve no other purpose than to cause offence." As for freedom of expression, Sampaio proclaimed that it "does not preclude the protection of people from discriminatory and xenophobic language. . . . Let us remember that freedom of expression and the protection against racist and xenophobic language can, and have to, go hand in hand, as only the two together make democracy meaningful." The Dutch media damned *Fitna* too: Wilders, pronounced *de Volkskrant*, "has done the debate over integration of Muslims into Dutch society a disservice." And Dutch businesses chimed in: Bernard Wientjes, chairman of the Dutch employers' organization VNO-NCW, told *Het Financieele Dagblad* that companies might sue Wilders if his film led to a boycott of their products in Muslim countries. After being targeted by threats, Liveleak, the Web site that hosted *Fitna*, took the film offline, replacing it with a statement saying that "this is a sad day for freedom of speech on the net but we have to place the safety and well being of our staff above all else. . . . We stood for what we believe in, the ability to be heard, but in the end the price was too high."

Surprisingly, the opinion page of the *Washington Post* asked writer Sam Harris, a critic of Islam, to write about the *Fitna* controversy; unsurprisingly, the editors rejected his piece as "too critical of Islam"— this from a newspaper that had published op-eds by Mousa abu Marzook of Hamas and Muhammad Hussein Fadlallah of Hezbollah, and that in April would give op-ed space to yet another Hamas member, Mahmoud al-Zahar. In short, Harris was too extreme for the *Post*, but Hamas wasn't.[11]

---

[11]To their credit, the editors of the often PC Web site *Huffington Post* ran an expanded version of Harris's rejected *Washington Post* piece in May 2008. In it, Harris lamented a "whitewash of Islam" that had appeared in *Nature* magazine, "arguably the most influential scientific journal on the planet." The editors of *Nature* agreed to run a letter from Harris taking issue with the article—which, absurdly, called Islam "intrinsically rational" and blamed its current irrationality on Western colonialism—yet according to Harris his letter "was only published after perfectly factual sentences deemed offensive to Islam were expunged." Even scientific publications famous for their scholarly rigor, in short, have chosen to exchange truth for propaganda when addressing Islam.

In May 2008, acting on a 2005 complaint by an imam named Abdul-Jabbar van de Ven (a Dutch convert to Islam), approximately ten Dutch police officers burst into the home of a cartoonist who goes by the name Gregorius Nekschot; searched his possessions; confiscated his computer, cell phone, and some drawings; arrested him on charges of "publishing cartoons which discriminate against Muslims and people with darker skin"; and dragged him away brutally. According to *NIS News*, some members of the Dutch Parliament "suggested that the arrest of Nekschot was an appeasement signal from the Netherlands to the Arab world after *Fitna*." (Remarkably, even the chairman of the Union of Moroccan Imams criticized the arrest, saying that the Dutch cabinet "is more afraid of criticism of Islam than the Dutch Muslims" and declaring that "freedom of expression is a core value of Dutch society.")

Meanwhile there were other dhimmi developments on the part of the Dutch government. In May 2008, in a patent attempt to please Muslims, Welfare State Secretary Jet Bussemaker proposed that schools and teacher training programs pay greater attention to the role supposedly played by Muslims in liberating the country in World War II—even though Muslims in fact played a minimal role in that effort.[12]

Official attitudes are no different in Belgium. Freddy Thielemans, the socialist mayor of Brussels—where innumerable Muslim demonstrations and riots have taken place—banned a peaceful public gathering planned for September 11, 2007, in memory of the victims of 9/11. According to a press release issued by the event organizers, a group called Stop Islamization of Europe (SIOE), "the reason for the prohibition is that he says he cannot guarantee public safety and that he won't disturb the Islamic section of the population in Brussels." As SIOE noted (in an observation that anticipated Wilders's remark about the Dutch government's stance on his film), Thielemans's explanation for his decision only underscored the urgency of the group's cause: "SIOE's message . . . is exactly to warn against conditions such as these, where people no longer can use their freedom of expression and feel

---

[12]In June 2008, an "expertise center for urban policy" called Nicis Institute recommended that the Netherlands, far from trying to integrate Muslims, encourage separation. Distinctive Muslim neighborhoods, Nicis argued, could reduce the Muslim unemployment rate (which stood at around 47 percent), reduce welfare dependency, aid tourism, and lure investment. A proposal more divorced from reality was not easy to imagine.

secure." What's ludicrous about decisions like Thielemans's is that such politicians ban nonviolent gatherings one day because they fear violent Muslim reactions and the next day resume insisting that European Muslims are peace-loving and well-integrated.

When British Tory leader David Cameron stood up in Parliament in July 2007 and called for a ban on the radical Muslim organization Hizb ut-Tahrir, a ban that the government had promised to put into effect two years earlier, the newly installed prime minister Gordon Brown claimed that evidence of the organization's extremism was still insufficient—despite such rather unambiguous Hizb ut-Tahrir statements as "Jews should be killed wherever they are found." In February 2008, the British government capitulated to sharia law in a remarkable way, announcing that the marriages of individuals with multiple spouses would be recognized for purposes of welfare disbursement, provided the marriages were performed in countries where polygamy is permitted. In other words, Muslim men with more than one wife would be permitted to collect additional state benefits. (British immigration law had previously allowed a Muslim husband to import a second wife, even if he still lived with his first wife and remained married to her under Islamic law, so long as he had obtained a secular divorce from the first wife.) While polygamy by non-Muslims in Britain would continue to be a crime, then, polygamy by Muslims would be rewarded. (Such a policy was already in place, by the way, in Ontario.) British citizens were up in arms. "This country has gone truly mad," complained one reader at the *Daily Telegraph* Web site. "This is self-destroying madness," wrote another. The decision was widely recognized for exactly what it was—a major step on the road to sharia in Britain. Indeed, inasmuch as it accorded privileges to Muslims that were denied to infidels, the new policy was a model of sharia lawmaking.

Later in 2008, Ann Cryer, a member of Parliament, lamented publicly that MPs representing Muslim constituencies were "keeping quiet" about forced marriages "because they don't want to lose votes." And the headline of a September article in the *Mail on Sunday* about terrorists living in London at British taxpayers' expense gave voice to a widespread outrage: "Are we mad? Every organ of the state now seems intent on protecting those who would destroy us." The article, by Ruth Dudley Edwards, spelled out the situation: "The system does not just allow people in who hate the country, but it subsidises them, turns a blind eye to their activities until forced to act, foots the bill for lawyers to find loopholes in laws that were designed to keep the public safe, and has judges who take such lofty absolutist positions that it is almost impossible to deport even the vilest of the vile."

I've mentioned the case of Sweden's Lars Vilks, whose drawings of Muhammed as a dog motivated several Muslim countries to file official protests. Prime Minister Fredrik Reinfeldt replied that under Sweden's political system "we don't make political decisions about what gets published in the newspapers" and that he wished "to ensure we keep it that way." So far, so good. But then Reinfeldt received the now-obligatory letter from Muslim ambassadors. "Muslims around the world have yet again been greatly hurt by this deliberate mischief," the ambassadors (twenty-two in all) wrote, and proceeded to lecture Reinfeldt on freedom: "It is most unfortunate that the universally accepted principle of freedom of expression and press has been used to offend over 1.3 billion Muslims around the world." Universally accepted? (Shall we take another look at those Freedom House ratings?) "Freedom of speech," the ambassadors maintained, "is not a license to abuse other people or their most cherished values." On the contrary, that's exactly what it is. The ambassadors claimed that their letter was not "a demand for the respect for religion" but "a demand not to be deliberately insulted." Not a request, mind you—a demand.

"Is that too much to ask?" they asked. Yes, in a free society that *is* too much to ask, let alone demand. "Muslims welcome an informed debate or dialogue over religion," the ambassadors claimed, but insisted that "vulgar satires do not constitute scholarly discourse. That is sheer mischief and should not be confused with art or artistic expression." (This comment reflects the crucial importance in Islam of the role of the Islamic scholar, who alone is empowered to settle questions about what is and isn't permitted in the eyes of Allah, as well as the assumption that Islamic rules about such matters should apply in the West— namely, that people who aren't Islamic scholars should have no right to make any kind of pronouncement on Islam.)

Some of the emissaries, when speaking to the media, had additional points to make. "We reject all forms of violence, psychological as well as physical," said Hassan Ghashghavi of Iran. "Causing offense does not belong to the concept of freedom of speech"—a freedom which, of course, doesn't exist in his country. Ghashghavi added that free speech should be used to promote integration, not "Islamophobia." As noted, Reinfeldt, unlike Fogh Rasmussen, chose to meet with his cohort of Muslim ambassadors. Prior to the meeting, the Egyptian envoy, Mohamed Sotouhi, talked tough: "We want to see action, not just nice words. We have to push for a change in the law." He called for the establishment by the Swedish government of "a permanent parliamentary committee . . . to tackle Islamophobia." (It was interesting to see that the multicultural nonsense word "Islamophobia" had entered the vocabularies of both the Iranian and Egyptian ambassadors.) Ekmeleddin Ihsanoglu, the secretary-general of the Organization of the Islamic Conference, agreed: according to the *Arab News*, he believed "there was a need for a legal mechanism for stopping the recurrence of such extreme provocation" as Vilks's dog drawings.

Sotouhi claimed that he and his fellow ambassadors had drawn up a list of demands for legislative reform—plainly along sharia lines—and would present it to Reinfeldt. After the meeting, however, Reinfeldt insisted he had received no such list. He'd explained to the ambassadors, he told the media, "that Sweden is an open country and an open society," that Sweden's system of government didn't "permit politicians to interfere" with the media, and that "we don't have elected representatives making editorial decisions." Reinfeldt didn't deny reports, however, that he'd expressed "regret" that Vilks's cartoons had offended Muslims. In any event, Algeria's ambassador, Merzak Bedjaoui, praised Reinfeldt for having approached the exchange "in a spirit of appeasement."

In April 2008, Arshad Mubarak Ali, a city councilman in Stavanger, Norway, proposed a total ban on alcohol in downtown Stavanger as a first step toward making the city 100 percent alcohol-free. While Ali's father, Mubarak Ali, who is also a member of the city council, supported his son's proposal, Mayor Leif Johan Sevland dismissed it; but when Progress Party member Trond Birkedal said (quite reasonably) that the idea sounded like something the Taliban would have cooked up, Sevland turned on him, insisting that "such language does not belong in the city council"; the younger Ali, for his part, claimed his suggestion had "nothing to do with religion."

Efforts to forbid and punish criticism of Islam are under way not only at the national but also at the international level. In 2006, Flemming Rose expressed concern that the Organization of Islamic Countries and

Muslim clerics were "working systematically in all international organizations including the UN to make insulting the prophet a criminal offense all over the world." Many of those organizations have proven eager to cooperate. Benita Ferrero-Waldner, European Commissioner for External Relations and European Neighborhood Policy (meaning, essentially, relations with the Arab world), actually instructed European journalists in 2006 to "regulate [them]selves" in the cause of "mutual respect and understanding" between cultures. Such self-censorship, she insisted, was "a vital part of the fight against racism and xenophobia." Echoing the familiar refrain that "[f]reedom of expression is not the freedom to insult or offend," she pronounced that "[h]ate speech is always abhorrent." In April 2007, the EU criminalized "incitement of racism, xenophobia, or hatred against a racial, ethnic, or religious group," and set a penalty for violations of up to three years in prison. The law, which stipulates that member states "may choose to punish only conduct" that "is threatening, abusive or insulting," was especially disturbing given the multicultural tendency to define "incitement," "racism," and "xenophobia" in ways designed to silence the politically incorrect. Agence France-Presse characterized the EU's decision as having been "tempered by caveats to appease free speech concerns" on the part of representatives of Britain, Ireland, and the Scandinavian nations—meaning that in the eyes of somebody at Agence France-Presse, those who expressed concerns about the free-speech implications of this appalling measure were the ones being "appeased." It was one more Orwellian inversion of reality. (In any event, it was difficult to see how the EU's outrageous new prohibition was "tempered" in the slightest by "free-speech concerns.") There was one bright spot: at a September 2007 meeting of the Council of Europe, member countries voted that freedom of speech should be valued higher than religious considerations. But *bien pensant* observers frowned on this vote; a Danish professor of law, Gorm Toftegaard Nielsen, of Aarhus University, spoke for many when he said, "This is a very unfortunate signal to send. . . . It creates discord rather than peace."

If anything, the UN has been even more consistently craven on this front than the EU. When the UN was founded, it purportedly stood for human rights, including freedom of expression. It never *really* did, of course, because it pretended that the Soviet bloc was free; but at least it paid lip service to the idea of liberty. Now, however, the UN has openly scrapped the pretense of standing for democratic principles, and has supplanted freedom of speech with the concept of "respect for religion"—which, needless to say, was never an Enlightenment value.

At an April 2005 meeting of the UN Human Rights Commission, its Islamic members refused to condemn those who kill in the name of religion, and in fact said that criticism of Muslim terrorists amounted to "defamation of religion." In July of that year, after the bombings in London, David Littman of the International Humanist and Ethical Union tried to persuade the UN Sub-Commission on Human Rights in Geneva to condemn murders committed in the name of religion, but members from Muslim countries interrupted his speech so often that it was impossible for him to finish. The fact that the Human Rights Commission's member nations were mostly unfree countries, and that it repeatedly condemned Israel while remaining silent about terrorism, actually caused enough of a scandal that the commission was disbanded and replaced with a new body, the Human Rights Council. Alas, its biases proved to be identical to those of its predecessor. In March 2007, in an action seen as a response to the *Jyllands-Posten* controversy, and again in March 2008, the council passed resolutions calling for a worldwide ban on the defamation of religion. (The earlier resolution, which decried "attempts to identify Islam with terrorism, violence, and human rights violations," was proposed by the Organization of the Islamic Conference and mentioned no religion other than Islam.)

In September 2007, Reuters reported that "the United Nations investigator on racism" had "condemned a rising trend of Islamaphobia [sic], especially in Europe." The "investigator," a Senegalese lawyer named Doudou Diène who works under the auspices of the UN Human Rights Council and bears the impressive title of United Nations Special Rapporteur on Contemporary Forms of Racism, Racial Discrimination, Xenophobia and Related Intolerance, said that "in the current context, Islamaphobia constitutes the most serious form of religious defamation." Forget that Muslims in Europe are beating Jews and desecrating Jewish cemeteries, and making it impossible for Jewish children to get an education; no, "the most serious form of religious defamation" is Islamophobia—even though actual examples of Muslims being seriously abused anywhere in the West are precious few and far between. Diène complained that politicians, journalists, and intellectuals were "equating Islam with violence and terrorism"—as if the real problem were not precisely the opposite, namely that politicians, journalists, and intellectuals were systematically seeking to obscure the very real connections between Islam and acts of violence and terrorism. Diène urged journalists to contribute actively to the formation of a multicultural society and urged governments to prevent anti-immigration parties from gaining power. If in his comments Diène seemed to claim for the UN powers it has never had, and seemed also to be recommending courses of action that were not only blatantly undemocratic but might well have been formulated by jihadists themselves, this was only par for the course for today's UN, which seems determined to cripple resistance to jihad.[13]

In December 2007, the UN General Assembly passed a "Resolution on Combating Defamation of Religions" in which, as Elizabeth Samson pointed out in the *Wall Street Journal*, "the only religion mentioned by name was Islam." Six months later, David Littman appeared at a meeting of the UN Human Rights Council to read a statement on behalf of the Association for World Education and the International Humanist and Ethical Union. The statement addressed honor killings, the stoning of women, and the marrying off of young girls in Muslim countries, and explained that a fatwa by an Islamic scholar decrying these sharia-sanctioned practices could help reduce their incidence.

But Muslim members of the council interrupted Littman's remarks sixteen times. The Egyptian delegate warned that "Islam will not be crucified in this council"; his Pakistani colleague stated that "we have strong objections on any discussion . . . on the Shari'a law in this council. I would request the president to exercise his judgment and authority and request the speaker not to touch the issues which have already been deemed barred from discussion in this council." And indeed the council president, Doru Romulus Costea of Romania, complied thoroughly with the Muslim members' demands, calling on speakers to "refrain from making judgments or evaluations of a particular religion" and promising that "at the next evaluation of a religious creed, law, or document, I will interrupt the speaker and we'll go on to the next one." The IHEU's Web site summed up the day's lesson: "The UN Human Rights Council is not allowed to judge religions. . . . Criticism of Sha-

---

[13] In 2008, Diène traveled around the United States meeting with leading Muslims in preparation for an expected 2009 report on Islamophobia in America.

ria law or fatwas is now forbidden." As Littman observed, moreover, "the implication of the Egyptian complaint is that it is not necessary for Sharia law to be mentioned explicitly. It is enough that a speaker criticizes any human rights abuse sanctioned by the Sharia to be accused of insulting Islam and being forced to stop."

Then there's the American Civil Liberties Union (ACLU), which was once famous for defending even the rights of Nazis to march in Jewish neighborhoods, but which in recent years appears to have decided that when Islam is in the picture, liberty must yield to "respect." In 2007, Wendy Kaminer lamented this transformation, recalling in the *Wall Street Journal* that she had once "loved the ACLU" for being "a reliable defender of *everyone's* speech rights," but that the organization's agenda had become selective. These days, she explained, the ACLU only rarely stood up for the politically incorrect, and had been "remarkably quiet in several important free-speech cases and controversies." In the case of the Muhammed cartoons, for example, the ACLU had not only kept mum but advised its press office not to answer media questions on the topic. Even after a donor complained about this pusillanimous posture and the ACLU's board was asked to explain it, the organization's executive director, Anthony Romero, brought up the cartoons in only one low-profile dinner address and in a letter supporting the editors of a student paper that the University of Illinois sought to punish for reprinting the cartoons. Romero justified his near-total silence on the topic by saying that "rather than put out a hortatory statement that no one would read (except insiders) but might make us feel good about ourselves, we have tried to engage in thoughtful forums and discussions that relate to the issue. Speaking out on an issue involves more than slapping a paragraph together and posting it on a Web site." Yet as Kaminer noted, the ACLU "regularly posts slapped-together paragraphs . . . about the abuses of the Bush administration, among other subjects." One can only assume from Romero's preference in this case for "thoughtful forums" over "a hortatory statement" that he believed that in this case free speech needed to be "balanced" by consideration for Muslim sensitivities.

Suggesting that there was increasing sympathy in ACLU ranks "for restricting what many liberals condemn as hate speech," Kaminer quoted a 2006 statement by Romero to the effect that the ACLU believed in free speech but that "we do not believe in or condone speech that attacks minorities"—which pretty much says all you need to know about the ACLU's betrayal of the very values it was established to defend. In stark contrast to its silence on the cartoon crisis, in November 2007 the ACLU reacted swiftly and vigorously to news that the Los Angeles Police Department's antiterrorism bureau planned to identify the Muslim neighborhoods in L.A. (which has a Muslim population of about half a million). According to the *Los Angeles Times*, a letter that the ACLU sent jointly with several "community groups"—in other words, Muslim organizations—complained that "the mapping of Muslim communities . . . seems premised on the faulty notion that Muslims are more likely to commit violent acts than people of other faiths." Ramona Ripston, the ACLU's executive director, invoked the 1950s Red Scare, declaring: "This is nothing short of racial profiling." Within days, thanks to the furious protests by the ACLU and those "community groups," the LAPD's plan had been scrapped.

Other independent associations and non-governmental organizations have also taken highly worrying steps. In January 2008, for example, it was reported that the Swedish group Rädda Barnen (Save the Children) had censored its own report on honor-related violence in Palestine, Lebanon, and Yemen, for it was worried that researcher Pernilla Ouis's conclusions and word choices would "polarize" and "lead to a 'we and them' thinking." Ouis protested that Rädda Barnen had "removed everything" from the report "that explains honor thinking and honor violence," and explained that "if you don't write about the honor culture, you can't understand the acts of violence." Among the things Rädda Barnen had edited out was Ouis's description of those three countries' societies as patriarchal—a decision that Sanna Johnson of the organization's Beirut office defended with a deliciously absurd example of multicultural moral equivalence, asserting that "all societies are patriarchal. Sweden is a patriarchal society."

V

Cops, Courts, Civil Service

If the dhimmification of politicians, diplomats, and international bureaucrats may not be terribly shocking, consider the degree to which law-enforcement officers have yielded to Islamic pressure. When, after van Gogh's murder, a Rotterdam artist named Chris Ripken drew a street mural featuring a dove of peace and the words "Thou shalt not kill," that city's mayor, fearing Muslim displeasure, ordered police to destroy the mural. The police not only carried out this order; they also arrested a cameraman, Wim Nottroth, who tried to save the mural, and they confiscated and destroyed a videotape showing the mural's destruction.

In August 2007, it was announced that a British police investigation was under way as a result of the Channel 4 program *Undercover Mosque*, an unusually frank exposé which used hidden video cameras to catch supposedly moderate Muslim imams on tape calling for the beating of wives and daughters and the murder of gays and apostates. No, the police weren't investigating the imams (who had also called for war on Britain and justified the July 7 bombings); they were investigating Channel 4, which, the imams charged, had taken their comments out of context. Eventually the police reported Channel 4 to the Crown Prosecution Service for possible violation of the Public Order Act of 1986; and when they were told that there was insufficient evidence for a conviction, they reported Channel 4 to the government communications authority, Ofcom, on charges of stirring up racial hatred. Ofcom, to its credit, rejected the complaint.

What's worth noting here is that Channel 4's program consisted almost entirely of videotape footage of imams saying things—it was, in other words, pure reportage, a straightforward effort to show Britons what was going on behind the closed doors of mosques. As such, the documentary not only represented a stunning exception to the mainstream media's standard approach to Islam; it amounted to an exemplary act of public service. Yet instead of being commended, Channel 4 got in trouble with the authorities. The police reaction, noted James Forsyth in the *Spectator*, revealed "a mindset that views the exposure of a problem as more of a problem than the problem itself." And that wasn't all: days after *Undercover Mosque* was broadcast—in a colossal sign of indifference to the reality it exposed—Metropolitan Police Commissioner Sir Ian Blair announced plans to share antiterrorist intelligence with Muslim community leaders. (This plan, thankfully, was later "shelved.") Fortunately, this wasn't the end of it: Channel 4 sued the West Midlands police for libel, and in May 2008, as part of an out-of-court settlement, the police department agreed to apologize for its action—which, it turned out, had been the work of an assistant chief constable named Anil Patani (who apparently went unpunished for his abuse of police power).

Alas, examples of dhimmitude—and even jihadism—by British police abound. In July 2007 a planned television appeal by police to help capture a Muslim rape suspect was canceled to avoid "racist backlash." The next month, the London *Times* reported that "Asian" men (British for "Muslims") in the U.K. were having sex with perhaps hundreds of "white girls as young as twelve," but authorities wouldn't take action for fear of "upsetting race relations." (Typically, neither the *Times* nor government officials acknowledged that the "Asian" men's contempt for the "white" girls was a matter not of race but of religion—in their eyes the girls, being unbelievers, merited no respect.) In early 2008, a study by the think tank Social Cohesion reported that Muslims on the Britain police force and in other official positions were actively resisting efforts to prevent honor killings. According to an account in the *Daily Mail* by Miles Goslett and Daniel Boffey, Muslim police were "not only failing to help desperate women trying to flee abuse and arranged marriages" but also "return[ing] women to their abusive families" and encouraging "punishment for those they believe are breaking traditional taboos." Non-Muslim officials and police, for their part, were "scared of acting against families who abuse their relatives for fear of being branded as racist."

In February 2008, a police community support officer (PCSO) in Birmingham ordered two preachers to stop handing out Bible tracts because they "were in a Muslim area" and told them that their evangelism constituted a "hate crime." "You have been warned," he told them. "If you come back here and get beaten up, well you have been warned." According to the *Daily Telegraph*, the West Midlands police "refused to apologize" for the PCSO's conduct; by contrast, the police department in Tayside, England, fell all over itself apologizing in July 2008 when it landed in trouble for using a picture of a puppy on postcards advertising its new phone number. Islam, of course, views dogs as unclean.

In May 2008 the *Guardian* reported that according to a report by the British Prison Service's Directorate of High Security, officers at Whitemoor, a maximum-security prison, "are losing control to Muslim gangs." The *Guardian* quoted the report as saying that staff members "appeared reluctant to challenge inappropriate behaviour" by prisoners "for fear of doing the wrong thing" and that "this was leading to a general feeling of a lack of control and shifting the power dynamic towards prisoners." In a familiar move, the writers of the report, instead of focusing on the developing chaos itself, professed concern that this nightmarish situation might result in "hostility and Islamophobia." What was the authorities' solution to this nightmare? A spokeswoman for the Ministry of Justice outlined a "programme" that had been formulated with the intention of "increas[ing] mutual understanding between staff and prisoners," and that included "a development day for staff on the Muslim faith, focus groups in which staff and ethnic minority prisoners will discuss prison community issues, and diversity events."

Britain may be at the cutting edge of this kind of institutional dhimmitude, but such outrages are hardly unique to the sceptered isle. The Canadian feminist writer Irshad Manji, herself an open lesbian and reformist Muslim, has noted that in 2006, when seventeen terrorists were arrested in Toronto on the verge of giving Canada "its own 9/11," "the police did not mention that it had anything to do with Islam or

Muslims, not a word." In January 2008, Canada's *National Post* reported that a Bangladeshi-Canadian university student in Ontario had been posting Internet messages calling Canadian soldiers "legitimate targets to be killed"; but though police officers spoke with him, he was not arrested—and continued to incite violence against that country's troops. The *Post* noted that "Canada's Anti-Terrorism Act (ATA) does not specifically outlaw incitement of terrorism"—which meant that even as Canadian writers like Mark Steyn and Ezra Levant (as we shall see) were being hauled before official commissions for criticizing Islam, jihadists were free to engage in online terrorist recruiting.

Similarly, while American immigration officials are desperate not to do anything that might be construed as "racial profiling," an Icelandic woman who was obviously above suspicion (Iceland has virtually no Muslims) was detained by immigration personnel at JFK Airport in 2007 simply because she'd briefly overstayed a visa more than a decade earlier. Officials interrogated her for hours, arrested her, and locked her in a cell. One can only conclude from such actions by government functionaries that not only are they determined *not* to deal with the real threat—they may also be thinking, either consciously or subconsciously, that if they're seen to abuse harmless non-Muslim women from places like Iceland, it will serve to dispel any suspicion that they might be guilty of so dastardly a multicultural offense as "racial profiling."

The "problem of legitimizing radical Muslims," counterterrorism expert Steven Emerson has observed, "extends right up through the highest levels of our top law enforcement agency" (that is, the FBI). Emerson has enjoined readers to "be very suspicious" when confronted with claims not only by the media but also by the FBI that this or that person is a "mainstream Muslim" who supports "'inter-faith' activities." In October 2007, a *New York Post* article by Emerson and Stephen M. Flatow described an October 2007 "counterterrorism conference" sponsored by the New Jersey Department of Homeland Security as "a textbook case of exactly what's wrong with many U.S. counterterror and outreach efforts—a farce that had apologists for terrorism and radical Islam writing the 'script' for how to protect Americans from the terrorist threat." Citing one of the post-conference report's conclusions—that "[u]niversities can be breeding grounds for radicalization" and that academia needs an "anti-radicalization strategy"—Emerson and Flatow agreed, but noted that one of the speakers at the event was none other than John Esposito, director of Georgetown University's Prince Alwaleed bin Talal Center for Muslim-Christian Understanding, who, they observed, "should be a case study in *how* universities can promote radicalism, not a member of a panel discussing 'anti-radicalization' strategies."

In September 2007, Rita Karlsen reported on a panel discussion about "Muslims, Norway's Security, and Surveillance" that had been sponsored by the Muslim Student Association in Oslo. Karlsen focused on the comments made by one of the panelists, Jørn Holme, head of the Norwegian Police Security Service (PST), who seemed to Karlsen "to be most concerned with telling Muslims in Norway that they themselves mustn't link terror to Islam. For Norwegians are too stupid to understand that there is no connection." She quoted Holme's remarks to the Muslim audience: "90 percent of the Norwegian population doesn't understand the difference between Islam and Islamism," he told them. "When it's asserted that there's 'widespread surveillance of Muslims,' yeah, there's a guy sitting, for example, in Fauske"—a town of 10,000 in northern Norway (Holme was bonding with Oslo Muslims by sneering at rural Norwegian hicks)—"and thinking: 'It's great that they're keeping an eye on the Muslims.'" Holme went out of his way to avoid connecting Islam with any wrongdoing, but was eager to point out that Christianity has been responsible for many wrongs. As an example, he said that "in the United States in the Sixties, blacks were raped by whites who went to church the next day." Whites, Christians, Americans: Holme managed to insult all three in a single sentence before an audience of Muslims.

According to Karlsen, Holme received plenty of laughs, especially when he slurred what he called "human-rights-violation-country number one," namely the United States. Holme went on to point out that 90 percent of those *affected* by terror are Muslims, but he said nothing about who *carries out* the terror. As for the terror danger in Europe, he claimed that at present it comes *from within*. "For it's not as if Osama bin Laden will come sailing a boat into Oslo Fjord," said Holme, to fresh laughter from the audience. He pointed out that there's a small number of people in Norway who represent a terror danger, in the sense that they support terror abroad; he added that some of these individuals had become Norwegian citizens, which seemed to imply that they had come from somewhere else—but he didn't say where. Nor did he explain exactly what he meant by "support terror abroad." Did he mean, Karlsen wondered, that only a small number belonged to violent organizations, or was he actually suggesting "that only a tiny minority of Muslims in Norway support Hamas or Islamic jihad?" Holme emphasized that PST had no interest in Islamism, fundamentalism, or the desire for a sharia state; all it cared about was the possibility of violence. (As Karlsen dryly observed, "Holme's approach to security in Norway didn't seem particularly preventive.")

Most sensational of all was Holme's disclosure that one of PST's greatest concerns was this: "What will happen with Norway in case of a possible terror attack?" Holme, wrote Karlsen, "was not in doubt: 'What we fear is that there will be a lynch-mob atmosphere against Muslims. There will be a polarization in the society, and violence will be used, in which extreme right-wing forces will go on the attack against Muslims.'" Thus did Holme slide past the prospect of Muslim violence itself to focus instead on the supposed possibility of retributory violence by non-Muslims. Holme criticized the Dutch for what he saw as their illiberal response to the murder of van Gogh and praised Britain for reacting to 7/7 and other attacks (in Karlsen's paraphrase) "in a more nuanced and calm manner." Karlsen, who wondered if Holme was aware that "13 percent of young British Muslims support terror groups like al-Qaeda," concluded as follows:

> Scared? Yes, I was scared by PST head Holme. That we have a
> leader of the PST whose greatest concern is that a terror action
> on Norwegian soil will lead to the stigmatizing of Muslims,
> rather than that a terror action on Norwegian soil *may happen*,
> is something I consider nothing less than frightening.

Karlsen noted wryly that Holme, after having labored so hard to disconnect terrorism from Islam, essentially admitted in the end that any terrorist act in Norway would of course be performed by Muslims— "for otherwise there's hardly any reason, is there," she pointed out, "to fear that Muslims generally would be subjected to stigmatization and polarization after a terror plot?"

Even military leaders aren't immune to the virus of dhimmitude. In 2005, *Washington Times* columnist Diana West noted that America's then commander in Iraq, Lt. Gen. John R. Vines, was educating his staff in Islam by giving them a reading list that "whitewashes jihad, dhimmitude and sharia law with the works of Karen Armstrong and John Esposito"; two years later, West noted the unwillingness of a U.S. counterinsurgency advisor, Lt. Col. David Kilcullen, to mention the word jihad. Replying to her column, Kilcullen told West that she "may not like Muslims, and that's your choice"—implying that to acknowledge the reality of Islamic jihad was to be a bigot. In early 2008, officials at a Royal Air Force base in Cambridgeshire advised servicepeople not to wear uniforms off-base in order to avoid abuse by members of the public. (Prime Minister Gordon Brown, to his credit, condemned this advice.) In February 2008, it was reported that Saudi Arabia's Prince Bandar, in a 2003 conversation with then Prime Minister Tony Blair, had threatened to withhold information from Blair's government about Saudi terrorists if British investigators did not cease looking into allegations of corruption in Saudi arms deals. According to the *Guardian*, "The threats halted the fraud inquiry"; Lord Justice Moses said it was "just as if a gun had been held to the head" of the British government.

In early 2008, it was reported that the Pentagon had fired Stephen Coughlin, its resident expert on sharia and jihad, supposedly because his open acknowledgment that terrorism is motivated by jihad had antagonized an influential Muslim aide to Deputy Secretary of Defense Gordon England. "That Coughlin's analyses would even be considered 'controversial,'" wrote Andrew Bostom, editor of *The Legacy of Jihad*, "is pathognomonic of the intellectual and moral rot plaguing our efforts to combat global terrorism." Apparently as a result of the outcry over this dismissal, the Pentagon ended up keeping Coughlin after all, though it moved him to a different job in another office. Meanwhile the Muslim aide who had apparently been behind the firing—and who, it emerged, had violated U.S. policy by arranging for his boss to meet representatives of both the Syrian government and the Muslim Brotherhood—remained firmly ensconced in his highly sensitive position.

In February 2008, a Web site run by the U.S. military in Afghanistan published an attack on Geert Wilders's film about Islam. Since the film had not yet been released, it was clear that the article, entitled "Stirring the Hate," was not taking issue with any specific details of the production, but with the very idea of it. As far as the article's author, M. Sgt. Allen Ness, was concerned, it was simply "stupid and irresponsible" for someone in the West to make a film critical of Islam. Explaining his position, Ness told UPI that Afghan riots over the *Jyllands-Posten* cartoons had "caused great damage and loss of life" and also "damaged the trust that we had built up with the Afghans," and was concerned that Wilders's film might do the same. In other words: don't say they're violent, or they'll get violent. Ness seemed not to realize that a "trust" between two nations that could be destroyed by a movie was fragile, if not entirely illusory. It was disturbing that a man supposedly fighting for freedom could so blithely condemn someone else for exercising that freedom—and for fighting for it, too, in his own way.

Increasingly, courts in the West have handed down rulings contrary to democratic principle—but entirely in line with sharia. Indeed, there have even been moves toward enshrining sharia as a parallel system of jurisprudence in the West. Back in 1999, Daniel Pipes wrote in a prescient *Commentary* article about Western Muslims' legal efforts "to build an inviolate wall around Islam, endowing it with something like the sacrosanct status it enjoys in traditionally Muslim countries." Pipes noted that French bishop Marcel Lefebvre had already been fined nearly $1,000 for warning about his country's Islamization, and that a Canadian who had distributed "leaflets protesting the Muslim persecution of Christians" was convicted of hate speech and "sentenced to 240 hours of community service and six months of probation."

Since then, this tendency to charge citizens of supposedly free countries with violating sharia-like laws has only intensified. Ruling in 2005 on a petition by the Muslim Union of Italy, a magistrate in the northern Italian city of Bergamo ordered writer Oriana Fallaci to stand trial for disparaging Islam in her book *The Force of Reason*. Fallaci had previously been tried for a similar offense in France; that she was ultimately found not guilty in both cases did not mitigate the outrage of being tried on such charges in the first place. In the same year, the European Court of Human Rights affirmed a Turkish court's conviction of a publisher for issuing a novel, Abdullah Riza Ergüven's *Yasak Tümceler*, that purportedly insulted Muhammed and the Koran. In 2006, the Islamic Society of Denmark, a group tied to the Muslim Brotherhood, sued Danish politician Pia Kjærsgaard for defamation. Her crime? She had used the word "traitors" to describe the Danish imams who'd traveled abroad to stir up anti-Danish sentiment over the *Jyllands-Posten* cartoons. Kjærsgaard, like Fallaci, was eventually acquitted, but not before putting a good deal of time, effort, and money into her defense. Thus do traitors use the system they seek to destroy to intimidate its defenders. After the verdict in Kjærsgaard's case, the Islamic Society called for a fatwa against *Jyllands-Posten*, and its spokesman Kasem Ahmad said: "We have been subject to so many provocations by you in the West. The latest example is the knighting of Salman Rushdie. Before that *Jyllands-Posten* insulted our prophet. Now we want directions from authoritative clerics in the Middle East on how to react."

In Britain, where imams preach holy war without being arrested, schoolgirl Codie Scott was hauled into court in 2006 on charges of racism because she'd been told to work on a project with a group of Pakistani students and made the mistake of saying that she couldn't communicate with them because they didn't speak English. British police protect Islamists when they take to the streets and call for the murder of Bush and Blair, but at least one Englishman has been convicted of a crime for hanging a banner outside his home calling for the death of Islamists (who are, after all, Britain's declared enemies in Afghanistan and Iraq). And in 2002, *Daily Telegraph* columnist Robin Page was arrested in Gloucestershire on charges of hate speech for having begun a speech by saying: "If you are a black, vegetarian, Muslim, asylum-seeking, one-legged lesbian lorry driver, I want the same rights as you." This in a country where every day imams preach *real* hatred. In February 2008, it was reported that prosecutions of jihadists in Britain might "collapse" because judges were watering down or defying counterterrorism laws by requiring that prosecutors prove "that terror suspects not only possessed potentially dangerous material but were intent on using it in an attack."

In Canada, both publisher Ezra Levant and journalist Mark Steyn were ordered to face human-rights tribunals, the former for reprinting the *Jyllands-Posten* cartoons in his magazine, the *Western Standard*, the latter for writing about Islam in *Maclean's*. The Levant case began with a complaint by Syed Soharwardy, an imam in Calgary and founder of the Islamic Supreme Council of Canada (ISCC). First Soharwardy had gone to the police, insisting that they arrest Levant for reprinting the cartoons. (It is interesting that though Soharwardy had lived in North America for more than two decades, he expected Canadian police to behave like their counterparts in Saudi Arabia.) When the police refused, Soharwardy turned to a more receptive body—Alberta's so-called Human Rights Commission, which is empowered by a Canadian hate-speech law and which, as Lee Duigon noted in an article at MichNews.com, had "a 100% conviction rate" because "the accusation alone is enough to find the defendant guilty." (As Duigon put it, "the fact that some doofus says he found the defendant's speech offensive is proof that it offended somebody and therefore must be punished.")

Among the many outrageous aspects of this system is that the state pays the plaintiff's expenses, but not the defendant's. Nor does it permit the accused to be accompanied to his hearing by a lawyer. The media are banned, too. But Levant did take along a videocamera—and afterward posted the video of the entire interrogation online. It was a remarkable spectacle, precisely because every aspect of the situation was so perfectly and chillingly banal, from the drab office setting to the "bovine indifference" (as Duigon aptly put it) of Levant's inquisitor, who plainly didn't recognize that she was an instrument of terrifying freedom-crushing forces; it was obvious that she saw herself as a provincial official simply doing her job. While Levant eloquently explained to her his rights as a citizen of a democracy and the outrageous overstepping of government powers that her commission represented, the woman just sat there looking fatuous and apathetic—the very picture of the clueless bureaucrat.

In February 2008, Soharwardy tried to withdraw his complaint, claiming that he had not previously recognized the importance of free speech; in an interview on the CBC, however, he explained that he wanted to drop the complaint because Levant was becoming "a martyr of freedom of his [sic] speech." (This martyrdom, incidentally, had cost Levant over $100,000 in legal and other expenses.) Licia Corbella of the *Calgary Herald*, who had interviewed Soharwardy, noted that Soharwardy had "wanted to be the hero and martyr"—and that when things had turned out otherwise, he had backed off. Corbella's article was illuminating: though Soharwardy fiercely denied Levant's charge that he wanted to see Canada under sharia law, it turned out that he had written in 2004 that "Sharia cannot be customized for specific countries. These universal, divine laws are for all people of all countries for all times." With a bluntness about these matters that is rare in a mainstream journalist, Corbella wrote: "Soharwardy is a charmer.

He convinced me that I must have misread his columns. But relistening to the tape of our meeting and rereading his original texts, one thing is clear: he cannot be believed." One wishes the *New York Times'* coverage of Tariq Ramadan were half as frank as Corbella's coverage of Soharwardy.

As for Steyn, he was reported to the human-rights commissions in Ontario and British Columbia as well as to Canada's federal Human Rights Commission (HRC). Apropos of the last-named complaint, Jonathan Kay reported in the *National Post* in March 2008 that Dean Steacy, the investigator for the federal commission, had dismissed a question about free-speech considerations, saying that "freedom of speech is an American concept, so I don't give it any value." The complaints against Steyn were filed by Mohamed Elmasry, head of the Canadian Islamic Congress, and a group of law students. In April the Ontario commission announced that it would not be pursuing the case against Steyn—but nonetheless took the opportunity to condemn his article as "Islamophobic." Under public pressure, the federal HRC, too, dropped its complaint. But Steyn's show trial in British Columbia went ahead in June 2008. Reporting on it, Petti Fong of the *Toronto Star* gave special Andrea Elliott–style attention to a Muslim woman in the public gallery, Lazina Yasir, who "began weeping quietly . . . when the lawyer for the CIC read some of the blog responses to [Steyn's] article" (never mind that Steyn could hardly be held responsible for reader comments on a blog) and whose husband argued that free speech wasn't the only issue that mattered here (plainly, we were meant to understand that his wife's tears trumped freedom of expression). In the end, British Columbia, too, let Steyn go—a verdict that might have turned out differently had Canadians (alerted largely by blogs) not made clear their outrage at this abuse of state power. If found guilty, Steyn could have been forced to stop writing his column for *Maclean's*, one of Canada's oldest and most venerable magazines. For such an assault on free speech to take place in a modern democracy was profoundly disturbing; yet many major Canadian media seemed not to care very much, and the mainstream U.S. media all but entirely ignored the whole business.

In a June 2008 *New York Times* article, Adam Liptak used these Canadian cases as the starting point for a comparison of American and foreign approaches to free speech. The piece's original headline captured Liptak's view of America as a freakish exception to the rule: "Out of Step with Allies, U.S. Defends Freedom to Offend in Speech." (The headline was later altered online to "Unlike Others, U.S. Defends Freedom to Offend in Speech"; some readers noted it should simply have been entitled "Unlike Others, U.S. Defends Free Speech.") Though Steyn's *Maclean's* article had been largely factual, Liptak avoided any account of its content, instead focusing on Muslim charges that it "stirr[ed] up hatred against Muslims" and linking it to statements by Nazis and the KKK in such a way as to lead readers to assume that he belonged in the same category as those groups. Slipping right past the question of whether Steyn's piece was hate speech, Liptak implied throughout that it unquestionably was, and concentrated instead on exploring whether hate speech should be banned. (Needless to say, at no point in Liptak's piece did he provide these events with the proper context by noting that Muslim leaders around the West are using every stratagem they can think of to try to limit free expression.)

Several complaints have been made under the Racial and Religious Tolerance Act in the Australian state of Victoria. The Islamic Council of Victoria, for example, sued pastors Danny Nalliah and Daniel Scot and their ministry for "vilification of Muslims"; in December 2004, they were found guilty and ordered to apologize in print and on the Internet. (The estimated cost of the print apology was over fifty thousand U.S. dollars.) The verdict was awash in irony, since a major factor, if not *the* major factor, in Scot's conviction was apparently that he had quoted from the Koran and had dared to suggest that Muslims today still read that book literally and revere every word of it as immutable divine truth—a fact that the judge simply refused to accept. Scot told *Time* magazine that he believed his real offense was having discussed "the parts of the Koran that Muslims want to hide from people." In June 2007, after the pastors had spent five years and more than half a million dollars in their defense, an appeal ended with a mediated settlement.

In Ontario in 2003, retired lawyer Syed Mumtaz Ali announced that he was establishing a sharia court to handle family-law cases. The news caused an uproar, and in 2005 religious courts were prohibited in Ontario. Elsewhere in the West, however, sharia has continued to make inroads. In November 2006, citing a new report, Joshua Rozenberg wrote in the *Telegraph* that "Islamic sharia law is gaining an increasing foothold in parts of Britain." When several young Somali men were accused of stabbing a Somali teenager in London, the police granted the request of the victim's family that the suspects be released, and the case was adjudicated by a court of family elders. Noting that there are already sharia courts in Britain's major urban areas, Rozenberg wrote that some attorneys "welcomed" this "legal pluralism." For example, Prakash Shah, who teaches law at Queen Mary University, said that such trials might be "more effective than the formal legal system," while barrister Faizul Aqtab Siddiqi agreed: "I think there is a case to be made under which the elders sit together and reprimand people, trying to get them to change."

I've mentioned Archbishop of Canterbury Rowan Williams's proposal that Parliament forbid insensitive utterances. This was fatuous enough; but as it turned out, Williams wasn't through. In February 2008 he proposed—first in a speech, then in a BBC radio interview—that sharia law be formally introduced in Britain. To be sure, the Islamic Sharia Council had already been operating in that country for many years, handing down judgments on marriages and divorces; and local sharia courts take on cases that range from family and neighborhood disputes to crimes of rape and assault. What Williams now suggested, however, was "a much enhanced and quite sophisticated version of such a body, with increased resources." The flavor of Williams's lecture on the subject, a masterly six-thousand-word exercise in euphemism and circumlocution given at the Royal Courts of Justice in London, is suggested by the following passage:

It would be a pity if the immense advances in the recognition of human rights led, because of a misconception about legal universality, to a situation where a person was defined primarily as the possessor of a set of abstract liberties and the law's function was accordingly seen as nothing but the securing of those liberties irrespective of the custom and conscience of those groups which concretely compose a plural modern society.

What Williams seemed to be saying was that he found it more attractive to see a human being as a submissive member of a group than as a free individual. Language like the archbishop's, which reduces harsh reality to bland academic abstraction, effectively removes from view the fact that, for example, as the *Telegraph* had reported a couple of weeks before the archbishop's lecture, "36 per cent of young British Muslims believ[e] that a Muslim who converted to another religion should be 'punished by death.'" *That's* sharia for you—but you would never have known it from reading Williams's reassuringly gray, depersonalized prose. George Orwell might well have been describing Williams's lecture when, in his 1945 essay "Politics and the English Language," he imagined

> some comfortable English professor defending Russian totalitarianism. He cannot say outright, "I believe in killing off your opponents when you can get good results by doing so." Probably, therefore, he will say something like this:
>
> "While freely conceding that the Soviet régime exhibits certain features which the humanitarian may be inclined to deplore, we must, I think, agree that a certain curtailment of the right to political opposition is an unavoidable concomitant of transitional periods, and that the rigours which the Russian people have been called upon to undergo have been amply justified in the sphere of concrete achievement."
>
> The inflated style is itself a kind of euphemism. A mass of Latin words falls upon the facts like soft snow, blurring the outlines and covering up all the details. The great enemy of clear languge is insincerity. Where there is a gap between one's real and one's declared aims, one turns as it were instinctively to long words and exhausted idioms. . . .

Williams urged his audience to recognize "that if we are to think intelligently about the relations between Islam and British law, we need a fair amount of 'deconstruction' of crude oppositions and mythologies, whether of the nature of sharia or the nature of the Enlightenment." This is a popular means nowadays of obscuring the very clear distinctions between living in freedom and living under sharia—to dismiss those distinctions as "crude," unsophisticated, lacking in intellectual seriousness and nuance. It was only appropriate that the first person Williams cited in his lecture was none other than Tariq Ramadan, whose brilliantly vague and pretentious definition of sharia ("the expression of the universal principles of Islam [and] the framework and the thinking that makes for their actualization in human history") made it a perfect fit for Williams's essay.

Williams's comments about his proposal on BBC radio were more direct. The country, he said, should "face up to the fact" that Muslims prefer sharia law to British law, that instituting at least some aspects of sharia would improve relations (for it was unfair to expect Muslims to decide between "the stark alternatives of cultural loyalty or state loyalty"), and that the eventual establishment of some form of sharia in Britain was, in any event, "unavoidable." Using Buruma's and Garton Ash's favorite term, Williams called for a "constructive accommodation" with Islamic law. Ruth Gledhill of the *Times* of London was so incensed by the archbishop's proposal ("Has the Archbishop Gone Bonkers?" was the headline on her column) that she decided to write about a phenomenon she had recently learned about from a human-rights advocate: the commitment of Muslim women to psychiatric hospitals by their husbands, with the connivance of male Muslim physicians and psychiatrists, not because they were mentally ill, but because they were insufficiently submissive or overly Westernized, or simply because their husbands had tired of them. "There are lots of these women in there, locked up in these hospitals," the advocate had told Gledhill. "Why don't you people write about this?" Gledhill had declined, because she required evidence and wanted the advocate to go on the record; but the advocate couldn't: "I would be killed. And so would the women." Gledhill concluded: "So there you have it. After weeks of wondering what to do, inspired by the Archbishop, I've taken her word that she is telling the truth, respected her anonymity, and written it anyway.

"And this, I imagine, is what the Archbishop wants for the whole of England."

Both the *New York Times* and the *Washington Post* responded to the controversy over Williams's speech by running pro-sharia pieces. The *Times'* contribution, which appeared in the issue of the *Times Magazine* dated March 16, 2008, took the form of an essay by Noah Feldman, a law professor at Harvard and adjunct senior fellow at the Council on Foreign Relations. With this essay, "Why Shariah?," the *Times* outdid itself. The piece was a mind-boggling whitewash of Islamic law.

"For most of its history," wrote Feldman, "Islamic law offered the most liberal and humane legal principles available anywhere in the world." Feldman blamed criticism of sharia on Westerners' need for an enemy: "It sometimes seems as if we need Shariah as Westerners have long needed Islam: as a canvas on which to project our ideas of the horrible, and as a foil to make us look good." The passage in which Feldman pretended to acknowledge sharia's downside was brief and dishonest: "Some rules associated with Shariah are undoubtedly old-fashioned and harsh. . . . The prohibition on sodomy, though historically often unenforced, makes recognition of same-sex relationships difficult to contemplate." Feldman didn't bother to mention that sharia doesn't just mean no gay marriage: it means executing gays. Such details were apparently of small significance to Feldman, who in his next sentence sought to cheer readers with the news that "Shariah also prohibits bribery or special favors in court" and that it demands "equal treatment for rich and poor." (But not, as he neglected to point out, equal treatment for Muslim and non-Muslim or for man and woman.) "In its essence," asserted Feldman, "Shariah aspires to be a law that applies equally to every human, great or small, ruler or ruled." Feldman acted as if this were tantamount to saying that it's *just*. No, it's exactly the opposite: it's totalitarian, reaching into every corner of life. Feldman concluded that "the Islamists' aspiration to renew old ideas of the rule of law while coming to terms with contemporary circumstances is bold and noble."

Which, one wondered, was more staggering: that a Harvard law professor had written such an obscene essay, or that the *New York Times* had published it?

Meanwhile, the *Washington Post*'s response to Williams's speech was to run a piece on its Web site by Feisal Abdul Rauf headlined "Archbishop of Canterbury Was Right." "It is time for Britain to integrate aspects of Islamic law," wrote Rauf, author of a book entitled *What's Right with Islam: A New Vision for Muslims and the West.* Among his arguments was that "the integration of Sharia law would provide some modicum of equilibrium among Jewish law, Christian law and Islamic law," thus providing "an aggregated legal framework that represents all three Abrahamic traditions, Jewish, Christian and Muslim. By doing so, Britain would ensure that Muslims stay engaged, not isolated or estranged, and assume active ownership in civic participatory duties and responsibilities." In other words, Muslims in the West don't *want* to live under secular democratic law, so give them sharia—whose integration into Western jurisprudence would only be fair anyway, since it would balance out the Judeo-Christian influence. (Equal time for "all three Abrahamic traditions": what a terrific justification for annihilating modern freedom!) Like Feldman, then, Rauf swept the horrors of sharia totally under the rug—and did so with the imprimatur of one of the nation's most respected newspapers.

Not until September 2008, several months after the flap over Rowan Williams's sharia comments, did it emerge that not only were there already sharia courts in several British cities, but that their rulings, according to Abul Taber in the *Times* of London, had been "enforceable with the full power of the judicial system" since August 2007—meaning that no matter how unjust a decision a sharia judge might make, British authorities were obligated to enforce it.

Germany's legal system, too, was under assault. In March 2007, Christa Datz-Winter, a family-court judge in Frankfurt, refused to expedite a divorce between a young Moroccan-German woman whose Moroccan husband had reportedly beaten her and threatened to kill her. Datz-Winter argued that the wife should have been prepared for such treatment given that her husband's religion granted him the "right to use corporal punishment." Armin Laschet, minister of integration in North Rhine Westphalia, told *Der Spiegel* that this was only one "in a chain of horrific rulings" in which German courts had taken sharia into account (by, for example, treating honor killings as manslaughter rather than murder). Seyran Ates, a Berlin lawyer who has fought to secure the democratic rights of Muslim women in the face of efforts by the political and judicial establishment to keep them trapped in sharia, said she was almost grateful that Datz-Winter had grounded her decision so explicitly in the Koran, for by doing so she had exposed "an undercurrent that already exists in our courts" whereby tolerance for Muslim intolerance was gradually leading to the introduction of a parallel, sharia-based legal system. Yet though Datz-Winter's ruling was reversed—and widely reported and condemned—the trend continues. One of the surprises of this case was *Der Spiegel*'s frank, extensive exposé itself. "For decades," it read, "German judges essentially paved the way for Islamic fundamentalists to form a parallel society." *Der Spiegel* might have added that this process was aided by the German media's failure to sound the alarm about it—and its frequent vilification and misrepresentation of those, like Ates, who did.

On another of the rare occasions when German media have tried to report honestly on the reality of creeping sharia, the judicial system stepped in. In May 2006, the Web site of the ZDF television network described a Berlin imam who had called Germans "stinking infidels" as a "hate preacher." The imam took ZDF to court, and Judge Klaus Feldmann barred ZDF from describing him in that way. It's permissible in Germany, then, for a Muslim to spew hate at non-Muslims, but for a non-Muslim to call it hate is verboten.

Judges across Europe routinely give the perpetrators of honor killings not heavier sentences because their crimes are premeditated, but lighter sentences because the crimes, according to their native cultures, are not crimes at all. For some dhimmis, even this is insufficiently multicultural. In late 2007, Norway's most celebrated lawyer, Tor Erling Staff, proposed that the punishment for honor killing be *officially* set lower than that for other murders. Why? Because, he explained, we are doing the Muslim man a disservice: he acts in accordance with his own sense of honor and we call his acts dishonorable. This, Staff said, is sheer arrogance: we expect the Muslim to conform to *our* society's norms when instead we should be striving, humbly and respectfully, to understand *his* society's norms.

In recent years, the would-be silencers of Islam's critics have discovered the joys of "libel tourism"—they sue the critics in British courts, even if neither party is British, because libel laws in that country strongly favor plaintiffs. In 2007, the *Chronicle of Higher Education* reported that at least four books detailing the financing of jihad terrorism had been the targets of libel suits in Britain. Cambridge University Press, the publisher of one of the books, *Funding Evil: How Terrorism Is Financed—and How to Stop It* by Rachel Ehrenfeld, had received a threatening letter and (according to Ehrenfeld) "immediately caved in and said, Do whatever it takes. Pay them whatever they want. Ban the book, destroy the book, we don't want this lawsuit." In fact Cambridge pulped all the unsold copies of Ehrenfeld's work. In another case, involving the book *Alms for Jihad*, the same publisher not only sent a letter of apology to Sheikh Khalid Bin Mahfouz in Saudi Arabia, obligingly avowing that a number of statements in the book about his family, businesses, and charities were "entirely and manifestly false," according to Gary Shapiro in the *New York Sun*, but also posted an apology on its Web site and promised to pay damages and legal costs—all this even though the book's authors had reportedly provided documents supporting the statements made in their book about Mahfouz. Deborah Lipstadt, another author sued by Saudis, told the *New York Sun* that the Saudis were "systematically, case by case, book by book," taking such action against authors who drew links between Saudis and terrorism.

In 2007, the member nations of the European Union signed the Lisbon Treaty, which will take effect in 2009. One of its provisions is the implementation throughout the EU of the "European Arrest Warrant," whereby the list of crimes for which one can automatically be arrested and extradited included "racism and xenophobia." Thus, as Serge Trifkovic observed, "a Muslim-friendly judge in, say, Leicester or Birmingham could issue a warrant for my arrest in Greece" for giving a speech critical of Islam in Austria, and Greek authorities "would have to comply, no questions asked." Under the treaty, additional criminal charges could be leveled for having given such a speech to an audience, for having given it under the auspices of an organization, and for having posted it on a Web site.

As part of their efforts to control speech about Islam, governments as well as various non-governmental or supragovernmental authorities have sought to restrict or forbid the use of certain words and expressions. At one point in 2007, President George W. Bush dared to use the expression "war on Islamofascism," but after Muslims and dhimmis protested he quickly reverted to the meaningless term "war on terror." In his 2008 State of the Union address, Bush seemed to be trying even harder to placate Muslims, pointedly avoiding words like "Islamic" or even "Islamist" to characterize terrorism. This represented a departure from his earlier State of the Union addresses, and marked the intensification of an already colossal act of irresponsibility—namely, a refusal to make clear to Americans the nature of the enemy's beliefs and motives. The very least that a president owes people whom he is asking to fight a war, after all, is a clear, honest, and complete explanation of whom and what they are up against, and why.

Bush wasn't alone. In 2007, British Prime Minister Gordon Brown, who (as we have seen) refused to ban the radical Islamic group Hizb ut-

Tahrir, *did* forbid the use by cabinet ministers of the phrase "war on terror" (which is itself, of course, a euphemism for something that should actually be called "war with Islamofascists" or "war with jihadists") and the use of the word "Muslim" in discussions of terrorism. The goal, according to the *Daily Express*, was to "improve community relations and avoid offending Muslims." The EU was thinking along the same lines: in July 5, 2007, a *Daily Express* headline read: "Europe tells Britain: Don't Say 'Muslims.'" The article, by Alison Little, explained that "secret EU guidelines have been drawn up warning governments not to link Islam and terrorism" and banning the words "jihad," "Islamic," and "fundamentalist." Little noted that neither Brown nor his home secretary, in interviews about the recent car-bomb attacks in London and Glasgow, had used the word "Muslims" or "Islam." (Indeed, British officials and media had dutifully echoed the "explanations" by Muslim "leaders" that the attacks reflected Muslim discontent over British foreign policy, the knighting of Salman Rushdie, and other issues.) According to Little, "EU officials said the 'common lexicon' aimed to stop the distortion of the Muslim faith and alienation of its followers in Europe. European governments had previously agreed on the need to develop a 'non-emotive lexicon' for use in discussion to avoid 'exacerbating division.'"

Conservative MP Philip Davies complained, "If we believe in anything in this country we should believe in free speech." But a Foreign Office source, according to Little, "insisted the 'common lexicon' was not an exercise in 'political correctness' but an attempt to find a 'common vocabulary and definitions' for statements about terrorism." In *1984*, George Orwell imagined a society with a "common vocabulary and definitions," too.

Indeed, official language about Islam has grown increasingly Orwellian. In February 2008, the *Daily Mail* reported that the British government had compiled a counterterrorism phrasebook designed to ensure that "civil servants no longer blame fanatical extremism on Islam, for fear of upsetting the Muslim community." The guide, according to Alan Travis in the *Guardian*, "tells civil servants not to use terms such as Islamist extremism or jihadi-fundamentalist but instead to refer to violent extremism and criminal murderers or thugs to avoid any implication that there is an explicit link between Islam and terrorism." Travis approvingly described this as a "new sophistication"—presumably an accompaniment to Paul Vallely's "new sensitivity"—and cited home secretary Jacqui Smith's recent declaration that "violent extremism [is] 'anti-Islamic'" (as if it were a democratic government's job to say that adherents of any faith have gotten their theology wrong). There was certainly no understanding on the part of the *Guardian* that this "new sophistication," far from winning Muslim hearts and minds, could hardly have been better designed to muddle the real issues, thicken the fog of war—for the friends of freedom, anyway—and thereby lend aid to jihad.

In March 2008, the U.S. State Department issued a set of guidelines for "counterterrorism communication," among them a directive that employees not use "terms such as 'Islamo-fascism'" because it is "considered offensive to Muslims." Also: "Avoid the term 'caliphate,' which has positive connotations for Muslims." Also, since jihad means "striving in the path of God," "calling our enemies jihadis and their movement a global jihad unintentionally legitimizes their actions" in the eyes of Muslims. The Department of Homeland Security issued a similar list of no-nos, which drew on meetings between DHS Secretary Michael Chertoff and Muslim leaders and Islam scholars and was designed, as Steven Emerson wrote in May, to "shape a softer approach to a government lexicon about terrorists and their ideological motivations." Emerson revealed several previously unreported items in both reports, including this statement in the DHS document: "The experts we consulted debated the word 'liberty,' but rejected it because many around the world would discount the term as a buzzword for American hegemony." Think about this: the very principle on which America was founded, and for which generations of American soldiers have given their lives, is not to be mentioned. The DHS report also included this eye-opening, history-defying claim: "Islam and secular democracy are fully compatible—in fact, they can make each other stronger."

The importance to the foreign-policy establishment of enshrining an Orwellian rhetoric about jihad was underscored by the appearance in the *New York Times*, on June 2, 2008, of a breathtakingly dishonest op-ed by P. W. Singer of the Brookings Institution and Elina Noor of the Institute of Strategic and International Studies in Malaysia. Utterly ignoring the full meaning and history of jihadism, they defined jihad as "a quest to find one's faith or an external fight for justice," and argued that using the word "jihadist" to described Muslim terrorists is to alienate "the tens of millions of Muslims who condemn the violence that has been perpetrated in the name of Islam." This is an increasingly popular stratagem: pretending that any Muslim who doesn't commit terrorism can be assumed to have condemned it. (Never mind that "tens of millions" are less than one-tenth of the world's Muslims.)

Perhaps the most unsettling action taken in recent years by a Western court occurred in January 2009, when the Amsterdam Court of Appeals announced its intention to put Geert Wilders on trial for "incitement to hatred and discrimination" against Islam. Particularly at issue was Wilders's comparison of the Koran to *Mein Kampf*. Now, for a court to try any citizen simply for expressing his opinions about a religion or its scriptures is an outrageous violation of democratic principles; but to see a Member of Parliament hauled into court for such an "offense" is particularly disquieting. One observer who did not find Wilders's impending prosecution worrisome, however, was—surprise!—Ian Buruma, who in an op-ed published in the *New York Times* (where else?) mocked the courageous MP and denied that the court's decision represented an assault on free speech. Quoting a Dutch law professor who "said he found it 'strange' that a man should be prosecuted for 'criticizing a book,'" Buruma sniffed that "this seems a trifle obtuse. Comparing a book that billions hold sacred to Hitler's murderous tract . . . suggests that those who believe in the Koran are like Nazis, and an all-out war against them would be justified. This kind of thinking, presumably, is what the Dutch law court is seeking to check." And for Buruma, clearly, this was just as it should be. Pronouncing it a "misconception" that "people should be totally free to insult," Buruma ruled Wilders's *Mein Kampf* comparison over the line. Of course, what Buruma was doing here was drawing a new line. Both the court's action and Buruma's ignoble defense of it served only to underscore the truth of what Wilders had been arguing all along: that fear and "sensitivity" to Islam are fast eroding Western freedoms.

VI

"I'm not Spartacus!"

Some days after a car bomb exploded outside Denmark's embassy in Islamabad on June 2, 2008, killing eight, al-Qaeda took credit and confirmed its motive: the Muhammed cartoons, which had been reprinted by a raft of Danish dailies on the previous February 13 in a show of solidarity with turban-bomb cartoonist Kurt Westergaard, the target of three would-be assassins who had been arrested the day before. The bombing came on the same day that Norway's foreign minister, Jonas Gahr Støre, was booked for a panel discussion on the Norwegian elite's favorite topic, racism. Arriving late, Gahr Støre told the audience he'd just been asked by an interviewer whether Pakistanis in Denmark had condemned the explosions. The audience laughed. His point was clear: of course they had; it was racist even to ask! In fact the Muslim "condemnations" had almost invariably come with the usual "but"—violence was wrong, but the bombers' rage was "understandable." Meanwhile, Norwegian Muslim politician Ali Khan was congratulating Norway for having spared itself Denmark's fate through its wise actions—namely, the display of dhimmi groveling at Selbekk's notorious press conference. In short, Norway needn't fear terrorist attacks—it had already surrendered.

But there was a new wrinkle. Trondheim's *Adresseavisen* daily ran a cartoon which, though not depicting Muhammed, angered "moderate"

Muslim lawyer Abid Q. Raja, who—apparently feeling that *Adresseavisen* had obeyed the word but not the spirit of the *Magazinet* accords—argued that the cartoon shouldn't have been published because it would be "misunderstood" by Muslims. Pakistani ambassador Rab Nawaz Khan agreed, calling the cartoon an "act of terror" that can "endanger the lives of Norwegian citizens." When a cartoon is terrorism and a bomb is a form of expression, you know you're in Orwell country.

Yet the star of the moment was Norwegian novelist Dag Solstad, who only days before the bombing made the argument that free speech is actually undesirable, since it drowns meritorious works (such as his novels, presumably) in a sea of vulgarity (a category to which he relegated the Muhammed cartoons). Several highly placed members of Norway's cultural elite essentially seconded Solstad's thumbs-down on free speech. For example, Andreas Skartveit, former director-general of the Norwegian Broadcasting Corporation and chairman of Gyldendal, a major publishing house, complained in an op-ed that Per Edgar Kokkvold calls free speech "sacred." This, Skartveit argued, is the problem: we've made free speech holy, and are clinging to this new "religion" in an unhealthy way. Skartveit argued for what he plainly saw as a more historically sophisticated view: "The world is changing. It always has been. Sacred things come and go . . . Once it was the kings who fought for our faith, as the Swedish Gustavus Adolphus, the lion of the North, fought for Protestantism. Now it is prime ministers, such as Denmark's Fogh Rasmussen, today's lion of the North, who fight for our new faith, freedom of expression."

Skartveit called this determination to fight for free speech "scary." No, what's scary is that Fogh Rasmussen has been essentially alone among European prime ministers in taking responsible steps against the gradual closing down of liberty. What's scary is that the head of a major publishing house can draw a fatuous moral equivalence between a so-called "religion" founded on individual freedom—the "religion," that is, of the Enlightenment, the U.S. Declaration of Independence and Constitution, and the Universal Declaration of Human Rights—and oppressive faiths that restrict expression, subordinate women, and demand the execution of apostates. Solstad and Skartveit weren't alone: apropos of the Danish cartoons and other such actions, politician and author Janne Haaland Matlary wrote an op-ed arguing that "it is both stupid and dangerous to challenge others by insulting them." And

Anders Giæver, the newly anointed U.S. correspondent for Norway's largest paper, *VG*, made a similar argument in a magazine piece. It was striking, if in an altogether gruesome and dispiriting way, to see one member after another of a free country's elite rise up and, as it were, declare—proudly, firmly, defiantly—"I'm not Spartacus!"

It would be impossible to enumerate all the spheres of life in the West that have felt the influence of soft jihad. I've scarcely touched here on the banking and financial sectors, whose entire way of doing business is being radically transformed in order that procedures may be made consistent with sharia. Then there's the hotel business: the *Gulf Daily News* of Bahrain reported in May 2008 that the Jasper Capital Group in Britain was involved in plans to develop "an international chain of Sharia-compliant hotels."

Along with fear and ideology, of course, money often plays a significant role in the determination to prettify Islam. The flow of Saudi millions into the coffers of American politicians (and former politicians now working as lobbyists) should be a matter of the utmost concern. It is also reasonable to wonder at the extraordinary amount of ad time purchased on networks like CNN Europe by the tourist boards and chambers of commerce of countries like Dubai and Malaysia.

Even a sector as seemingly ideology-neutral as public transportation faces the challenge of jihad. For example, growing numbers of cabbies—a job category that, in cities around the world, is dominated by Muslims—are turning away passengers who carry liquor or are accompanied by guide dogs (both of which sharia law regards as "unclean"). In Minneapolis, where conflict over these matters arose between taxi drivers and airport officials, there were attempts to broker a compromise, but Katherine Kersten of the *Star-Tribune* had some valid questions: "What if Muslim drivers demand the right not to transport women wearing short skirts or tank tops, or unmarried couples? After taxis, why not buses, trains and planes?" Kersten plainly understood something that many observers of soft jihad do not—namely, that jihadist demands for accommodation, however modest and even reasonable they may seem, are never ends in themselves, but are only the beginning of what is intended to be an extended pattern of demand and compromise, demand and compromise, ending ultimately in full capitulation to sharia, and that to give in to the first demand is simply to hasten the arrival of the second.

Nor is it only in the cab line that jihad has had an impact at airports: inside the terminals, meeting rooms and ecumenical prayer rooms have been converted without permission into Muslim prayer rooms to which infidels are forbidden access.

Not every Westerner in a position of influence or authority, to be sure, has been hopelessly crippled by dhimmitude. In February 2008 a British think tank, the Royal United Services Institute, issued a report prepared by a panel of politicians, diplomats, and military and academic experts. This refreshingly non-dhimmi document concluded that multiculturalism had done profound damage to Britons' sense of national identity and to their self-confidence as a people. Contrasting British diffidence and timidity in the face of Islamism with the "implacability" of the Islamist enemy, it warned that the inability of Britons to "lay down the law" with immigrant groups was endangering the country. "The United Kingdom," it stated unequivocally, "presents itself as a target, as a fragmenting, post-Christian society, increasingly divided about interpretations of its history, about its national aims, its values, and in its political identity. . . . We look like a soft touch. We are indeed a soft touch, from within and without." There could hardly be a better summing-up of the dilemma with which not only Britain but the entire Western world is confronted.

It's not a pleasant fact, but it's true: the jihadists *do* hate us for our freedoms—because those freedoms are a violation of the sharia law that they're determined to impose on all of us. So far, they've been less successful at rolling back freedom, including freedom of speech, in the United States than in Europe—partly because the First Amendment makes that freedom a good deal stronger in America than anywhere else on earth, and partly because Americans have traditionally possessed a deeply ingrained appreciation for their freedom that many Europeans, alas, do not. In *Democracy in America* (1835, 1840), Alexis de Tocqueville put his finger on a key weakness of the monarchical European governments of his day—and the statist governments of today's Western Europe—when he wrote that

> The most important change which extensive government
> control produces is a psychological change, an alteration in the
> character of the people . . . the will of man is not shattered but
> softened, bent and guided; men are seldom forced by it to act,

but they are constantly restrained from acting. Such a power does not destroy, but it prevents existence; it does not tyrannize, but it compresses, enervates, extinguishes, and stupefies a people, till each nation is reduced to be nothing better than a flock of timid and industrial animals, of which government is the shepherd.

There is in this nineteenth-century observation a deep truth about twenty-first-century Europe: societies in which collectivism is celebrated and individualism often demonized are societies in which people learn to think differently about the individual's freedom and the individual's responsibility. Americans traditionally respond to things that aren't the way they should be by rolling up their sleeves and doing something; Western Europeans today see things that aren't the way they should be and are, all too often, helpless. The necessary price of a free life is the willingness to die for it; and for some of us who were raised in America during the Cold War, and who were intensely aware that, through no virtue or effort on our part, we were fortunate enough to enjoy freedom for which hundreds of thousands of Americans had died and of which millions of our contemporaries behind the Iron Curtain could only dream, this was a no-brainer. For many Europeans and, alas, not a few Americans today, such thinking is utterly alien. Willing to die for something? How primitive! How warlike!

In 2006, the German writer Thomas Kleine-Brockhoff put it this way in *Die Zeit:* Americans "chose liberal democracy as the best of all systems, while many Europeans embraced liberalism because more exciting alternatives had disappointed them." While Germans, he points out, are annoyed by the idea of American troops putting their lives on the line for other people's freedom, for Americans this is precisely what America is all about. Or, at least, such was the case until multiculturalism came along, diminishing many people's appreciation for their liberty and rendering their societies susceptible to jihadist pressures. Recently, recalling the triumphant reconciliation, in Britain's Glorious Revolution of 1688, of government authority and property rights with free speech and individual rights, Lee Harris lamented that "we in the West have completely forgotten what a remarkable achievement our ancestors bequeathed to us." Nor do most of us have a clue of the kind of despotism, official cruelty, and general misrule we are inviting by our lazy and cowardly acts of day-to-day dhimmitude.

We live in a time when Tariq Ramadan, the very personification of the shariafication of the West, is awarded respect and positions of honor while Ayaan Hirsi Ali, the embodiment of individual liberty, lives under twenty-four-hour armed guard. Today, when the Rushdie fatwa can seem like ancient history, Rushdie himself, as Paul Berman puts it, "has metastasized into an entire social class" of men and women who live under round-the-clock police protection in Western democracies because of what they have said or written about Islam—a class of which Hirsi Ali is only the most prominent member. In early 2008, while Ramadan was settling into a professorship at a prestigious Dutch university, Hirsi Ali—who had been thrown out of her apartment in The Hague because her neighbors didn't want to live near a terrorist target, and who had later felt obliged to leave the Netherlands for her own safety—was cold-bloodedly informed by the Dutch government that it had decided to stop paying for her security. At the time, Hirsi Ali was living in Washington, D.C., and working for the American Enterprise Institute, but the U.S. government refused to take over responsibility for her protection. Hirsi Ali thereupon returned to Europe in search of a government that might, in addition to spending millions in welfare support for people who look forward to a Europe under sharia law, be willing to set aside a tiny portion of its budget to keep alive freedom's most eloquent living advocate.

Hirsi Ali is the heroine of our age, but in 2008 she was a woman without a country.

The question before us is this: Do we love our freedoms as much as they hate them? At least one thing seems certain: against people who are ready to die in the cause of destroying freedom, people who are unwilling to speak up for freedom for fear of being called a racist or Islamophobe don't stand much chance of victory. Many free people, alas, have become so accustomed to freedom, and to not having to stand up for it, that they're simply incapable of defending it when it's imperiled—or even, in some cases, of recognizing that it *is* imperiled. And there seems to be a corollary problem: that the more civilized a civilization gets, the harder it is for some of its most civilized members to recognize that there is, in fact, such a thing as barbarism; and that most of those who do recognize this fact consider it uncivilized to say so.

In an October 2007 issue of the *Washington Post*, columnist Anne Applebaum—one of the few oases of reason and courage in a desert of media dhimmitude—described the West as facing a "fundamental test, maybe even a turning point." The fundamental question, she argued, was this: "Are prominent, articulate critics of radical Islam . . . entitled to the same free speech rights enjoyed by other citizens . . . ?" This is indeed the question we face today. Free speech is in crisis. To respond with the "accommodation" recommended by so many journalists, politicians, and intellectuals would be simply to submit—to abandon freedom, embrace dhimmitude, and hope for the best from our new overlords. The West's unwavering principle, rather, must be a refusal to sacrifice or compromise liberty—*no matter what*. Simple as that.

No, there's no guarantee that Western Muslims, in meaningful numbers, will ever openly and actively champion freedom and defy jihadists; to do so, after all, is alien to every value with which many of them were raised. But we certainly can't expect them to take a stand for liberty if the rest of us don't stand up for it ourselves.

AFTERWORD
to the Anchor Books Edition

Given all the criticism I've leveled in these pages against the *New York Times*—particularly regarding its failure to review books that are critical of Islam—it is perhaps appropriate to begin this afterword by mentioning that the *Times* not only reviewed *Surrender* but gave it a very positive write-up. I hoped at the time that this might mark a broader change of direction in the Gray Lady's approach to Islam-related issues; alas, it didn't. By contrast, the review of *Surrender* by Islam apologist Paul A. Barrett in the *Washington Post Book World* provided a textbook example of exactly the kind of media mendacity I have described in this book. Indeed, the review was so insistently and breathtakingly in denial about basic facts that I felt moved to examine it at length in a piece for Pajamas Media, in which I noted that Barrett "treated the hard facts" presented in *Surrender* "as if they were the feverish delusions of a crackpot." For example, Barrett insisted that "Bawer veers into self-parody when he asserts that Muslims have cowed skeptics into self-censorship and inaction." "It is," I wrote in my Pajamas piece, "as if the countless examples that I cite in my book simply did not exist. We are, make no mistake, deep into Orwellian territory here."

Deeper and deeper, in fact. As 2009 wore on, not only did new examples of the pattern of appeasement described in *Surrender* continue to accumulate; it seemed that members of the Western creative community were increasingly blasé about the whole business, confessing to their acts of capitulation matter-of-factly, with no sign of discomfort or shame. In November, a *New York Times* article about *2012,* director Roland Emmerich's latest movie about the destruction of the world, described how Emmerich "razed Rio de Janeiro; Rome; California; Washington, D.C.; Tibet; Las Vegas; Yellowstone National Park; and more, but decided against destroying Islamic symbols." Emmerich explained that his cowriter, Harald Kloser, had said, "I'm not writing this to get a fatwa on my head." Emmerich noted that his film showed "Jesus falling apart in all kinds of forms. The Vatican falls on people's heads, and we can do that because we're a free, Western society, but if there would be, like, Mecca destroyed, there would be an outrage. And so you don't do it."

Turnabouts, too, seemed to be happening faster and faster. In August, British novelist Sebastian Faulks, whose new novel, *A Week in December*, featured Muslim characters, dared to air his views about the Koran: "It's a depressing book. . . . It's just the rantings of a schizophrenic. It's very one-dimensional . . . the English translation I read was, from a literary point of view, very disappointing." He also criticized "the barrenness of the message," saying that unlike the Old Testament the Koran contains "no stories" and that unlike the New Testament "it has no ethical dimension . . . no new plan for life. It says 'the Jews and the Christians were along the right tracks, but actually, they were wrong and I'm right, and if you don't believe me, tough—you'll burn for ever.' That's basically the message of the book.'" In response, imam Ajmal Masroor, a spokesman for the Islamic Society of Britain, issued a not-so-veiled threat: "The consequences of saying things like this could be quite severe." The prominent British Muslim Anjem Choudary called for Faulks's death. Within hours Faulks recanted, insisting that his novel presented "a hugely sympathetic and loving Muslim family" and that "it is . . . made clear that the parents' kindness and good citizenship spring not just from being naturally good eggs but from their devotion to the Koran. . . . It was never my intention to offend my Muslim friends or readers, and if you read my novel I think you will see how I have shown the positive effects of the Koran on a kind and typical Muslim family." Faulks agreed with Masroor that it was problematic to "navigate solo with our own cultural compasses" and said he "would be pleased to learn more about Islam" and would willingly enter into dialogue with Masroor "with a degree of humility and plenty of respect for his religion and his scripture." Meanwhile the *Telegraph* story containing Faulks's original remarks was removed from that newspaper's website without explanation.

In August it emerged that a forthcoming book about the Muhammed cartoons, written by Jytte Klausen and published by Yale University Press, would not actually include any of the cartoons. The press said its decision was based on a fear of Islamist reprisal, and had been made after consultation with "two dozen authorities, including diplomats and experts on Islam and counterterrorism," who had unanimously advised that the cartoons be omitted from the book. Islam expert Martin Kramer noted that back in 2006 one of Yale's "experts," Marcia Inhorn, had written an article condemning American "fear-mongering" about the Muslim world; yet it was she who told Klausen that including the cartoons in the book would involve "a serious risk of instigating violence," and who was quoted in a Yale statement as saying that publishing the pictures was "likely to provoke a violent outcry." For those who missed the irony, Kramer spelled it out: "The last time we encountered Professor Inhorn, she was telling us to ignore the fear-mongering, not to let the media dupe us into expecting the worst.... Now ... she's telling an expert author ... that Yale's press absolutely must expect the worst." (A further irony, one might add, is that Klausen herself is no critic of Islam but rather an apologist much in the manner of Karen Armstrong.)

Yet Yale's profession of editorial cowardice turned out to be only a cover story. Soon after the announcement that her book would be cartoon-free, Klausen revealed that the decision to exclude the pictures had been made by university officials, not by the press itself. Commentators suggested that the fear in New Haven had not been over the possibility of violence but over the possible alienation of potential Muslim donors; citing "Yale's courting of Saudi Prince Alwaleed bin Talal," who had funded multimillion-dollar Islamic programs at Harvard and Georgetown, Kramer noted that as recently as April 2009 Yale had named Muna AbuSulayman, executive director of the Alwaleed Bin Talal Foundation, a "Yale World Fellow" for 2009—a transparent effort to butter up the royal philanthropist. This was, of course, no isolated case: Yale was far from the only American university that was prepared to compromise free expression in order to please Islamists with deep pockets.

One surprising and cheering development came in August 2009. In the wake of news that Tariq Ramadan had been hosting a weekly talk show on official Iranian government TV, the leaders of the Rotterdam city government—which had been employing Ramadan for two years as an integration consultant, and which also subsidized his professorship at Erasmus University—decided to relieve him of his duties. Yet Ian Buruma continued to see Geert Wilders, not Ramadan, as the embodiment of the problems facing the Netherlands. The headline and subhead of an op-ed he published in August said it all: "When the blood starts flowing, where will the Wilders voters be? Do the many supporters of anti-Islam politician Geert Wilders fully realise the dangers of a divided society? When people feel rejected, they will start to display hostile behaviour." *Start?* Buruma's message was clear: appease, or end up like Theo van Gogh. With his usual flair for euphemism, Buruma acknowledged that Muslim immigrants to Netherlands "often have ideas about women and homosexuals that are out of touch with the more progressive ideas we have come to accept as normal," but added that

intolerance against homosexuals, though reprehensible, is not the same as revolutionary extremism. As long as no violence is involved, that kind of intolerance is something we can live with, just like we live with orthodox Christians or ultra-orthodox Jews. Good education can help there, and of course everything needs to be done to prevent aggression against women or homosexuals. But normative differences will always exist; it comes with being a pluralistic society.

In other words, forget about protecting the equal rights of Muslim women—and forget that Islam calls for the execution of gays. *Execution.* How many times, one wondered, did that word have to be repeated before it sank in? The plain fact was that Muslims who explicitly refused to reject the Islamic death penalty for gays, or who even explicitly embraced it, were being welcomed with open arms into the European elite—and their barbaric views on women and gays were being treated by elitists like Buruma as "normative differences" that simply had to be accepted in order to avoid full-scale bloodshed.

The saga of Geert Wilders continued. In February 2009, Wilders, who had been invited to screen and discuss *Fitna* in the House of Lords, was denied entry into the United Kingdom on the orders of Home Secretary Jacqui Smith, on the grounds that he was an extremist; in October, Britain's Asylum and Immigration Tribunal reversed Smith's decision and Wilders traveled to Britain as planned. (In the meantime, his party triumphed in the June elections for the European Parliament, going from zero to four seats, putting it only one seat behind the leading Dutch party.) Britain's wasn't the only Western government to reach new heights in its efforts to placate Islamists. On June 4, 2009, Barack Obama gave a highly touted "speech to the Muslim world" at Al-Azhar University that was widely hailed as epochal and bridge-building. In fact it amounted to an implicit announcement that his administration's policy toward the Muslim world would be one of shameless appeasement. A self-described "student of history," Obama served up a staggering pastiche of half-truths, exaggerations, and utter nonsense about Islamic history. Even in his supposedly gutsier moments—as when he criticized the treatment of women in Muslim societies—he was hardly as forceful as the circumstances warranted. (Instead of defending the right of women to dress as they wished, he defended their "right" to wear hijab.) His flattering account of Islam—the celebration of imaginary Islamic achievements in science and culture, the evocation of a golden-age Andalusia where Christians and Jews were treated with respect and equality, and the references to the Koran that made it sound like the Sermon on the Mount—was of a piece with the pretty fictions about Islam found regularly in the mainstream media.

Increasingly, governments targeted not Islamic jihad but its critics. In August 2009 Norwegian Foreign Minister Jonas Gahr Støre asserted that "radical Islam is not a problem in Norway today," and that "we must strike down all rhetoric that ties Islam to danger, violence, and terror." Not strike down jihadist terrorists, mind you—but strike down any honest acknowledgment of their motives. Then there was the Irish government, which in July 2009 passed a defamation bill outlawing the publication or utterance of any "matter that is grossly abusive or insulting in relation to matters held sacred by any religion, thereby causing outrage among a substantial number of the adherents of that religion." The law also punished the *intention* "to cause such outrage" and authorized Irish police to enter—forcibly if necessary—any workplace or residence where there was reason to believe that printed matter offensive to religion might be found and to seize such materials. Fines ran up to €25,000. Reading about the law, one could not help recalling Ray Bradbury's dystopic novel *Fahrenheit 451*, in which books themselves are forbidden. As Padraig Reidy wrote in the *Guardian*, "Irish law has now enshrined the notion that the taking of offense is more important than free expression."

Then there was the UN, where the Organization of the Islamic Conference was busy pressuring the Human Rights Council to pass a resolution prohibiting the defamation of religion. The United States sent mixed signals about this effort. On the one hand, Secretary of State Hillary Clinton said on October 26 that "[s]ome claim that the best way to protect the freedom of religion is to implement so-called anti-defamation policies.... I strongly disagree." Differences about religious questions, Clinton asserted, "should be met with tolerance, not with the suppression of discourse." Yet only weeks earlier, on October 2, the United States had joined Egypt in sponsoring a Human Rights Council resolution that contained the following language: "The Human Rights Council ... expresses its concern that incidents of racial and religious intolerance, discrimination and related violence, as well as of negative racial and religious stereotyping continue to rise around the world, and condemns, in this context, any advocacy of national, racial or religious hatred that constitutes incitement to discrimination, hostility or violence, and urges States to take effective measures, consistent with their obligations under international human rights law, to address and combat such incidents...." As Stuart Taylor, Jr., noted in the *National Journal*, this resolution "could plausibly be read as encouraging or even obliging the U.S. to make it a crime to engage in hate speech, or, perhaps, in mere 'negative racial and religious stereotyping.' This despite decades of First Amendment case law protecting such speech."

Meanwhile, the continued failure of Western judicial systems to stand up to Islamist pressures was reflected in the resolution of the "flying imams" case. With the help of CAIR, the imams had brought a lawsuit against US Airways, against the officials who had detained and questioned them, and against their fellow passengers on Flight 300. Thanks to a new law that shielded individuals from being sued for reporting suspicious activities, the passengers were removed as defendants. In July, however, Federal Judge Ann Montgomery denied motions by law enforcement officials to dismiss charges against them, maintaining, in Scott W. Johnson's summary, that "the flying imams were the subject of an unlawful arrest and that no reasonable law enforcement officer could have believed otherwise." This was a curious argument, given that, as Johnson observed, over a dozen law officers had "participated in the detention or questioning of the imams," including "six MAC [Metropolitan Airports Commission] officers, one federal air marshal, three FBI special agents, at least one Social Service officer, and four other law enforcement officers." Had they *all* been unreasonable? In October it was announced that the imams had reached an out-of-court settlement with the airline, which agreed to pay them an undisclosed sum. Though some media, such as the *New York Daily News,* considered this outcome a victory for flyer safety, CAIR Executive Director Nihad Awad declared it a victory for the imams, whom he compared to Rosa Parks. Investigative journalist Paul Sperry, for his part, called the settlement "a victory for future hijackers. . . . Even pilots will now think twice about bouncing from flights any Arabs or Muslims acting suspiciously and threateningly." The fact that one of the flying imams, Omar Shahin, was head of the North American Imams Foundation—described by journalist David Kupelian as "a sister organization to CAIR" and a subsidiary, as it were, of "the international Muslim Brotherhood, which federal authorities recognize as the parent organization of both al-Qaeda and Hamas"—did nothing to assuage concerns that the whole event had been staged so that the imams could be represented as victims, file charges, and end up using the judicial system to weaken antiterrorism efforts.

As I've noted, documents introduced at the Holy Land trial demonstrated conclusively the connection between CAIR and the Muslim Brotherhood. Nonetheless, CAIR continued to be treated respectfully by government authorities. On November 9, 2009, it was reported that although the FBI had supposedly cut "formal contacts" with CAIR, Attorney General Eric Holder would be giving a keynote speech at a Detroit awards banquet held by the Advocates and Leaders for Police and Community Trust (ALPACT), a coalition of several groups including CAIR's Michigan chapter, and that the dinner would be cochaired by the FBI's top Detroit official, Andy Arena. Josh Gerstein quoted the CAIR chapter's executive director, Dawud Walid, as saying that "[w]e meet every month and included with us is the U.S. Attorney's Office, the FBI." Walid added that an ALPACT meeting had in fact been held the previous Friday at the Detroit office of the U.S. Attorney. Gerstein quoted former terrorism prosecutor Andrew McCarthy as saying that he wasn't surprised by any of this: "When [the FBI] said they cut off formal ties with [CAIR], whenever they say something like that you have to look very carefully at the way it's worded. . . . The last administration was guilty of it, this administration is guilty of it—they have determined it is more important to have what it can publicly hold out as ties to the Muslim community than it is to be careful about who you have the ties with."

As far as Islam-related censorship and self-censorship were concerned, the most grimly illuminating event of 2009 was surely the response to the Fort Hood massacre of Thursday, November 5—not only by the media, political, and cultural elite, but also by military leaders. Even after having cataloged in this book scores of examples of establishment pusillanimity in the face of Islamism, I was stunned by the blatant dishonesty of the official narrative that began to take shape immediately after Major Nidal Malik Hasan's act of jihad. In a piece posted on Pajamas Media a few hours after the atrocity, I observed that the brave soldiers who were massacred at Fort Hood had trained to fight the jihadist enemy abroad only to end up being murdered by the same enemy on American soil—murdered, apparently, because a series of military and medical officials had recognized that Hasan was indeed an enemy within but had chosen to do nothing. And now the mainstream media, too, were turning away from the obvious truth. Throughout the evening, military and other authorities kept saying, and talking heads on CNN kept repeating, that there was no sign that this was "a terrorist act"—as if Nidal Malik Hasan had to be officially connected to al-Qaeda to be a jihadist.

Repeatedly, CNN reporters hammered home the line that Hasan had been the victim of anti-Muslim prejudice by his military colleagues. Repeatedly they read out, and showed onscreen, a long statement from CAIR condemning the massacre—never mentioning, of course, CAIR's terrorist links. Online I found telling details: Hasan had been a devout Muslim; Arabic words, reportedly a Muslim prayer, had been posted on his apartment door in Maryland; in conversations with colleagues he had expressed sympathy for suicide bombers; hours before the massacre, he had handed out copies of the Koran to neighbors. A couple of these facts eventually surfaced on CNN, but only briefly; they were rushed past, left untouched, unexamined; the network seemed to be making a masterly effort to avoid giving this data a cold, hard look. Meanwhile it engaged in heavy-handed spin—devoting several minutes, for example, to an inane interview with a forensic psychiatrist who talked about the stress of treating soldiers bearing the emotional scars of war, as if this had anything whatsoever to do with the case of Hasan, who had never spent a single moment in a theater of war. The obvious intention was to turn viewers' eyes away from Islamism and toward psychiatric instability as a motive.

On *Anderson Cooper 360*, Anderson Cooper quoted a posting by Hasad on an Islamist website about martyrdom and jihad. Case closed, one would think—but no, Cooper immediately glided from this damning evidence into a description of Hasad not as a jihadist but as a man deeply troubled (just as you or I might be) by "the war in Iraq" and by disagreement with "U.S. foreign policy." It was also reported on Cooper's program that Hasan had sometimes worn traditional Muslim garb—a surveillance camera even showed him wearing such an outfit in a convenience store hours before the massacre. Yet this information was left hanging. Cooper said nothing to indicate that this revelation suggested any particular interpretation of Thursday's events. On the contrary, after wrapping up this story, he reiterated for the umpteenth time that we still don't know anything—other than that this had been a day no one at Fort Hood would ever forget. And after Cooper came *Larry King Live* with guest host Wolf Blitzer, who by way of "illuminating" Hasan's actions interviewed a panel of—no, not experts on Islamic jihad, but psychiatrists. Blitzer endlessly repeated the mantra that Hasan had been "taunted" for being Muslim, had feared going to a war zone, and had ultimately gone "berserk," and the doctors echoed this line. "He did not reach for help when he should have," lamented one panelist. Another opined: "It sounded like it got to be too much for him." Yet another told us: "All kind of people need help who aren't getting help. . . . He was feeling picked on by his colleagues. . . . He was strained. He was scared."

Even as I e-mailed my piece to Pajamas Media, I hoped that as the days went by, the mass-scale denial would dissipate in the face of the facts. But no: the refusal of establishment institutions and individuals to call this jihadist massacre by its own name only intensified—even as the evidence mounted that Hasan was indeed a jihadist. On the Sunday after the massacre, the *New York Times* ran a story by Joseph Berger whose principal focus was on concerns by Army Chief of Staff George Casey, Jr., "that speculation about the religious beliefs of Maj. Nidal Malik Hasan, accused of killing 12 fellow soldiers and one civilian and wounding dozens of others in a shooting rampage at Fort Hood, could 'cause a backlash against some of our Muslim soldiers.'" By 2009, needless to say, this "backlash" line had become a staple of life in the West: after every Islamist atrocity, the media were quick to shift focus from the real, mostly non-Muslim victims of actual acts of jihad to the potential Muslim victims of imaginary acts of retaliation. This "backlash" had never yet materialized, yet the hand-wringing—the reflexive transformation of perpetrators into victims and vice versa—had become a grotesque reflex. Of course, to play such rhetorical games in the case of the Fort Hood massacre was nothing less than an obscenity, and to pretend that Hasan's religious beliefs had absolutely nothing to do with his actions was an affront to the memories of his victims, to their loved ones, and to the intelligence of the American public. Indeed, it was a betrayal of all of the men and women who were risking their lives in a war in which the identity, nature, and motive of the enemy was constantly being euphemized. The blogger at Mudville Gazette pointed out a particularly breathtaking example of dishonest reporting. In an interview with CNN, one of the soldiers wounded by Hasan, Private Joseph Foster, said that Hasan had shouted "Allahu akbar" during the shooting. Two minutes later Foster was asked, "[Y]ou were shot in the hip and didn't recognize it at the time?" and he replied: "I had realized it at first, but with that much adrenaline, you tend to forget things." Presto: next thing you knew, CNN—manifestly eager to cast doubt on the "Allahu akbar" story—ran a report stating that Foster "said he wasn't clear about whether the gunman said those exact words, noting that 'with that much adrenaline, you tend to forget things.'" In short, as Mudville Gazette's blogger put it, CNN "willfully and intentionally rewrote an eyewitness account to make it fit their narrative."

One of the few challenges to the mainstream-media narrative to appear was a *Wall Street Journal* op-ed that ran five days after the massacre. In it, Dorothy Rabinowitz deplored the "instant flow of exculpatory media meditations on the stresses that must have weighed on the killer who mowed down 13 Americans and wounded 29 others." Rabinowitz observed that while Hasan had been advertising his anti-American, pro-jihadist sympathies for some time, military higher-ups had refused to deal with this ticklish problem, and now that Hasan had acted on his beliefs those same officials, along with a veritable army of journalists and psychiatric experts, were busy serving up all kinds of absurd explanations for actions whose actual motivation was as clear as day. By now, she noted, the blatant denial of uncomfortable Muslim-related facts in the corridors of power was a familiar enough phenomenon; but never before had it been exhibited "in such naked form" as in the case of Fort Hood.

On November 10, 2009, the day on which the President of the United States was to deliver a eulogy at the memorial service for Hasan's victims, Ralph Peters asked in the *New York Post*: "As President Obama belatedly appears at Fort Hood today, will he dare to speak the word 'terror'?" Peters added, "He won't use the word 'Islamist.' If he mentions Islam at all, it'll be to sing its praises yet again." Peters proved correct. That day at Fort Hood, President Obama spoke many pretty words. But he did not speak of terrorism or Islamism. He mentioned that the United States was at war, but refrained from naming the enemy. And he said this: "It may be hard to comprehend the twisted logic that led to this tragedy. But this much we do know: No faith justifies these murderous and craven acts." To say this was, quite simply, to ignore the Koran's explicit injunction to commit jihad. For the President of the United States to leaven his public tribute to Hasan's victims with a pathetic effort to exculpate Islam was not only morally despicable: it was chilling in its wholesale denial of the fundamental reality of what had happened at Fort Hood as well as of the guiding ideology of the enemy that confronts the West both at home and abroad.

—Bruce Bawer,
November 2009

NOTES

To make it easy for readers to verify my assertions and quotations, I've listed sources, wherever possible, that are written in English and available online.

PART ONE: *A New Brand of Jihad*

CHAPTER I: *"Send him to hell"*

4 **"founded on the Laws":** Letter of March 28, 1786. Thomas Jefferson Papers, Library of Congress.

5 **"I inform the proud":** Peter Murtagh, "Rushdie in Hiding after Ayatollah's Death Threat," *Guardian*, 15 February 1989 (http://www.guardian.co.uk/books/1989/feb/15/salmanrushdie).

6 **"It was ironic":** Chapter three of Martin Kramer's *Ivory Towers on Sand: The Failure of Middle Eastern Studies in America*. Washington: The Washington Institute for Near East Policy, 2001 (http://www.geocities.com/martinkramerorg/IslamObscured.htm).

6 **"deals only incidentally":** Michiko Kakutani, "Books of the Times; A Simple Miracle to Start, Then High Complexity." *New York Times*, 27 January 1989 (http://query.nytimes.com/gst/fullpage.html?res=950DE2DE163CF934A15752C0A96F948260).

6 **"two or three Muslim politicians":** Salman Rushdie, "India Bans a Book for Its Own Good," *New York Times*, 19 October 1988 (http://query.nytimes.com/gst/fullpage.html?res=940DE1DF163FF93AA25753C1A96E948260&scp=2&sq=Rushdie%20%22two%20or%20three%20Muslim%20politicians%22&st=cse).

7 **"and tell him exactly":** Craig R. Whitney, "Cat Stevens Gives Support to Call for Death of Rushdie," *New York Times*, 23 May 1989 (http://www.nytimes.com/books/99/04/18/specials/rushdie-cat.html?_r=1&oref=slogin).

7 **"Death, perhaps"**: Peter Murtagh, "Rushdie in Hiding after Ayatollah's Death Threat," *Guardian*, 18 February 1989 (http://www.guardian.co.uk/books/1989/feb/18/fiction.salmanrushdie).

7 **"his upbringing"**: Ursula Owen, "Essay: A Victory for Literary Freedom," *The Independent*, 27 September 1998 (http://findarticles.com/p/articles/mi_qn4158/is_19980927/ai_n14182705).

8 **"Even if Salman Rushdie"**: Eliot Weinberger, "The Month of Rushdies," *Boston Review*, 15 March 1989 (http://bostonreview.net/BR14.4/rushdie.html).

8 **"a megalomaniac"**: Associated Press, "Rushdie Slams Support of Film Protesters," *Boston Globe*, 30 July 2006 (http://www.boston.com/news/world/europe/articles/2006/07/30/rushdie_slams_support_of_film_protesters/).

8 **"would not shed a tear"**: Melanie Phillips, "After the Rushdie Affair, Islam in Britain Became Fused with an Agenda of Murder," *Guardian*, 28 May 2006 (http://www.guardian.co.uk/commentisfree/2006/may/28/religion.islam).

8 **"in an open society"**: Richard Bernstein, "Ideas and Trends; After a Pause, Writers Stood Up for Rushdie and Themselves," *New York Times*, 26 February 1989 (http://query.nytimes.com/gst/fullpage.html?res=950DE7DA113DF935A15751C0A96F948260&sec=&spon=&pagewanted=all).

9 **"the overwhelming consequence"**: Ibid.

10 **"as a spiritual"**: Farshad Kholghi, *Verden er ét land*. People's Press, 2007.

CHAPTER II: *From Mill to Multiculturalism*

16 **"Persecution for the expression"**: Oliver Wendell Holmes, Jr., Dissenting Opinion in Abrams vs. United States (http://www.law.cornell.edu/supct/html/historics/USSC_CR_0250_0616_ZD.html).

18 **"decency and consideration"**: Anthony Browne, *The Retreat of Reason*, Coronet, 2006.

19 **"a racism of the anti-racists"**: Pascal Bruckner, "Enlightenment Fundamentalism or Racism of the Anti-Racists?" *Sign and Sight*, 24 January 2007 (http://www.signandsight.com/features/1146.html).

20 **"they, in the many domains"**: Richard Bernstein, *Dictatorship of Virtue: Multiculturalism and the Battle for America's Future*, Knopf, 1994.

CHAPTER III: *The Dialectical Scam*

22 **"I tested freedom of speech"**: http://IndyMedia.org

22 **"free expression is under attack"**: Stephen Lendman, "The War on Free Speech," The Populist Party blog (http://www.populistamerica.com/the_war_on_free_speech).

22 **"the Bush administration assault"**: http://pandagon.blogsome.com/.

23 **"Just as Christianity"**: Alvin Rosenfeld, "Progressive Jewish Thought and the New Anti-Semitism," American Jewish Committee Web site (http://www.ajc.org/atf/cf/%7B42D75369-D582-4380-8395-D25925B85EAF%7D/PROGRESSIVE_JEWISH_THOUGHT.PDF).

23 **"there really hadn't"**: Alvin Rosenfeld, "Rhetorical Violence and the Jews," *TNR Online*, 28 February 2008 (available at Scholars for Peace in the Middle East Web site, http://www.spme.net/cgi-bin/articles.cgi?ID=1884).

23 **"conservative"**: Patricia Cohen, "Essay Linking Liberal Jews to Anti-Semitism Sparks a Furor," *New York Times*, 31 January 2007 (http://www.nytimes.com/2007/01/31/arts/31jews.html?scp=1&sq=%22essay%20linking%20liberal%20jews%22&st=cse).

23 **"hysterical, verging on McCarthyism"**: Roger Cohen, "Jews and Evangelicals Find Common Political Ground," *International Herald Tribune*, 10 February 2007 (available at http://select.nytimes.com/iht/2007/02/10/world/IHT-10globalist.html).

23 **"Stalinist tactics":** Alvin Rosenfeld, "Rhetorical Violence and the Jews," op.cit.

23 **"a shocking tissue":** Jonathan Tobin, "Running with the Jackals of Hate," *Jewish World Review*, 19 February 2007 (http://www.jewishworldreview.com/0207/tobin021907.php3?printer_friendly).

24 **"an honest analysis":** Gil Troy, "Israel's Critics Protest Too Much," *Jewish Week*, 27 March 2007 (http://togetherwithisrael.org/2007/03/israels-critics-protest-too-much.html).

24 **"How does joining":** Bret Stephens, "Anti-anti-Semitism Defended," *TNR Online*, 12 February 2007 (http://www.tnr.com/doc.mhtml?i=w070212&s=stephens021207).

24 **"dialectical scam":** Alvin Rosenfeld, "Rhetorical Violence and the Jews," TNR Online, 28 February 2008 (available at Scholars for Peace in theMiddle East Web site, http://www.spme.net/cgi-bin/articles.cgi? (ID=1884).

24 **"distinguished British-born historian":** Gaby Wood, "The New Jewish Question," *The Observer*, 11 February 2007 (http://www.guardian.co.uk/world/2007/feb/11/religion.uk).

25 **"non-mainstream views":** http://pandagon.blogsome.com/.

27 **"It's a sad commentary":** http://news.bbc.co.uk/2/low/entertainment/6094446.stm.

28 **"That this is being censored":** http://thinkprogress.org/2006/10/27/dixie-chicks-advertisement-nbc/.

29 **"I think people are using":** "49th Annual Grammy Awards," 11 February 2007, CBS.

29 **"Nazi book-burners":** Jacob Sullum, "Play Politics. Free Speech Isn't Free, Even for the Dixie Chicks." *Reason Online*, 11 July 2003 (http://www.reason.com/news/show/35775.html).

CHAPTER IV: *"Who the hell are we to point fingers?"*

33 **"When is the West":** Comments on Dominic Kennedy, "Gays Should Be Hanged, says Iranian minister," *Times Online*, 13 November 2007 (http://www.timesonline.co.uk/tol/news/world/middle_east/article2859606.ece).

CHAPTER V: *Fortuyn*

36 **"has been taken over":** Bruce Bawer, "Europe's Champion of Liberty," *New York Sun*, 4 May 2007 (http://www.nysun.com/opinion/europes-champion-of-liberty/53818/).

36 **"dangerous man":** Marlise Simons, "Rotterdam Journal; Proudly Gay, and Marching the Dutch to the Right," *New York Times*, 22 March 2002 (http://query.nytimes.com/gst/fullpage.html?res=9D05E6DB1E38F931A15750C0A9649C8B63).

36 **"by standing up":** Bruce Bawer, *While Europe Slept*, Doubleday, 2006, p. 168.

36 **"danger":** Ibid., p. 169.

CHAPTER VI: *Van Gogh*

39 **"crossed the limits":** Bruce Bawer, "Tolerance or Death!," *Reason Online*, 30 November 2005 (http://www.reason.com/news/show/33002.html).

39 **"Is freedom of expression":** Iqbal Sacranie, "We Need Protection from the Pedlars of Religious Hatred," Muslim Council of Britain Web site (http://www.mcb.org.uk/library/article_12-01-05.php).

39–40 **"I can see how":** Ian Buruma, *Murder in Amsterdam*, Penguin, 2006, p. 118.

40 **"There were no significant":** Peter Whittle, "Islam: The Silence of the Arts," New Culture Forum Web site (http://www.newcultureforum.org.uk/home/?q=node/136).

41 **"Does this mean I'm yielding":** Marlise Simons, "Militant Muslims Act to Suppress Dutch Film and Art Show," *New York Times*, 31 January 2005 (http://www.nytimes.com/2005/01/31/international/europe/31netherlands.html).

CHAPTER VII: *The Cartoons*

43 "one of the most serious": Flemming Rose, Northern Light blog, 14 July 2007 (http://pajamasmedia.com/flemmingrose/2007/07/14/post_2/).

43 "the interest of inter-faith harmony": http://www.filtrat.dk/grafik Letterfrom ambassadors.pdf.

43 "It is so self-evidently clear": Helle Merete Brix and Lars Hedegaard, "Islamic Extremists and Their Western Allies on the Offensive against Free Speech in Denmark," Sappho Web site, 3 January 2006 (http://www.sappho.dk/Den%20 loebende/ekstremister_english.htm).

44 "Our right to say": "Muslim Anger at Danish Cartoons," BBC News Web site, 20 October 2005 (http://news.bbc.co.uk/2/hi/europe/4361260.stm).

45 "adding fuel to the flames": Charles Moore, "If You Get Rid of the Danes, You'll Have to Keep Paying the Danegeld," *Daily Telegraph*, 4 February 2006 (http://www.telegraph.co.uk/opinion/main.jhtml?xml=/opinion/2006/02/04/do0402.xml&sSheet=/opinion/2006/02/04/ixop.html).

45 "We will never apologize": *France Soir*, 1 February 2006.

46 "debated whether or not": Peter Whittle, "Islam; The Silence of the Arts," New Culture Forum Web site (http://www.newcultureforum.org.uk/home/?q=node/136).

46 "a reasonable choice": "Those Danish Cartoons," *New York Times*, 7 February 2006 (http://www.nytimes.com/2006/02/07/opinion/07tue2.html).

46 "a characteristically pompous": Gerard Baker, "Free Speech in America," *Times Online*, 8 February 2006.

CHAPTER VIII: *The* Magazinet *Case*

48 "Has it come this far": Vebjørn Selbekk, *Truet av islamister*, Genesis, 2006.

51 "*Magazinet* has the legal right": Kaja Korsvold, "—Be om unnskyldning!," *Aftenposten*, 27 February 2008 (http://www.aftenposten.no/nyheter/uriks/article1218389.ece).

51 "to take part in a defense": "Ytringsfrihet og demokrati," *Dagbladet*, 31 January 2006 (http://www.dagbladet.no/tekstarkiv/artikkel.php?id=5001060036757&tag=item& words=forsvar%3BMagazinet).

51 "problems": Tommi Rudihagen, "Ytringsfrihet medfører ansvar," *Teknisk Ukeblad*, June 2006 (http://www.tu.no/meninger/article47765.ece).

51 "demands in our time": "Må ta følsomhet på alvor," *Aftenposten*, 26 January 2006 (http://www.aftenposten.no/nyheter/iriks/article1206745.ece).

51 "freedom of expression": Bjørnar Hellen, "Gahr Støre kritiserer israelsk publisering," VG, 6 February 2006 (http://www.vg.no/pub/skrivervennlig.hbs?artid=181871).

52 "prostration before": Vebjørn Selbekk, *Truet av Islamister*.

52 "constructive for building": Kristoffer Egeberg, "Mohammed-brevet Norge ikke skulle se," *Dagbladet*, 26 January 2006 (http://www.dagbladet.no/nyheter/2006/01/26/455939.html).

52 "the cartoon has never": Kokkvold made these remarks on Norwegian television.

53 "a display of cowardice": Tore Gjerstad, "Oppildner fundamentalister," *Dagbladet*, 13 February 2006 (http://www.dagbladet.no/nyheter/2006/02/13/457665.html).

53 "how wounding": "Selbekks budskap til muslimene," VG, 10 February 2006 (http://www.vg.no/nyheter/innenriks/artikkel.php?artid=182179). Audio of the press conference is at http://www1.nrk.no/nett-tv/klipp/144791.

55 "responsibility": Elisabeth Breien Ellingsen, "—Vil ikke spre beklagelsen," VG, 10 February 2006 (http://www.vg.no/nyheter/innenriks/artikkel.php?artid=302132).

55 *Aftenposten* cheered: "Forsoning," *Aftenposten*, 11 February 2006 (http://www.aftenposten.no/meninger/leder_morgen/article1220516.ece).

55 "Norway went a long way": Vebjørn Selbekk, "Brukt av regjeringen," *Aftenposten*,

3 October 2006 (http://www.aftenposten.no/meninger/kronikker/article1480033.ece).

55 **"To meet Yusuf al-Qaradawi":** Mina Hauge Nærland, "—Al-Qaradawi godtok beklagelsen," *Dagbladet*, 14 February 2006 (http://www.dagbladet.no/nyheter/2006/02/14/457855.html).

55 **"a warm person":** Halvor Tjønn, "Islamist godtar unnskyldningen," *Aftenposten*, 27 February 2008 (http://www.aftenposten.no/nyheter/uriks/article1224136.ece).

56 **"we had a responsibility":** Vebjørn Selbekk, "Ytringsfrihet kan aldri Beklages," *Aftenposten*, 15 February 2006 (http://www.aftenposten.no/meninger/debatt/article 1224401.ece).

56 **"frightful that a small":** Robert Holender and Clas Svahn, "Muhammedteckningar borta efter Säposamstal," *Dagens Nyheter*, 2 October 2006 (http://www.dn.se/DNet/jsp/polopoly.jsp?d=147&a=520257&previousRenderType=6).

56 **"For the first time":** Per Edgar Kokkvold, "Ytringsfrihed bør finde sted" (http://www.tv2.no/arkiv/magasiner/dokument2/article756850.ece).

56 **"I would guess":** Interview with *Bergens Tidende*, 1 February 2006 (http://www.bt.no/utenriks/article240521.ece).

56 **"limitless when the utterances":** Per Edgar Kokkvold, foreword to *Truet av Islamister*.

57 **"What Norwegian editor":** Vebjørn Selbekk, "Ytringsfrihet kan aldri beklages," *Aftenposten*, 15 February 2006 (http://www.aftenposten.no/meniger/debatt/article 1224401.ece).

57 **"a lesson learned":** Jan M. Olsen, "Muslim's Party Could Decide Danish Vote," Associated Press (http://unityconquer.wordpress.com/2007/11/16/muslims-party-could-decide-danish-vote/).

58 **"no leading Norwegian":** http://www.regjeringen.no/nb/dep/ud/dep/utenriks minister_jonas_gahr_store/taler_artikler/2006/Magazinets-rett-og-ansvar .html?id=273544.

58 **"believe in the freedom":** "-Ytringsfrihet er religion i Vesten," NRK Web site, 10 February 2006 (http://www.nrk.no/nyheter/utenriks/5476565.html).

PART II: *Censors and Self-Censors*

CHAPTER I: *The Ripple Effect*

64 **"no longer be given an education":** "Les signes et manifestations d'appartenance religieuse dans les etablissements scolaires" is now available online at the Web site of the French education department: ftp://trf.education.gouv.fr/pub/edutel/syst/igen/rapports/rapport_obin.pdf.

64: **wrote it up in the *New York Times*:** Craig S. Smith, "Jews in France Feel Sting as Anti-Semitism Surges Among Children of Immigrants," *New York Times*, 26 March 2006 (http://www.nytimes.com/2006/03/26/international/26antisemitism.html?_r=2&scp=1&sq=obin%20report&st=cse&oref=slogin&oref=slogin).

CHAPTER II: *The Media in the Driver's Seat*

65 **"If you're wondering":** Tim Rutten, "Where Is the West's Outcry?," *Los Angeles Times*, 23 June 2007 (http://articles.latimes.com/2007/jun/23/entertainment/et-rutten23).

66 **"a deep-rooted hatred":** Andrew Norfolk, "Hardline Takeover of British Mosques," *Times Online*, 7 September 2007 (http://www.timesonline.co.uk/tol/comment/faith/article2402973.ece).

66 **"tells a story":** Jane Lampman, "In Many Ways, US Muslims Are in Mainstream

America," *Christian Science Monitor*, 24 May 2007 (http://www.csmonitor.com/2007/0524/p02s01-ussc.html).

66 "Muslim Americans are largely": "Muslims 'Well Integrated' in US," *BBC News*, 22 May 2007 (http://news.bbc.co.uk/2/hi/americas/6680939.stm).

66–67 "By an almost": "Midwest Lutherans Largely Reject Violence," Iowahawk blog, 23 May 2007 (http://iowahawk.typepad.com/iowahawk/2007/05/midwest_luthera.html).

67 "a religious president": Laurie Goodstein, "Ahmadinejad Meets Clerics, and Decibels Drop a Notch," *New York Times*, 27 September 2007 (http://www.nytimes.com/2007/09/27/world/middleeast/27clerics.html?_r=2&ref=world&oref=slogin&oref=slogin).

CHAPTER III: *The "American Imam"*

68 "The imam begins": Andrea Elliott, "A Muslim Leader in Brooklyn, Reconciling 2 Worlds," *New York Times*, 5 March 2006 (http://www.nytimes.com/2006/03/05/nyregion/05imam.html). "To Lead the Faithful in a Faith under Fire," appeared on 6 March (http://www.nytimes.com/2006/03/06/nyregion/06imam.html?_r=1&oref=slogin); part three, "Tending to Muslims' Hearts and Islam's Future," on March 7 (http://www.nytimes.com/2006/03/07/nyregion/07imam.html).

73 "to reconcile this ecstatic": Diana West, "The Media and Islam," *Washington Times*, 9 March 2006 (http://www.washingtontimes.com/news/2006/mar/09/20060309-085706-2287r/).

73 "intimate, richly textured portrait": http://en.wikipedia.org/wiki/Pulitzer_Prize_for_Feature_Writing.

73 "does possess religious opinions": Gal Beckerman, "The Sun's Wafer-thin Attack on Elliott's Pulitzer Prize," *Columbia Journalism Review*, 20 April 2007 (http://www.cjr.org/politics/the_suns_waferthin_attack_on_e.php).

74 "Just from the between-the-lines": Gary Shapiro, "Pulitzer for Imam Feature Called 'Outrageous,'" *The Sun*, 20 April 2007 (http://www.nysun.com/new-york/pulitzer-for-imam-feature-called-outrageous/52867/).

CHAPTER IV: *Redefining Moderation*

76 "in the anxious": Robert S. Leiken and Steven Brooke, "The Moderate Muslim Brotherhood," *Foreign Affairs*, March/April 2007 (http://www.foreignaffairs.org/20070301faessay86208/robert-s-leiken-steven-brooke/the-moderate-muslim-brotherhood.html).

76 "engage the [Muslim Brotherhood]": James Traub, "Islamic Democrats?," *New York Times Magazine*, 29 April 2007 (http://www.nytimes.com/2007/04/29/magazine/29Brotherhood.t.html?scp=1&sq=islamic+democrats%3F&st=nyt).

76 "there are no extremists": Inger Anne Olsen, "Fatwabrødrene," *A-magasinet*, *Aftenposten*, 12 June 2007 (http://www.aftenposten.no/amagasinet/article1824132.ece).

77 "Does the *Times* even mention": Hugh Fitzgerald, "Help the New Duranty Times See the Light," *Dhimmi Watch* Web site, 30 April 2007 (http://www.jihadwatch.org/dhimmiwatch/archives/2007/04/016252print.html).

77 "the words 'Assailants'": *Dhimmi Watch* Web site, 30 April 2007 (http://jihadwatch.org/dhimmiwatch/archives/016252.php).

77 "charitable work for orphans": http://www.internet-haganah.com/harchives/003022.html.

77 "support for jihad": Internet Haganah Web site, 13 December 2006 (http://www.internet-haganah.com/harchives/005797.html).

78 **"home to Britain"**: Alan Cowell and Raymond Bonner, "4 Held in Scottish Attacks as British See Broader Plot," *New York Times*, 1 July 2007 (http://www.nytimes .com/2007/07/01/world/europe/01britain.html?scp=1&sq=home%20to%20 Britain%20fears%20of%20homegrown%20terrorist%20attacks%20among%20 its%20disenfranchised%20&st=cse).

79 **"cracked where it was broken"**: Nicholas Kulish, "New Terrorism Case Confirms That Denmark Is a Target," *New York Times*, 17 September 2007 (http://www .nytimes.com/2007/09/17/world/europe/17denmark.html?scp=1&sq=cracked%20 where%20it%20was%20broken%20open%20by%20a%20police%20battering%20 ram&st=cse).

79 **"a pipe bomb"**: Gretchen Parker, "A Family in Despair," *Tampa Tribune*, 2 September 2007 (http://www.tbo.com/news/metro/MGBRKZY036F.html).

80 **"MacFarquhar not only"**: Steven Emerson, "MacFarquhar Strikes Again," *National Review Online*, 6 September 2007 (http://article.nationalreview.com/?q=mdzjogiyn wvjnme4mmi5ymzimzvlzmyzztq4yzk0mdc).

81 **"was listed as a member"**: "CAIR Identified by the FBI as part of the Muslim Brotherhood's Palestine Committee," Counterterrorism Blog, 8 August 2007 (http:// counterterrorismblog.org/2007/08/cair_identified_by_the_fbi_as.php).

81 **"It's disgraceful"**: Charles Johnson, "CAIR: Part of the Muslim Brotherhood's Palestine Committee," *Little Green Footballs* blog, 8 August 2007 (http://littlegreenfootballs. com/weblog/?entry=26584_CAIR-_Part_of_the_Muslim_Brotherhoods_Palestine_ Committee&only&headline).

81 **"Charitable giving"**: Gretel C. Kovach, "Charity or Terror?," *Newsweek*, 26 July 2007 (http://www.newsweek.com/id/32751).

82 **"like the government"**: Robert Spencer, "A Trying Time for CAIR," *FrontPage Magazine*, 28 August 2007 (http://frontpagemagazine.com/Articles/Read.aspx? GUID=2C78DA37-AE8A-4DFF-A59C-86AB1CCF9986).

82 **"deceptive and ridiculous"**: Charles Johnson, "Newsweek Shills for Radical Islam (Again)," *Little Green Footballs*, 28 July 2007 (http://littlegreenfootballs.com/ weblog/?entry=26439_Newsweek_Shills_for_Radical_Islam_(Again)&only).

82 **"the HLF trial is exposing"**: Rod Dreher, "What the Muslim Brotherhood Means for the U.S.," *Dallas Morning News*, 9 September 2007 (http://www.dallasnews.com/ sharedcontent/dws/dn/opinion/columnists/rdreher/stories/DN-dreher_09edi.ART. State.Edition1.4235f88.html).

83 **"found her spiritual home"**: Cathy Lynn Grossman, "The Face of Islam in America," *USA Today*, 21 August 2007 (http://www.usatoday.com/news/religion/2007-08-20- mattson-islam_N.htm).

CHAPTER V: *Carrying Islamists' Water*

84 **"attempts to answer"**: Dennis Wagner, "Maker of Documentary Cries Foul," *Arizona Republic*, 10 April 2007 (http://www.azcentral.com/news/articles/0410crossroads0410 .html).

84 **"is futile"**: Brendan Bernhard, "Across the Great Divide," *New York Sun*, 13 April 2007 (http://www.nysun.com/arts/across-the-great-divide/52406/).

85 **"Muslims, like people everywhere"**: *CNN Presents. God's Warriors*, aired on CNN, 21, 22, and 23 August 2007. (Transcripts: http://transcripts.cnn.com/TRANSCRIPTS/ 0708/21/cp.01.html, http://transcripts.cnn.com/TRANSCRIPTS/0708/22/cp.01.html, http://transcripts.cnn.com/TRANSCRIPTS/0708/23/cp.01.html.)

85 **"no counterpart"**: "God's Jewish Warriors—CNN's Abomination," CAMERA: Committee for Accuracy in Middle East Reporting in America, 22 August 2007 (http://www.camera.org/index.asp?x_context=3&x_outlet=14&x_article=1354).

86 **"shameful advocacy"**: "MSNBC Live with Dan Abrams," 27 August 2007. (A partial transcript of Abrams's comments is here: http://insidecable.blogsome. com/2007/08/28/abrams-vs-amanpour-2/.)

86 **"the most dishonest"**: "MSNBC Live with Dan Abrams," 27 August 2007. (Emerson's MSNBC comments are cited here: http://newsbusters.org/blogs/brad-wilmouth/2007/08/28/msnbcs-abrams-hits-cnns-amanpour-defending-islamic-fundamentalism.)

86 **"Vilks should have"**: Paula Newton, "Artist Defiantly Draws Prophet Muhammed," CNN Web site, 16 October 2007 (http://edition.cnn.com/2007/WORLD/europe/10/16/artist.controversy/index.html).

86 **"dialogue"**: "Gone to the Dogs," *The Economist*, 13 September 2007 (http://www .economist.com/world/europe/displaystory.cfm?story_id=9803885).

87 **"when we as Americans"**: Ann Sorkowitz and Julie N. Hays, "Witness to Discrimination: What Would You Do?," ABC Web site, 26 February 2008 (http:// abcnews.go.com/Primetime/WhatWouldYouDo/Story?id=4339476&page=1).

88 **"oppressed and forced"**: "Common Misunderstandings about Muslims," ABC Web site, 26 February 2008 (http://abcnews.go.com/Primetime/WhatWouldYouDo/story?id=4339516&page=1).

88 **"no content or images"**: Caroline Davies, "Wikipedia Defies 180,000 Demands to Remove Images of the Prophet," *Observer*, 17 February 2008 (http://www.guardian. co.uk/technology/2008/feb/17/wikipedia.islam).

88 **"threat culture"**: "Internettleverandører sensurerte Muhammed-tegninger," Human Rights Service Web site, 21 February 2008 (http://www.rights.no/publisher/publisher. asp?id=45&tekstid=1558).

CHAPTER VI: *The European Media*

89 **"other orthodox religions"**: "Imam Accused of Gay-Death Slur," BBC News Web site, 26 October 2006 (http://news.bbc.co.uk/2/hi/uk_news/england/manchester/6087430.stm).

89 **think tank's report:** A video of the BBC's report is here: http://news.bbc.co.uk/player/nol/newsid_7140000/newsid_7142200/7142296.stm? Also see this: http://www.bbc.co.uk/blogs/newsnight/2007/12/richard_watsons comment _on_the_policy_exchange_row.html.

90 **"How can we expect"**: James Chapman, "BBC's Newsround Fed Youngsters Al Qaeda propaganda, Claims Ex-Spy Chief," *Daily Mail*, 29 September 2007 (http://www. dailymail.co.uk/news/article-484577/BBCs-Newsround-fed-youngsters-Al-Qaeda-propaganda-claims-ex-spy-chief.html. See also "Broadcasters in BBC reporter plea," BBC News, 11 April 2007 (http://news.bbc.co.uk/2/hi/middle_east/6543773. stm).

90 **"An organisation which"**: Paul Revoir, "BBC Pays £200,000 to 'Cover Up Report on Anti-Israel Bias,'" *Daily Mail*, 22 March 2007 (http://www.dailymail.co.uk/news/article-444074/BBC-pays-200-000-cover-report-anti-Israel-bias.html).

90 **"reputation for accuracy"**: Julian Glover, "Poll Reveals How Trust in BBC Has Plummeted after Scandals," *Guardian*, 28 July 2007 (http://www.guardian.co.uk/media/2007/jul/28/broadcasting.bbc).

90–91 **"a stunning whitewash"**: Charles Johnson, "Video: Don't Panic, I'm Islamic," Little Green Footballs blog, 24 October 2007 (http://littlegreenfootballs.com/weblog/?entry=27679_Video-_Dont_Panic_Im_Islamic&only).

91 **"Muslims who speak openly"**: This text was originally at http://www.bbc.co.uk/religion/programmes/misc/islamic.shtml and has apparently been removed; it can still be found at "Dhimmitude at the BBC: 'Don't Panic, I'm Islamic,'" *Dhimmi Watch*

Web site, 13 June 2005 (http://www.jihadwatch.org/dhimmiwatch/archives/2005_06. php).

91 it emerged that five of the show's participants: See Adam Sherwin, "BBC 'Took Terrorist Trainers Paintballing,'" 5 December 2007 (http://www.timesonline.co.uk/ tol/news/uk/crime/article3001102.ece), Charles Johnson, "BBC Knew of Terrorist Activity, Didn't Tell Cops," Little Green Footballs blog, 5 December 2007 (http:// littlegreenfootballs.com/weblog/?entry=28174_BBC_Knew_of_Terrorist_Activity_ Didnt_Tell_Cops&only).

91 "opposes inter-faith dialogue": Andrew Norfolk, "BBC 'Censored Christian Party Broadcast,'" *Times Online*, 29 April 2008 (http://www.timesonline.co.uk/tol/news/ politics/article3835551.ece).

92 "intentionally and in cold blood": "Statement under oath by a photographer of France 2 television," 3 October 2000, posted at Palestinian Centre for Human Rights Web site (http://www.pchrgaza.org/special/tv2.htm).

93 "lifting his arm": "Raw Footage Shown in Al-Dura Case," JTA Web site, 15 November 2007 (http://www.jta.org/cgi-bin/iowa/breaking/105344.html).

93 "Every French citizen": "Karsenty on His Win over France 2 on the Al-Dura Hoax," Meryl Yourish blog, 21 May 2008 (http://www.yourish.com/2008/05/21/4845).

93 "smear campaign": http://hebdo.nouvelobs.com/hebdo/parution/p2274/articles/ a376434-.html.

93 "the guild . . . closing ranks": Anne-Elisabeth Moutet, "L'Affaire Enderlin," *Weekly Standard*, 7 July 2008 (http://www.weeklystandard.com/Content/Public/ Articles/000/000/015/284xawsb.asp?pg=1).

93 "a fatwa against": Bruce Crumley, "Wife No Virgin; Annulment Allowed," *Time*, 3 June 2008 (http://www.time.com/time/world/article/0,8599,1811460,00.html).

93 "used to diminish": Charles Bremner, "Outrage as French Judge Annuls Muslim Marriage over Bride's Virginity Lie," *Times Online*, 31 May 2008 (http://www .timesonline.co.uk/tol/news/world/europe/article4034908.ece).

94 "destroying our country": "Bardot Fined over Racial Hatred," *BBC News*, 3 June 2008 (http://news.bbc.co.uk/2/hi/entertainment/7434193.stm).

94 Afshan Rafiq: "Gudene Vet," TV2, 27 April 2008 (http://webtv.tv2.no/webtv/ sumo/?progId=234098).

94–95 "You know, these Muslims": The ad can no longer be found on *Morgenbladet*'s site, but the Ghozlan interview is here: Simen Sætre, "En voldelig religion?," *Morgenbladet*, 25 August 2006 (http://www.morgenbladet.no/apps/pbcs.dll/ article?AID=/20060825/OAKTUELT001/108250028).

96 "embraces the dream": http://honestthinking.org/no/pub/HT.2005.04.JTA.Ghozlan _extra_info.html.

96 her ideal is a sharia state: Helle M. Brix, "Søstre i Brødrenes tjeneste," Human Rights Service Web site, 30 January 2007 (http://www.rights.no/publisher/publisher. asp?id=54&tekstid=1193). See also Hans Rustad, "Program for islamiseringen av Norge," Document no, 24 June 2006 (http://www.document.no/2006/06/program_ for_islamiseringen_av.html).

96 Ghozlan also has close ties: Hege Storhaug, "Basim Ghozlan om muslimske jentebarn og skilsmisse på TV2 igår," Human Rights Service Web site, 17 April 2007 (http:// www.rights.no/islam_gen/hrs_25.20_070417_113.htm).

CHAPTER VII: *"Sowing Pain"*
97 "Europe . . . appears to be": Dan Bilefsky and Ian Fisher, "Across Europe, Worries on Islam Spread to the Center," *New York Times*, 11 October 2006 (http://www.nytimes. com/2006/10/11/world/europe/11muslims.html?_r=1&oref=slogin).

97 "neoconservatives": Henrik Thune, "Nykonservatisme på norsk," *Dagbladet*, 3 October 2006 (http://www.dagbladet.no/kultur/2006/10/03/478527.html).

97 "Something is obviously": Morten A. Strøksnes in Stavanger *Aftenblad*, 14 October 2006, quoted at http://www.rights.no/publisher/publisher.asp?id=31&tekstid=211.

97–98 "risks further isolating": Tom Heneghan, *Reuters*, 23 October 2006 (originally at http://today.reuters.co.uk/news/articlenews.aspx?storyid=2006-10-23T092915Z_01_NOA334134_RTRUKOC_0_RELIGION-EUROPE-MUSLIMS.xml&type=reutersEdge&WTmodLoc=Editors+Choice-C3-More-2; available at http://www.gulf-times.com/site/topics/article.asp?cu_no=2&item_no=114273&version=1&template_id=46&parent_id=26).

98 "elevating cultures": Interview with Johann Hari, "Ayaan Hirsi Ali: My Life under a Fatwa," *The Independent*, 27 November 2007 (http://www.independent.co.uk/news/people/ayaan-hirsi-ali-my-life-under-a-fatwa-760666.html).

98 "sow[n] pain": "The Pope's Words," *New York Times*, 16 September 2006 (http://www.nytimes.com/2006/09/16/opinion/16sat2.html?scp=2&sq=pope%20heal%20words%20pain&st=cse).

99 "seek to compel Europe": Robert Redeker, "Face aux intimidations islamistes, que doit faire le monde libre?," *Le Figaro*, 19 September 2006 (full text available at http://villiers2007.over-blog.com/article-4005448-6.html and http://www.20minutes.fr/article/111437/Toulouse-Le-texte-de-Robert-Redeker-qui-fait-polemique.php).

99 "unacceptable": "Entretien du Premier Ministre, M. Dominique de Villepin, avec 'RMC'—Extraits," 29 September 2006 (http://www.ambafrance-uk.org/Entretien-du-Premier-ministre-sur.html).

99 Gilles de Robien declared "solidarity": Alain Auffray and Gilbert Laval, "L'auteur de la Tribune Satanique Menace," *Libération*, 29 September 2006 (http://www.liberation.fr/actualite/societe/207448.FR.php).

99 Pierre Rousselin similarly vowed "solidarity": "Le Figaro s'excuse pour la publication de l'article islamophobe," *Agence PAF*, 23 September 2006 (http://www.agence-paf.net/article.php3?id_article=266).

100 "only a pretext": Angelo Panebianco, "Fondamentalismo e Libertà d'opinione," *Corriere della Sera*, 19 September 2006 (http://terzotriennio.blogspot.com/2006_09_01_archive.html).

100 "champions of freedom": Paul Vallely, "Has the West Been Silenced by Islam?," *The Independent*, 4 October 2006 (http://www.independent.co.uk/news/world/politics/has-the-west-been-silenced-by-islam-418629.html).

101 "adding fuel": "Leading Article: Beware Loose Talk about a Clash of Civilisations," *The Independent*, 4 October 2006 (http://www.independent.co.uk/opinion/leading-articles/leading-article-beware-loose-talk-about-a-clash-of-civilisations-418605.html).

101 "rights—like the freedom of the press" (footnote): Neal Ascherson, "A Carnival of Stupidity," *Open Democracy*, 6 February 2006 (http://www.opendemocracy.net/faith-terrorism/cartoons_3242.jsp).

102 Philip Bennett delivered a speech: Philip Bennett, "Covering Islam," Center for the Study of Democracy, University of California at Irvine, 2008 (http://repositories.cdlib.org/cgi/viewcontent.cgi?article=1168&context=csd/).

102 Hizb ut-Tahrir: Martin Ejlertsen, "DR bøjede seg for islamister," *Kristeligt Dagblad*, 11 March 2008 (http://www.kristeligt-dagblad.dk/artikel/280232:Danmark—DR-boejede-sig-for-islamister).

CHAPTER VIII: *Profiles in Courage*

103 TV2 . . . documentary: *Truet til Taushet*, TV2, 2 October 2006.

103 German courts: Matthias Bartsch, Andrea Brandt, Simone Kaiser, Gunther Latsch,

Cordula Meyer, and Caroline Schmidt, trans. Christopher Sultan, "Paving the Way for a Muslim Parallel Society," *Der Spiegel*, 29 March 2007 (http://www.spiegel.de/international/germany/0,1518,474629,00.html).

103 **"Why can't we call":** George Weigel, "The War against Jihadism," *Newsweek*, 4 February 2008 (http://www.newsweek.com/id/105583).

104 **violent revolt in Windsor:** "Race Clashes Hit Windsor," *This Is London*, 5 October 2006 (http://www.thisislondon.co.uk/news/article23369687-details/Race+clashes+hit+Windsor/article.do).

104 **Amsterdam bus attack:** "Media Silence on Attack on Amsterdam Bus," *NIS News*, 24 October 2006 (http://www.nisnews.nl/public/241006_2.htm).

105 **"Even though Jamaat ul-Fuqra":** Paul Williams, "Radical Muslim Paramilitary Compound Flourishes in Upper New York State," *Canada Free Press*, 14 May 2007 (originally at http://www.canadafreepress.com/2007/paul-williams051107 .htm, available at http://www.frontpagemag.com/Articles/Printable.aspx?GUID= ec5933a9-cfa2-4faf8d67-34958a623392).

105 **"sites of Jewish interest":** Mike Brooke, "Holocaust Day Marred by 'Racist' Stone-throwing," *East London Advertiser*, 30 January 2008 (http://www.eastlondonadvertiser. co.uk/content/towerhamlets/advertiser/news/story.aspx?brand=ELAOnline&cate gory=news&tBrand=northlondon24&tCategory=newsela&itemid=WeED30%20 Jan%202008%2020%3A51%3A30%3A863).

106 **"seven of the men":** Annie Jacobsen, "Terror in the Skies—Again?," Womens WallStreet.com, 16 July 2004 (originally at womenswallstreet.com; available at http:// frontpagemag.com/Articles/Read.aspx?GUID=D5D05E65-4E21-47C5-BDEF-8FB592C917E1).

106 **"the air marshals":** Eric Leonard, "Air Marshals Say Passenger Overreacted," KFI640 AM News, 22 July 2004.

107 **"far-fetched":** http://trishwilson.typepad.com/blog/2004/07/airline_lesson__3 .html.

107 **"a story about nothing":** Patrick Smith, "The Hysterical Skies," *Salon*, 21 July 2004 (http://archive.salon.com/tech/col/smith/2004/07/21/askthepilot95/index.html).

107 **"But nothing happened":** http://jihadwatch.org/archives/002532.php.

107 **dismissive business-travel column:** Joe Sharkey, "Business Travel: On the Road; What Really Happened on Flight 327?," *New York Times*, 20 July 2004 (http://query .nytimes.com/gst/fullpage.html?res=9F01EFD71538F933A15754C0A9629C8B63&s ec=&spon=&&scp=12&sq=annie%20jacobsen&st=cse).

107 **"flight crews are being":** Joe Sharkey, "Business Travel: On the Road; Now Boarding, Cultural Misperceptions," *New York Times*, 27 July 2004 (http://query.nytimes.com/gst/ fullpage.html?res=9906EFD71538F934A15754C0A9629C8B63&sec=&spon=&&sc p=1&sq=%93flight%20crews%20are%20being%20routinely%20warned%22%20 that%20terrorists%20are%20%22testing%20the%20system%22&st=cse).

108 **"The Federal Agents who were there":** Annie Jacobsen, *Terror in the Skies: Why 9/11 Could Happen Again*, Spence Publishing, 2005, p. 163.

108 **"pretended not to notice":** Originally at http://insider.washingtontimes.com/ articles/normal.php?StoryID=20070530-121308-3365r; quoted at http://www .captainsquartersblog.com/mt/archives/010096.php.

109 **redacted version:** "Security Flaws Confirmed on Flight 327," *Washington Times*, 29 May 2007 (http://washtimes.com/news/2007/may/29/20070529-040125-8213r/).

109 **"resembled a dry run":** "Report Confirms Terrorist Dry Run," *Washington Times*, 30 May 2007 (http://www.washingtontimes.com/news/2007/may/30/20070530-121308-3365r/).

109 **"to downplay and cover up":** "Report Confirms Terror Dry Run," *Washington Times*, 30 May 2007.

109 **"He has had many"**: *Terror in the Skies*, p. 43.

109 **"because its contents embarrass"**: Annie Jacobsen, WomensWallStreet.com, 18 April 2007.

110 **"falling down on the job"**: Tobin Harshaw, "It's Not Paranoia if They're Really Out to Get You," *New York Times*, 30 May 2007 (http://opinionator.blogs.nytimes.com/2007/05/30/its-not-paranoia-if-theyre-really-out-to-get-you/).

110 **"To practice your faith"**: Bob Von Sternberg and Pamela Miller, "Uproar Follows Imams' Detention," *Minneapolis Star-Tribune*, 22 November 2006 (http://www.startribune.com/local/11585901.html).

111 **"no stranger"**: Jessica Bennett and Matthew Philips, "Flying while Muslim," *Newsweek*, 22 November 2006 (http://www.newsweek.com/id/44711?tid=relatedcl).

112 **"a terrorist probe"**: "How the Imams Terrorized an Airliner," *Washington Times*, 28 November 2006 (http://www.washingtontimes.com/news/2006/nov/28/20061128-122902-7522r/).

112 **"chose to make a spectacle"**: "A Profiling in Courage," *Investor's Business Daily*, 22 November 2006 (http://www.investors.com/editorial/editorialcontent.asp?secid=1501&status=article&id=249091839930090).

CHAPTER IX: *Buruma*

116 **"potential menace"**: Ian Buruma, *Murder in Amsterdam*, p. 69.

116 **"echoes . . . enthusiasm"**: Ibid., p. 158.

116 **"9/11 was a Jewish plot"**: Ibid., p. 258.

117 **"is not Islam"**: Ibid., p. 239.

117 **"uprooted rural people"**: Ibid., p. 239.

117 **"accommodation with the Muslims"**: Ibid., p. 246.

117 **"of orthodox Muslims"**: Ibid., p. 235.

118 **"opinions and habits"**: Ibid., p. 244.

118 **"deserves the benefit"**: Ibid., p. 246.

118 **"Attacking religion"**: Ibid., p. 246.

118 **"Perhaps Western civilization"**: Ibid., p. 234.

CHAPTER X: *"Angry White Men"*

120 **"racism as criticism"**: Patricia Cohen, "In Books, a Clash of Europe and Islam," *New York Times*, 8 February 2007 (http://www.nytimes.com/2007/02/08/books/08circ.html?ref=books).

121 **"said several times"**: Lars Hedegaard, "Foghs forunderlige sammenhængskraft," *Sappho*, n.d. (http://www.sappho.dk/Nr.%203%20juni%202006/burka.htm).

121–122 **"become a bible"**: Dag Herbjørnsrud, "Falskt USA-alibi," *Ny Tid*, 9-15 March 2007, p. 33 (http://www.nytid.no/arkiv/artikler/20070320/falskt_usa_alibi/).

122 **"Are the Islam critics"**: Thomas Berg, "Sinte, hvite menn," *Ny Tid*, 16-22 March 2007, p. 48–51.

CHAPTER XI: *"An Islamic superstar"*

124 **"a more glorious"**: Paul Berman, "Who's Afraid of Tariq Ramadan?," *The New Republic*, 4 June 2007 (www.tnr.com/politics/story.html?id=fd52e6a4-efc5-42fd-983b-1282a16ac8dd).

127 **"were he to condemn"**: Spengler, "Europe in the House of War," *Asia Times*, 11 February 2008 (http://www.campus-watch.org/articleid/4780).

127 **"bridge-builder"**: Ian Buruma, "Tariq Ramadan Has an Identity Issue," *New York Times*, 4 February 2007 (http://www.nytimes.com/2007/02/04/magazine/04ramada

n.t.html?sq=tariq%20ramadan%20has%20an%20identity%20issue&st=cse&scp=1 &pagewanted=all).

130 **"He is neither one"**: Daniel Pipes, "Tariq Ramadan Exposed," Daniel Pipes blog, 23 September 2004 (http://www.danielpipes.org/blog/2004/09/tariq-ramadan-exposed .html).

132 **"Yes, you read it right"**: Pascal Bruckner, "A Reply to Ian Buruma and Timothy Garton Ash," *Sign and Sight*, 26 March 2007 (http://www.signandsight.com/ features/1263.html).

132 **"From the start"**: Rosemary Bechler, "Reinventing Islam in Europe: A Profile of Tariq Ramadan," Open Democracy blog, 6 July 2004 (http://www.opendemocracy. net/faith-europe_islam/article_1996.jsp), quoted in David Thompson, "Squinting at Extremists," David Thompson blog, 28 March 2007 (http://davidthompson.typepad. com/davidthompson/2007/03/squinting_at_ex.html).

132 **"Charismatic"**: Elizabeth Bryant, "Message of Islamic Pride Resonates with Europe's Muslims," *San Francisco Chronicle*, 13 March 2004 (http://www.sfgate.com/cgi-bin/ article.cgi?file=/c/a/2004/03/13/MNG905K1DR1.DTL).

133 **"advocating a sweeping ban"**: Stéphanie Giry, "The Faces of Tariq Ramadan," *New York Times*, 1 April 2007 (http://www.nytimes.com/2007/04/01/books/review/ Giry.t.html?ref=review).

CHAPTER XII: *"A caricature of sweetness and light"*

138 **"a trifle overblown"**: Ian Buruma, "Against Submission," *New York Times*, 4 March 2007 (http://www.nytimes.com/2007/03/04/books/review/04buruma.html? pagewanted=print).

140 **"one of Europe's most infamous"**: Lorraine Ali, "The Controversial Memoir of a Muslim Woman," *Newsweek*, 26 February 2007 (available at http://www.somaliweyn. com/pages/news/Feb_07/18Feb15.html).

140 **"throwing a rhetorical"**: http://news.bbc.co.uk/2/hi/programmes/hardtalk/ 6335401.stm.

140 **"Euro-Gaullists"**: Timothy Garton Ash, *Free World*, Penguin, 2005, p. 50.

141 **"populist, anti-immigrant parties"**: *Free World*, p. 197.

141 **"Garton Ash does a sudden"**: Bruce Bawer, "Crisis in Europe," *Hudson Review*, Winter 2006, p. 594.

141–142 **"It's no disrespect to Ms. Ali"**: Timothy Garton Ash, "Islam in Europe," *New York Review of Books*, 5 October, 2006 (http://www.nybooks.com/articles/article- preview?article_id=19371).

142 **"It is five minutes to twelve"**: a video of Fortuyn's famous "five minutes to twelve" statement is at http://www.youtube.com/watch?v=i_keH3Gn5Ok.

144 **"in the eyes of our genteel"**: Pascal Bruckner, "Enlightenment Fundamentalism or Racism of the Anti-racists?," *Sign and Sight*, 24 January 2007 (http://www .signandsight.com/features/1146.html).

144 **"I admire Ayaan Hirsi Ali"**: Ian Buruma, "Freedom Cannot be Decreed," *Sign and Sight*, 29 January 2007 (http://www.signandsight.com/features/1161.html).

145–146 **"Euro-Islam . . . is impossible"**: Bassam Tibi, "Europeanisation, Not Islamisation," *Sign and Sight*, 22 March 2007 (http://www.signandsight.com/ features/1258.html).

146 **"exemplary"**: Tariq Ramadan, "Blair Can No Longer Deny a Link Exists Between Terrorism and Foreign Policy," *Guardian*, 4 June 2007 (http://www.guardian.co.uk/ commentisfree/2007/jun/04/comment.politics).

146 **"spent quite a lot of time"**: David Goodhart, "Open Letter to Tariq Ramadan,"

Prospect, June 2007 (http://www.prospect-magazine.co.uk/article_details.php?id=9641).

147 "a slippery figure": Ian Buruma, "His Toughness Problem—and Ours," *New York Review of Books*, 27 September 2007 (http://www.nybooks.com/articles/20590).

147 "lent respectability": Ian Buruma, "Lucky Little Countries?," *Project Syndicate*, 2007 (http://www.project-syndicate.org/commentary/buruma6).

147–148 "huge admiration": Debate between Ayaan Hirsi Ali and Timothy Garton Ash at Royal Society of Arts, London, 21 November 2007 (http://www.axess.se/web/main.nsf/0/FA53330E9EB4DA68C12573B000600CE9).

148 Ramadan was fined: http://www.danielpipes.org/blog/2004/09/tariq-ramadan-exposed.html.

148 Edward Said . . . throwing a rock: Karen W. Arenson, "Columbia Debates a Professor's 'Gesture,'" *New York Times*, 19 October 2000 (http://www.nytimes.com/2000/10/19/nyregion/19COLU.html?ex=1219118400&en=8cebdb5).

CHAPTER XIII: *Apologists Aplenty*

149 "it can be difficult": Jon Meacham and Sally Quinn, "Why 'Muslims Speak Out' Matters," *Newsweek/Washington Post* Web site, 22 July 2007 (http://newsweek.washingtonpost.com/onfaith/muslims_speak_out/2007/07/why_muslims_speak_out_matters.html).

149 "pulling out all the stops": Charles Johnson, "Tariq Ramadan at the Washington Post," Little Green Footballs blog, 25 July 2007 (http://littlegreenfootballs.com/weblog/?entry=26398&only&a-mp;rss).

150 Johnson quoting Timmermann: Charles Johnson, "Washington Post Continues the Parade of Whitewash," Little Green Footballs blog, 29 July 2007 (http://littlegreenfootballs.com/article/26452_Washington_Post_Continues_the_Parade_of_Whitewash), quoting Kenneth Timmermann, "Pipes Objects to Fox in Henhouse," *Insight*, 19 March 2004 (available at http://www.danielpipes.org/article/1650).

150 "efforts to help sanitize": Steven Emerson, "Muzammil the Moderate," Counterterrorism Blog, 30 July 2007 (http://www.investigativeproject.org/article/276).

151 "Esposito, more than any other": Martin Kramer, "Georgetown Yankees in Prince Alawaheed's Court," Sandbox blog, 2 January 2006 (http://sandbox.blog-city.com/georgetown_yankees_in_prince_alwaleeds_court.htm).

151 "a world hegemonic discourse": Martin Kramer, "Terrorism? What Terrorism?," *Wall Street Journal*, 15 November 2001 (http://www.campus-watch.org/article/id/1037).

151 "reshaping of the concept": Martin Kramer, "Islam Obscured," chapter three of *Ivory Towers on Sand: The Failure of Middle Eastern Studies in America* (Washington: The Washington Institute for Near East Policy, 2001), pp. 44–60 (http://www.geocities.com/martinkramerorg/IslamObscured.htm).

151 "media were the real fanatics": Ibid.

151 "international sources": Ibid.

152 "The treatment of women under Islam": John Esposito, "Want to Understand Islam? Start Here," *Washington Post*, 22 July 2007 (http://www.washingtonpost.com/wp-dyn/content/article/2007/07/20/AR2007072002137.html).

152 "a magnet for Arab and Muslim money": Martin Kramer, "Georgetown Yankees in Prince Alawaheed's Court," Sandbox blog, 2 January 2006 (http://sandbox.blog-city.com/georgetown_yankees_in_prince_alwaleeds_court.htm).

152 "educational": Julia Duin, "Saudis Give Big to U.S. Colleges," *Washington Times*, 10

December 2007 (http://snuffysmithsblog.blogspot.com/2007/12/saudis-give-big-to-us-colleges.html).

152 **"some 210 Islamic centers":** *Ain-al-Yaqeen*, 1 March 2002 (excerpts at http://memri.org/bin/articles.cgi?Page=archives&Area=sd&ID=SP36002#_edn1).

152 **"political and economic grievance":** Cinnamon Stillwell, "Esposito at Stanford," *FrontPage Magazine*, 15 February 2008 (http://www.meforum.org/article/1855).

CHAPTER XIV: *"Secular fundamentalists"*

154 **"honor killings, cutting":** Paul Vallely, "View from England: Overcoming Islamophobia," *On Faith: Muslims Speak Out, Newsweek/Washington Post* Web site, 25 July 2007 (http://newsweek.washingtonpost.com/onfaith/muslims_speak_out/2007/07/the_symptoms_of_islamophobia.html).

156 **"For a fruitful discussion":** "Muslims Speak Out: Tariq Ramadan," *On Faith: Muslims Speak Out, Washington Post/Newsweek* Web site, 25 July 2007 (http://newsweek.washingtonpost.com/onfaith/muslims_speak_out/2007/07/tariq_ramadan.html).

157 **"the liberal deity":** Mark Lilla, "The Politics of God," *New York Times Magazine*, 19 August 2007 (http://www.nytimes.com/2007/08/19magazine/19Religion-t.html?scp=1&sq=mark%20lilla%20%22politics%20of%20god%22&st=cse).

159 **"No need for studies":** Tariq Ramadan, "Reading the Koran, *New York Times Book Review*, 6 January 2008 (http://www.nytimes.com/2008/01/06/books/review/Ramadan-t.html?scp=1&sq=tariq%20ramadan%20%22reading%20the%20koran%22&st=cse).

160 **"Armstrong argues":** Laurie Goodstein, "Seeing Muhammed as Both a Prophet and a Politician," *New York Times*, 20 December 2006 (http://www.nytimes.com/2006/12/20/books/20goods.html?scp=2&sq=%22laurie%20goodstein%22%20karen%20armstrong&st=cse).

161 **"what they perceive":** David Thompson, "Karen Armstrong: Islam's Hagiographer," Butterflies and Wheels Web site, 2006 (http://www.butterfliesandwheels.com/articleprint.php?num=202).

162 **"The criminal activities":** Karen Armstrong, "Balancing the Prophet," *Financial Times*, 27 April 2007 (http://www.ft.com/cms/s/0/4a05a4a4-f134-11db-838b-000b5df10621.html?nclick_check=1).

163 **"non-Western immigrants":** Mark S. Berger, "Mener Norske Jenter Frister til Sex," *Dagbladet*, 6 September 2001 (http://www.dagbladet.no/nyheter/2001/09/06/279676.html).

164 **Yousef op-eds:** Ahmed Yousef, "What Hamas Wants," *New York Times*, 20 June 2007 (http://www.nytimes.com/2007/06/20/opinion/20yousef.html); Ahmed Yousef, "Engage with Hamas," *Washington Post*, 20 June 2007 (http://www.washingtonpost.com/wp-dyn/content/article/2007/06/19/AR2007061901736.html).

164 **"good ideas prosper":** Clark Hoyt, "The Danger of the One-Sided Debate," *New York Times*, 24 June 2007 (http://www.nytimes.com/2007/06/24/opinion/24pubed.html).

164 **"propaganda from a designated":** Brian Hecht, "Hamas' Mystery Media Representative in the U.S.," Counterterrorism Blog, 12 July 2007 (http://www.investigativeproject.org/article/289).

164–165 **SPJ guidelines:** http://www.spj.org/divguidelines.asp.

CHAPTER I: *Jihad on Campus*

170 **"He was clearly terrified":** Abigail Thernstrom, "The Massacre of Innocence," *Wall Street Journal*, 6 September 2007 (http://www.opinionjournal.com/la/?id=110010564).

170 **Summers invitation withdrawn:** "U. of California Regents Disinvite Lawrence Summers as Dinner Speaker," *Chronicle of Higher Education* news blog, 15 September 2007 (http://chronicle.com/news/article/3034/u-of-california-regents-disinvite-lawrence-summers-as-dinner-speaker).

170 **"one out of every four":** "Religious Liberty in Peril on Campus, National Surveys Reveal," Foundation for Individual Rights in Education Web site, 10 November 2003 (http://www.thefire.org/index.php/article/167.html).

170 **"the last generation's":** Stuart Taylor Jr., "It's Time to Junk the Double Standard on Free Speech," *Atlantic Monthly*, 25 January 2002 (http://www.theatlantic.com/politics/nj/taylor2002-01-25.htm).

170 **"the resolution didn't reflect":** Scott Jaschik, "Historians, War, Responsibility," Inside Higher Ed blog, 8 January 2007 (http://www.insidehighered.com/news/2007/01/08/aha).

170–171 **"We are not censoring":** Joe Light, "Universities Challenge Free Speech after Sept. 11," *Yale Herald*, 19 October 2001 (http://www.thefire.org/pdfs/4135_2454.pdf).

171 **"Vassar deserves credit":** Joseph Berger, "Film Portrays Stifling of Speech, But One College's Struggle Reflects a Nuanced Reality," *New York Times*, 27 June 2007 (http://www.nytimes.com/2007/06/27/education/27education.html).

171 **"making one of censorship's":** Greg Lukianoff, "'New York Times' Disappoints," *Fire's The Torch*, 27 June 2007 (http://thefire.org/index.php/article/8180.html?PHPSESSID=901d625f16d7685ffb2549facb665181).

172 **"spur hate crimes":** Karen W. Arenson, "Film's View of Islam Stirs Anger on Campuses," *New York Times*, 26 February 2007 (http://www.nytimes.com/2007/02/26/movies/26docu.html).

172 **"the question about radical Islam":** Ibid.

172 **"reinforced a negative stereotype":** "Quick Takes," Inside Higher Ed blog, 6 December 2007 (http://www.insidehighered.com/news/2007/12/06/qt).

172 **"two valid sides":** Suruchi Sharma, "Muslim Radicals to Justify Violence at Student Debate," *Guardian*, 17 October 2006 (http://www.guardian.co.uk/education/2006/oct/17/highereducation.uk2).

173 **"Ayatollah rethinks":** "Fears Magazine Could Fuel Racial Tension," *Cambridge News*, 12 February 2007 (originally at http://www.cambridge-news.co.uk/news/city/2007/02/09/ef79ee97-fec1-4f00-babf-dbd17447b40b.lpf; available at http://www.news.faithfreedom.org/index.php?name=News&file=article&sid=1064). Also see Alexandra Smith, "Religion Editor Sent Student Newspaper into Hiding," *Education Guardian*, 12 February 2007 (http://www.guardian.co.uk/education/2007/feb/12/students.highereducation).

173 **"anti-Islamic material":** "Muslims Outraged by Use of Cartoon," *Cambridge News*, 10 February 2007 (http://www.cambridge-news.co.uk/cn_news_cambridge/displayarticle.asp?id=293145).

173 **"The College chaplain":** Matthew Beard, "Student Editor in Hiding as Religious Satire Backfires," *Independent*, 12 February 2007 (http://findarticles.com/p/articles/mi_qn4158/is_20070212/ai_n17222236).

174 **Islamic Academy:** Olga Craig, "'The People Who Cure You Will Kill You,'" *Daily Telegraph*, 7 July 2007 (http://www.telegraph.co.uk/news/uknews/1556802/'The-people-who-cure-you-will-kill-you'.html).

174 **Kafeel Ahmed, Rowan Williams:** Adam Lusher and Jasper Copping, "Islamic Charity Linked to Car Bomb Suspect," *Daily Telegraph*, 8 July 2007 (http://www.telegraph .co.uk/news/uknews/1556813/Islamic-charity-linked-to-car-bomb-suspect.html).

174–175 **"You . . . are a nation":** Assad [Julio] Pino, "Violence Over Cartoon Justified for Muslims," Letter to the Editor, *Kent State News*, 28 February 2006 (http:// media.www.kentnewsnet.com/media/storage/paper867/news/2006/02/28/Opinion/ Letters.To.The.Editor-1640071.shtml). See also Carol Biliczky, "Kent State Denies Ties to Jihadi Site," *Akron Beacon Journal*, 1 March 2007 (originally at http:// www.ohio.com/mld/ohio/living/education/16808652.htm?template=content Modules/printstory.jsp, available at http://www.kentnewsnet.com/home/index. cfm?event=displayArticleComments&ustory_id=3270868a-9f55-42b3-ad59- d7a456391878).

175 **"Mr. Al-Arian's supporters":** Neil MacFarquhar, "Professor in Deadlocked Terrorism Case Could Face a New Indictment," *New York Times*, 18 April 2008 (http://www. nytimes.com/2008/04/18/washington/18professor.html?scp=15&sq=sami%20al- arian&st=cse).

175 **"I assume you have security":** Andrea Levin, "Eye on the Media: MSNBC Follies," *CAMERA: Committee for Accuracy in Middle East Reporting in America*, 20 September 2002 (http://www.camera.org/index.asp?x_context=6&x_article=342).

175 **"two charges of criminal mischief":** Audrey Hudson, "Koran Abuse Draws Hate- Crime Charge," *Washington Times*, 31 July 2007 (http://www.washingtontimes.com/ news/2007/jul/31/koran-abuse-draws-hate-crime-charge/).

176 **"pressure from Muslims":** *Paula Zahn Now*, CNN, 31 July 2007 (transcript at http:// transcripts.cnn.com/TRANSCRIPTS/0707/31/pzn.01.html).

177 **"security reasons":** John Steele, "Freedom of Speech Row as Talk on Islamic Extremists Is Banned," *Daily Telegraph*, 15 March 2007 (http://www.telegraph.co.uk/ news/uknews/1545591/Freedom-of-speech-row-as-talk-on-Islamic-extremists-is- banned.html).

177 **"there is no such thing":** "Islam? Perfectly Compatible with Women's Rights," Martha Nussbaum interviewed by Elisabetta Ambrosi, *ResetDOC*, 5 April 2007 (http://www.resetdoc.org/EN/Nussbaum-interview.php).

178 **"become a regular":** Walter Olson, "Over the Edge," *City Journal*, 5 October 2007 (http://www.city-journal.org/html/eon2007-10-05wo.html).

178 **"it would be going against":** The student, Alex Paige, is quoted in Leora Falk, "Columbia Is Divided by Bollinger Remarks," City Room, *New York Times*, 24 September 2007 (http://cityroom.blogs.nytimes.com/2007/09/24/columbia-is- divided-by-bollinger-remarks/).

178 **"very dire human rights situation":** Helene Cooper, "Ahmadinejad, at Columbia, Parries and Puzzles," *New York Times*, 25 September 2007 (http://www.nytimes .com/2007/09/25/world/middleeast/25iran.html?fta=y).

179 **"It should never be thought":** "President Lee C. Bollinger's Introductory Remarks at SIPA-World Leaders Forum with President of Iran Mahmoud Ahmadinejad," *Columbia News*, 24 September 2007 (http://www.columbia.edu/cu/news/07/09/ lcbopeningremarks.html).

181 **"Bollinger has disgraced":** See reader comments at http://cityroom.blogs .nytimes.com/2007/09/24/columbia-is-divided-by-bollinger-remarks/.

183–184 **"The president's address":** "Columbia University Faculty Action Committee Statement of Concern," *New York Sun*, 12 November 2007 (http://www.nysun.com/ new-york/columbia-university-faculty-action-committee/66314/).

183 **David Horowitz at Emory (footnote):** Salvador Rizzo, "Outside Group Stifles Horowitz Speech," *Emory Wheel*, 25 October 2007 (http://www.emorywheel.com/ detail.php?n=24510).

184 **"to deflect criticism"**: David Bernstein, The Volokh Conspiracy blog, 3 March 2008 (http://volokh.com/archives/archive_2008_03_02-2008_03_08.shtml#1204592536).

185 **"was more disturbing"**: Hillel Stavis, Solomania blog, 6 March 2008 (http://www.solomonia.com/blog/archive/2008/03/hillel-stavis-preaching-the-sharia-just/index.shtml).

185 **"MESA has over"**: Hugh Fitzgerald, Jihad Watch blog, 25 January 2005 (http://jihadwatch.org/archives/2005/01/004791print.html).

185 **"a well-known Hate Mongerer"**: Charlie Sykes, "Shut Up. They Explained," 620 WTMJ radio Web site, 27 November 2007 (http://www.620wtmj.com/shows/charliesykes/11853126.html).

186 **"application of Sharia law"**: Jonathan Constantine Movroydis and Reut R. Cohen, "UC Irvine Still Enforcing Sharia Law," *Pajamas Media*, 22 May 2008 (http://pajamasmedia.com/blog/uc-irvine-still-enforcing-sharia-law/#comment-45713).

186 **"a new generation"**: Event announcement on University of California, Irvine, Web site (http://www.socsci.uci.edu/newsevents/event.php?eid=952).

187 **"The word** *jihad*": Bob Unruh, "Textbook: Islamic 'Jihad' Means Doing Good Works." *World Net Daily*, 16 January 2008 (http://www.worldnetdaily.com/news/article.asp?ARTICLE_ID=59707).

188 **"provocative"**: "Dutch Flag Prohibited," Dutch Report blog, 1 February 2005 (http://dutchreport.blogspot.com/2005/02/dutch-flag-prohibited.html).

188 **"for wearing sweaters"**: Sune Sundahl, "Stoppade av rektorn," *Expressen*, 27 May 2004 (http://www.expressen.se/1.105114).

188 **"xenophobic"**: "'Racist' Sports Shirts Banned from School Pic," *The Local*, 5 September 2007 (http://www.thelocal.se/8401).

188 **separate . . . inspectorate**: Graeme Paton, "Muslim Schools to Conduct Own Inspections," *Daily Telegraph*, 4 February 2008 (http://www.telegraph.co.uk/news/newstopics/politics/education/1577137/Muslim-schools-to-conduct-own-inspections.html).

188 **Ofsted complaint**: Graeme Paton, "Government Drops Plan to Allow Muslim Schools to Police Themselves," *Daily Telegraph*, 21 July 2008 (http://www.telegraph.co.uk/news/newstopics/politicseducation/2439866/Government-drops-plan-to-allow-Muslim-schools-to-police-themselves.html).

188 **"service dog"**: "SCSU Student Leaves Project," *SC Times*, 12 May 2008 (originally posted at http://www.sctimes.com/apps/pbcs.dll/article?AID=/20080512/NEWS01/105120058; now behind a pay wallat http://search.sctimes.com/sp?eId=122&gcId=11009641&rNum=3&url=http%3A%2F%2Fnl.newsbank.com%2Fcgi-bin%2Fngate%2FSCTB%3Fext_docid%3Dstc22820311%26ext_hed%3DSCSU+student+leaves+project%26s_site%3Dsctimes%26ext_theme%3Dgannett%26pubcode%3DSCTB%26usefield%3Dsqn&siteIdType=2; excerpts at http://www.scsuscholars.com/2008/05/when-rights-collide.html).

189 **"Islamic Awareness"**: Bob Unruh, "Texas Children Roped into Islamic Training," *World Net Daily*, 30 May 2008 (http://www.wnd.com/index.php?fa=PAGE.

189 **"Islamists have taken"**: Cinnamon Stillwell, "Islam in America's Public Schools: Education or Indoctrination?," *San Francisco Chronicle*, 11 June 2008 (http://www.sfgate.com/cgi-bin/article.cgi?f=/g/a/2008/06/11/cstillwell.DTL).

189 **"For one night"**: "'Open Tent' at Amherst Middle School," Cabinet Press Web site, 31 May 2007 (http://www.cabinet.com/apps/pbcs.dll/article?AID=/20070531/MILFORD01/70531004/-1/Milford01).

192 "not acceptable": "Muslim Head Says Gays 'Harmful,'" *BBC News* Web site, 3 January 2006 (http://news.bbc.co.uk/1/hi/uk/4579146.stm).

192 "After more than": Kirsten Damgaard's 2005 letter, originally published in *Jyllands-Posten*, appears in full at http://dansk-svensk.blogspot.com/2005/07/muslimer-og-homoseksualitet.html.

192 Dutch-Moroccan imam interviewed: Khalil el-Moumni, a Rotterdam imam, made the remarks in a TV interview on NOVA (transcript at http://www.novatv.nl/index .cfm?ln=nl&fuseaction=artikelen.details&achtergrond_id=39).

193 "when it comes to the Muslim world": Rob Anderson, "How America's Gay Rights Establishment Is Failing Gay Iranians: The Quiet Americans," *The New Republic*, 6 October 2005.

193 "ever eager to show": Richard Rosendall, "The Queer Left's Palestinian Folly," *FrontPage Magazine*, 2 February 2006 (http://www.frontpagemag.com/Articles/ Printable.aspx?GUID={3E3FA710-7C62-455F-BF5A-29BB354C47A2}).

194 "barmy": Patrick Barkham, "Gay Magazine in Race Row after Calling Islam a 'Barmy Doctrine,'" *Guardian*, 2 January 2006 (http://www.guardian.co.uk/uk/2006/ jan/02/pressandpublishing.gayrights).

194 "chosen to shift": Ghazzam Makarem, "Gay Rights: Who Are the Real Enemies of Liberation?," *Socialist Review*, February 2006 (http://www.socialistreview.org.uk/ article.php?articlenumber=9662).

196 "Is she blind": "The Trouble with Irshad Manji," *Palestine Solidarity Review*, Fall 2004 (http://www.psreview.org/content/view/26/72/).

196 "any incident": Daniel Pipes and Sharon Chadha, "CAIR: Islamists Fooling the Establishment," *The Middle East Quarterly*, Spring 2006 (http://www.meforum.org/ article/916).

196 "saw flyers and posters": David Skinner, "Behind CAIR's Hate-Crimes Report," *Weekly Standard*, 6 May 2004 (http://www.weeklystandard.com/Content/Public/ Articles/000/000/004/054aycfi.asp?pg=1).

196 "Mohammed pedophile": Nate Karlin, "Clarksville Muslims Experience Hate Crime: Defaced Quran Found at Center," *Tennessean*, 10 April 2007. The article is no longer on the *Tennessean* site but is available at http://www.jihadwatch.org/ dhimmiwatch/archives/016015.php.

197 "I have faced": Nathan C. Walker, "American Islam and Queer Solidarity" (http://www .natewalker.org/images/islam%20in%20america%20by%20nathan%20c%20 walker.pdf).

198 "Israel: Stop persecuting Palestine!": "Gays Attacked at Palestinian Rights Protest," 17 May 2004. A press release by *OutRage!* Available at http://www.thevillage.org.uk/ displaystory.php?recordID=384.

198 "so carefree and liberal": "Comment: My Holiday in Iran Challenged Perceptions," *Pink News*, 7 June 2008 (http://www.pinknews.co.uk/news/articles/2005-7859 .html).

199 "several leading black": Peter Tatchell, "Religion and Rights," *Guardian*, 1 October 2004 (http://www.guardian.co.uk/world/2004/oct/01/gayrights.religion?gusrc=rss& feed=global).

199 "the disgusting racism": These comments were at the gay and lesbian Muslim site Imaan (imaan.org.uk), but are no longer posted there. The first one ("disgusting racism") was also posted on 9 August 2005 at Indymedia UK (http://www.indymedia. org.uk/en/2005/08/320466.html?c=on); the second ("Outrage's campaign") was quoted in Livingstone's document *Why the Mayor of London Will Maintain Dialogues with All of London's Faiths and Communities* (see below).

199 "a coalition of Muslim": Peter Tatchell, "Defend Muslims—Oppose Qaradawi & Islamic Fundamentalism," http://www.petertatchell.net/religion/qaradawi .htm.

200 "We fear for the future": Tatchell, "Religion and Rights," *Guardian*, 1 October 2004 (http://www.guardian.co.uk/world/2004/oct/01/gayrights.religion?gusrc=rss&feed= global).

200 "reminiscent of the various": *Why the Mayor of London Will Maintain Dialogues with All of London's Faiths and Communities*, Greater London Authority, 2005 (http://www.london.gov.uk/news/docs/qaradawi_dossier.pdf).

201 "perverted act": Yusuf al-Qaradawi, *The Lawful and the Prohibited in Islam*, American Trust Publications, 1994, pp. 169–70.

201 "We should be prepared" (footnote): Inayat Bunglawala, "So Much for Free Speech," *Guardian*, 7 February 2008 (http://www.guardian.co.uk/commentisfree/2008/feb/07/ somuchforfreespeech).

202 "responding to every criticism": Johann Hari, "Don't call me an Islamophobe: The poisonous attacks on gay people by 'Islamophobia Watch,'" JohannHari.com, 6 June 2006 (http://www.johannhari.com/archive/article.php?id=897).

202 "Fucking fags": Chris Crain, "Looking Hate in the Face," Washington Blade blog, 6 May 2005 (http://www.washblade.com/blog/index.cfm?blog_id=523).

202 "the Amsterdam Tourist Board": Anthony Browne, "It May Be Europe's Most Liberal City—But If You Are Gay, You Had Best Beware," London *Times*, 14 May 2005 (http://www.timesonline.co.uk/tol/news/world/article522264.ece).

204 "commissioned the University": "Growing Hate: Amsterdam to Study Gay Bashers," *Der Spiegel*, 30 November 2007 (http://www.spiegel.de/international/ europe/0,1518,520601,00.html).

204 du Pree incident: "Opstootje bij show homos in Adam," *NRC Handelsblad*, 2 May 2008; B. Daniel Blatt, "Gay Bashing in Amsterdam Goes Unnoticed in the US," Gay Patriot blog, 5 June 2008 (http://www.gaypatriot.net/2008/06/05/gay-bashing-in- amsterdam-goes-unnoticed-in-us/).

204 "the huge spike": "Gays in the Netherlands Turning Conservative," Newsvine Web site, 21 April 2008 (http://krishna109.newsvine.com/_news/2008/04/21/1443304- gays-in-the-netherlands-turning-conservative).

205 "when it comes to the oppression": Rob Anderson, "How America's Gay Rights Establishment Is Failing Gay Iranians: The Quiet Americans," *The New Republic*, 6 October 2005.

205 "while we condemn": Faisal Alam, "Rush to Judgment Feeds Islamophobia," *Southern Voice*, 5 August 2005 (http://www.southernvoice.com/2005/8-5/view/ columns/column_ALAM.cfm).

205 Asghar Ali and gays: "Avviser ikke homo-dødsstraff," *NRK* Web site, 8 November 2007 (http://www.nrk.no/nyheter/distrikt/ostlandssendingen/1.3988084).

205 "as a Muslim in Norway": Tore Letvik, "Ber fatwaråd gi råd om homo-dødsstraff," *Dagsavisen*, 3 December 2007 (http://www.dagsavisen.no/innenriks/article323752 .ece).

206 "there is a significant difference": Rita Karlsen, "Islamskråd rådvill i homofilisak— ber om fatwaråd," *Human Rights Service* Web site, 3 December 2007 (http://www .rights.no/publisher/publisher.asp?id=36&tekstid=1226).

206 "I am neither a theologian": "Kokende debatt om homofili og Islam," *Universitas*, 14 November 2007 (http://www.universitas.no/kultur/49954/).

206 "tone down their religiosity": Mohammad Usman Rana, "Den sekulære ekstremisten," *Aftenposten*, 25 February 2008 (http://www.aftenposten.no/meninger/ kronikker/article2274868.ece).

207 "Islam is Islam": Hege Storhaug, "Hvilket makabert svik!," *Aftenposten*, 25

February 2008 (http://www.aftenposten.no/meninger/debatt/article2277486.ece). Rana's "Islam is Islam" statement originally appears in Astrid Meland, "Vil danne internasjonalt muslimsk Nettverk," *Dagbladet*, 16 February 2006 (http://www .dagbladet.no/nyheter/2006/02/16/458056.html).

208 **"100 percent certain"**: NTB, "For eller mot dødsstraff for homofile?," *Vårt Land*, 4 August 2008 (http://www.vl.no/samfunn/article3699505.ece).

208 **"can't see the difference"**: Bjørn Lecomte, "Oslo Arbeidersamfunn: - Forstår at folk blir skremt," *Østkantavisa*, 8 November 2007 (http://www.ostkantavisa.no/apps/ pbcs.dll/article?AID=/20071108/NYHETER/71108005/1002).

208 **"as a Norwegian Muslim"**: Asghar Ali, "Saken tatt ut av sammenheng," press release, Electricians' and IT Workers' Union Web site, 9 November 2007 (http://www.elogit .no/asset/9214/1/9214_1.doc).

208 **"satisfied"**: "Forbundet glad for avklaring Ali tar avstand fra dødsstraff," press release, Electricians' and IT Workers' Union Web site, 9 November 2007 (http://www .elogit.no/index.gan?id=9174&subid=0&serchDone=1).

209 **"Ali emphasizes"**: "Islamsk råd overrasket," *Dagsavisen*, 19 February 2008 (http:// www.dagsavisen.no/innenriks/article336321.ece).

209 **"Travel-Happy Imam"**: Kristin Høiland, "Reiseglad imam," *Aftenposten*, 12 April 2008 (http://www.aftenposten.no/reise/article2360369.ece).

209 **"reportedly threatening"**: Frederik Pleitgen, Mohammed Tawfeeq and Wayne Drash, "Gays in Iraq Terrorized by Threats, Rape, Murder," CNN.com, 24 July 2008 (http://www.newsweek.com/id/155656).

209 **"government, security forces"**: Lennox Samuels, "Don't Ask, Don't Tell, Do Kill," *Newsweek* Web site, 26 August 2008 (http://www.newsweek.com/id/155656).

210 **"Ammar, a young"**: Doug Ireland, "Shia Death Squads Target Iraqi Gays," *Gay City News*, 23 March 2006 (http://gaycitynews.com/site/index.cfm?newsid=17008100&B RD=2729&PAG=461&dept_id=568864&rfi=8).

210 **"one gay Iraqi"**: Rob Anderson, "How America's Gay Rights Establishment Is Failing Gay Iranians: The Quiet Americans," *The New Republic*, 6 October 2005.

210 **"produce homosexuals"**: Joseph Massad, "Re-Orienting Desire: The Gay International and the Arab World," *Public Culture* 14:2, Spring 2002, 361–85.

210–211 **"a 'missionary' campaign"**: Brian Whitaker, "Distorting Desire," *Gay City News*, 13 September 2007 (http://gaycitynews.com/site/news.cfm?newsid=1881493 0&BRD=2729&PAG=461&dept_id=569346&rfi=6).

212 **"This thesis claims"**: http://www.amazon.com/Desiring-Arabs-Joseph-Massad/ dp/0226509583.

212 **"Massad's intellectual project"**: James Kirchick, "Queer Theory," *New Republic*, 15 October 2007 (http://www.tnr.com/politics/story.html?id=b41d10c0-1bfb-4d8f- 83fa-47ae8776b2b5).

212 **HRW briefing paper:** "The Netherlands: Discrimination in the Name of Integration," *Human Rights Watch*, May 2008 (http://www.hrw.org/backgrounder/2008/ netherlands0508/netherlands0508web.pdf).

CHAPTER III: *Docile Provocateurs*

215 **"comparison of Danny's abduction"**: Judea Pearl, "Moral Relativism and *A Mighty Heart*," *New Republic* Web site, 3 July 2007 (originally at http://www.tnr.com/doc .mhtml?i=w070702&s=pearl070307; now available at http://www.danielpearl.org/ news_and_press/articles/moral_relativism.html).

215–216 **"the ordinary, quiet"**: Jonathan Foreman, "War Heroes in Hollywood," *National Review Online*, 24 August 2007 (http://article.nationalreview.com/?q=ZjM 4NWUwZTM0NjM1M2Y1MmU0NDczNWNlZTIxYjVhNDg=).

216 "somber drama": Cusack's remarks were made on *Bill Maher Realtime*, 28 March 2008 (transcript at http://www.billmaher.com/?page_id=230).

216 "brief for moralistic": Ross Douthat, "The Return of the Paranoid Style," *Atlantic Monthly*, April 2008 (http://www.theatlantic.com/doc/200804/iraq-movies).

217–218 "the reluctance to speak": Pat Sajak, "Selective Freedom of Speech," *Human Events* Web site, 11 December 2006 (http://www.humanevents.com/article .php?id=18429).

218 *Little Mosque on the Prairie* . . . and *Aliens in America*: Mrinalini Reddy, "Muslims on TV, No Terror in Sight," *New York Times*, 11 November 2007 (http:// www.nytimes.com/2007/11/11/arts/television/11redd.html?pagewanted=2&_r=1); Scott Collins, "Comedy Doers," *Los Angeles Times*, 20 August 2007 (http://articles. latimes.com/2007/aug/20/entertainment/et-channel20); Lisa de Moraes, "A Woman in the White House—For 24 Hours," *Washington Post*, 21 July 2007 (http://www .washingtonpost.com/wp-dyn/content/article/2007/07/20/AR2007072002396_ pf.html).

218 "a complete parcel": Richard Littlejohn, "Truth Is the First Casualty at the BBC," *Daily Mail*, 20 August 2007 (http://www.dailymail.co.uk/debate/columnists/ article-476626/Truth-Casualty-BBC.html).

219 "a young Muslim": Mark Edward Manning, "BBC: Animal Rights Extremists More of a Threat than Radical Muslims," *Blogcritics*, 10 September 2007 (http://blogcritics .org/archives/2007/09/10/133340.php).

219 "the story of the clash": *White Girl* information page, BBC Web site (http://www .bbc.co.uk/white/white_girl.shtml?dnafrom=0&dnato=9).

219 "bias toward Islam": Jerome Taylor, "Sikhs and Hindus Accuse BBC of Pro-Muslim Bias," *Independent*, 8 September 2008 (http://www.independent.co.uk/news/media/ sikhs-and-hindus-accuse-bbc-of-promuslim-bias-922482.html).

220 "Why is Hollywood": Reihan Salam, "The Sum of All PC," *Salon*, 28 May 2002 (http://www.slate.com/id/2066272/).

220 "not a single movie": Farshad Kholghi, *Verden Er ét Land*, People's Press, 2007.

220 "one of our national icons": Lousewies van der Laan, "Islamic Bullfighting," *Expatica*, 11 December 2007 (http://www.expatica.com/nl/life_in/feature/Islamic-bullfighting.html).

220 "state-subsidized courage": Harald Jähner, "Selbstzensur i Moll und Dur,"*Berliner Zeitung*, 27 September 2006 (http://www.berlinonline.de/berliner-zeitung/archiv/ .bin/dump.fcgi/2006/0927/meinung/0012/index.html). English version, "Self-censorship in Major and Minor," at http://www.signandsight.com/features/970.html (trans. Naomi Buck).

221 "We are enthusiastic": Marlise Simons, "Dutch Group Calls Off an Opera After Muslims Pressure Cast," *New York Times*, 10 December 2000 (http://query.nytimes. com/gst/fullpage.html?res=9A04E4DD173FF933A25751C1A9669C8B63&partner= rssnyt&emc=rss).

221 "Our supposedly 'fearless'": Peter Whittle, "Islam: The Silence of the Arts," New Culture Forum Web site (http://www.newcultureforum.org.uk/home/?q= node/136).

221 "somewhat . . . idealise[s]": Benedict Nightingale, "King of Hearts," London *Times*, 6 March 2007 (http://entertainment.timesonline.co.uk/tol/arts_and_entertainment/ stage/theatre/article1475233.ece).

221 "dark satire": Kelsey Munro, "Be Very Afraid," *Sydney Morning Herald*, 30 June 2007 (http://www.smh.com.au/news/arts/be-very-afraid/2007/06/28/1182624066917 .html).

222 "has its boundaries": Carolyn Palmer, "Muslims Unhappy at German 'Satanic

Verses' Staging," *Reuters*, 28 March 2008 (http://www.reuters.com/article/newsOne/idUSL2889008620080328).

222 **"an insult to the entire"**: Andrew Higgins, "Muslims Ask French to Cancel 1741 Play by Voltaire, *Wall Street Journal*, 6 March 2006 (available at http://www.post-gazette.com/pg/06065/666058.stm).

223 **"This is the play"**: Charles Spencer, "Now or Later: Gripping and Daring Work Brings Passion to Politics," *Daily Telegraph*, 15 September 2008 (http://www.telegraph.co.uk/arts/main.jhtml?xml=/arts/2008/09/15/btlater113.xml).

223 **"The arts . . . are increasingly"**: Peter Whittle, "Islam: The Silence of the Arts," New Culture Forum Web site (http://www.newcultureforum.org.uk/home/?q=node/136).

223 **"but very few people"**: Ben Hoyle, "Artists Too Frightened to Tackle Radical Islam," London *Times*, 19 November 2007 (http://entertainment.timesonline.co.uk/tol/arts_and_entertainment/visual_arts/article2896431.ece).

223–224 **"Arts establishments"**: Brendan O'Neill, "How a Sensitivity Stasi Is Eroding Artistic Freedom," *Spiked*, 6 December 2007 (http://www.spiked-online.com/index.php?/site/article/4159/).

224 **"space constraints"**: "Whitechapel Gallery . . . the Importance of Self-Censorship," *The New Culture Forum*, 10 October 2006 (http://newcultureforum.blogspot.com/2006/10/whitechapel-gallery-importance-of-self.html).

224 **"response to Muslim"**: Mats Lilja, "Dödshot stopper kärlekstavlan," *Expressen*, 17 August 2008 (http://www.expressen.se/1.171798).

224 **"in the light of events"**: David Smith, "Artist Hits at Tate's 'Cowardice' over Ban," *Observer*, 25 September 2005 (http://www.guardian.co.uk/uk/2005/sep/25/arts.religion).

224 **Religion at Tate Modern:** Alastair Sooke, "Illuminations at Tate Modern: Light Cast on the Power of Religion," *Daily Telegraph*, 15 January 2008 (http://www.telegraph.co.uk/arts/main.jhtml?xml=/arts/2008/01/15/basooke115.xml).

224 **"Shark" in Middelkerke:** "Belgium Town Bans 'Saddam Shark,'" *BBC News*, 7 February 2006 (http://news.bbc.co.uk/2/hi/entertainment/4688402.stm).

224 **"a gang of young Muslims"**: "Muslim Gang Forces Paris Café to Censor Cartoon Show," *Middle East Times*, 31 March 2006 (originally at http://www.metimes.com/articles/normal.php?StoryID=20060331-084337-4435r; available at http://www.coxandforkum.com/archives/2006_04.html).

225 **"The Birmingham Museum"**: Paul Sims, "Photo Exhibition 'Censored' as Semi Naked Picture Offends Muslims," *Daily Mail*, 28 August 2006 (http://www.dailymail.co.uk/news/article-402604/Photo-exhibition-censored-semi-naked-picture-offends-Muslims.html).

225 **"certain people in our society"**: "Hague Museum Pulls Offensive Muslim Art," *Sydney Morning Herald*, 3 December 2007 (http://www.theage.com.au/news/World/Hague-museum-pulls-offensive-Muslim-art/2007/12/03/1196530582874.html).

225 **"to become part of a political debate"**: Wim van Krimpen, "Gay-Mohammed Exhibition Turned Down for the Third Time," *NIS News*, 26 April 2008 (http://www.nisnews.nl/public/260408_1.htm).

225 **"great professionalism"**: Matthew Campbell, "Woman Artist Gets Death Threats over Gay Muslim Photos," London *Times*, 6 January 2008 (http://www.timesonline.co.uk/tol/news/world/europe/article3137510.ece).

225 **"was very afraid"**: Ibid.

226 **"Freedom of expression . . . has become"**: Jana Winter, "Iranian Artist Fights to Have Muhammed Art Displayed in Dutch Museums," Fox News, 3 May 2008 (http://www.foxnews.com/story/0,2933,354075,00.html).

226 **"a misrepresentation of Islam":** Amir Taheri, "The West's Self-Imposed Censorship," *FrontPage Magazine*, 13 October 2006 (http://frontpagemag.com/Articles/Read. aspx?GUID=5EC03F38-63C0-4179-8FBB-3FDBC8203334).

226 **"a group of angry Muslims":** Madeline Chambers, "Berlin Gallery Shuts After Muslim Threats," *Reuters*, 28 February 2008 (http://africa.reuters.com/wire/news/ usnL28921281.html).

226 **"The reason I haven't gone all out":** Ben Hoyle, "Artists Too Frightened to Tackle Radical Islam," London *Times*, 19 November 2007 (http://entertainment.timesonline. co.uk/tol/arts_and_entertainment/visual_arts/article2896431.ece).

226 **"It has come to the point":** Lousewies van der Laan, "Islamic Bullfighting," *Expatica*, 11 December 2007 (http://www.expatica.com/nl/life_in/feature/Islamic-bullfighting. html).

CHAPTER IV: *Our Fearless Leaders*

227 **"just the way an Islamist":** Hege Storhaug, *Størst av alt er friheten*, Kagge, 2006, p. 237.

228 **"Islamic dress":** Margaret Talbot, "The Agitator," *The New Yorker*, 5 June 2006 (http://www.newyorker.com/archive/2006/06/05/060605fa_fact?currentPage=1).

228 **"who I am told is a staunch":** Bernard Lewis, "The 2007 Irving Kristol Lecture by Bernard Lewis," American Enterprise Institute, 7 March 2007 (http://www.aei.org/ publications/pubID.25815,filter.all/pub_detail.asp).

229 **"the British government and its circle":** Pascal Bruckner, "Enlightenment Fundamentalism or Racism of the Anti-Racists?," *Sign and Sight*, 24 January 2007 (http://www.signandsight.com/features/1146html).

230 **"the leading opposition group":** Bill Zlatos, "Local Educators Learn about Islam on Trip to Egypt," *Pittsburgh Tribune-Review*, 3 September 2007 (http://www .pittsburghlive.com/x/pittsburghtrib/search/s_525507.html).

230 **"endorsed the OIC's fulminations":** Andrew Bostom, "Losing Our Soul to the Islamintern," Andrew Bostom Web site, 22 March 2008. http://www.andrewbostom .org/blog/2008/03/22/losing-our-soul-to-the-islamintern/.

230 **"harassment on the grounds":** The text of Norway's Discrimination Law is at http://www.lovdata.no/all/nl-20050603-033.html.

232 **Belgian government harassing blogger:** http://www.brusselsjournal.com/ node/1251; http://standaard.typepad.com/kreten_en_gefluister/2006/07/politie_ teverge.html.

232 **"female holy warrior":** Elaine Sciolino, "Al Qaeda Warrior Uses Internet to Rally Women," *New York Times*, 28 May 2008 (http://www.nytimes.com/2008/05/28/world/ europe/28terror.html?_r=1&scp=3&sq=ELAINE%20SCIOLINO%20SOUAD%20 MEKHENNET&st=cse&oref=slogin).

232 **Alejandro de Llano:** http://elrincondelalibertad.blogspot.com/2006/10/juicio-poltico.html; http://toastedbread.wordpress.com/2006/10/24/galician-blogger-charged-for-supporting-israel/.

232 **"if Holliday were to film":** Peter Sayer, "Law Could Lead to Imprisonment of Amateur Videographers and Web Site Operators Who Publish Their Images," *Infoworld*, 6 March 2007 (http://www.infoworld.com/archives/emailPrint.jsp?R=printThis&A=/ article/07/03/06/HNfrancecitizenjournalists_1.html).

232–233 **"For telling a good and incisive":** Rowan Atkinson, "Religion as a Fit Subject for Comedy," London *Times*, 17 October 2001 (originally at http://www.thetimes .co.uk/article/0,,59-2001361433,00.html; now available here: http://www.mail-archive.com/man-bytes-dog).

233 **"keep before our eyes":** Rowan Williams, "Archbishop's Lecture—Religious Hatred

and Religious Offense," 29 January 2008 (http://www.archbishopofcanterbury
.org/1561).

233 **"People who believe that the answer"**: Rachel Sylvester, "We Must Talk to the
Taliban, Says Des Browne," *Daily Telegraph*, 30 March 2008 (http://www.telegraph
.co.uk/news/uknews/1583196/We-must-talk-to-the-Taliban,-says-Des-Browne
.html).

233 ***"You don't have to use violence"***: "A Glimpse Ahead," David Frum's
diary, *National Review Online*, 30 March 2008 (http://frum.nationalreview.com/post
/?q=MzZlM2ZkNDgxMTBmM2IzNzZjZjVmNzM5OTYzYmE1YTI=).

234 **"ideologically encapsulate"**: "PvdA Tries to Muzzle Muslim Apostate," *NIS News*, 5
June 2007 (http://www.nisnews.nl/public/050607_1.htm).

234 **"Not for nothing"**: "Crown Prince Calls for Mild Tone on Islam," *NIS News*, 2 May
2007 (http://www.nisnews.nl/public/020507_2.htm).

234 **"interior and justice ministers"**: "Dutch Lawmaker Plans Film Criticizing the
Quran," AP story, 28 November 2007 (http://www.iht.com/articles/ap/2007/11/28/
europe/EU-GEN-Netherlands-Anti-Quran-Film.php).

234 **"misusing his position"**: Doekle Terpstra, "'Nee' Tegen Kwade Boodschap
Wilders," *Trouw*, 30 November 2007 (http://www.trouw.nl/deverdieping/podium/
article856996.ece/Nee_tegen_kwade_boodschap_Wilders_opinie).

235 **"Wilders is the evil"**: This comment was originally reported in *De Telegraaf* (http://
www.telegraaf.nl/binnenland/2671490/Verzetsbeweging _tegen_Wilders.html?p=6,1);
it is no longer there, but is available at http://www.geencommentaar.nl/index.php/
quotes_van_de_dag_terpstra_vs_wilders.

235 **"a new balance"**: Terpstra's statement is at http://www.trouw.nl/hetnieuws/
nederland/article882058.ece.

235 **"the youths on the street"**: Michael van der Galiën, "Holland: Likely to Be the Next
Target of Islamic Rage," *Pajamas Media*, 24 January 2008 (http://pajamasmedia.com/
blog/geert_wilders/).

235 **"with imams and other leaders"**: "Wilders' Film on Koran to Be Shown on Internet,"
Expatica, 7 January 2008 (http://www.expatica.com/nl/articles/news/Wilders_-film-
on-Koran-to-be-shown-on-internet.html).

235 **Tjibbe Joustra**: "Wilders Should Leave the Netherlands," *Expatica*, 23 January 2008
(http://www.expatica.com/nl/articles/news/_Wilders-should-leave-the-Netherlands
_.html).

235 **"private companies have joined"**: Michael van der Galiën, "Holland: Likely
to Be the Next Target of Islamist Rage," *Pajamas Media*, 24 January 2008 (http://
pajamasmedia.com/blog/geert_wilders/).

235 **"it would be a disgrace"**: "Donner: Sharia moet kunnen," *Ad.nl*, 12 September 2006
(http://www.ad.nl/binnenland/article622846.ece).

235 **"openly distanced itself"**: "Wilders Says Islam Film to be Released in March,"
Expatica, 28 January 2008 (http://www.expatica.com/nl/articles/news/Wilders-says-
Islam-film-to-be-released-in-March-.html).

235 **Job Cohen accusation**: "Cohen: 'PVV zet aan tot haat,'" *Het Parool*, 30 January
2001(available at http://mobiel.marokko.nl/index.php?p=1&n=9268).

236 **"freedom of expression doesn't mean"**: Jason Burke, "Violence Fear over Islam
Film," *The Observer*, 20 January 2008 (http://www.guardian.co.uk/world/2008/
jan/20/film.religion).

236 **"reactions that endanger"**: "Dutch MP Warned over Islam Film," *BBC News*, 23
January 2008 (http://news.bbc.co.uk/2/hi/europe/7204452.stm).

236 **"stressed that 'provocations'"**: "EU Ministers Express Concern about Dutch Anti-
Islam Film," ABC [Australian Broadcasting Corporation] News, 27 January 2008
(http://www.abc.net.au/news/stories/2008/01/27/2147371.htm).

236 **"The serious threats":** Geert Wilders, "'Angst voor islam regeert Nederland,'" *De Volkskrant*, 23 January 2008 (http://www.volkskrant.nl/binnenland/article497246 .ece).

236 **"hour of intimidation":** "Wilder beticht ministers van intimidatie," *NRC Handelsblad*, 28 February 2008 (http://www.nrc.nl/binnenland/article1884054.ece/ Wilders_beticht_ministers_van_intimidatie).

236 **"legal consequences":** "Wilders accuses ministers of intimidation," *Expatica*, 28 February 2008 (http://www.expatica.com/nl/articles/news/Wilders-accuses-ministers-of-intimidation.html).

236 **"polarization":** "PKN wil gesprek met Geert Wilders," *Trouw*, 14 February 2008 (http://meer.trouw.nl/nieuws-en-debat/pkn-wil-gesprek-met-geert-wilders).

237 **"new breed of right-wing":** Ian Traynor, "'I Don't Hate Muslims. I Hate Islam,' says Holland's rising star," *The Observer*, 17 February 2008 (http://www.guardian.co.uk/ world/2008/feb/17/netherlands.islam).

237 **"anti-Muslim":** "Dutch TV Stations Refuse Anti-Muslim Film," *Washington Times*, 7 March 2008 (http://www.washingtontimes.com/news/2008/mar/07/dutch-tv-stations-refuse-anti-muslim-film/).

237 **"warned the film could spark":** "Muslims Condemn Dutch Lawmaker's Film," *CNN*, 28 March 2008 (http://edition.cnn.com/2008/WORLD/europe/03/28/islam. film/).

237 **Fogh Rasmussen . . . condemned:** "Fogh fordømmer Wilders' film," *Jyllands-Posten*, 28 March 2008 (http://jp.dk/indland/indland_politik/article1305091.ece).

237 **"offensively anti-Islamic":** Ban Ki-moon's statement is at http://www.un.org/News/ Press/docs/2008/sgsm11483.doc.htm.

238 **Louise Arbour . . . agreed:** http://www.kuna.net.kw/NewsAgenciesPublicSite/ ArticleDetails.aspx?Language=en&id=1895163.

238 **"an insulting film":** Sampaio's statement is at http://www.unaoc.org/content/ view/236/73/lang,english/.

238 **"has done the debate":** "Commentaar: Wilders op herhaling in harde propaganda film," *De Volkskrant*, 27 March 2008 (http://www.volkskrant.nl/binnenland/ article520347.ece/Commentaar_Wilders_op_herhaling_in_harde_propagandafilm).

238 **Wientjes' comments:** "Vil saksøke 'Fitna'-skaperen," *Dagbladet*, 29 March 2008 (http://www.dagbladet.no/nyheter/2008/03/29/530961.html).

238 **"too critical of Islam":** Sam Harris, "Losing Our Spines to Save Our Necks," *Huffington Post*, 5 May 2008 (http://www.huffingtonpost.com/sam-harris/losing-our-spines-to-save_b_100132.html).

239 **"publishing cartoons":** "Furore over Cartoonist Arrested for Discrimination," *NIS News*, 17 May 2008 (http://www.nisnews.nl/public/170508_1.htm).

239 **"suggested that the arrest":** "Imams: Governments More Afraid Than Us of Islam Criticism," *NIS News*, 28 May 2008 (http://www.nisnews.nl/public/280508_1.htm).

239 **Bussemaker and the war:** "Bussemaker wijst op rol allochtonen bij bevrijding," *FOK*, 4 May 2008 (http://frontpage.fok.nl/nieuws/91766).

239 **SIOE press release:** http://www.petitiononline.com/ulfkotte/.

240 **"Jews should be killed":** Ann Treneman, "He's in the Driving Seat, but He Still Needs L-plates," London *Times*, 5 July 2007 (http://www.timesonline.co.uk/tol/ news/politics/article2028652.ece).

240 **British government capitulated to sharia:** Jonathan Wynne-Jones, "Multiple Wives Will Mean Multiple Benefits," *Daily Telegraph*, 18 April 2008 (http://www.telegraph. co.uk/news/newstopics/politics/1577395/Multiple-wives-will-mean-multiple-benefits.html).

240 **"keeping quiet":** Martin Beckford, "MPs Too Scared to Talk About Forced Marriage 'in Case They Lose Muslim Votes,'" *Telegraph*, 2 September 2008 (http://www

.telegraph.co.uk/news/newstopics/politics/2661385/MPs-too-scared-to-talk-about-forced-marriage-in-case-they-lose-Muslim-votes.html).

240 **"Are we mad?":** Ruth Dudley Edwards, "Are We Mad? Every Organ of the State Now Seems Intent on Protecting Those Who Would Destroy Us," *Mail on Sunday*, 3 September 2008 (http://www.mailonsunday.co.uk/news/article-1051984/Are-mad-Every-organ-state-intent-protecting-destroy-us.html).

241 **"we don't make political decisions":** "Reinfeldt månar om yttrandefrihet," *Expressen*, 31 August 2007 (http://www.na.se/artikel.asp?intId=1211267).

241 **"Muslims around the world":** The text of the ambassadors' letter is at "Hemliga brevet til Reinfeldt," *Expressen*, 8 September 2007 (http://www.expressen.se/nyheter/1.831654/hemliga-brevet-till-reinfeldt).

241 **"We reject all forms of violence":** "Muslim Ambassadors 'Made No Demands,'" *The Local*, 7 September 2007 (http://www.thelocal.se/8424/20070907/).

242 **"We want to see action":** "Muslim Ambassadors: 'Sweden Needs to Change Its Laws," *The Local*, 6 September 2007 (http://www.thelocal.se/8412/20070906/).

242 **"there was a need":** Siraj Wahab, "Swedish Envoy Apologizes for Caricature," *Arab News*, 13 September 2007 (http://www.arabnews.com/?page=1&section=0&article=101123&d=13&m=9&y=2007).

242 **"that Sweden is an open country":** "Sweden Seeks to Cool Tensions over Muhammed Cartoon," *Agence France-Presse*, 7 September 2007 (http://afp.google.com/article/ALeqM5jmgaRDJtc5a_4iAsFdDpVjz361mQ).

242 **"in a spirit of appeasement":** "Muslim Ambassadors: 'Sweden Needs to Change Its Laws,'" *The Local*, 6 September 2007 (http://www.thelocal.se/8412/20070906/).

242 **"such language does not belong":** Elisabeth Seglem, "Ali ville tørrlegge hele byen," *Aftonbladet*, 28 April 2008 (http://aftenbladet.no/lokalt/article632407.ece?service=print).

243 **"working systematically":** Flemming Rose, "Danish Politician Acquitted of Defamation against Muslims," Northern Light blog, 14 July 2007 (http://pajamasmedia.com/flemmingrose/2007/07/14/post_2/).

243 **"regulate [them]selves":** http://europa.eu/rapid/pressReleasesAction.do?reference=SPEECH/06/321&format=HTML&aged=0&language=EN&guiLanguage=en.

243 **"tempered by caveats":** "EU Makes Racism, Xenophobia Illegal," *Herald Sun*, 20 April 2007 (http://www.news.com.au/heraldsun/story/0,21985,21589292-5005961,00.html).

243 **"This is a very unfortunate":** "Europårådet vil have love mod blasfemi afskaffet," *Kristeligt Dagblad*, 18 September 2007 (http://www.kristeligt-dagblad.dk/artikel/261973).

244 **"defamation of religion":** http://www.un.org/News/Press/docs/2004/hrcn1082.doc.htm.

244 **Littman speech:** http://www.iheu.org/node/1751; http://www.bigpicweblog.com/exp/index.php/weblog/comments/david_littman_calls_on_the_un_to_condemn_killing_in_the_name_of_religion/.

244 **Council replaces Commission:** http://news.bbc.co.uk/2/hi/europe/4810538.stm; http://www.nytimes.com/2006/02/26/opinion/26sun2.html?_r=2&n=Top%2fOpinion%2fEditorials%20and%20Op%2dEd%2fEditorials&oref=slogin&oref=slogin.

244 **2007 HRC resolution on religion:** Associated Press, "U.N. Rights Council Adopts Resolution against Religion Defamation at Muslim Prodding," *International Herald Tribune*, 30 March 2007 (http://www.iht.com/articles/ap/2007/03/30/news/UN-GEN-UN-Islam.php).

244 **2008 HRC resolution on religion:** "Vote on Freedom of Expression Marks the End of Universal Human Rights," *International Humanist and Ethical Union*, 30 March 2008 (http://www.iheu.org/node/3123).

244 **"attempts to identify"**: European Centre for Law and Justice, "Combating Defamation of Religions," June 2008 (http://www.meforum.org/pics/ECLJ_submission_to_OHCHR_on_Combating_Defamation_of_Religions.pdf).

24 **"the United Nations investigator"**: Stephanie Nebehay, "Islamophobia on Rise, Especially in Europe—U.N. Envoy," *Reuters India*, 14 September 2007 (http://in.reuters.com/article/worldNews/idINIndia-29537020070914).

245 **"the only religion"**: Elizabeth Samson, "Criminalizing Criticism of Islam," *Wall Street Journal Europe*, 10 September 2008 (http://online.wsj.com/article/SB122099204692716155.html?mod=googlenews_wsj).

245 **"Islam will not be crucified"**: "Discussion of Religious Questions Now Banned at UN Human Rights Council," 23 June 2008, Web site of the International Humanist and Ethical Union (http://www.iheu.org/node/3193). A webcast of this debate can be heard at http://www.un.org/webcast/unhrc/archive.asp?go=080616#pm.

246 **"loved the ACLU"**: Wendy Kaminer, "The American Liberal Liberties Union," *Wall Street Journal*, 23 May 2007 (http://www.opinionjournal.com/editorial/feature.html?id=110010111).

247 **"community groups"**: Paul Pringle, Richard Winton, Jean-Paul Renaud, "LAPD to Build Data on Muslim Areas," *Los Angeles Times*, 9 November 2007 (http://articles.latimes.com/2007/nov/09/local/me-lapd9).

247 **LAPD plans had been scrapped**: Teresa Watanabe and Richard Winton, "LAPD's Muslim Mapping Plan Killed," *Los Angeles Times*, 15 November 2007 (http://articles.latimes.com/2007/nov/15/local/me-muslim15).

247 **"polarize"**: Kinga Sandén, "Rädda Barnen censurerar rapport om våld," *Sydsvenskan*, 15 January 2008 (http://sydsvenskan.se/sverige/article293498.ece).

CHAPTER V: *Cops, Courts, Civil Service*

248 **"Thou shalt not kill"**: Ron Meerhof, "'Gij zult niet doden' ligt anno 2004 te gevoelig," *De Volkskrant*, 5 November 2004 (http://www.volkskrant.nl/binnenland/article188354.ece/Gij_zult_niet_doden_ligt_anno_2004_te_gevoelig).

249 **"a mindset that views"**: James Forsyth, "Stand Up for Channel 4 and Press Freedom," *Spectator*, 16 August 2007 (http://www.spectator.co.uk/coffeehouse/93266/stand-up-for-channel-4-and-press-freedom.thtml).

249 **Anil Patani**: Alasdair Palmer, "A State in Denial Needs Reality Checks," *Daily Telegraph*, 18 May 2008 (http://www.telegraph.co.uk/opinion/main.jhtml?xml=/opinion/2008/05/18/do1804.xml).

249 **"racist backlash"**: Patrick Phelvin, "TV Appeal over Afghan Rapist Cancelled," *Daily Telegraph*, 19 July 2007 (http://www.telegraph.co.uk/news/uknews/1557788/TV-appeal-over-Afghan-rapist-cancelled.html).

249 **"white girls as young"**: Lucy Bannerman and Richard Ford, "Grooming of White Girls for Sex Is Exposed as Two Asian Men Jailed," London *Times*, 11 August 2007 (http://www.timesonline.co.uk/tol/news/uk/crime/article2237940.ece).

249–250 **"not only failing to help"**: Miles Goslett and Daniel Boffey, "Asian PCs Blocking Crackdown on Honour Killings," *Daily Mail*, 3 February 2008 (available at http://www.freerepublic.com/focus/f-news/1964131/posts).

250 **"were in a Muslim area"**: David Harrison, "Christian Preachers Face Arrest in Birmingham," *Daily Telegraph*, 2 June 2008 (http://www.telegraph.co.uk/news/uknews/2058935/Police-advise-Christian-preachers-to-leave-Muslin-area-of-Birmingham.html).

250 **"are losing control"**: Jamie Doward, "Muslim Gangs 'Are Taking Control of Prison,'" *Guardian*, 25 May 2008 (http://www.guardian.co.uk/society/2008/may/25/prisonsandprobation.ukcrime).

250–251 "the police did not mention": Kaja Korsvold, "Threats from Norway," *Aftenposten*, 11 May 2007 (http://www.aftenposten.no/english/local/article1782355 .ece).

251 "legitimate targets to be killed": Stewart Bell, "Police Visit Fails to Stop Web Postings," *National Post*, 30 January 2008 (http://canadiancoalition.com/forum/ messages/28054.shtml).

251 Icelandic woman at JFK: Associated Press, "Iceland Complains about Treament of Tourist," MSNBC Web site, 14 December 2007 (http://www.msnbc.msn.com/ id/22263392/).

251 "problem of legitimizing": Steven Emerson, "Muzammil the 'Moderate,'" Counterterrorism Blog, 30 July 2007 (http://www.investigativeproject.org/article/276).

251 "counterterrorism conference": Steven Emerson and Stephen M. Flatow, "Jersey's Counterterror Farce," *New York Post*, 12 November 2007 (http://www.nypost .com/seven/11122007/postopinion/opedcolumnists/jerseys_counterterror_ farce_382583.htm).

252 "to be most concerned": Rita Karlsen, "Dumme og uvitende nordmenn kan lynsje muslimer," *Human Rights Service* Web site, 27 September 2008 (http://www.rights. no/publisher/publisher.asp?id=43&tekstid=792).

254 "whitewashes jihad": Diana West, "Military on the Mall," *Washington Times*, 20 January 2005 (http://www.washtimes.com/news/2005/jan/20/20050120-083547- 3406r/).

254 "may not like Muslims": Diana West, "Call It Like It Is," *Washington Times*, 6 July 2007 (http://www.washingtontimes.com/news/2007/jul/06/call-it-like-it-is/).

254 not to wear uniforms off-base: "Brown Condemns No-uniform Advice," *BBC News*, 7 March 2008 (http://news.bbc.co.uk/1/hi/england/cambridgeshire/7282943.stm).

254 "The threats halted": Louise Radnofsky and agencies, "Government Rolled over to Saudi BAE Threats, Says Judge," *Guardian*, 14 February 2008 (http://www.guardian .co.uk/world/2008/feb/14/bae.armstrade).

254 "That Coughlin's analyses": Andrew Bostom, "Eaton Agonistes, Redux?," at Andrew Bostom blog, 5 January 2005 (http://www.andrewbostom.org/blog/2008/01/05/ eaton-agonistes-redux/).

254 "Stirring the Hate": Shaun Waterman, "Analysis: U.S. Cuts Critique of Islam Film," *Middle East Times*, 6 February 2008 (http://www.metimes.com/Security/2008/02/06/ analysis_us_cuts_critique_of_islam_film/7efc/).

255 "to build an inviolate wall": Daniel Pipes, "How Dare You Defame Islam," *Commentary*, November 1999 (http://www.danielpipes.org/article/321).

255 Fallaci trial in Bergamo: "Trial over Italian Islam 'Insult,'" *BBC News*, 24 May 2005 (http://news.bbc.co.uk/2/hi/europe/4576663.stm).

255 *Yasak Tümceler*: Birthe Pedersen, "Religionsfrihed overtrumfer ytringsfrihed," *Kristeligt Dagblad*, 15 September 2005 (http://www.kristeligt-dagblad.dk/artikel/ 64324:Kirke---tro--Religionsfrihed-overtrumfer-ytringsfrihed).

256 "We have been subject": Flemming Rose, "Danish Politician Acquitted of Defamation against Muslims," Northern Light blog, 14 July 2007 (http://pajamasmedia.com/ flemmingrose/2007/07/14/post_2/).

256 Codie Scott: "You're Nicked," Nanny Knows Best blog, 24 October 2006 (http:// nannyknowsbest.blogspot.com/2006/10/youre-nicked.html).

256 "If you are a black": Paul Stokes, "Robin Page Compensated over 'Race' Arrest," *Daily Telegraph*, 16 January 2008 (http://www.telegraph.co.uk/news/uknews/1575619/ Robin-Page-compensated-over-'race'-arrest.html).

256 "that terror suspects not only": "Multiculturalism Is Making Britain 'a Soft Touch for Terrorists,'" *Daily Mail*, 15 February 2008 (http://www.dailymail.co.uk/news/ article-514523/Multiculturalism-making-Britain-soft-touch-terrorists.html).

257 **"the accusation alone"**: Lee Duigon, "Watch Canada Strangle Free Speech!" *MichNews.com*, 17 February 2008 (http://www.michnews.com/cgi-bin/artman/exec/view.cgi/432/19413).

257 **posted the video . . . online:** http://www.youtube.com/watch?v=AzVJTHIvqw8.

257 **"a martyr of freedom"**: Licia Corbella, "Imam Undercuts Himself by Twisting His Own Words," *Calgary Herald*, 16 February 2008 (http://www.canada.com/calgaryherald/news/theeditorialpage/story.html?id=5162d29c-ffe4-4f4a-8d25-fe5e097c0963&p=2).

258 **"freedom of speech is an American concept"**: Jonathan Kay, "A Disaster for Canada's Human Rights Commission," *National Post*, 28 March 2008 (http://www.nationalpost.com/news/story.html?id=405744).

258 **"Islamophobic"**: Jacob Laksin, "Free Speech on Trial," *FrontPage Magazine*, 16 June 2008 (http://frontpagemag.com/articles/Read.aspx?GUID=F95EB00F-2B31-4629-A6B2-012044A95444).

258 **"began weeping quietly"**: Petti Fong, "Emotions Run High over Maclean's Article," *Toronto Star*, 7 June 2008 (http://www.thestar.com/News/Canada/article/439111).

259 **"stirr[ed] up hatred against Muslims"**: Adam Liptak, "Under Others, U.S. Defends Freedom to Offend in Speech," *New York Times*, 12 June 2008 (http://www.nytimes.com/2008/06/12/us/12hate.html?scp=1&sq=%94Unlike%20Others,%20U.S.%20Defends%20Freedom%20to%20Offend%20in%20Speech&st=cse).

259 **"the parts of the Koran that Muslims"**: Elizabeth Keenan, "All Fired Up About Faith," *Time*, 27 June 2005 (http://www.time.com/time/magazine/article/0,9171,1077728,00.html?iid=chix-sphere).

259 **Syed Mumtaz Ali:** DeNeen L. Brown, "Canadians Allow Islamic Courts to Decide Disputes," *Washington Post*, 28 April 2004 (http://www.washingtonpost.com/ac2/wp-dyn/A47735-2004Apr27?language=printer).

259 **"Islamic sharia law is gaining"**: Joshua Rozenberg, "Sharia Law Is Spreading as Authority Wanes," *Daily Telegraph*, 30 November 2006 (http://www.telegraph.co.uk/news/uknews/1535478/Sharia-law-is-spreading-as-authority-wanes.html).

260 **"It would be a pity"**: http://www.archbishopofcanterbury.org/1575.

261 **"some comfortable English professor"**: George Orwell, "Politics and the English Language," *Horizon*, April 1946 (http://www.george-orwell.org/Politics_and_the_English_Language/0.html).

262 **"So there you have it"**: Ruth Gledhill, "Has the Archbishop Gone Bonkers?," *Times Online*, 7 February 2008 (http://timescolumns.typepad.com/gledhill/2008/02/has-the-archbis.html).

262–263 **"For most of its history"**: Noah Feldman, "Why Shariah?," *New York Times Magazine*, 16 March 2008 (http://www.nytimes.com/2008/03/16/magazine/16Shariah-t.html?scp=1&sq=feldman%20why%20shariah?&st=cse).

263 **"It is time for Britain"**: Feisal Abdul Rauf, "The Archbishop of Canterbury was Right," *Washington Post/Newsweek* Web site, 13 March 2008 (http://newsweek.washingtonpost.com/onfaith/feisal_abdul_rauf/2008/03/archbishop_of_canterbury_was_r.html).

264 **"enforceable"**: Abul Taher, "Revealed: UK's First Official Sharia Courts," *Times Online*, 14 September 2008 (http://www.timesonline.co.uk/tol/news/uk/crime/article4749183.ece).

264 **"right to use corporal punishment"**: Matthias Bartsch, Andrea Brandt, Simone Kaiser, Gunther Latsch, Cordula Meyer and Caroline Schmidt, "Paving the Way for a Muslim Parallel Society," *Der Spiegel*, 29 March 2007 (http://www.spiegel.de/international/germany/0,1518,474629,00.html).

265 **Tor Erling Staff:** Gunnar Hultgreen, "Gi strafferabatt for aeresdrap," *Dagbladet*, 29 November 2008 (http://www.dagbladet.no/nyheter/2007/11/29/519655.html); "Staff

vil gi strafferabatt for 'aeresdrap,'" *Aftenposten*, 29 November 2008 (http://www
.aftenposten.no/nyheter/iriks/article2126407.ece).

265 "immediately caved": David Glenn, "Cambridge U. Press Seeks to Destroy All Copies
of Book on Terrorism to Settle Libel Lawsuit by Saudi Businessman," *Chronicle of
Higher Education*, 10 August 2007 (http://chronicle.com/daily/2007/08/2007080104n.
htm; free at http://www.campus-watch.org/article/id/3779).

266 "entirely and manifestly false": Gary Shapiro, "Libel Suit Leads to Destruction of
Books," *New York Sun*, 2 August 2007 (http://www.nysun.com/foreign/libel-suit-
leads-to-destruction-of-books/59706/).

266 "a Muslim-friendly judge": Srjda [Serge] Trifkovic, "The European Union, a
Prisoner of Nations," *Chronicles*, 6 June 2008 (http://www.chroniclesmagazine
.org/?p=613).

267 "improve community relations": Macer Hall, "Brown: Don't Say Terrorists
Are Muslims," *Daily Express*, 19 August 2008 (http://www.express.co.uk/posts/
view/12172/Brown:-Don).

267 "secret EU guidelines": Alison Little, "EU Tells Britain: Don't Say 'Muslims,'" *Daily
Express*, 5 July 2007 (http://www.express.co.uk/posts/view/12236).

267 "civil servants no longer": "'Don't Mention Islamic Extremists': Government
Phrasebook Tries to Avoid Upsetting Muslims," *Daily Mail*, 5 February 2008 (http://
www.dailymail.co.uk/news/article-512377/Dont-mention-Islamic-extremists-
Government-phrasebook-tries-avoid-upsetting-Muslims.html).

267 "tells civil servants not to use": Alan Travis, "Whitehall Draws Up New Rules
on Language of Terror," *Guardian*, 4 February 2008 (http://www.guardian.co.uk/
politics/2008/feb/04/uk.terrorism).

268 State Department directives: http://www.investigativeproject.org/documents/
misc/127.pdf.

268 "shape a softer approach": Steve Emerson, "Investigative Project Releases Gov't
Memo Curtailing Speech in War on Terror," *IPT News*, 2 May 2008 (http://www
.investigativeproject.org/article/659).

268 "a quest to find one's faith": P.W. Singer and Elina Noor, "What Do You Call a
Terror(Jihad)ist?," *New York Times*, 2 June 2008 (http://www.nytimes.com/2008/06/02/
opinion/02singer.html).

CHAPTER VI: *"I'm not Spartacus!"*

270 Gahr Støre at racism debate: complete video of debate at http://www.nrk.no/
nett-tv/klipp/372714.

271 "misunderstood": Amund Trellevik, "Muslimer i Midtøsten Vil Tolke Dette Som en
Fornærmelse," *Aftenposten*, 4 June 2008 (http://www.aftenposten.no/nyheter/uriks/
article2464371.ece).

271 "act of terror": Kadafi Zaman, "Dette er terror," *TV2 News* Web site, 6 June 2008
(http://tv2nyhetene.no/innenriks/article1967041.ece).

271 Dag Solstad on free speech: Dag Solstad, "Om ytringsfriheten," *Samtiden* 2 (2008).

271 "The world is changing": Andreas Skartveit, "Vår nye religion?," *Dagbladet*, 10 June
2008 (http://www.dagbladet.no/kultur/2008/06/10/537706.html).

271 "it is both stupid and dangerous": Janne Haaland Matlary, "Ytringsdumhet?,"
Aftenposten, 13 June 2008 (http://www.aftenposten.no/meninger/signert/article
2481262.ece).

272 Anders Giæver: Anders Giæver, "Modigst på avstand," *VG Helg*, 21 June 2008.

272 "an international chain": "New Move on Sharia-Compliant Hotel Chain," *Gulf
Daily News*, 4 May 2008 (http://www.gulf-daily-news.com/Story.asp?Article=21633
7&Sn=BUSI&IssueID=31045).

272 **"What if Muslim drivers"**: Katherine Kersten, "A Two-Tiered Airport Taxi System Could Lead to 'Chapter Two,'" *Minneapolis Star-Tribune*, 16 October 2006 (http://www.startribune.com/local/11585696.html).

273 **"implacability"**: Robert Winnett, "Britain 'a Soft Touch for Home-Grown Terrorists,'" *Daily Telegraph*, 18 April 2008 (http://www.telegraph.co.uk/news/uknews/1578785/Britain-'a-soft-touch-for-home-grown-terrorists'.html).

273–274 **"The most important change"**: Alexis de Tocqueville, *Democracy in America*, chapter 4 (http://xroads.virginia.edu/~HYPER/detoc/ch4_06.htm).

274 **"chose liberal democracy"**: Thomas Kleine-Brockhoff, "Who Are Our Friends?" *Die Zeit*, 13 May 2005 (http://www.zeit.de/2005/20/aussenpolitik_englisch).

275 **"has metastasized into an entire"**: Paul Berman, "Who's Afraid of Tariq Ramadan?," *The New Republic*, 4 June 2007 (www.tnr.com/politics/story.html?id=fd52e6a4-efc5-42fd-983b-1282a16ac8dd).

276 **"fundamental test"**: Anne Applebaum, "A Dutch Retreat on Speech," *Washington Post*, 8 October 2007 (http://www.washingtonpost.com/wp-dyn/content/article/2007/10/07/AR2007100701031.html).

AFTERWORD

277 *New York Times*: Stephen Pollard, "The Appeasers," *New York Times*, 24 July 2009 (http://www.nytimes.com/2009/07/26/books/review/Pollard-t.html). The *Times* also gave Christopher Caldwell's *Reflections on the Revolution in Europe* a big thumbs-up (which was perhaps not entirely surprising, given that Caldwell is a *Times Magazine* contributing editor).

277 **"treated the hard facts"**: "Media Takes Whitewashing of Islam to a Whole New Level," Pajamas Media, 9 June 2009 (http://pajamasmedia.com/blog/media-takes-whitewashing-of-islam-to-a-whole-new-level/).

277 **"Bawer veers"**: Paul A. Barrett, "Bracing for a Cultural Takeover," *Washington Post*, 7 June 2009 (http://www.washingtonpost.com/wp-dyn/content/article/2009/06/05/AR2009060501189.html).

278 **"razed Rio de Janeiro"**: Tyler Gray, "Destroying the Earth, Over and Over Again," *New York Times*, 6 November 2009 (http://www.nytimes.com/2009/11/08/movies/08gray.html?pagewanted=2&8dpc&_r=1).

278 **"It's a depressing book"**: Sophie Freeman, "Author Sebastian Faulks risks Muslim fury by describing the Koran as the 'depressing rantings of a schizophrenic,'" *Daily Mail*, 24 August 2009 (http://www.dailymail.co.uk/news/article-1208629/Author-Sebastian-Faulks-risks-Muslim-fury-describing-Koran-depressing-rantings-schizophrenic.html).

278 **Anjem Choudary**: "UK hate preacher demands Koran-bashing author's trial under sharia court," *Thaindian News*, 4 September 2009 (http://www.thaindian.com/newsportal/world-news/uk-hate-preacher-demands-koran-bashing-authors-trial-under-sharia-court_100242817.html).

278 **"a hugely sympathetic"**: Sebastian Faulks, "Sebastian Faulks: The book I really can't put down," *Telegraph*, 24 August 2009 (http://www.telegraph.co.uk/news/newstopics/religion/6083338/Sebastian-Faulks-The-book-I-really-cant-put-down.html).

279 **"two dozen authorities"**: Patricia Cohen, "Yale Press Bans Images of Muhammed in New Book," *New York Times*, 12 August 2009 (http://www.nytimes.com/2009/08/13/books/13book.html).

279 **"experts . . . fear-mongering"**: Martin Kramer, "Fear-Mongering at Yale," Sandbox blog, 17 August 2009 (http://sandbox.blog-city.com/fear_mongering_at_yale.htm).

279 **Klausen revealed:** "University Presses Wary over Editorial Interference," Bookseller

.com, 20 August 2009 (http://www.thebookseller.com/news/94899-university-presses-wary-over-editorial-interference.html).

279 Commentators suggested: Diana West, "Yale Economics 101: Crush Cartoons, get Sharia-Backed Gold," Townhall.com, 20 August 2009 (http://townhall.com/columnists/DianaWest/2009/08/20/yale_economics_101_crush_cartoons,_get_sharia-backed_gold?page=2); Roger Kimball, "Yale & the Danish Cartoons: The Plot Thickens," Roger's Rules blog, 15 August 2009 (http://pajamasmedia.com/rogerkimball/2009/08/15/yale-the-danish-cartoons-the-plot-thickens/).

279 "Yale's courting": Martin Kramer, "Some Day Yale's Prince Will Come," Sandbox blog, 19 August 2009 (http://sandbox.blog-city.com/some_day_yales_prince_will_come.htm. In October 2009, a German publisher, Droste, cancelled the publication of a murder mystery because it contained the line of dialogue, "You can shove your Koran up . . ." ("Publishing House Under Fire for Self-Censorship over Koran Comments," *Deutsche Welle*, 6 October 2009, http://www.deutsche-welle.de/dw/article/0,,4767411,00.html).

280 Ramadan firing: Mark Hoogstad, "Rotterdam Fires Tariq Ramadan over Iranian TV Show," *NRC Handelsblad*, 12 November 2009 (http://www.nrc.nl/international/article2332245.ece/Rotterdam_fires_Tariq_Ramadan_over_Iranian_TV_show).

280 "When the blood": Ian Buruma, "When the Blood Starts Flowing, Where Will the Wilders Voters Be?" *NRC Handelsblad*, 25 August 2009 (http://www.nrc.nl/international/opinion/article2339000.ece/When_the_blood_starts_flowing,_where_will_the_Wilders_voters_be).

281 "radical Islam is not": Anders Børringbo, "Støre ønsker multikulturelt Norge," NRK Nyheter, 12 August 2009 (http://nrk.no/nyheter/innenriks/valg/valg_2009/1.6728709).

282 "Irish law has now": Padraig Reidy, "Who Asked for Ireland's Blasphemy Law?" *Guardian*, 9 July 2009 (http://www.guardian.co.uk/commentisfree/libertycentral/2009/jul/09/ireland-blasphemy-laws).

282 "[s]ome claim": "U.S. Opposes Bid to Bar Religious Defamation," AP story, (http://today.msnbc.msn.com/id/33486054/ns/world_news-world_faith/).

282 "The Human Rights Council . . .": The text of the resolution is at http://daccess-dds-ny.un.org/doc/RESOLUTION/LTD/G09/161/50/PDF/G0916150.pdf?OpenElement.

282 "could plausibly be read": Stuart Taylor, Jr., "Troubling Signals on Free Speech," *National Journal*, 31 October 2009 (http://www.nationaljournal.com/njmagazine/or_20091031_1700.php).

283 "the flying imams were the subject": Scott W. Johnson, "Ascent of the Flying Imams," Powerline Blog, 28 July 2009 (http://www.powerlineblog.com/archives/2009/07/024145.php).

283 CAIR . . . declared victory: "Rosa Parks they ain't: The case of the flying imams ends as it should: with flier safety first," Editorial, *New York Daily News*, 28 October 2009 (http://www.nydailynews.com/opinions/2009/10/28/2009-10-28_rosa_parks_they_aint.html#ixzz0WcfyIhHChttp://www.nydailynews.com/opinions/2009/10/28/2009-10-28_rosa_parks_they_aint.html).

283 "sister organization": David Kupelian, "'Flying imams' rewarded for ominous airline 'stunt'?" *World Net Daily*, 21 October 2009 (http://www.wnd.com/index.php?fa=PAGE.view&pageId=113579).

283 "[w]e meet": Josh Gerstein, "Despite Ban, Holder to Speak to CAIR-Linked Group," Politico blog, 9 November 2009 (http://www.politico.com/blogs/joshgerstein/1109/Despite_ban_Holder_to_speak_to_CAIRlinked_group.html).

284 In a piece posted: Bruce Bawer, "Fort Hood Massacre: A Day of Courage and

Cowardice," Pajamas Media, 6 November 2009 (http://pajamasmedia.com/blog/fort-hood-massacre-a-day-of-courage-and-cowardice/).

286 **"that speculation":** Joseph Berger, "Army Chief Concerned for Muslim Troops," *New York Times,* 8 November 2009 (http://www.nytimes.com/2009/11/09/us/politics/09casey.html?_r=2&hp).

286 **"made the mistake":** "Greyhawk," "What the 'C' Stands For," Mudville Gazette, 9 November 2009 (http://www.mudvillegazette.com/032881.html).

286 **"instant flow":** Dorothy Rabinowitz, "Dr. Phil and the Fort Hood Killer," *Wall Street Journal,* 10 November 2009 (http://online.wsj.com/article/SB10001424052748704404 24045745258317857244114.html?mod=wsj_share_facebook#printMode).

287 **"As President Obama":** Ralph Peters, "Deadly Denial," *New York Post,* 10 November 2009 (http://www.nypost.com/p/news/opinion/opedcolumnists/deadly_denial_nta 2v3RwY9bjnkRWrAyoJP).

287 **"It may be hard to comprehend":** Peter Baker and Clifford Krauss, "President, at Service, Hails Fort Hood's Fallen," *New York Times,* 10 November 2009 (http://www.nytimes.com/2009/11/11/us/11hood.html?hp).

INDEX

ALSO BY BRUCE BAWER

WHILE EUROPE SLEPT

How Radical Islam Is Destroying the West from Within

As an American living in Europe since 1998, Bruce Bawer examines the challenges posed by radical Islam. Across the continent he encounters Muslim enclaves in which women are oppressed and abused, homosexuals persecuted and killed, "infidels" threatened and vilified, Jews demonized and attacked, barbaric traditions (such as honor killing and forced marriage) widely practiced, and freedom of speech and religion firmly repudiated, to which the European political and media establishment turns a blind eye in order to pacify radical Islamists and preserve the illusion of multicultural harmony. *While Europe Slept*, a brave and invaluable book—with its riveting combination of eye-opening reportage and blunt, incisive analysis—is essential reading for anyone concerned about the fate of Europe and what it portends for the United States.

Political Science/978-0-7679-2005-6

ANCHOR BOOKS
Available at your local bookstore, or visit
www.randomhouse.com

Meet with Interesting People
Enjoy Stimulating Conversation
Discover Wonderful Books

VINTAGE BOOKS / ANCHOR BOOKS
Reading Group Center
THE READING GROUP SOURCE FOR BOOK LOVERS

Visit ReadingGroupCenter.com where you'll find great reading choices—award winners, bestsellers, beloved classics, and many more—and extensive resources for reading groups such as:

Author Chats

Exciting contests offer reading groups the chance to win one-on-one phone conversations with Vintage and Anchor Books authors.

Extensive Discussion Guides

Guides for over 450 titles as well as non–title specific discussion questions by category for fiction, nonfiction, memoir, poetry, and mystery.

Personal Advice and Ideas

Reading groups nationwide share ideas, suggestions, helpful tips, and anecdotal information. Participate in the discussion and share your group's experiences.

Behind the Book Features

Specially designed pages which can include photographs, videos, original essays, notes from the author and editor, and book-related information.

Reading Planner

Plan ahead by browsing upcoming titles, finding author event schedules, and more.

Special for Spanish-language reading groups
www.grupodelectura.com

A dedicated Spanish-language content area complete with recommended titles from Vintage Español.

A selection of some favorite reading group titles from our list

Atonement by Ian McEwan

Balzac and the Little Chinese Seamstress by Dai Sijie

The Blind Assassin by Margaret Atwood

The Devil in the White City by Erik Larson

Empire Falls by Richard Russo

The English Patient by Michael Ondaatje

A Heartbreaking Work of Staggering Genius by Dave Eggers

The House of Sand and Fog by Andre Dubus III

A Lesson Before Dying by Ernest J. Gaines

Lolita by Vladimir Nabokov

Memoirs of a Geisha by Arthur Golden

Midnight in the Garden of Good and Evil by John Berendt

Midwives by Chris Bohjalian

Push by Sapphire

The Reader by Bernhard Schlink

Snow by Orhan Pamuk

An Unquiet Mind by Kay Redfield Jamison

Waiting by Ha Jin

A Year in Provence by Peter Mayle